Galax Remembered

By John J. Nunn
and Judith Nunn Alley

Local History collected from many sources: old scrapbooks, old newspapers and personal files of friends.

A special thanks to Ravin Bilbrey for the use of his wonderful watercolor of Galax's Main Street at night in the Winter of about 1910.

And another thanks to Becky Webb Guynn for her Oil Painting of the most recognizable landmark of Galax, "Bolens Drug Store".

All of this information will be posted to www.Galaxscrapbook.com sometime in 2014

Acknowledgements…………

After the great reception received for our photo book about the first 50 years of Galax history we realized that the story was unfinished. Since then, we have both worked independently to continue this project. I completed and published the history of the first residents in town and John has compiled this book of historical data that has been shared with him. The book includes old newspaper articles, items at the Matthews Museum and items copied from privately owned albums of photographs and clippings that were so graciously made available to him. You will also read about the fires, floods, sporting events, class reunions, visiting dignitaries, famous residents, church and social activities that have taken place over the years. As would be expected, occasionally, there are discrepancies from one article to the next, depending on the information available at the time each article was written. Except for a rare editor's note (…), they have been presented as they were written.

Encouraged by our first book, people began to search around their homes for old newspapers, family scrapbooks, photo albums and any other items they thought might be of interest. In many cases, John was allowed to take the old newspapers to the Matthews Museum to be placed in special archival, acid free boxes. Tony and Joyce have spent many hours preparing an index for each box to make searching easier. These newspapers are a valuable link to our past and will be treasured for years to come.

An important addition is the excellent history written by C. L. Martin. It is a summary of events and residents during the early years and was graciously made available by Mr. Martin's brother Roger. It served as a major source of information when we were working on the photo history book.

Doug Saunders has graciously loaned John photographs of his relatives who were early Galax residents of the Black community. These include Bryants, Bryans and others.

John has also included articles and photographs from the three Rotogravure publications that provide an excellent history of our local furniture, textile and other industries. At one point in the 1950s, Galax was reputed to have more manufacturing per capita than any other town in the country. Beside the industry publications, he has included a small amount of information about the local music and how it has played an important part in the economic development of the community. While John has a highly respected and successful business background neither of us can carry a tune. We also failed to follow through with all those piano lessons Mother insisted that we take so we don't feel that we are the ones to write a complete history of the local music. We hope someone will compile a book about our very talented musicians and our world famous Fiddlers Convention.

Recognition should be given to John's dedicated and hardworking "behind the scene" support team. The two people who questioned the spelling, demanded organization, asked for articles to be included or deleted, and nitpicked him through the entire project. Without wife Mariah and sister Judy this book would still be floating around in the never-never land in his computer.

A special thank you to Mary Ann Spinks Dotson, Susan Parsons Fackrell, Ruby Lindamood, Elwood Newman, Laura and John Waugh, Nancy Waugh, Jay Guynn, Nell Frye and daughters Annelle Frye Williams and Patti Frye Meredith, Roger and Pat Martin, Bill Brannon, Mary Ann Ward Deaton, Gary Leagan, Hershal Murphy, Bill Murphy, Jackie Gentry McGrady, Ed Burcham, Bob Bryant, Nicky Felts, Hattie Bob Felts Wilson, Dedee Ward, Jerry Wolford, Lona Mae Cox, Mary Lee McCoy, Mary Roberts Guynn, Odell Hampton, Bill Nuckolls, Pat Hampton Bolt, Carole Waddell, Chicken Chappell, Jewel Amburn Melton, Frances Eads Halsey, Mike Brown, Irene Alderman, John Ashby, Ken Rosenbaum, Skip Henderson, Rebecca Webb Guynn, Ravin Bilbrey, Brian Funk, Randy Mayes, Sharon Martin Blevins and Zeke Morton. Your generosity and support is greatly appreciated.

Judith Lucinda Nunn Alley   May 2013

Table of Contents

People

Galax Schools

Scouting

Businesses

Events and Galax History

Young Men About Town
Judith Nunn Alley

The names of the young men were noted on the back of this old photograph. Listed were Elmer Jones, Clyde Henderson, Rob Rhudy, Raymond Vass, Earley Smith, Clyde Schooley, Edwin Dodd, Rex Wright, David Bolen, Paul Kapp and Joe Todd. The date, location and event for the picture are unknown at this time.

My brother John Nunn and I had planned to use this photograph in our book on early Galax that was published by Arcadia several years ago. It was one of our favorites, but for some unknown reason it was rejected by the publisher. We felt it was an important photograph so we immediately set it aside for a future project. The photograph fascinates me because it represents the second generation of Galax. Most of the parents of these young men were involved in building the foundation of our beautiful community. For example, the fathers of Rex Wright, Paul Kapp and David Bolen were members of the first town council.

I decided to research each young man and write a brief "sketch" to add human interest to the photograph; to make it more than just a picture of a gathering. By going through documents, records and census reports I was able to determine that Clyde Schooley was born in 1885 and Elmer Jones was born in 1888 while the rest of the young men were born between 1899 and 1903. The names of the eleven are written on the back, but their exact position in the group is not known. The date can only be estimated to be between 1915 and 1920. Considering the difference in age of Clyde and Elmer and the others it is possible that the two older men were mentors, teachers or sponsors of some kind. A photograph of the GHS senior class of 1917 included Paul Kapp, Rex Wright, and Joe Todd.

Elmer Jones
Elmer Sterling Jones was born on 9 January 1888. His WWI draft registration card dated 5 June 1917 indicated he was single. He was the only surviving child of Thomas and Cora Jones and inherited the family home on Washington Street after their deaths. He married Grace Edwards on 22 September 1920. They were the parents of three daughters Iva Jones Bourke, Kitty Jones Halsey, and Peggy Jones, a very popular Galax High School teacher. The 1940 census indicated that the Jones family was still residing in the same house on Washington Street where

they were living in 1935. Elmer was employed as an automobile dealer and Grace was a clerk in a dry goods store. Elmer died on 30 March 1945 and Grace and Peggy remained in the family home.

Arthur Clyde Henderson
According to North Carolina birth records, Clyde was born on 8 January 1899 in Alleghany County to Marcus L. and Myrtie Helbrook Henderson. He was living with his parents in 1930 and was employed in the family's jewelry store in Galax. Clyde was residing with his Uncle Lee Henderson in North Wilkesboro North Carolina in 1940. His WWII draft registration card indicated his birthdate as 18 January 1899. At that time he was residing at Rt. 2, North Wilkesboro North Carolina. The card, dated 16 February 1942, indicated he was not employed and his permanent contact was C. H. Henderson, Galax Virginia. Clyde died in 1964 and was buried with his parents in Felts Cemetery, Galax.

Rob Rhudy
Rob Roy Rhudy was the son of attorney J. Hicks Rhudy and his wife Hattie Fulton Rhudy. His WWI military registration dated 12 September 1918 indicated he was a student at V.M. I. and provided the names of his parents. He married Helen Elizabeth Pheobus on 1 June 1925 and divorced in Florida in 1936. He was listed on the Florida 1935 census as a lawyer. He later married Vera Blanton Freeman on 29 December 1941 and divorced her in Highland Florida in 1944. According to Utah military records, Rob Roy Rhudy was born in Independence Virginia on 30 June 1900. He enlisted in the army on 12 September 1942 and his service was terminated on 13 December 1943. His wife was listed as Vera Blanton Rhudy. The obituary of his mother Hattie Fulton Rhudy, who passed on 5 December 1939, indicated her son Rob Roy Rhudy was a resident of Miami Florida. He died at age 64 on 3 July 1964 in Fulton County Georgia.

Raymond Vass
Frank Raymond Vass was born on 1 July 1902 to Dennis Shelby and Laura Vass. He was 18 years old when he married Mayme Brown on 9 January 1921. They were the parents of one son, Frank Raymond Vass Jr. who was born on 3 April 1925. By 1930, Mayme and Raymond Jr. were living with her parents on north Main Street. She later married Jessie Ivey Palmer in May 1935. In 1940 they were still residing in Galax. Raymond returned to Galax and lived with his parents in their later years. He passed away on 11 August 1977 and was buried in Felts Cemetery with his parents and other members of the Vass family.

Earley Smith
Lemuel Earley Smith was one of four children born to James D. and Valeria Smith. James died in 1913 and by 1920 daughter Ada had left home; her brothers Glenn H., Earley and James H. remained with their mother in the family home located in the northern area of Galax. By the 1930 census, Earley was the only son remaining at home. According to his WWI draft registration card he was born on 13 June 1899 but his gravestone indicated he was born on 13 June 1900. The draft card, dated 12 September 1918, and the 1930 census indicated he was a clerk at the post office. He died on 1 January 1964 and was buried in Christiansburg Virginia. His parents were buried in the Gladeville Methodist Church cemetery.

Clyde Schooley
In 1900 Clyde and his widowed father Joseph, grandmother Clarissa and two siblings were living in Tucker West Virginia where Joseph was employed as a store clerk. Around 1907 Clyde married Bertha and they were still residing in Tucker where he was employed as a bank teller in 1910. According to his WWI draft registration card, he was living in Wise County Virginia and employed as an assistant payroll clerk for the Stone Gap Coke and Coal Company. He was listed as being married and the father of four children. The 1920 census indicates he was a 33 year old garage book keeper in Galax. Dorothy Burnett Peterson wrote in her memories of early Galax that Clyde was the book keeper for Felts Motor Company at the time and was living on Center Street across from the old Waugh Hotel. According to his WWII draft registration card he was born in Deer Park Maryland and his wife Bertha was born in West Virginia. He was listed as married with 4 children and employed by W. M. Bassett Furniture Company in Martinsville as a traveling salesman. An obituary for Joseph Schooley on 16 December 1937 indicated that he had been visiting his son Clyde in Galax at the time of his death. Rev. Sidney McCarty and Rev.

W. M. Bunts conducted the funeral service that was held at the Clyde Schooley home. Joseph was also survived by a daughter Mrs. J. F. Williams (Gladys D.) of Majestic Kentucky, a sister Miss Elizabeth Schooley and a brother William Schooley, both residents of Maryland. By 1940 Clyde, Bertha and their three sons were residing in Charlottesville Virginia. The family later returned to Galax where Jack, a graduate of the Medical College of Virginia, was a druggist at Bolen Drug Store and Arch, a graduate of Emory and Henry, was a science teacher at Galax High School. Curtis was killed in action while serving with the 38th Infantry Regiment during the Korean War. Daughter Connie married Hobert Boyer. They were the parents of one son and resided in Fries in 1940 where Hobert was employed at the cotton mill. The couple later divorced and Connie and her son resided with her parents. Clyde, Bertha and their four children are all buried in Felts Cemetery.

Edwin Nuckolls Dodd

Edwin Jr was born on 5 Feb 1901 to Edwin and Susan Nuckolls Dodd.in Virginia and lived on Grayson Street at the time of the 1920 census. In 1930 he and his wife Louise Arrington had been married approximately five years and were the parents of 9 month old son Phillip. Edwin was employed as a safety engineer. He and his family were listed in the Des Moines Iowa city directory in 1932. The 4 May 1933 issue of the Kingsport Times in Tennessee included a court ordered publication in regard to the divorce of Edwin and Louise. By 1940 he was living in Atlanta Georgia. He passed away in Atlantic Beach, Duval County Florida on 6 July 1979 and was buried in Kingsport with his parents.

Rex Wright

Ronald Rex, born 2 Jan 1901, was a son of Elbert and Leona Wright, pioneer citizens of Galax. Mr. Wright, a highly respected builder in town, had probably constructed the family home on West Grayson Street. By 1910, the family circle included five sons and one daughter. Rex indicated on his WWI draft registration card dated 12 Sept 1918, that he was working as a commissary clerk at the Field Scott Coal Company in Richlands, Tazewell County Virginia and his mother was Mrs. Leona Wright of Galax. In 1920 all six children were still living at home. Burtrand and Katie were teachers, Greek was a carpenter, Raymond was a bookkeeper and Rex and Dick did not list their employment. Mrs. Wright had also taken in a boarder. By 1930 Rex had moved to Roanoke where he was boarding with the Shelton family on Virginia Avenue and employed as a book keeper in a clothing store. Rex married Carrie Ward (1909-1996) and they were the parents of at least one son (Charles). Cemetery records indicate Rex died on 10 April 1977 and was buried in Roanoke Virginia.

David Bolen

David W. Bolen was born on 28 October 1901 to John W. and Nettie Bolen. It was difficult to locate the family on the 1910 census because the name had been incorrectly transcribed on the index as "Rolon." David's father John Wesley Bolen was a physician, owned a drug store, and had been one of the earliest residents in the new town of Galax. In 1920 the Bolens were living near Dr. A. G. Pless, Sr. a local dentist. By 1930, 28 year old David had completed dental school at Emory University in Atlanta, established his dental practice and set up housekeeping with his 23 year old bride Louise Marcella Hagan Bolen. Dr. Bolen and his childhood friend Dr. Paul Kapp established a joint dental practice that was located on the second floor of the Bolen Drug Company building on Main Street. David and Louise were the parents of two sons John and David. Dr. Bolen died in 1985 and his wife died in 1990; both are buried in Felts Cemetery, Galax.

Paul Kapp

Paul Homer Kapp was born on 5 September 1899 to John Harden and Julia May Hoffman Kapp. The family resided on Main Street in 1910 and John Harden was listed as a hardware merchant. He and Julia May had been married eleven years and were the parents of one child. On Paul's WWI draft registration card, dated 12 September 1918, he indicated he clerked in a furniture store for C. L. Smith. In 1920 he was still residing with his parents but was listed as having no occupation. Between 1920 and 1930, Paul graduated from dental school, established a dental practice and married Katherine Vass. His father had died in 1921 so Julia May was listed as "head of household" in 1930. At that time, Paul and Katherine and Julia May's brother John Hoffman were residing in the Kapp home. By 1940 the family home consisted of Paul, Katherine, their 2 year old son John Paul, his mother Julia May and her brother John

Hoffman. Paul Kapp shared a dental practice with his childhood friend and neighbor David Bolen. Paul Kapp died in 1988 and Katherine died in 1990; both are buried in Felts Cemetery, Galax.

Joe Todd

Joseph Earl Todd was born on 21 December 1899 to Henry Harden and Mallie Cornett Todd. His WWI 12 September 1918 draft registration card indicated he was a student at Galax High School at the time. His father passed away in 1918 so his mother was listed as a widow on the 1920 census where she resided on Main Street with her children. By 1930 Joe and his wife Opal were residing in Marion Virginia where he was employed as an insurance salesman. Apparently the couple did not have any children. They were residing in Floyd County Virginia by 1935 and in 1940 Joe was working as an interviewer for the state unemployment service.

In the 1932 Galax city directory the David Bolen family resided at 503 N. Main St. while the Paul Kapp family was across the street at 410 North Main; Rex Wright's mother Leona was residing at 412 West Grayson and Clyde and Bertha Schooley were at 201 Virginia St. Clyde Henderson was working at the family jewelry store on Main Street. Rob Rhudy's widowed mother Hattie was residing at 307 West Grayson Street. Edwin Dodd's parents had passed and he was residing in Kingsport with his wife and son. Out of this group of eleven there were two dentists, two bookkeepers, an automobile dealer, a safety engineer, a postal clerk, a government employee, and one who worked in the family's business. They all made positive contributions to the world around them; after all, they were "Galax boys!"

Sources: U. S. census reports, Florida Census Reports, WWI and WWII draft card registrations, 1932 Galax City directory, cemetery records, old Galax Gazette articles, 1925 Galax City directory, marriage records, and various web research sites.

TWO GALAX OLD-TIMERS RECALL OLDTOWN STREET 50 YEARS AGO

In 1906,the appearance of Oldtown street was vastly different and two of the men who best remember it are familiar sights 'around Galax-- Fields Bryant with his cap, his pleasant smile, and his gracious courtesy to everyone, old or young-and Fred "Date" Day, who as a boy grew up in Galax, knows its history and stories from A to Z and who helped lay the bricks for most of the buildings of a brick nature in Galax.

Both Fred (left) and Fields (right) lived on Oldtown Street and remember it as it was in 1906.

The Gazette photographer took these men down to Oldtown street recently and listened as they recalled the way it looked fifty years ago -particularly interesting now as Galax prepares for the Golden Anniversary celebration on August 11, 1956

Fields Bryant came to Galax as a very young fellow and says that he is 75 years old now. Born in Alleghany County, N.C., he was brought to this area by a Mr. John Bowman who reared him on a farm in the airport section.

About 1903 Fields drifted down to Galax where he has worked at both regular and odd jobs ever since.

Now you'll see him around the Rex theatre, but when he was younger and more agile and when the passenger train ran into Galax, Fields Met every train and worked for all the hotels, carrying baggage, running errands, and making himself useful.

Mr. Day came as a boy from Mt. Airy and his father was a bricklayer and mason — one of the best—and taught his boys to lay bricks from just about the time they could heft one off the ground.

Fred Day first remembers Fields Bryant from an unimportant incident ,regarding a cat. The Days lived on the corner of Carroll and Oldtown where a brick building belonging to McCamant Higgins now stands. Fields was working at a bowling alley just across the street on the present Mirror plant site.. Day remembers Fields calling his father and him for help early one morning and on rushing across the street found that Fields' kitten had its head stuck in a salmon can.

It was sitting on the corner Oldtown in the cool of the April sun that the two men gave this reporter a picture of Oldtown and Carroll Streets fifty years ago. Down where lower part of the Mirror plant is located was a camp ground where teamsters and visitors to Galax camped overnight. They would haul bark and produce in from Low Gap and other parts of the surrounding country, take back groceries for the country stores, and spend the night cooking. eating and telling yarns. Mr. Day remembers the cook shack with the tin roof and how he and his brothers and men such as Lawrence Patton and Sid Dotson would sneak close and shower the roof with rocks and then run for their lives.

There is nothing that will bring back remembrances to old-timers more than the mention of a livery stable. Any man who lived in any small town fifty or sixty years ago can remember the livery stable with its exciting chores, the chance to lead the steeds to water, the chance to see the drummers coming in to rent horses and buggies, and the importance they assumed over other lads when they were allowed to do the feeding—usually for nothing.

So the men remembered first the livery stable operated by Uncle Luke Bishop where Globman's now stands. They remembered that the horses had to be watered at the little branch that runs down Calhoun street and what fun it was taking the horses there twice a day.

He recalled too a small Jersey cow that was lost for 14 days and finally found under the feedway of the stable. It belonged to a John Anders and since cows ran loose in those days, it no doubt wandered into the stable for a free handout. In some manner it got under the runway and lived for 14 days without water but eating from the feed that dropped through the cracks. Mr. Day recalled that one of the boys had crawled up under the runway to hide some whiskey when he put his hand out and thought he had come upon a hibernating bear.

Other recollections are Where the Higgins Oil Co. parking lot is now, Jim Reavis had a foundry and planing mill; where the Shell station stands was a planing mill and machine shop operated by Tyree and Andrew Gillesie; and on the same site after that burned was a livery stable operated by Watt Bishop; the corner occupied by the Levi Todd home and Krogers was a camping lot; the first blacksmith shop in Galax was where the Pontiac used car lot is now located, operated by John Chaffin, later J. L. Hawkins, later John Kenney; a saddle and harness shop operated by a Mr. Draper where Bemie Harris' restaurant is located; a grist mill and saw mill where Coca Cola plant now stands; a produce house operated by E. Lane Whitley, later by B. D. Beamer, on the site now occupied by Rex Sage.

"Date" Day also recalls as a boy being paid 25 cents a day for sitting under a locust tree where the Milo Cockerham filling station now is—his job- keeping cows from feeding in the cornfields of the Anderson farm.

This appeared in th Galax Gazette during the Golden Jubilee Celebration in 1956

White Chevrolet Sales 301 South Main Street, Galax VA

1. David W. Spraker
2. J.W. Dalton
3. E.R. Odell
4. Harold Sharp
5. Virginia Cox
6. Bruce Galyean
7. Hubert S. White
Behind Mr. White but not numbered is Richard Carico
8. Walter Gillespie
9. Royce Frye
10. Eldridge J. Allen
11. C. N. "Tiny" Hedrick
12. Eugene Frye
13. Melvin Mayberry
14. James Wilson
15. Robert Thomas
16. Thomas Sullivan
17. Grady Stoneman
18. Robert "Wimpy" King
19. Lee Cox
20. Johnny Reavis
21. James Maxwell
22. Raleigh Brown
23. Robert Brown
24. Paul Hash
25. Charlie Maxwell
26. Robert Lee Higgins
27. Oren Edwards
28. Cleatus Newman
29. Victor Osborne
30. C. H. Frazier
31. Bill Sells
32. Harley Rippey
33. Herman Hackler
34. Elbert "Pete" Killon
35. Lewis Newman
36. Junior Maxwell

WHITE CHEVROLET SALES, INC.

Dealers in Chevrolet, Oldsmobile and Cadillac automobiles, sales and service for Galax, Carroll and Grayson counties, and adjoining territory, is one of the largest motor agencies in Southwest Virginia. With America's largest and fastest selling car, the Chevrolet, supplemented by the aristocratic Cadillac and the popular Oldsmobile, it is easy to understand why this agency' is ranked with the most aggressive and substantial automobile businesses in the State.

A large and imposing plant, attractive display rooms, a most complete Parts department, the most complete and scientific equipment for all other departments, which are operated by skilled and experienced mechanics, are some of the factors that contribute to this concern's high reputation.

The White Chevrolet Sales is also dealer for the popular Chevrolet trucks and Maytag Washing Appliances.

The company normally employs over 50 persons, the majority being in the high salaried brackets of salesmen and skilled mechanics.

The White Chevrolet Sales began business November 20, 1931, with an organization--of five persons, including the owner and founder.

On its Twentieth Anniversary in 1951, with its large and most modern plant, one of the foremost in this respect in the nation, and a trained and skilled organization of over fifty persons, President White has justifiable grounds for his pride in his agency and its enviable record of progress and growth with the enterprising town of Galax and Southwest Virginia.

Hubert S. White,
Owner.

This is one of the very few agencies in the country selling Chevrolet, Oldsmobile and Cadillac cars, and only top flight agencies get this prized recognition from General Motors. Hubert S. White is manager and owner of this successful enterprise.

Mr. White is also president of the B. & L. Chevrolet Company, of Hillsville, the Old Dominion Knitting Company, Huwal's Frozen Foods Locker Plant; vice-president of the Merchants and Farmers Hank, past president and current executor of the Galax Chamber of Commerce, past president of the Galax Retail Merchants Association, past chairman of the Board of Stewards of the First Methodist Church, ,a 32nd degree Scottish Rite Mason, Shriner and Rotarian, past president Rotary Club, and deeply interested and active in all civic affairs.

13

Station WBOB in Galax Has Big Opening Saturday 2-1-1947

Radio station WBOB, located on E. Oldtown St., or the Poplar Knob Road, when on the air at 6 o'clock Saturday
morning, and during the day Saturday,
and yesterday (Sunday), hundreds of
persons visited the new station, which
operates on a frequency of 1400
kilocycles on the radio dial. Following
the announcement that radio station
WBOB was on the air for the first time
and the playing of the Star-Spangled
Banner, prayer was offered by the Rev.
D.R. Weiglein, pastor of the
Presbyterian Church in Galax.

JOE CROCKETT, SECOND GENERAL MANAGER   MURIEL BELL, FIRST PROGRAM DIRECTOR   BRICE PARKS, SALES MANAGER SINCE 1951

The first regularly scheduled program
was a string musical band program by the "Blue Mountain Boys" from station WMVA, Martinsville.
At 8 AM Sunday the Sacred Hour was presented by the Twin Counties Evangelistic Club in charge of Rev. Otte Utt,
pastor of the East Side Brethren Church Galax and his evangelistic singers. This program continued until 8:30 when
a 30 minute religious broadcast was concluded by Rev. John D Scott Mount Airy, North Carolina and his singers.

From 10 to 10:30 AM, the Progressive Men's Bible Class of the First Methodist Church was on the air and from 11
to 12 o'clock, the morning worship service at the first Methodist Church was broadcast. Rev. W Kyle Cregger,
pastor the church preached on the subject "Facing Christ's most pressing question", using as a scripture text the
words of Christ when he said to Peter "Feed My Sheep."

From 8:45 to 9 o'clock Saturday morning, a devotional program was conducted by Rev. William P. Taylor pastor of
the first Christian church, who will conduct the morning devotional program, at the same time, throughout this
week, with other Galax ministers to follow in coming
weeks.

The new Galax radio station has consummated a contract
with the Mutual Broadcasting System for the carrying of
various mutual network programs on the WBOB schedule,
but the local broadcasting of these programs has been held
up by temporary delay in getting the telephone line
facilities necessary for such broadcasting into operation. It
is expected however that MBS programs will be heard
over WBOB in the near future.

Included the personnel of the WBOB staff are Johnny
Schultz, manager Carl F Duckett, chief engineer Miss
Jewel Cullop, bookkeeper, Ms. Muriel Bell receptionist,
William White and John Horton engineering department,
Frank Osborne announcer and Joe Crockett commercial
manager. February 1, 1947

Photo on left:
Staff members of WBOB in 1997
Include (from left to right) Public Relations Director,
Jerry Sprinkle, News Director, Ralph Gatchel, Sales
Manager, Brice Parks, and Station owner, Debby Sizer.

Gazette Photo on left by Brian Funk.

14

Two of Galax's musicians from different ages.

When 6-year-old Jimmy Edmonds, son of Mr. and Mrs. Nelson Edmonds of 132 Petty Road, goes over to Hillsville to "help out" his grandfather he takes along his violin and his bass fiddle because Grandfather Norman Edmonds has his own band, the "Old-timers", and Jimmy plays with them on the Saturday night Jamboree over the Radio Station in Hillsville.

Jimmy has never had lessons, he does have a lot of talent and he just "picked up" the dozens of folk tunes he plays from memory. The violin is his favorite instrument but not the only one he plays, or likes . . . he divides his time and interest between four other instruments . . the accordion, guitar, banjo, and mandolin.

Jimmy was just 6 years old this month . . about 6 weeks too late to enter school this year . . and like most boys his age is mostly noise, appetite, and band-aids, until he tucks that violin under his chin and starts playing -- then he displays a poise and charm far beyond his years.

In October he entered the Fiddling contest in the two day, old Fiddlers Convention in Pulaski where he delighted the audience with his rendition of "Boil that Cabbage down," Jimmy is also the grandson of Mr. and Mrs. James Claude Parks of Galax.

Wade Ward

Uncle Wade's Banjo To Smithsonian

Mr. and Mrs. Nelson Edmonds and son, Jimmy, left Galax Friday evening for Washington, D.C. where they presented the banjo used by-the late "Uncle Wade" Ward, of Independence, to the Smithsonian Institution.

 Mr. and Mrs. Edmonds were close friends and associates of "Uncle Wade", veteran old time country-music artist and old-time banjo-picker extraordinary, who passed away May 1971.

Jimmy Edmonds, Mr. and Mrs. Edmonds' young son and who, despite his tender age, is an accomplished fiddle and banjo player, was "Uncle Wade' s " protégé. Jimmy learned much about the art of banjo-picking'--the old-time claw hammer style, that is --from "Uncle Wade" Ward, just as he did about fiddling from the late "Uncle Charlie" Higgins, of Galax.

"Uncle Wade" was said to have requested that, after his death, the Edmondses take his trusty banjo, which he had used for many years at Fiddlers convention, Parson's Auction Co. land sales, ect. and present it to the Smithsonian Institution. In fact, "Uncle Wade" played the banjo in a national folk-music gathering held at the Smithsonian on at least one occasion. "Uncle Wade" had owned and used this banjo it is thought, since about 1935.

The Edmondses expected to make the delivery and presentation at the Smithsonian sometime Saturday evening and return home Sunday Two of "Uncle Wade's granddaughters, Dorothy and Christine accompanied Mr. and Mrs. Edmonds and Jimmy on their mission to Washington, thus carrying out the expressed desire of the long popular and greatly beloved Grayson County purveyor of the true, old time "Mountain Music".

Galax Gazette

A few photos from Mary Ann Spinks Dotson's school days

Left to right: Steps; Frances Lowe Hampton, Jim Hale Anderson, Judy Nunn Alley, Bob Pless, Shirley Branscome Crawford, Jim Reynolds

Galax YMCA (Rec. center) Girls Basketball team 1957: **Kneeling** YMCA Director, Pete Cregger, Ruby Morton, Sarah Price, Augusta Messer Anderson, Pat Exum Bassett, Jackie Hanks Morris Houghton, Charlotte Price Frye East.

Standing: Mary Ellen Kyle Philen, Frances Guynn Newman, Martha Smith Cox, Sue Morris Pearson, Allison Pollard Bertram, Mgr. Judy McGee Ward Gregory

Galax Music Club 1954-55: **4 in front**: Linda Lang Lure, Frances Dixon, Deanna Hartsock Goodson, Sally Hawks Hawks,

back 5: Sarah Price, Sue Morris Pearson, Mary Ann Spinks Dotson, Pat Exum Bassett, Charlotte Price Frye East..

Morning after slumber(less) party 1958: Allison Pollard Bertram, Augusta Messer Anderson, Sarah Price, Charlotte Price Frye East :**Three on the porch**: Bernie Edwards, Mary Ann Spinks Dotson and Jim Hale Anderson on poach of Youth Center.

Restaurant stop after Basketball game 1957: LtoR. R. A. Roberts, Warren Frye, Pat Exum Bassett, holding Bill Nuckolls, Jim Nuckolls, with Sally Hawks Hawks adjusting head, Ann Carico McMillian

Ruby Branscome during snow of 1960 at her Methodist Youth Center

Sharon Martin Blevins shares family pictures
while living on the corner of Madison and East Stuart Drive.
Madison is still a dirt street at this time

Top left-Sharon, Ron, Jim (standing) and Jean…….Top right- Mom (Betty Martin) and Jim
Bottom left- Floyd Landreth and Ron Martin………Middle-Mom with Ron and Jim in carriage
Middle right-back row Nancy Sprinkle, Jean Martin, ecky Sprinkle and Jim Martin. .Front row is Mary Gordon and Sharon.
Bottom right-Rayburn Martin, Betty Martin holding Sharon and Jean on couch, Ron on left and Jim on right.

Harry B. Zabriskie A Tribute

Harry B. Zabriskie

A TRIBUTE -- As these lines are being written, on Thursday, March 24, 1966, an atmosphere of solemnity overshadows the Gazette office. This is true because of the fact that, on the morrow, all that is mortal of "Mr. Z," as most of us around here who have known him many years have learned to call him, will be laid to rest in Felts Cemetery.

Though the life of Harry Brevoort Zabriskie, coming to a close, as it has, at the age of 84 years, has   been a long and useful one, and its end has not come unexpectedly, his departure from among us leaves a distinct void.

Though he had been in semi-retirement for more than half a dozen years, and absent in body from the office here at the Gazette during most of this time except for occasional visits during the summer seasons, mostly, the knowledge that he no longer mortally exists causes us to miss his presence. During the active years of his life, "Mr. Z" was active indeed. He believed in activity, and practiced it as long as he was physically able to do so.

I have known him since the Spring of 1933, and was in his employ, under his direct guidance, for over twenty years. Therefore, possibly I have learned to know him---the man, the newspaper editor and publisher, the friend--- as well as anyone outside of his family circle.

As a journalist, he had strong convictions relative to what constitutes good journalism, and he always sought to produce a newspaper in keeping with those convictions.

 I went to work for "Mr. Z" on June 5, 1933, when I had just received my diploma at Fries High School. Having been interested in newspapers and the products of journalism in general almost from the time of my earliest memories of childhood, I welcomed the opportunity that he offered me to get into actual newspaper work. I have retained my liking for the Fourth Estate, as the newspaper profession is known, through the years, and I have, of course, learned many things about newspapers and the journalistic profession during those years.

Basically, however, whatever special knowledge that I may possess relative to the gathering and dissemination of news--in short, the editorial treatment of news matter---"Mr. Z" taught me, by precept and example. Mr. H.B. Zabriskie was, by all reasonable standards, a newspaperman, and he was a good one. Not only was he a good newspaperman, but he was a good businessman. As a publisher, a man must, in order to be successful, be also a good businessman. "Mr. Z" possessed both of these qualities in large measure, and, sometimes in the face of many, he was successful.

He was interested in the betterment of Galax and the Twin Counties, and he gave unsparingly of his time and effort in support of such movements as he thought would lead to a more progressive area—a better citizenship, a better place in which to live, a better community.

Mr. Zabriskie was a good citizen, a patriotic citizen--in the truest and most meaningful sense of the word. To him, the word, "patriotism," meant exactly what our founding fathers had in mind when they set up our national government. The Flag of the United States of America had, for "Mr. Z," an almost special meaning, and he never missed what he considered an opportunity to emphasize the meaning of the Stars and Stripes, the good things of our American way of life for, and over, which Old Glory waves.

NEWSPAPER MAN – H. B. Zabriskie, owner of The Galax Gazette in 1931, was an experienced journalist.

(This article was from a scrapbook loaned to me, however the author was not a part of the   page nor the date or name of the publication)

18

Walter G. Andrews
Recognized for 20 years of Community Service

CITY MANAGER HONORED - Members of Galax City Council honored City Manager Walter G. Andrews at an informal dinner Tuesday night, marking his completion of 20 years as City Manager. Shown at the Midtowner Restaurant are, seated, Mayor McCamant Higgins, Andrews, Vice Mayor A. Glenn Pless. Standing: City Engineer Harold Snead and Councilmen Dr. William B. Waddell, John W. Sutherland, Henry L. Harris, Horace Cochran and Fred J. Roberts.

Walter G. Andrews was guest of honor at an informal dinner Tuesday night at the Midtowner in observance of his 20th anniversary as Galax City Manager.

Actually, Galax was a "town" when Andrews assumed the position of manager in 1947. However, seven years later, in 1954, the General Assembly approved the charter giving Galax the designation of City of the second class.

Mayor McCamant C. Higgins, who is completing his 16th year on Council, presented the City Manager with a special, embossed certificate, in a frame, commemorating his 20 years of service.

Members of Council were unanimous in praising the work of the City Manager during the past two decades, determining him "the best City Manager in the whole country".

The City Manager, in expressing appreciation for the honor, said the job of City
Manager was made easier by having "the type of good, sound businessmen serving on Council as we have had over the years."

"When the businessmen of the community won't serve on Council to look after the affairs of the community, you can expect the community to begin to slide backwards. We have been fortunate in Galax to have businessmen who will make the sacrifice to serve on the governing body. The advice and counsel of present members and others who have served before them make the City Manager's job easier."

The framed certificate presented to Andrews reads:

"Recognition Award presented to Walter G. Andrews in appreciation for twenty
years service as City Manager of the City of Galax 1947 -1967 12th Day of December,1967."

The certificate was signed by Mayor Higgins and the following other members of Council, all of whom were present at the dinner: Vice Mayor A. Glenn Pless, Dr. William B. Waddell, Henry L. Harris, Horace Cochran, John W. Sutherland, and Fred J. Roberts. Also attending the dinner were City Engineer Harold Snead and Galax Gazette Publisher Arthur Gurley.

19

Galax Cotillion Club 1965

The Galax Cotillion Club is a social club with a membership of 20 teenage boys under the sponsorship of Mr. R.O. Nelson. The club was organized many years ago under the sponsorship of Wyatt Exum who participated in the reorganization of the group in 1964. George Gillespie served as president that year.

Front row: Left to right

Doug Williams, Kay Reynolds, Jimmy Spinks, President David Morris, Vice-president Ted Brewer, Sect-Treasurer John Sutherland, Duane Alderman

2nd Row: Rudy Galyean, Allan Royal, Jimmy Galyean, Bill Lindsey, Larry Hackler, Mike Beamer and Ray Bedsaul

3rd Row: Johnny Funk, Chris Lineberry, Tommy Wilson, and Walter Mason.

Not Present: Mike Coomes, Sonny Morton, and Sponsor R.O. Nelson

Galax Gazette April 16, 1965

" Dr. Virgil Jefferson Cox
is one of the finest men I have ever known.
He has brought me through many sicknesses."

That's the way Howard Martin of Galax described Dr. Cox while he was getting his blood pressure checked recently.

This seems to be the trademark of Dr. Cox. To help his fellow man, especially in their time of need.

Cox, now 79 and slowly curtailing his practice of medicine, smiles a lot when he talks about his career which began almost 50 years ago.

"I have no idea of knowing how many patients I have treated," said Dr. Cox. "I do know that I have performed over 5,000 operations to remove tonsils and delivered more than 5,000 babies."

Although his hair has turned a light gray, Dr. Cox still has a very sharp mind and enjoys talking to his patients. His patients dearly love the man who has provided them with medical care for so many years, not worrying if they could pay his bill.

James Yates, a former resident of Galax who now lives in Columbus, Ga., remembers Dr. Cox as a kind man who came to his house at 2 a.m. when his wife went into labor.

Yates said he dreaded calling Dr. Cox at such an hour but his wife was going into labor. Dr. Cox came and Yates watched as the first baby girl was born. Yates was elated, but Cox told him to "just hold on old boy, there's another one coming."

Both girls were delivered healthy. When it came time to pay, Yates said he didn't have much money. Cox said just give me $20 and we'll call it even. Yates said he sold a pig to pay the $20.

This is the way people regard Cox. A man who is willing to help them regardless of the time of day or night, or the weather.

Cox recalls making house calls in the late 30s in his old V-8 Ford. "Shucks, if my car had broken down, or got stuck, I would have probably froze to death."

Cox was born in Peach Bottom, Va., near Baywood in Grayson County.

He attended nine different elementary schools before entering Baywood High School at the age of 16. "It seemed something always happened to our schoolhouse," said Cox.

One time, when I was in the first grade, we noticed flames coming from the flue leading from the old pot-bellied stove. My sister, Cleo Cox, screamed for everyone to grab their books that the schoolhouse was on fire. The kids got out safely but the one-room school was destroyed."

Cox said he attended several other schools in the community, including one in Nile, N. C., part of Alleghany County, just about two miles from his home.

21

"Sometimes we sat on benches in the schools," said Cox, "other times we had a desk and shared it with a second person, or desk-mate as we called them in those days."
After entering Baywood in the seventh grade, Cox remained there and completed the 11th grade.

"When it came time for my senior year, I decided to move to Fries, where my brother was a dentist," said Cox. "Baywood was not an accredited high school and Fries was, so I lived with my brother."

Cox said he was a senior in 1924 and William Tate was the principal of the school, which was a wooden structure then. He later pushed a wheelbarrow hauling cement to help build the present Fries school building. "I was paid 15 cents an hour and thought I was making big money," Cox said.

"I've always been interested in medicine," Cox said. "I entered Emory and Henry College in 1925 and washed dishes to make money to help pay my way there. I remember washing dishes about two weeks when one of the waiters quit his job. I moved up and was later made head waiter and made extra money for that."

Cox went to Emory and Henry for three summer sessions to gain officer at a transit camp in Fort Eustis, Va.

"I didn't make much money, $225 a month, but I did get some good experience at Fort Eustis."

Finding a place to open his first office was difficult for Cox. "At that time in Virginia, the ratio was one doctor for every 1,300 residents. In North Carolina, the ratio was one doctor for every 900 persons."

In 1936, Cox made the decision to return to Galax and opened his first office in the same building with Goodson's Cafe on Grayson Street. "I'll never forget the day," said Cox. "My first day in my office was July 11, 1936, and I made $11."

Cox describes himself as a general practitioner but he has performed several operations for fractures and other related injuries.

In 1953, he opened Blue Ridge Hospital and Clinic, with 24 beds. He later expanded the hospital to 44 beds and joined several other doctors in the venture. The name of the hospital was Galax General, which was closed when Twin County Community Hospital was opened.

Cox tried his hand at politics in 1962 when he was elected to the Virginia House of Delegates. He served two two-year terms, retiring in 1966 because it interfered with his practice.

During' his terms in the General Assembly, Cox helped to establish Mt. Rogers State Park, now known as Grayson Highlands State Park at Whitetop.

Cox said the medical profession had meant so much to him. He donated $25,200 to Emory and Henry College last year to be used as scholarships for students from Southwest Virginia who want to enter the medical profession.

Cox said he enjoyed his work, the patients who had meant so much to him during his career, and especially his wife, the former Gladys Guynn whom he married in 1930. "Gladys has been a real worker and stood beside me through my every endeavor." When asked about when he planned to retire, Cox only grinned. "I have curtailed my activities over the past several months, but I have no plans to retire all together.

"I just don't think I could live without going to my office every day," said Cox. "This is my life, and I certainly enjoy it every day." •

Larry Chambers, Editor in Chief. Galax Gazette

22

Employees of the Twin County Motor Company

Front Left to Right: Roy Manning, Jake Mink, Alvia Gilley, John Hackler, Lance Todd, Charles Carico, unknown, Clarence Bobbitt, unknown, E. G. Cummings, Duard Burnette.

Second Row: Charlie Bond, Ralph Jennings, Everett Faddis, Irwin King, Buford Lindamood,   W.B.. Lindamood, Orman Edwards, unknown, Frieda Watson, unknown, G.W. Todd.

Third Row: E.E. Richardson, Buford Crockett, Peyton Cock, McKinley Cox, Ross Boyer, Paul Crouse, Boyd Hawks, Ray Melton, Unknown, Garnett Bobbitt, unknown.

Glenn Pless

Galax community leader A. Glenn Pless, Jr. was born just one year after Galax became a city, and died a year before he would have witnessed the city's 90th anniversary.
Pless devoted his life to serving Galax.

Even in his younger years, Pless exhibited a drive to better himself and the community around him.
The Grayson County native attended the University of Florida and played baseball for the Gators. In 1928 he was picked up by the Class C Southeastern League and got a shot at being a professional baseball player. But upon returning to Galax for a visit, Pless was involved in a car wreck that caused him to lose his right hand.

His son, John, said that within a year his father learned to play baseball one-handed and was playing Class D ball for the Galax team.

That tenacity served him and Galax well in years to come.
In 1931 Glenn Pless took over the General Electric franchise in Galax. Two years later he added furniture to his business.

GLENN PLESS — his death came just short of the city's 90th birthday

John Pless recalls his father speaking of hardships and depressed conditions. He thinks his father was one of the first merchants to offer credit to customers during the trying times.

The senior Pless told of people asking to pay for their purchases with corn or potatoes. John said his father never doubted that people told the truth about their impoverished state.

But though his business concerns must have been overwhelming, Glenn Pless always made time to pay attention to other aspects of the community. He coached baseball and football at Galax High School for years.

When Galax flooded in 1940, Pless helped flood victims by canceling a majority of debts to his store. He then made a movie of the flood that he presented to a congressional appropriations committee. As a result, Chestnut Creek was widened and straightened and has not flooded to that degree since.

Pless also spent about 40 years on the board of the former Merchants and Farmers Bank in Galax - the bank that is now Signet Bank.

He also was president of the Galax Rotary Club and a member of the Sons of the American Revolution, Galax YMCA, Galax-Carroll-Grayson Chamber of Commerce and Galax Country Club .

He served on the board of Vaughn Memorial Library and Twin County Regional Hospital. Pless held elected office on what then was Galax Town Council.

Even though he spent hours serving the community, his down- town business also flourished. Pless Furniture Co., Inc., expanded to five stores over the years, including locations in Galax and Fries.

But the success did not mean he gave up on other efforts to bring commerce to the area.

Pless was president of the Galax Development Corp., an organization that bought a 26-acre tract and raised more than $1.2 million in a fund drive in an attempt to attract Hanes to Galax. The effort was successful and Hanes evolved into Sara Lee Knit Products - a major employer in the area.

John said that if there is one word to describe his father that word is "builder."

"He was the most fascinating man in my life - and that's not just because he was my old man," John said.
Glenn Pless said his father believed there was some good in everybody and that people had to be challenged to bring out the good in them.

He wouldn't let anyone feel defeated, according to his son. "He could pat you on the back and kick your butt at the same time," John Pless said.

By STEPHANIE JOHNSON Staff
Galax Gazette: "Celebrating 90 Years".
Monday/Tuesday July 1-2 1996
*Staff writer Larry Chambers also contributed information to this article.

The Pless complex on East Grayson street. The store on the right was occupied first with an empty lot on the left. Later, the second addition was built and filled in the empty space beside the Rex Theater.

Herm Lee Reavis started at WBOB in Galax

Herm was born in Reavistown, a small village in Grayson County, between Galax and Independence, Virginia, October 14, 1932, Reavis has been very influential in helping shape and guide Virginia radio and television. He entered into the broadcasting field more by accident than intent. At the age of 14, Herm began his broadcasting career in 1947 at WBOB in Galax. He happened to be listening to Bill White's "Club 300" show one night. White

announced that he needed "some young fella" to help out at the station. The following morning, Reavis walked three miles to apply for the job only to find that Mr. White had gone home upon completion of his shift the night before. Later that day, he again made the walk, met Mr. White and was hired. During high school, he worked part time at the station when he wasn't studying or playing football or baseball. He admits that radio made him a pretty popular guy around the small town. He began work at WBOB answering phones and then broke into on-the-air work, work which would gradually increase. Reavis was also emcee at the world famous Galax Fiddlers' Convention and of the Saturday Night Jamboree when he was still a teenager. He announced play-by-play of Galax High School football games and automobile racing long before the days of NASCAR. Yet, he says, the idea of making a radio career never really occurred to him.

Mayor B.D. Beamer and Johnny, the Phillip Morris "Call for Boy".
In 1953, a relative who was a radio and television engineer in Roanoke, told Reavis about the newly formed WRIS radio; he applied, was hired and signed the new station on the air in February of that year. He soon became a popular Icon known as "Uncle Herm" with his "Squirm With Herm" boogie and blues radio show gave way to the new bobby sox and drive-in generation which was witnessing the new Rock 'n' Roll revolution.

Some of his early experiences associated with his radio activities included traveling with Jimmy Dean and his band to Nashville for Dean's first recordings sessions with Mercury Records. During this time Dean's fiddle player, Buck Ryan, wanted to record an untitled song and titled it "Uncle Herm's Horn Pipe." He introduced well-known singer Wayne Newton and his brother Jerry, who as youngsters lived in Roanoke, to local radio audiences. They were regular visitors for a while to Reavis' early morning broadcast on WRIS. And in that same mid 50's period, he introduced a then-unknown man know as Elvis Presley before Presley's rise to fame and his celebrated appearance on the national Ed Sullivan Show. Presley was one of seven artist on the RCA Victor card playing in American Legion Auditorium and was so unknown that he was listed number 7 on the card.

Reavis gave up his personality status in 1956 to become general sales manager of WSLS AM/FM radio, part of Shenandoah Life Insurance Company's AM/FM/Television operation, which was later to become part of Park Broadcasting. In 1972 Reavis was named general manager of the newly formed WSLC-AM / WSLQ-FM when WSLS was sold to Mel Wheeler, Inc., the current owner of the two Roanoke stations. Reavis led WSLC at a time when block radio was the norm into a more contemporary format which included targeted country music, NASCAR motor racing and Virginia Tech sports, news and information. WSLC soon became the ratings leader in Roanoke radio, a position it held regularly until 1980 when FM radio signals became more numerous and listener acceptable. WSLQ at 200,000 watts is still one of the most powerful FM radio stations in the United States.

In April of 2007, Herm Reavis, joined the likes of fellow Virginians; Roger Mudd, John Harkrader, Ann Compton, James Kilpatrick, Earl Hammer, Willard Scott, Forrest Landon, Harry F. Byrd, Jr., and Lloyd Dobyns by being inducted into the 2007 Class of the Virginia Communications Hall of Fame. Pictured above, Dr. Judy Van Slyke Turk, Director, School of Mass Communications, Chair, Selection Committee, Virginia Communications Hall of Fame, with Herm Reavis

James Albert Eads

Every town has a man who is "street smart" and possesses a sharp business mind. James "Albert" Eads was just that man about town in the mid 20th century. He was born in Surry County North Carolina on 11 November 1905 to James Alexander Eads and Mary Alida Atkins. He belonged to the generation that was issued a delayed birth certificate because he was born during the period when the U. S. government did not require that births and deaths to be recorded. He and his wife Lulu were married in the late 1920s and were living in Madison North Carolina in 1930 where he was employed as an automobile mechanic. They had two daughters Helen and Frances, both born in North Carolina before they moved to Galax. By 1940 the family was living on Carroll Street in Galax and Albert owned his own mechanic business. This was about the time he built a rather unusual house for his family that centered around an old streetcar. It was located on Carroll Street behind what is now Hardy's. The house caught the attention of Hollywood and it was featured in one of the news reels that were shown in movie theaters before the main feature movie. The family later resided on East Stuart Drive.

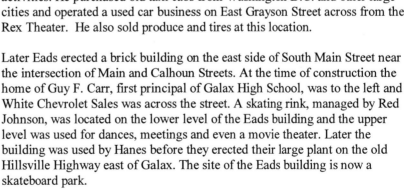

Like other successful, local men Albert owned many houses, buildings and lots around Galax. If one checks the deed books they will see how frequently ownership traded hands during this period of Galax history. Old timers will tell you that after the "great flood" Albert Eads traveled around the area east of Chestnut Creek in a rowboat as he bought property from people who were tired of

losing their homes to floods. As Eads conducted his business, he was rarely seen without his two pet monkeys. Not only were they constant companions they were featured in his ads.

If one took the time to read the old Galax Gazettes on microfilm at the library they would learn how patriotic residents were during World War II. All of the country's industry was focused on producing items for the war and Eads immediately recognized how profitable used cars could be for his business activities. He purchased old taxi cabs from Washington D.C. and other large cities and operated a used car business on East Grayson Street across from the Rex Theater. He also sold produce and tires at this location.

Later Eads erected a brick building on the east side of South Main Street near the intersection of Main and Calhoun Streets. At the time of construction the home of Guy F. Carr, first principal of Galax High School, was to the left and White Chevrolet Sales was across the street. A skating rink, managed by Red Johnson, was located on the lower level of the Eads building and the upper level was used for dances, meetings and even a movie theater. Later the building was used by Hanes before they erected their large plant on the old Hillsville Highway east of Galax. The site of the Eads building is now a skateboard park.

Mr. Eads passed away in Surry County in 1981 and his wife Lulu four years later in 1985. Both are buried in Monta Vista Gardens in Galax.

Blue Ridge Ladies End 1993 Season

Left to Right: Margaret Cheek, Martha Rose, Judy Chambers, Wilda Fayne and Janet Nuckolls

The Blue Ridge Country Club Ladies' Golf Association finished its golf season with the Hike Harter tournament on Oct. 2.

Martha Rose won the tournament following a two-hole playoff with Wilda Fayne after both ladies finished 18 holes tied with net scores of 64.

The Ladies' Championship tournament was won by Judy Chambers with rounds of 79 and 72 for a 151 total.   Pat Tickle was second with an 86-78-164. The Net Tournament was won by Janice McCullough with a 65-64-129. Fayne was runner-up with a 65-69-134.

Janet Nuckolls was the Most Improved Golfer with a two-stroke handicap improvement. Chambers won the "Birdie tree" in the 0-21 handicap division with 41 birdies scored on Ladies' Day. She also won for recording birdies on the most holes, 15. Rose and Janette Shockley tied for the most birdies in the 21-40 handicap division with three each.

Margaret Cheek won the Ringer tournament with a 54-stroke improvement from the beginning of the season.

Two golfers recorded eagles during the season. Chambers had one at Blue Ridge's 18th hole and another at Crestview's 15th, and Tickle recorded her eagle on the 18th at BRCC.
Galax Gazette October 24-25, 1993

28

Ladies End 1978 Season at Galax Country Club

Left to right: Margaret Hensley, Kit Ferguson, Opal Vaughan , Jackie Herman and Gladys Rhodes

The Ladies' Golf Association of Galax Country Club ended its season play Thursday, Sept. 28. To highlight the events, a dinner was held at the Rose Lane Motel at 6: 30 p.m. There were 14 ladies present along with guests, Dink Haley, pro, and Katherine Robinson.

Playing Match Play, defending Champion, Margaret Hensley, was again winner of the Club Championship for 1978. Kit Ferguson was runner-up.

Opal Vaughan was winner of the Handicap Tournament with Jackie Herman being runner-up.

The winner of the Hazel Waugh Tournament was: Gladys Rhodes.

Awards were given for various accomplishments as follows: RINGER BOARD -- 1st Low Score Margaret Hensley; 1st Most Improved - Lou Carson; 2nd Low Score – Kit Ferguson; 2nd Most Improved — Opal Vaughan. Silver Julep Cups were awarded for

low scores during the months of July, August and September.
Winners were: July —   Jackie Herman
             August —   Kit Ferguson
             September - Margaret Hensley

Kit Ferguson was named Most Improved Player of the Year. The Ladies' Golf Association presented the pro, Dink Haley, and his assistants with gifts to thank them for all their help during the year. In turn, Haley presented golf balls to all the ladies showing his appreciation for their participation in this year's activities.

Galax Gazette October 1978

Fire Department installs new Officials 1995-96

The Galax Volunteer Fire Department installed its newly elected officers recently. They are (from left) front, Chief

Mike Coomes, Honorary Chief Joe Crockett, and Assistant Chief Harvey Hennis; center, trustee Bays Roberts, Secretary/Treasurer David Hankley, Lieutenant Mark Burnett, Trustee James Talley; back, trustee Glenn Wilson, rescue squad Lieutenant

Neal Anderson, rescue squad Captain Charles Burnette, Captain Mac Higgins, and Chaplain Tom Whartenby.

BLUEMONT FIRE DRILL –

Employees of Bluemont Knitting Mills, Inc., were quickly and orderly evacuated from the plant Monday afternoon in another of a series of fire safety drills conducted by the company. A continuing fire and emergency safety program

is carried on by the company, with occasional fire drills.

Officials expressed pleasure at the orderly manner in which the employees carried out the drill. Lending realism to the drill was the presence of Galax Fire Chief E . C. Sutphin, and Assistant Chief Joe Crockett, with fire apparatus. Chief Sutphin commended the Bluemont officials on their safety program and urged other industries and business firms to take time to educate their personnel in the proper procedure in the event of an emergency Photo from Galax Gazette. **Galax Gazette date unknown**

Hats Off To Thomas Jeff Matthews

T.J. (Jeff) Matthews' offer of portions of his collections to the City of Galax is an act of generosity and deserves the gratitude of the citizens of Galax and of the surrounding community. Mr. Matthews' offer may be the spark needed to spur the city into acquiring a much-needed museum.

It may also serve to prompt others who have collections, antiques, etc. to give them to the city for exhibition.

Mr. Matthews properly qualified his offer, however. He will require the city to provide a place to exhibit his collections and also to take proper safeguards against loss or theft or fire. These are reasonable requests.

Mr. Matthews' collection of Indian artifacts is one of the finest in this section of the country. He has more than 6,000 arrowheads and spear points, plus about 100 tomahawks. They have been collected over a period of more than 30 years and most came from this general section. His collection of knives is believed to be unique. He houses his collection in a sturdy cinderblock structure in the yard of his home in Galax.

Thousands of people have viewed his collections through the years.

The other day Mr. Matthews invited Galax City Council to see his collections and while Council men were so doing he made his offer to the city. It was accepted with gratitude on the spot and later, in formal Council manic session, was accepted for the record.

Council, noting Mr. Matthews' request for protection, etc, of his gifts, appointed Councilman Ballard to study the matter and to make recommendations.

Among the city's needs, of course, is a museum which could be developed into a major tourist attraction. The sum of $5,000 a year is being set aside toward this purpose but it will take time to build up to the point that funds are sufficient in this manner.

One day, we will have a museum, but in the meantime the city needs a building in which it can house and exhibit collections such as those being given by Mr. Matthews.

Councilman Ballard would welcome suggestions-- or offers.

Whatever transpires, hats off to Mr. Matthews for his splendid and public-spirited offer!

An Editorial Opinion. Galax Gazette, Tuesday July 29, 1969

Jack E. Guynn ...Citizen

Galax Mayor Jack Guynn's first official words on assuming office were: "Come on, boys; let's get going."

With this admonition he opened the first meeting of Council in his new position of mayor, a title to which, as vice mayor, he fell heir upon the resignation of Mayor McCamant C. Higgins 14 weeks ago.

Although he was addressing his fellow Councilmen, his exhortation to "get going" may well become the hallmark of his administration.

Mayor Guynn in all probability doesn't recall his first words in office--but a newsman, bent on a personality feature such as this after the Mayor got his feet on the ground, jotted them down for future reference.

There is pride--a great deal of it--in Jack Guynn as he serves as mayor of Galax, there is also humility--a great deal of it--as he shoulders the responsibilities of the highest elective office the city has to offer.

The humility comes through when he expresses his feeling of "inadequacy in following such mayors as McCamant Higgins, Robert Nelson, B. D. Reamer, Walter Andrews (now city manager), Dr. Robert Bowie and other such men."

For a man who a year ago was saying that the last thing he would ever do would be to run for City Council, Jack Guynn has come a long way in a short time. Somewhere along the way he changed his mind, ran for Council, was elected last summer, and when Council reorganized in September was chosen vice mayor.

Today as probably the youngest mayor in the history of Galax (he's 43), he presides over what certainly is the youngest Council Galax has ever had (the average age is about 40).

It didn't take long for Mayor Guynn to realize that the position of mayor is much more time-consuming than that of Vice-Mayor.

As Mayor, he's called upon to welcome meetings of groups which include people who live outside Galax.

In addition to being the city's official spokesman, he's also its official "listener." Hardly a day passes but that he's not contacted--either by telephone or in person--by several citizens with problems or requests. You believe him when he says he enjoys those contacts.

As for his hopes of accomplishment during his tenure, Mayor Guynn admits to being a "nut" on two subjects: schools and municipal planning.

His goal for the city's school system is simple: "I want as fine a school system as there is anywhere." To this he added: "If you've got a good school system, the other things just naturally come along." The city's financial condition--and the community's booming economy--he thinks justify spending for a top-drawer school system.

He's deeply concerned because of the wide disparity between the city's ability to pay for its schools and its actual effort. According to statistics provided by the State Department of Education, of the 131 school divisions in Virginia, Galax ranks 26th in ability to pay but a woeful 103rd in actual local effort.

As for municipal planning, the city is already moving in the direction of acquiring a master plan which Mayor Guynn calls an absolute "must" for orderly and progressive growth of the city.

Particularly gratifying to Mayor Guynn is the way the Council operates as a close-knit, friendly group. What-ever differences of opinion have existed on issues facing Council have made no difference in the high regard which Councilmen hold for each other personally, he noted.

In business life, Jack Guynn is manager of Vaughan-Guynn Funeral Home. He's also involved in his family's chain of six furniture stores.

Jack Guynn was born 43 years ago in Hillsville, the son of Mr. and Mrs. Gilman E. Guynn, who now live at Woodlawn. He graduated from Hillsville High School where he played tackle on the football team (at 205 pounds instead of the present lithe 175). Incidentally, as a freshman he played on the Hillsville football team which was walloped by Galax High School, 81 to O. He also played on the Hillsville baseball team. In 1943 he played on the state champion Fork Union Military Academy football team and made all-state prep school tackle.

Then World War II intervened and he joined the Marines in 1944 in time to participate, as a member of a reconnaissance company of the Fifth Marine Division, in the bloody capture of Iwo Jima from the Japs.

After the war, he went to VPI (it was almost Auburn University under the lure of Coach Carl Voyles but a summer visit to hot and humid Alabama made him change his mind in favor of cool and windy Blacksburg. An injury his freshman year ended his football career. In 1949 he graduated from VPI and moved to Galax to become associates with Vaughan-Guynn.

Then came marriage to blond Mary Roberts of Galax and then came the children Flo, 14, Jay, 11, and Elizabeth, 7.

His wife and children, Jack Guynn says, have adjusted well his being mayor of their Town. "They keep me in my place," he said.

The mayor is a member of the First Presbyterian Church in Galax where he has served is a deacon. He's also a member of the Galax Country Club.

His hobby? Well, you might call it jogging. He learned it two years ago from a young ministerial student named David Morgan who was a summer guest in the Guynn home while the pastor of the First Presbyterian Church, the Rev. Robert Dendy, was overseas.

Every afternoon at 4 o'clock--regardless of the weather--Mayor Guynn runs precisely one mile. His "track" is a path he's worn around the outside of his house. It takes 24 times around the house to run the mile and neighbors have at last become accustomed to their Mayor's afternoon antics. Perhaps this explains why the crew-cut, iron-gray-haired, six-foot Mayor Glynn now weighs 175 pounds instead of the 205 pounds he weighed when he played tackle.

As for his 100 days as mayor of Galax, Jack Guynn sums it up thusly: "It's been an education in a big way. I'm really enjoying it,"

Talking to him about the job, you get the impression he means every word of it.

By STAFF WRITER Galax Gazette

James Piper Carico
Biographical Notes

-Born 26 August 1857 in Stevens Creek Community, Grayson County, VA

-Died 2 September 1936 following a meeting in Richmond VA while riding in a car travelling to Williamsburg. He passed while in the arms of his daughter, Nell, who was a nurse. (See the particulars regarding this in the newspaper accounts on the CD.)

-Father: John Stevenson Carico. (1816-1863); Mother: Lucy Hale Wright Carico (1820-1863). These individuals and their ancestors were all among the early pioneers of Grayson County.

-Seven siblings of J. P. Carico:

Miles H. (1843-1862). Died in Staunton, VA of disease while serving in the Confederacy

Amanda J. (1845-1909). Married a Wright?, no children.

Wiley H. (1847-?). Married Melissa Ann Lundy, 5 children.

Martha A. (1849-1928). Married 1886 to Robert S. Aker, no children.

Isabella A. (1851-1942). Never married.

Julina F. (1854-1863). Died age 9.

Emma C. (1860-1869). Died age 9.

NOTE: Notice the death dates of four family members including brother Miles (1862), mother, father, and sister Julina (1863) all within one year. Records show that Miles died of a "disease" in Staunton while serving in the confederate army and the deaths of the others less than a year later. It is assumed (not proven) that Miles may have visited home carrying some communicable disease contracted during his war service and passed it to the family members on the occasion of this visit. This left J. P. in the household at age 6 with the remaining brother Wiley and sisters Amanda, Isabella, and Emma. The census of 1870 listed J.P. at age 12 in a household with brother Hicks (Wiley H.) and sisters Amanda, Martha and Isabella. The census of 1880 indicated J.P. was "head of household" at age 22 living with his three sisters Amanda (age 34), Isabella (age 26), and Martha (age 28).

-Married 13 Dec 1883 to Elizabeth K Bourne (9 September 1865 – 3 May 1951) at the Curtis Bourne home place in Spring Valley, Grayson County, VA.

-Children of J. P. and Elizabeth Bourne Carico:

Lucy Blanche (1890-1927), Married Harry Edward Early. No children.

Harry Bourne (1893-1979), Married Helen Maude Carlan. One daughter. Worked for a chemical company in Asheville, NC. Was in World War I as a member of Army Ambulance Company in northern Russia in a campaign known as the "Polar Bear Expedition"

Eugene Hix (1897-1944), Married Clyde Harp. No children. Served in the World War I; died of cancer soon after coming home from service,

Nell Fries (1901-1994), Married Stirling Mann. No children. She was trained as a nurse.

James Khale (1905-1990), Married Juanita (Nita) Sue Cox. One son (James Edwin Carico), one daughter (Georgia Ann Carico McMillan). Employed in the Galax post office many years until retirement.

Kate McCollum (1907- unknown), married William Love Osborne. One son, one daughter. Housewife.

Role of J. P. Carico in the founding of Galax: He played a significant role in the founding of Galax by being part of a real estate venture that bought the land, had it surveyed for a town and sold lots. In addition to the clippings, see the Galax 100th anniversary site and others for some details;

Role of J. P. Carico in the founding of Fries: While trading horses in North Carolina, he persuaded Col. Fries to consider building a cotton mill and dam on the new river, This resulted in the development of a mill town, Fries. J.P. Carico is given the distinction of being the key person for the founding of this town which exists now long after the mill operation ceased to exist.

J. P. Carico Memorial Bridge: This bridge, spanning the New River between Galax and Fries via Rt. 94, was erected in 1927. Although there seems to be no documentation to support the contention, it was apparently named in 1942 in honor of J.P. Carico's role in the founding of both Galax and Fries among his other civic accomplishments. Since this bridge was, for several years, the only highway link across the New River between these two towns, the naming was a logical choice. This bridge is now scheduled to be replaced by a new bridge. The old bridge will be available for removal and reconstruction elsewhere by a private entity.

For your information, I am investigating with the Department of Transportation the possibility of leaving the old bridge in place and converting into a recreational park for observation of the river and fishing among other possibilities. If this is not possible, then I am looking into having the dedication and name transferred to the new bridge.

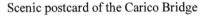

Scenic postcard of the Carico Bridge

River flooded , probably in the flood of 1940

Oral historical notes regarding J. P. Carico: There are only four items of oral history that I can recall. First, J.P. was a familiar site on various street corners in Galax with pocket knife in hand cutting bites off a block of cheese while chatting with citizens. Second, J. P. was the local contact for Harry F. Byrd when he made trips throughout the state, presumably while he was governor and later as US Senator. From this I assume J. P. was an important member of the Democratic Party representing the area. Third, J. P. was a horse trader supplying horses for (presumably) the First World War and toured the countryside buying up horses. Fourth, for a time he was either the owner of, or real estate broker for the sale of the famed old mansion at Fort Chiswell that is visible from I81 east of Wytheville, VA. My father (James Khale Carico) recalled that he and a friend stayed a night or two in the house and found several Civil War relicts in the **attic**.

Compiled by: James Edwin Carico, 15 Nov. 2008

Mrs. Slayton's 1965 Kindergarten class

Front row: L to R: Guynn Barr, Elaine Eller, Ronnie Kim, Ellen Kim, Dede Ward.
second row: Kemper Galyean, Richard Spurlin, David Foster, Ann Sage, Mark Poole, Eric Cox, Timmy Spraker,
Third Row: Jeanie Horn, John Augustin, Allen Brewer, Mark Carr, John y Combs, Beth Porter

Kindergarten Class enjoys:
Mrs. Hum Kim entertained the children of Mrs. Ed Slayton's Kindergarten Class at the First Methodist Church with an Easter Party at 10AM in the Kindergarten Room on Thursday April 15.

After an indoor Easter Egg hunt was enjoyed by the group, refreshments were served by the hostess assisted by Mrs. Slayton. Easter Baskets with sets of hens and chickens were given as favors. Cup cakes in fluted paper baskets decorated with jelly beans were served with ice cream and punch.

The children are shown with their Easter Baskets in the picture above.

Galax Gazette April 1965

Lance M. Todd

Someone once said that there was a story in everyone, if you just looked for it. Well, a person doesn't have to look too hard to see that Lance Todd certainly has a truly interesting story.

Mr. Todd was one of the charter members of the Galax Fire Department.

He started on the fire department when there were just 16 members and the streets of Galax were still dirt roads. At that time there were no fire trucks. The fire-fighting equipment used then consisted of two two-wheeled carts, with the fire hose rolled up on them and were pulled by hand. It took eight men to pull each cart, so the department was divided into two companies.

When a fire occurred each company tried to beat the other to the fire. They had what you might call a running competition. At this time one of the carts was kept at the present location of the Veteran's Cab Stand and the other was kept at the fire house.

LANCE M. TODD

Veteran machinist and former Fire Dept. Chief, Lance Todd, retired--but not for long

Mr. Todd recalls one quite interesting and humorous event connected with these carts. One day a fire broke out and each company started racing toward it. As fate would have it, both companies reached the intersection of Oldtown and South Main Street at the same time. This was a very unfortunate thing to happen because they collided throwing men and equipment in every direction.

In 1929 he was made fire chief and served thirteen years in succession. Later he served several other shorter terms as chief.

Lance Todd is a machinist, in fact he is considered to be one of the top machinists in the country. He went to work for Twin County Motor Company in 1918. He worked for them for 42 years.

He retired in 1960 and stayed retired for a few months. An energetic man, he soon found retirement to be pretty dull so he went to work for the M&M Saw Filing Company where he is presently employed.

He was also the first scout master in the Galax area. He began in 1914, just four years after scouting came to America. He served as scout master for almost three years.

Mr. Todd is almost 76 years old and he and his wife of 50 years, Ollie, live at 301 Anderson Road, Galax.

By JIMMY MILLER

Lance Todd home on West Oldtown

Mary Tidline Remembered

Mary Tidline was best known as she appeared in this 1998 Gazette photo: wearing her black felt hat and carrying her cake box and walking to town from her home in Oldtown to sell baked goods in downtown Galax.
Gazette file photo by Brian Funk

One of Galax's longest-lived and most beloved citizens passed away on March 17 at Waddell Nursing Home. Mary Tidline, who was 105 when she died, was a longtime resident of the Oldtown community of Galax, and was famous for walking to town — always impeccably dressed — with her boxes of cakes and pies to sell for many years.

Tidline was born in Crumpler, N.C., in 1908. She was married to the late Samuel K. Tidline and the couple had one son, John Neal. An obituary notes that she was preceded in death by both her son and her beloved cat, Buster.

Tidline was a church mother at Old Town Baptist in her community, as well as a choir member, missionary and "friend to everyone," her obituary says.
Below, we are reprinting a feature story on Tidline that ran in The Gazette in January 1998.

By BRIAN FUNK
Staff
Mary Tidline said she promised God that if she lived to see her 90th birthday, she would go jogging.
So, when Jan. 17 came, she took off down the road.

She ran around a church parking lot in her neighborhood, Galax's Oldtown section, and returned home.
"I got tired. By the time I got back to the gate, I was walkin' like a duck," Tidline says with a laugh.
Of course, she does most everything with a laugh and a mischievous smile.

Tidline has not let age take its toll on her. Her back is slightly bent from osteoporosis and her hair — which hangs in two braided pigtails across her shoulders — has turned gray, but her mind and wit are sharp and her hands are always busy.

She is best known for baking and delivering her cakes and pies around town, something she has been doing for years.
Tidline is hard to miss with her black felt hat and blue metal cake box, as she travels downtown Galax selling her wares.
She also crochets and makes sock monkeys — stuffed animals made from sewing together pairs of socks. She sells these and other items at Rooftop of Virginia's craft store in Galax.

"People talk about how I do all this stuff, but I don't do it for the money. I get enough money from Uncle Sam to get by
"It's just me and this cat."

With this, she calls to her constant companion, a fuzzy 7-year-old gray-and-white tomcat named Buster.
He saunters into the room like he owns it, eyeing a visitor with suspicion disguised as indifference.
Maybe it's the fact that she's so active at her age that makes other feel guilty. They don't have the energy and ambition to do half as much at a third her age.

"I believe people are just jealous. They think it's a sin or something to be out there."
She says she stays so busy to keep from being lonely.

"People ask me if I live by myself, and tell them, 'No — I have God, my

38

cat, devil and me!'"

Tidline has always been busy, she said, from the time she was a little girl.

That is one of her keys to staying so young at heart.

"I've worked hard all my life. I thank God I'm still in good health. I've never been seriously sick."

So what is her secret?

"It ain't no secret. God's got the secret to that. Faith in God strengthens me every day, and I just live one day at a time."

She does reveal that she never drank or smoked, and doesn't take too much medicine.

"I don't buy over-the-counter medicine — just what the doctor gives me. And if that helps in two or three days, I quit taking it."

Though she said she eats right, it's hard to resist her own cooking.

"I eat plenty of the sweet stuff!" she says with a sly grin.

For her birthday, she got lots of candy and cookies from friends, along with flowers and toys.

She loves any kind of wind-up, noise-making toy she can find — like the plastic parrot that sits in the living room and repeats whatever she says to it.

"Oh, quit mocking me!" she scolds the bird after demonstrating it to a guest.

On Tuesdays and Thursdays, Tidline loads her "sweet stuff" into the cake box, puts on her hat and heads to town.

She attends the seniors program at Rooftop and eats lunch there.

Then she heads across the street to the Galax Farmers' Market and sets up shop, weather permitting.

"I enjoy it down there. You meet a lot of people coming through from all over. One woman from Philadelphia bought $60 worth of stuff. "I don't think it was because she needed it. I think she was just trying to help."

In the summer she has her garden, and in the winter she sews her sock monkeys and crochets doilies and other items. Her work can last well into the night.

"I never go to bed until 1 or 2 o'clock. I always leave something to do at night."

Tidline said she is the oldest person who sells at the farmers' market.

"There was one lady two or three years younger than me, but she's in the nursing home now."

That's a place she never wants to go.

"There's a lot of people in there that don't need to be. They've just give up.

"I'm not going to give up!"

Tidline came to the area in 1963, after meeting and marrying Sam Tidline of Galax.

She was born in Crumpler, N.C., and moved to Jefferson, N.C., with her mother and siblings when she was 9 years old.

She was the youngest of seven children, and the only one left.

Her mother cooked at a hotel in Jefferson. She remembers standing on a stool so she could reach the table and help her mother sift flour.

"Back in those days, you didn't do nothing but cook and clean and wash for white families, and you might get 75 cents or a dollar.

"In those days, that's all the work black people and the poor classes of white people could get — cook in the house or work in the fields."

When she was 16, Tidline grew tired of working for pocket change and "shipped off" to North Wilkesboro.

"I got tired of it, so I took off. I worked in a café, and I was getting big money back then, $4 a week. That's back in what I call the good ole days."

She looks back on those days with fond remembrance, but also with some regret.

"When I was young and ran away from home, I was like a duck in a yard full of corn. I didn't do as I should do, and it took me 37 years to get back on the right track."

Her mother came one day to ask Tidline to come back home, but she refused.
Instead, she went to Winston-Salem, N.C., to work in a tobacco factory.

When her mother died, she returned home to stay with her brothers and sisters.
Years later, she met and married Sam Tidline, her second husband. In the 1960s, she moved to his farm in Oldtown, where Sam raised tobacco and cows.

"I never did any farming. I loved working in tobacco until I seen them big, green tobacco worms. I'm scared of them, so when I saw one, I went to the house."

So, she started a strawberry patch and a garden, which she still maintains in the summer. She also raised calves on a bottle.
Her husband died, but she still lives in the same little house on land that once was the farm.

Tidline says she enjoys living by herself, and never wanted to remarry. "When my husband died, I said I'd never want another man. When you've got a husband, all you've got is a big, overgrown child.

"You need to cook for him, keep his clothes clean and tell 'em when they need a haircut. "They're a lot of work."

Tidline said she didn't get much formal education, but she has a wisdom that can only come from living 90 years — and learning from some mistakes.

"We lived a mile and a half from the schoolhouse, but we had to walk and I didn't have sufficient clothes for the bad weather."
Most of what she learned came from her brother. "He got tired of me asking him what all these words meant, so he told et that when I came to a long word that I didn't understand, to just say 'elephant' and keep on reading."

She claps her knee and laughs, sighing at the end.

Tidline loves to tell stories and teach her visitors about the world and how it has changed.

"Lord, I can't begin to tell you how I've seen things change. The main thing is people. Back in those days, they didn't gossip like they do now."

When the evening news comes on television, Tidline shakes her head at reports of alleging presidential philandering. "But we can't judge. God doesn't want us to judge."

Opportunities for black people have grown since Tidline was a girl. She said her brother would get mad when white people made racist statements, but prejudice was something her mother taught her early on to ignore.

"She said that it doesn't matter what color you are. If you look in nature, there are black birds, black cows, black ants, black snakes and animals of all colors.

"It's not our outside appearance that we should look at. It's not what's in our heart; it's what's inside."
So now that she's passed the 90-year milestone, what's next?

"Well, I'm getting kindly tired of cooking now. I think I'm going to give it up when I get 91… or maybe 95."Then, when I turn 95, I'm going to join the army!"

Photographs Courtesy of the Doug Saunders Collection

Top..Left to right: Annie Wolf -Fannoy Tucker-Glen & Onnie Kyle
Middle: John Bolgins, Kansas Blair, Leota..1962
Bottom: Alonza Tidline & Walter Bryan, --Mack Wolf, Wife Nora and McKinnley and Bertie- Mary Robinson

Doug Saunders Family Photos   with letter about baptism

Top to bottom, left to right: Letter (typed out on next page) and Yvonne Blair.

Bottom; Neta Sue Bryan, --Walter Bryan and Uncle Roue Bryan with car, R. C. Cox.
Bottom Right : Tidline, Hale and Bryn.

The letter describes the activity in the River, a Baptism by Elder A. H. Bryan

Baptismal Service
This Baptizing was held on New River near where Mr. Sam Griggs has his summer home. It is Elder A. H. Bryan in the river with his members, followers. This was the only place for the Baptist to carry out their faith and beliefs. It has been said that he conducted one of the most beautiful , effective services. His voice echoing seemingly upon the water like it might have been a telephone system. People came for many miles both in Virginia and in North Carolina, often walking to attend one of his Baptismal Services. It is not known who was being baptized but one can almost feel the coolness of the River, it's silent beauty. It was there to help man to carry out the ordinance of Jesus Christ Who said " Ye must be Baptized of Water"

Early Galax Residents had Connection to Oldtown

By Muncy Poole, Gazette news editor

Dan B. Waugh

The history of the village of Oldtown, near Galax, which is formally the county seat of Grayson County, is closely interwoven with that of one of the real pioneer families of Galax----the Waugh family

Dan B. Waugh who resides on W. Center St. in Galax, is thought to be the only person now living in Galax who was born in Oldtown, one of Oldtown's pioneer families.

Mr. Waugh, a former mayor of Galax and who has long been engaged in the mercantile business here said in an interview recently that Oldtown which was a Grayson County seat in the early 1800s was settled by a number of pioneer families among those was that of Dr. B.F. Cooper whose home still stands there

Among others of the initial settlers of Oldtown, Mr. Waugh said, was a Mr. Howard, a Northerner who lived where the residents of the late Clayton H Higgins now stands. Howard, it was said, married a McCamant who was engaged in farming.

Another of the Oldtown pioneers was Dr. W.R. Duphey who was a large landowner. Dr. Duphey had two daughters, one of whom married the late J.H. Witherow who was a Galax merchant well into the 1930s, and the other of whom married the late Dr. B.S. Dobyns, who was a Galax physician, and practice medicine in Fries also for a time many years ago

Dr. B.F. Cooper was another of the Pioneer residents of Oldtown. His five daughters were Mrs. A.C. (May) Anderson and Mrs. C.E. (Lillie) Anderson both of Galax, Steve (Emma) Hale of Mount Airy North Carolina and Mrs. F.L.(Ettie) Warrick, Mrs. Jim (Lula) Dobyns and Mrs. A.F. (Nanny) Hoff all of Kingsport, Tennessee. A son died as an infant.

Another early-days Oldtown resident was Dr. C.A. Witherow, who was the father of the late J.H Witherow and B.G. Witherow who were well-known Galax citizens another son Dr. Touty Witherow died young.

Since Oldtown is so close to Galax, actually a suburban community, it may well be said that there has been a Waugh's store in (for what is now) Galax are almost a century and a half.

James Waugh, father of the late Capt. John Blair Waugh (Confederate States Army) began the operation of a store in Oldtown in 1827. He was the grandfather of Dan Blair Waugh, who is now associated with his sons, J. Blair

Waugh and Charles Waugh, in the operation of the Dan B Waugh and Co. store and their store is located on the original Waugh store site in Galax on the southeast corner of Main and Grayson streets.

William P Waugh brother of Capt. Waugh was wounded in the Civil War. He recovered however and opened a store in Oldtown after the close of the war. He had three daughters by his first marriage: Mrs. J.H. Dunkley wife of Dr. Dunkley, of Roanoke and Saltville, Mrs. Edgar Reeves of Jefferson North Carolina and Mrs. Ed Wolfe, who operated a store in Oldtown after William P. Waughs death in 1896.

William P. Waugh had two children by his second marriage, to Miss Leila Nuckolls. These were the late Miss Susie Waugh and the late Swift Waugh, both of Galax. Mrs. Lelia Waugh operated the old Waugh hotel in Galax where the Post Office now stands.

Lelia Waugh

Capt. John B Waugh opened a second Waugh store in Oldtown soon after his return from service in the Civil War.

(*Mrs. Lelia Waugh*)

Capt. Waugh and his wife Mrs. Jennie Perkins Waugh of Ashe County, North Carolina had four children. They were Charles Perkins Waugh of Galax, Ms. Berta Waugh who died at 21 or 22 years of age, Dan B. Waugh Galax, and the late Dr. Richard J Waugh of Pulaski, where he practiced dentistry.

(*Capt. J. B. Waugh*)

Having volunteered for service in the Confederate Army, Capt. Waugh commanded Company C the 63rd Virginia infantry Regiment. He fought in the famed Civil War battle of Missionary Ridge near Chattanooga, Tennessee and in various other engagements of that great conflict.

Capt. Waugh and his son Charles P, were together in the operation of the store J.B. Waugh and sons in Galax, In 1900. When the Norfolk and Western Railroad was extended to what was then Blair, now Cliffview, Charles B. Waugh opened a store there. The store at Oldtown was continued there for a while.

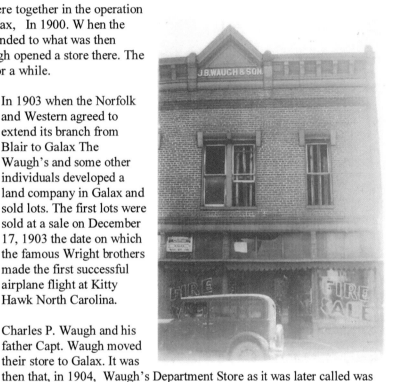

In 1903 when the Norfolk and Western agreed to extend its branch from Blair to Galax The Waugh's and some other individuals developed a land company in Galax and sold lots. The first lots were sold at a sale on December 17, 1903 the date on which the famous Wright brothers made the first successful airplane flight at Kitty Hawk North Carolina.

Charles P. Waugh and his father Capt. Waugh moved their store to Galax. It was then that, in 1904, Waugh's Department Store as it was later called was opened Galax.

The first J.B. Waugh and Son (as it was first known for several years) store Galax was destroyed by fire in the spring of 1905, it was rebuilt of brick construction, and was reopened in the summer of 1905.

After he returned from service in the U.S. Army during WW1 Dan B Waugh purchase what was then known as the Jones store (operate by Emmett Jones) on North Main St. and operated a store (The Dan B. Waugh store) there until 1933 The store site was then occupied by the A&Z store by the late W. A. Alderman and the late M.W. Zack.

Dan B. Waugh then moved to the present Waugh site at Main and Grayson.

Waugh's department stores cease to operate as such in the fall of 1932.

Charles P. Waugh operated Waugh's Warehouse until his death 27 years ago (1942) There on Rail Road Avenue, he bought beans, wool, berries, furs etc. for distant markets and sold feeds.

Charles P. Waugh, pioneered in the promotion of the Birdseye Bean Industry, which flourished in the Carroll and Grayson County area for some time in the early 1920s. During those years, almost every farmer raised a crop of Birdseye beans. During that period, Charles P Waugh also operated a warehouse at Speedwell in Wythe County.

Capt. J. B. Waugh

The Capt. John B. Waugh home was built in Galax and the Waughs moved here from Oldtown in 1912. This large Old Colonial style brick resident on West Stuart drive is now the home of Mrs. Charles B Waugh. The Dan B. Waugh home is south of the old Waugh residence on the south side of W. Center St. and just west of Stuart Drive. Capt. John B wall died in December 1934 and is buried at felt cemetery

Dan B. Waugh entered the U.S. Army air Corps in the spring of 1917 and was in England for 11 months. He had served at Kelly Field, Texas at San Antonio. He was discharged from Military service December 1918, following the German surrender at the end of World War I with the armistice of November 11, 1918. He was among the first of the overseas troops to return home after the close of the war.

Mr. Waugh married Hazel Phipps in 1925. Their sons J. Blair and Charles R. continue to operate the Dan B. Waugh and Co store Galax, doing business at the same "old stand" after 65 years

Dan B. Waugh was a member of the Galax town Council for a number of years and served a term as mayor about 10 years ago.

Among members of other pioneer families of Oldtown, which Mr. Waugh recalled were Dr. A.R. Grubb, a dentist who was the father of Miss Hattie Grubb Caldwell wife of the late J.K. Caldwell for many years a well-known Galax physician; Emmett Grubb, who married Miss Lou Grubb who is still living in Galax and Bud Kegley was a resident of Oldtown. In somewhat later years, Mr. Kegley was a father of Dewey J Kegley who now lives in Galax.

FIRST COUNTY SEAT

HERE AT OLD TOWN, IN 1794, WAS BUILT THE FIRST COURTHOUSE OF GRAYSON COUNTY. THE LAND WAS DONATED BY FLOWER SWIFT. A SECOND COURTHOUSE WAS BUILT IN 1838. THE COUNTY SEAT WAS REMOVED TO INDEPENDENCE ABOUT 1850.

Dan Waugh Studies Historical Marker at Oldtown

Troy Goodson

Troy Goodson Doesn't Wait Until December 25 to Put Christmas Into His Work

Christmas is a time for remembering, and not only is it a time for remembering but it is a time for doing---doing good deeds for our fellowmen, in keeping with the precepts of Him whose birth Christmas commemorates. "Inasmuch as ye did it unto one of the least of these my brethren, ye have done it unto me," said the Prince of Peace. These teachings are not limited, however, to the Christmas season, and in Galax there is a man who, through his many years in business here, has not waited until the happy Christmas season, but has brought, in a measure, "peace and good will" to many persons in need of kind words and kind deeds along the way---between Christmases! That man is Troy Goodson.

In his restaurant business, Mr. Goodson has been in a position where it has often been possible for him to extend acts of kindness to those who have come his way, to use the terminology of the day, "down on their luck." Whether or not many of them were deserving of the kind deeds extended, Mr. Goodson has not seriously questioned. Many hundreds of people he has fed, thus having made them happy as they went on their way, and Mr. Goodson has thereby been made happy too. And that was enough for him. For, again, did not the Prince of Peace say: "For I was an hungered and ye gave me meat."

Many have been the tired travelers who have enjoyed a free cup of coffee at his counter. In 1937 and 1938, twelve men who were working on the Blue Ridge parkway construction project were given room and board for $1 a day each. And, even so, Mr. Goodson said, "I made some money at it."

Mr. Goodson, who was born in Grayson county, in the Goodson settlement near the headwaters of Chestnut creek, came to Galax 'way back in "The Roaring Twenties." and set himself up in business. In that year, before Lindbergh flew the Atlantic and while "Silent Cal" Coolidge was in the White House, Mr. Goodson established a restaurant business on South Main street, where Harris' footwear store is now located. There he operated the eating place until 1932, when---in the midst of the Great Depression---he opened his restaurant, as the "Snappy Lunch," at his present location on (116) West Grayson street. He opened this business on October 8, 1932, and McCamant Higgins was the first man to eat there, said Mr. Goodson, "and he ate a five-cent sandwich and a Coca-Cola."

"I sold all kinds of sandwiches for eighteen months at five cents a-piece, and I didn't have a seat of any kind in the house for the first eighteen months," continued Mr. Goodson.

In those days, said Mr. Goodson, he bought pork ham at 11 cents a pound, hamburger sausage at six cent. "I made more on that five-cent sandwich than I am making today with hamburgers a quarter and paying 39 cents a pound for the meat that goes in 'em."

Now, his place of business, Goodson's Restaurant is large and modern, and well equipped, a far cry from the place opened October 8, 1932 (on his 46th birthday). Hundreds of people eat in it every week .

Looking over the restaurant room, with people contentedly partaking of the food served by Mr. Goodson and his staff of cooks, waitresses, etc., Mr. Goodson said: "I haven't done all of this by myself. The Good Lord has helped me. I thank Him today for it."

He explains also that Mrs. Goodson, the former Miss Bessie Lowe, has been with him all the way, and has done much to help him do whatever he has done.

Speaking of his family, he said he had reared one boy and two girls, and was "still raising three," who are with him. Two of these are now away at school. They are Rodger Goodson and Michael Goodson, Rodger attending King College, Bristol, and Michael, in school in New York. They are the children of Mr. Goodson's late son, Attorney Price Goodson. A daughter, Mrs. Ila York, passed away during the past year. The other daughter, Mrs. Beulah Harris, lives in Jackson, Tenn. He said he manages to "help some" from time to time the boys who are in school.

Mr. Goodson recalled that he has managed his business through "good times" and "bad times," and that during the years he had witnessed many changes. Before coming to Galax in 1925, Mr. Goodson worked in the T. N. Woodruff store at Low Gap, N. C., or two years, and it was this position that he left when he came to Galax.

Mr. Goodson's parents were the late Ben Goodson and wife, Mrs. Edna Lowe Goodson, and he mentioned that his grandfather, the late Kirby Lowe, was 106 years old at the time of his death.

Troy and Bessie Goodson

Galax Gazette

Galax, Grayson-Carroll Counties, Virginia Thursday, December 23, 1954 By Munsey M. Poole

"Pop" Goodson----A Tribute

(1886-1970)

If there is a generation Gap in Galax it is the fact that the younger generation does not remember the Snappy Lunch Cafe and Mr. Troy Goodson, who operated it for 28 years. They have missed knowing, first-hand, about an important part of Galax's history, for fire destroyed the restaurant in 1961, and death has taken Mr. Goodson from our midst this April, 1970.

Snappy Lunch was no ordinary restaurant, because its owner, Mr. Troy Goodson was no ordinary man. He would have been far richer in money if he had been paid for all the meals he gave away, but he was very rich in things that couldn't be counted in terms of dollars and cents. When we read in the Bible, " For inasmuch as ye have done it unto one of the least of these my brethren, ye have done it unto me" and "For I was an hungered and ye gave me meat," we know that Troy Goodson was one who based much of his philosophy of life on these words.

He came to Galax in the "roaring twenties," when Calvin Coolidge was in the White House. He had worked before that in the T. N. Woodruff store in Lowgap (NC) for two years. He first established a restaurant business on South Main Street, and then later in1932, he opened a restaurant on Grayson Street where the parking lot of Western Auto now is. It was a small, narrow building, and the menu was simple; hot dogs and hamburgers. Later, he enlarge his business and moved into a larger building that was where Western Auto now is. Benny Benfield, who is now employed at the Midtowner Restaurant, worked for Mr. Goodson from 1939 to 1960. He tells about Mr. Goodson and the restaurant this way:

"We always called him 'Pop' Goodson, and he was a good man to work for. He never got mad and he never turned anyone away if they were 'down on their luck' and broke, and needed a good meal. We were a three-man team at the first. 'Pop' operated the grill in the front, and Jack Todd and I waited on tables. We used a wood stove and everything, including the sink, was homemade. Coffee was 5 cents a cup, hot dogs 5 cents, and hamburgers 15 cents. ' Pop' had $4.00 to his name when he opened the restaurant, but he made it. 'Pop' Goodson was good to everybody. I never saw him get mad, and he had plenty of problems, but he took things as they came. This chair I'm sitting in is the one that was in the front of the restaurant for so many years. There were two. Mr. Pet Barlett occupied one for many years, and 'Pop' was often in the other one. One burned when the restaurant caught fire, but this one didn't and I brought it home with me. Restaurants came and went in this town, but Snappy Lunch just came and stayed, and people will never forget what it was like when it was the friendliest place in town."

As the business grew, so did the number of employees, and besides this family, which included his wife, Bessie, and children, grandchildren, nieces and nephews, there were others who worked there and are remembered and identified as having been a part of the "Goodson Cafe" years. Each of them can tell of so many ways in which their employer showed them acts of kindness and consideration. Among them are Charlie Harmon, John Tucker, Nora Davis, Jessie Davis, Nora Kinzer, Maude Mooney, Louise Grubb, Mamie Carpenter, Alice Bartlett, A. B. Cook, Leila and Marie Vass, and many, many others.

If there was a specialty of the house in his restaurant all through the years, it was the hamburgers. No "all meat" advertisement would have described the, for "Pop" Goodson made no pretense of serving an "all meat" hamburger. They were his own special mixture, and nobody is sure what all he mixed together, but one thing is for sure--- nobody else, then or now, has served such delicious hamburgers.

Mr. A. E. Doub, owner of the Galax Florist, and a long-time friend of Mr. Goodson, spoke very sentimentally about him recently, recalling the 32 years he had known him, and the 14 years he ate every meal in this restaurant after his wife died. He didn't talk so much about the food as about the man who ran the restaurant. Mr. Doub said, "I told him many times to his face that no man ever had a better heart. He raised about three families in that restaurant, and did it with a glad heart."

As we look back over the years, many of us perhaps, have forgotten, or neglected some of the fundamentals that were characteristic in the life of Troy Goodson, the willingness to work, respect for authority, consideration of the rights of others, the practice of thrift, and self reliance. We need to get back to and practice some of this things.

He was a religious man. His love for his fellow-man showed in his many acts of kindness to people in every walk of life, family, friends and strangers. One man recalls the time a stranger came to his restaurant at night---dirty, hungry, covered with lice, and broke. Mr. Goodson fed him, took him to his own home, bathed him himself, rid him of the lice, burned his clothes, and gave him a bed for the night. The next morning he bought him new clothes, and fed him again. When the man was leaving he said, "I don't know which way to turn now." Pop Goodson simply said, "I believe I'd turn to the Lord." Everyone remembers how he took care of Roby Patton. When the men gathered there in the morning for coffee, Roby was always in his place having his coffee, and those who went for meals often saw him on the stool having his favorite---a bowl of beans--compliments of the house. Pop's" daughter, Beulah, described his years of retirement---forced retirement because of the fire---as happy ones. He spent the winter months with her in Tennessee, enjoying his grandchildren, fishing, going to ball games, gardening, and - of all things, jogging. Beulah said every neighbor in her community had a freezer full of salad greens her father had taken them before he came back to Galax in April. His interest in politics remained active, and he always made certain his vote was counted, whether he was in Tennessee or Virginia. There was never any doubt about the political party he favored, and his friends, both Democrats and Republicans, respected his loyalty. He has two 5-month-old great-grandchildren, named Kimberly Ann Frazier and Tamala Denyse Smith, and because he had trouble remembering their names, he simply started calling them "R. N.." It was only after 3 or 4 weeks of wondering why, that his family got his confession. The "R. N." stood for Richard Nixon. "After all," he said, "they were born in the Nixon Administration."

Few people enjoyed their work as Mr. Goodson did his, and his work was constant and demanding. When his restaurant burned, Benny Benfield asked him if he would start over again. He thought for only a minute and said, "No, Benny, but if I were 20 years younger, I'd do it all over again."

50

Dr. Virgil Cox is probably the best friend Troy Goodson ever had. Only last week, they were at Dr. Cox's cabin, and Troy was doing what he liked to do best---cooking for his friends. No one could describe the kind of man Troy Goodson was better than Dr. Cox did only a few days later. "No man or person in Galax ever did so much for so many deserving people and said so little about it. He was a gentleman in every way. Of the many men I've known in the past 33 years, I have never known one who did so much for his family, friends, grandchildren, and relatives. Troy was a man that had great respect for the man who was 'down and out.' As far as I know he did not have one enemy, and everyone who know him had a high regard for him. He was always respectable and congenial in large or small groups. I never heard him say one harmful word about anyone. It was noticeable that if anyone made a statement that he didn't agree with, regardless if it concerned religion or politics or any other controversial subject, he kept silent, giving them due respect for their opinions. The motto he seemed to live by was 'Service Above Self.'

In all the things people in this area have been saying about Troy Goodson this week were written down, books would be filled and it would be a fine tribute to him. But the greatest tribute to him was shown when his much-loved family gathered around the table in his kitchen after the funeral and talked of their love and respect for him. Everyone had his own happy memories and talked of how their lives had been shaped by a very respectable, kind, generous, unforgettable "Pop" Goodson.

Galax Gazette Virginia Thursday, April 23, 1970 By: Mary Guynn

Walter G. Andrews

Walter Andrews spoke softly as he sat on the couch in his home which overlooks the City of Galax. He is now retired but he well remembers serving both the town and city as its manager through the bad and the good times.

Andrews retired as Galax City Manager in 1970 and has "just enjoyed life" the past 11 years. He will be 90 years old November 3 and terms his health as good.

Andrews said many people have had a hand in the success of Galax and he pays tribute to never working with a bad Council during his years as manager.

Andrews was born near the Fox community in Grayson County in 1891. He went to school at Potato Creek, which is near the N. C.-Va. line and later to Maple Shade and Bridle Creek High Schools. He remembers attending what was then called the Galax Normal School for eight weeks to receive his certificate to teach school. -
"Teaching school was tough in those days and you only received $25 a month," Andrews said.

Andrews felt that teaching school was not his life's calling and decided to take a business course from Draughan's Business College in Knoxville, Tenn. The course took eight months to complete. His first job after completing the course was for Southern Express Co. in Bluefield, W. Va. as a stenographer where he worked for a year in 1914 before taking a job with Pocahontas Fuel Co. in 1915 and working there for three years before joining the Navy

His tour in the Navy was short lived, lasting just under a year when the armistice was signed. When he was discharged from the Navy, he returned to Pocahontas Fuel Co. and was sent to eastern Kentucky in 1919 to help organize mines and also serve as bookkeeper and storekeeper. Andrews was promoted to manager and ran the mines until 1932 when times got hard and he returned to Galax.

Andrews and his wife, the former Annie Bagwell who he married in. 1920, planned to stay for only a short time until times got better in the mines but he soon found that he liked it in Galax and decided to stay. After he arrived in Galax, he opened the first shoe store in the city and operated it until 1942 when he went into the lumber cutting business with the late Warren B. Giersh. He was working in the lumber "business when he assumed the job as town manager. Andrews got his first' taste of political life in Galax in 1934 when he ran for a seat on Town Council and won. He served for four years and served as mayor in 1940 and 194!.

In 1947, Harvey Todd who had served for 22 years as Galax Town Manager retired and Andrews got the job .

Andrews said his first big project was to straighten Chestnut Creek and stop the flooding. "Every time it came a big rain it would flood the people out. So we started just above the present Webb Furniture Plant number two," Andrews said. But it wasn't easy to build such a project since the town had no money and it would cost approximately $1 million dollars to build. "That was a lot of money back in those days,' Andrews said.

The first thing Galax did was to solicit the help of late State Senator Floyd Landreth. Joining in were Buck Higgins of Vaughan Bassett Furniture, Glenn Pless and the late John Messer Sr. who owed Galax Mirror and Webb Furniture. "We made several trips to Washington to talk with U. S. Senator Thomas Stanley, who was a real friend of Galax," Andrews said. The project was finally funded for $600,000 and work started in 1950. Andrews said the contract was awarded to Albert Brothers Construction Co. of Salem. "They had the project completed, the banks seeded with grass and were in Galax the night before the project was to receive final approval the next day. That's when disaster struck. Galax received a heavy downpour that same night and the banks were washed away, "Andrews said. This required a second project to "rip-rap". the bank and place huge rocks, which are still there today, on the banks. This was when the city purchased what is now called the rock quarry to obtain rock for the project which cost an additional $400,000 to complete. Both projects were funded with federal funds because Galax had no money.

Andrews said back in the early twenties, Galax Had a bond issue and the town took just enough tax money in the following years to pay the interest on the bonds with very little to apply against the principal. Andrews said in 1935, the town actually ran out of money and the city employees were faced with no paychecks. "We went to a local bank and every councilman had to sign the note to borrow the money to make the payroll," he said. Things got better for Galax in 1940 when they hired Jack Matthews as town attorney. Matthews later went on to become a Circuit Court Judge.

A problem the town had was collecting tax money. "If a man wanted to pay his taxes, it was fine. If he didn't want to pay them, that was fine too," Andrews said. But Matthews decided that wasn't the way it should be and started collecting the back taxes. "Matthews was a real friend to Galax," Andrews said.

CITY MANAGER HONORED - Members of Galax City Council honored City Manager Walter G. Andrews at an informal dinner Tuesday night, marking his completion of 20 years as City Manager. Shown at the Midtowner Restaurant are, seated, Mayor McCamant Higgins, Andrews, Vice Mayor A. Glenn Pless. Standing: City Engineer Harold Snead and Councilmen Dr. William B. Waddell, John W. Sutherland, Henry L. Harris, Horace Cochran and Fred J. Roberts.

Gazette Photo-Chambers

From 1940 to 1956, Galax managed to accumulate enough money to pay off the remaining $200,000 of the bond issue and burn the bond during the Golden Anniversary celebration . 1956 . .. It was a glorious day as everyone gathered in Felts Park to burn the bonds; They were carried and placed on the fire by long time Galax Treasure Mildred Cornett," Andrews said.

Andrews said the men on council at that time were all businessmen who wanted the town to prosper and grow. He praised the work of Henry Harris and Edd Matthews who served on Council for 22 years, McCamant Higgins who served 20 years, Clarence Alderman, 18 years and Fred Roberts, 10 years. One of the Council: policies of the fifties was to build what they had money for, Andrews said. Another project Andrews is proud of is when Galax became a city in 1956. "We only had a population of 3,400 people and needed 5,000 to become a city of the second class so we had to annex two different times to get enough people," Andrews said.

Besides serving as manager of Galax, Andrews served as Commissioner of Revenue for ten years before retiring in 1962. He was replaced by Henry Puckett who ran for the seat and was elected. Puckett still holds the position today. Andrews is also an honorary member of the Virginia Association of Commissioners of Revenues Many buildings were constructed under his administration including the water and sewer Plants, elementary and high school and the new Galax Volunteer' Fire Department building. Because of Andrews' hard work and dedication, the firemen named the new fire station the "Walter G. Andrews Fire Station. "

Andrews now resides on Poplar Street, a street where he purchased 10 acres and eventually constructed every house but one and resold them. He has been involved in civic clubs, is a 5O-year Mason and life member of the Galax Lions Club. He attends the First United Methodist Church in Galax. Andrews has three children, Linton Andrews, who lives near Independence, Mrs. Bill McCarter and W. G. Andrews Jr., who live in Galax. He has six grandchildren and four great-great grandchildren.

What lies ahead for Andrews-"I still enjoy mowing my yard and me and this groundhog have a garden," Andrews said with a smile.

"I just plan to take it easy." **By Larry Chambers, Editor-in-Chief Galax Gazette**

Nathan Potolsky

One of the most visible signs of tough times that marked 1991 was the closing of Globman's on July 4. Earlier that year the employees had been informed that all of the Globman's stores would cease operations. This announcement caught Galax downtown supporters by surprise. They were relying on the store as a keystone of the downtown revitalization. The store closed while still financially solvent, according to company leaders, in an effort to avoid cash flow problems and prevent bankruptcy.

Galax was only 23 years old and the Great Depression was taking hold of the nation's finances when Nathan and Rose Potolsky arrived in town. Two old postcards offer before and after views of Globman's arrival on the northeast corner of South Main and Oldtown Streets. The major streets in town had only been paved for a few years and the roads in the rural areas adjacent to the little community were still muddy, but Nathan Potolsky and his brother-in-law Abe Globman had faith that the town would grow and prosper. And they were right! They selected a "front row seat" on which to build their store and then proceeded to stock it with merchandise of the highest quality at reasonable prices. One could say that Globman's dressed Galax residents from infancy to their senior years. When the store opened for its first day of business Mr. Potolsky was there as manager and 46 years later he was still there... making his daily rounds to see that everything was running smoothly and customers were finding what they needed. He knew everyone by name and everyone respectfully called him "Mr. P." He was a short little man in statue, but a big man in heart because, like most community leaders of his day, he believed in giving back to the community that had given so much to him.

Mr. Potolsky was born on September 5, 1903 in Tzarz Russia where his father kept books for a large landowner. There were no schools in the area so Nathan's father hired a teacher to board with the family and teach his eight children. They started learning from the Bible and went on to the basics of education.

There was great upheaval going on in the world during the first 20 years of the 20th century. It was a very dangerous time, especially if one was Jewish. In 1905 or 1906 The government in St. Petersburg ordered that any Jew who was not a blacksmith, carpenter or shoemaker could no longer live on a farm and must move to the nearest town to live. Fortunately, the Potolskys' landowner had political power and arranged for the family to remain on his farm. During World War I food became very scarce so all the members of his family still living at home became farmers. Nathan recalled that one could not buy food because there was no place to buy it and nobody had any money to buy it. In spite of the conditions, the Potolskys never went hungry when many others did. They grew the food for their table and the flax for the fabric of their clothing. From an early age, Nathan learned the importance of hard work and respecting others; two traits he lived by throughout his life.

By 1920 three of Nathan's brothers had immigrated to the United States and in 1921 the rest of the family joined them. They sailed from Europe on September 29, 1921 and 11 days later they arrived in New York where they were processed through Ellis Island. Mr. Potolsky described his immigration experiences with great clarity. They were met by one of his brothers who had immigrated earlier. They had to pass physicals and literacy tests and be checked for lice. They also had to sign a bond that their mother would not become a public charge since she would not be permitted to work. Nathan could not speak English when he arrived so after working all day he went to school at night with about 30 other recently arrived immigrants of all ages. The class lasted two hours a night, three nights a week. Those who had any language that used the Latin alphabet had less trouble learning English than those from Greece or Russia whose alphabet was Cyrillic. By March 1922 he was able to go Federal Court and fill out an application for his citizenship papers.

While working at a variety of jobs in New York City he met the charming Rose Globman who spent winters there and summers with her brother Abe in Martinsville, Virginia. Nathan recalled that they belonged to the same organizations and soon started keeping company. When her brother came to New York on a buying trip in 1927 he approved the match. A few months later he sent word that he wanted Nathan to come and work in his store. After they were married it was decided Nathan and Rose would move to Galax and open another Globman's store. Their first home in town was an apartment over the store next door. Later they built a home in the northwestern section of

town. They quickly earned for themselves a special place in the life of the community. They had two children Rita and Gerald. Rita married and moved to Atlanta and Jerry was lost in a tragic accident in 1946. Mr. Potolsky had long been involved in Boy Scout activities, from Scoutmaster to membership on the Executive Board of the Blue Ridge Council. He was one of just a few Scouts in the Twin Counties to be presented the coveted Silver Beaver Award for noteworthy service to Scouting, He received the Silver Beaver in 1963. His son had been a Cub Scout at the time of his death in 1946 and Mr. Potolsky vowed to devote the rest of his life to helping boys in memory of his son.

Al Zachary presents Nathan with an Appreciation award for Service to the Boy Scouts of America, present is James Tucker staff member running the scouting Department of Globman's

He was a member the Ohew Zion Congregation in Martinsville for over 47 years and was a member of B'nai B'rith. He was a member of 0ldtown Lodge No. 68, AFM which he was a Past Worshipful Master, and was a member of Kazim Temple of the Shrine in Roanoke. He was a past president of Galax Retail Merchants Association, past president of the Galax Rotary and a member of Galax Country Club. He also served as a director of the Community Fund and other fund-raising campaigns in town.

While some immigrants were reluctant to talk about their life before coming to the States Mr. P was always ready to share his experiences. When he arrived in Galax the town was still in its early growing years. He said that everyone made him feel at home. He was not afraid to declare his Jewish religion and looked forward to being able to do all the different things that he hadn't been allowed to do in Russia or Poland. He stated in an interview in the 1970s that when he first came to town if a person told you he was going to do something, you didn't have to have a signed contract. People did what they had promised.

I grew up in Galax during the mid-20th century. I know that Mr. Potolsky and Globman's were woven into the personality and spirit of Galax. His life was about what one leaves behind… its about their legacy. No one would hesitate to say "Well done Mr. Potolsky, well done!! You came, you left your mark, you left the world a better place, and you made a difference in the lives of your fellowmen.
Source: Information taken from a variety of newspaper articles and the Internet. Judith Nunn Alley

Upper left photo show a Globman's sign over the building and the future Globman's building under construction. This corner lot once being a Livery Stable.

Middle image is cropped cut showing the Globman's sign and empty storefront

Upper right photo shows the Globman's store occupying the large corner building where they remained until going out of business in July 1991.

Kenneth Tomlinson
Three articles that track his career:

Gets Scholarship: Kenneth Tomlinson, rising senior at Galax High School, and president of the Galax Student Cooperative association, has been selected for a scholarship with "Human Events" in Washington D.C. "Human

Events" is a conservative publication especially for young people with conservative leanings. Kenneth is the first high school student to be selected for a scholarship, all others having been college students. Kenneth also is Vice President of the State SCA. He left Sunday for Washington.
Galax Gazette June 1960

Ken Tomlinson, sophomore, at Randolph College, Ashland, VA. and a member of Young Americans for Freedom, is the State Chairman of a group of young Virginians with a conservative viewpoint who have organized to promote the Presidential candidacy of Sen. Barry Goldwater.

Ken spent last summer working in Washington as a contributing editor for "Human Events" the weekly Washington Report, a position he still holds on a part-time basis while keeping up with his studies. He is also the assistant news editor of the college paper, "The Yellow Jacket"

The picture shown of Ken Tomlinson was taken in Washington, D.C. He is the son of Mrs. Mattie Tomlinson of Galax. **Galax Gazette 1963**

A native of Grayson County, Virginia, Tomlinson began his career in journalism working as a reporter for the Richmond Times-Dispatch in 1965. In 1968 he joined the Washington bureau of *Reader's Digest*.

He was a correspondent in Vietnam, and co-authored the book P.O.W., a history of American prisoners of war in the Vietnam War. In 1977 and 1978, he worked out of the *Digest's* Paris bureau covering events in Europe, Africa and the Middle East.

In September 1982, President Reagan nominated Tomlinson to be his fourth Director of the Voice of America (VOA), where he served through August 1984.

In October 1986, President Reagan nominated Tomlinson to be the fourth chairman of the National Commission on Libraries and Information Science (NCLIS), where he served until May 1987.

In May 1987, President Reagan nominated Tomlinson to be a member of the Board for International Broadcasting (BIB) where he served until 1994 when the BIB was dissolved by the International Broadcasting Act of 1994 and replaced by the Broadcasting Board of Governors (BBG). Tomlinson became a close friend of Karl Rove while they served together on the BIB after President Bush nominated Rove to be a member of the BIB in 1989.

Following his work at VOA, Tomlinson returned to *Reader's Digest* as managing editor in 1984. He was named executive editor in 1985 and became editor-in-chief in 1989.

Tomlinson was the Virginia Press Association's Virginian of the Year in 1994 and is a member of the Virginia Communications Hall of Fame.

Tomlinson retired as editor-in-chief of *Reader's Digest* in 1996. After moving to Virginia soon after, Tomlinson was named president and director of the National Sporting Library in Middleburg, Virginia in 1999.

Mr. Tomlinson is a former board member of the Corporation for Public Broadcasting, and served as chairman from September 2003 to September 2005. During his time as chairman, he pursued aggressive policies of adding a conservative viewpoint to CPB's programming.
Allamerican Speakers Bureau

The Life of G. A. Holder

If variety is the spice of life, then Granville A. Holder of 307 West Center Street, Galax, has lived eighty-five mighty tangy years. Mr. Holder has held many jobs and resided in several locations in southwestern Virginia and northwestern North Carolina during his lifetime.

It all began on July 9, 1880, in the Round Peak section of Surry County, North Carolina, when a boy named Granville Anderson was born to the Holder family. Granville's parents had another boy named Samuel A. and a girl that everybody fondly called "Babe". Mr. Holder says about his family, "We were just farm folks; I wasn't born with any silver spoon in my mouth", "I used to walk three miles across a mountain to get to school", recalls Mr. Holder. "Of course we only had school for three months out of the year then, he added. Mr. Holder recalls that his schoolmaster, Thomas Golden, received a salary of eighteen dollars a month for teaching school and that the schoolmaster "kept four or five switches standing in the corner of the school room all of the time." Work on the farm kept Mr. Holder from his schooling to such an extent that he estimates his formal education to have been about three grades of the three "R"s. "What I have learned," he comments, " I learned through experience."

At the age of seventeen, he stopped working on his father's farm and walked a mile daily to help John R. Greenwood in his General Store near Round Peak. "When I first started working for Mr. Greenwood, I received a salary of seven dollars a month', he recalled, "but soon I worked up to where I was payed ten dollars a month plus board at my employer's house." Ten dollars bought a lot more in those days. "Ten dollars a month made me a rich boy then", says Mr. Holder.

After gaining experience in the mercantile business, he went to work in a general store for John J. Mathis in Hooker, North Carolina. Mr. Holder also served as Postmaster while running the store since most of the post offices at that time were found in conveniently located general stores scattered over the countryside. The Mathis store didn't fare too well financially, so Mr. Holder went to work running a store for Steve M. Hale. "We made profit enough' he says of the venture, "to build a new store building to replace the old dilapidated structure we started in." According to Mr. Holder, the general stores of the early nineteen hundreds sold about everything and received about everything as payment for goods since "not much money changed hand, at that time."

Mr. Holder married Miss Ida Blevins on March 9, 1902.

While at Hooker, North Carolina, Mr. Holder experimented with selling relatively unknown plants called "Galax leaves" to florists for use in flower arrangements. He travelled to New York, Baltimore, Philadelphia and other large cities to promote his idea of Galax leaves in floral arranging and developed a market for the leaf. The idea caught on. Soon he was selling Galax leaves quite successfully both in the United States and abroad. Mr. Holder still laughs about the time a cashier in a Mount Airy bank refused to cash a check in payment for Galax leaves sent to England because the money to be paid was in pounds and shillings. It was from Mr. Holder's lucrative leaves that the then town of Galax derived its name, A Norfolk and Western Railroad agent at Blair named Anderson became interested in the leaves when Mr. Holder began shipping them to out-of-town customers by rail. The town was in the process of being renamed so Agent Anderson promoted the idea of naming the community "Galax" because the leaves were unique to the area. Through Anderson's efforts "Galax' was chosen over "Grayson City" and other prospective titles as a new name for the town.

Meanwhile Mr. Holder sold his general store in Surry County and came to Galax. He wasn't in town long before he bought the Oscar Higgin's general store business on the corner of Oldtown and Main streets. He ran the store for about a year and then sold out to "Carico and South". After leaving the store business, Mr. Holder went to work for the Galax Ice and Cold Storage Company. In this capacity he sold ice from a wagon to Galax residents for use in their "ice boxes."

Then Mr. Holder in partnership with Fred Barker, opened a produce business in the Welch Building on Main Street. He journeyed to West Virginia twice each month to sell produce to the coal companies there.
However in 1918, he sold the produce establishment and took his wife Ida, who was afflicted with a rheumatic illness, to Hot Springs, Arkansas, for treatment. The Holders remained in Hot Springs for three months. Upon returning to Galax, Mr. Holder bought out Galax's only meat market on the corner of Main and Center streets from M.B. Jennings. He worked in the meat business until World War I came along.

During the war, Mr. Holder worked under civil service as a laborer foreman at the U.S. Navy base at Hampton Roads, Virginia.

After the war, he and Andrew Gillespie owned and operated an auto repair garage for about a year and a half.

Continuing in the garage business, Mr. Holder went to work for Twin County Motor Company where he served as parts and merchandise manager for about fourteen years. In 1942, his first wife Ida passed away.

When World War II came about, he served on the U.S. Rationing Board for the City of Galax.

Mr. Holder opened a Mick or Mack store at 118 South Main Street which he ran until his retirement in 1956.

In 1945, he married Mary Smith of Elkin, North Carolina,. She died in 1959.

Mr. Holder is a former town-councilman, he belongs to the Masonic Blue Lodge 423 in Sparta, North Carolina. As a Shriner, he is a member of the Kazim Temple in Roanoke; and is classed as a Permanent Contributing Member to the Shriner's hospital for crippled children. He has received the Scottish Rite degree.

He is married to the former Rae Quillen, originally of Wise, Virginia.

According to Mr. Holder, reading is his favorite hobby because "my leg trouble doesn't allow me to walk much to exercise my body; so I exercise my mind."
The picture below is the inside of the Mick or Mack store on South Main Street. Many will remember Helen Truitt who later operated Truitt's, A Ladies Store in that location. The store had the automatic door opener which is still there and in use today. At one time, earlier, Appalachian Power has an office in that location.

By MIKE WRIGHT

THE MUSIC MAN
By Victoria Vandegelder

Galax Gazette, Tuesday February 18, 1975

The butcher, the baker, the candlestick maker...folks from all walks of life...are putting it all together these nights and weekends at the Galax High School.

Carol Waddell Producer

Playbill design Al Victor
After a day's work at their own professions they all become part of the newly formed local theatrical group, The New River Players....and on the stage of the high school auditorium they sweat and strain to become polished actors and actresses so we can have live theater in Galax.

There's no form of entertainment that's more exhilarating than live theater. . . as Shakespeare said, "The play's the thing. . ." and he was so right. There's nothing to compare and it's coming to Galax.

But it's hard work. Unbelievably hard work. . . the music, the dances, the costumes, the dialogue, the comedy routines, the sets, the lighting, the timing and on and on. It's all got to go together to produce a fast-paced musical play. . .and the play chosen is perhaps the fastest musical ever to appear on the Broadway stage --THE MUSIC MAN!

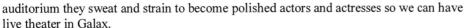

It's a gay, colorful, musical romp about the modes and morals of a small town in Iowa called River City around the turn of the century. It's a fun-filled story with lots of laughs and a great musical score featuring such songs as "76 Trombones," "Till There Was You, " "Trouble" and a host of other top hits.
The New River Players have taken on a great challenge and this reporter has been privileged to watch their rehearsals for the past five weeks. It's been a great experience. We have so much talent in our area and when you see your friends and neighbors performing you'll get the thrill of a life-time.

This has become truly a community project. It belongs to all of us in this area. Lumber for stage sets was donated. Costumes have been loaned by dedicated patrons and money has been provided by the proverbial angels, and more funds are needed so please become an angel. We need you _

One of the most rewarding experiences of this whole stage dream has been the transformation of raw talent into skilled Broadway performers. For example, developing a well-coordinated professional chorus is critical to a musical extravaganza. Two weeks ago when the youngsters in the chorus got together for the first time it was just plain havoc. Trying to perform the intricate steps and routines one of the girls twisted her ankle, another sprained

59

her back . . . but with all the pain and anguish they stuck with it and in the most recent rehearsal this reporter couldn't believe her eyes. . . this chorus was dramatically professional in every way. They were just plain great!

And who's making this magic, this beautiful magic... turning raw amateurs into professionals? Who is the master, teaching butchers and bakers how to sing, dance, act, walk, talk, so that when the curtain goes up on opening night we all will be in River City, Iowa, in 1912 and loving every minute of it.

This is the magic of the director. . .how to play the scene. It's an exhausting task, an impossible task and one that requires an intimate knowledge of human beings, one who can show how each part should be played and plays it to demonstrate. ..and finally, one who has an understanding of the range of emotions in every facet of human behavior.

For the New River Players the skills of the director are handled by Mrs. Sue Nunn. She is the magician turning lumps of clay into beautiful sculpture. There'll be more about Sue Nunn in future columns so stay with us.

Serving as producer of Music Man and president of the Galax Theater Guild is Carol J. Waddell, a newcomer to Galax.

Carol has had several roles in the theater in Chicago in leading and supporting roles in such plays as "Come Blow Your Horn"."Can-Can.""Peter Pan" and others. In addition to live theater, Carol has been in TV commercials, films, fashion shows, convention and trade shows and professional modeling in recent years working for Shirley Hamilton, Inc. of Chicago.

Carol is a member of the American Federation of TV and Radio Association. Music Man will be Carol's first experience in producing.

Well, see you all next week when we'll tell you more about the cast and production team. Till then. . .THINK MUSIC, MAN!

Another article later....

Live theater is in the air – – word is just reached me as I prepare this column, that our own Galax high school Thespian Society was awarded a superior rating at recent district competition in Blacksburg.

They perform their version of "The Flattering Word", a sparkling one-act play starring Connie Hilliard, Jayne Victor, Steve Nuckolls, Sandra Norman and Jeannie Horne. The production was staged by Tom McAllister and Linda Anderson under the direction of Dana Mooney with the supervision and tutelage of Ms. Lois Goad. And now the whole troupe goes on to Gate City for the regional competition. Good luck from all of us to all of you... Or as they say in theater parlance... Break a leg.

Theater, live theater, it's beautiful and as the glamour and excitement of opening-night nears for our Music Man production, tension mounts, patience dwindles and tempers fly. But it's all getting done, fitting together, blending like the colors of a great piece of art. Sets are being giving their finishing touch, entrances and exits are being timed, and music is blessed with lyrics and suddenly the lights dim, the orchestra strikes up the overture and its opening night. Opening-night for Music Man is only a few days away so please get your tickets. Don't miss this chance to see talented performers beyond your wildest expectations.

And we have so much talent here. Actors, singers, dancers that put Broadway to shame. In the female lead as Marian, Theresa Cardinale is delightful. She sings beautifully with a voice that throws tingles up your spine. Theresa comes from a musical family of seven children. Born in West Union, Iowa, and reared in Elmira, New York, Theresa has been musically inspired throughout her life. Starring high school drama, singing choruses, she attended the State University of New York at Albany and was involved in various college productions. She is currently in her third year as speech therapist in this area with project Score. She has sung with the Carroll Community Chorus in their presentation of the Messiah, performing various community and church programs and has had seen engagements at Cascades Mountain resort.

Talent is not confined to the performers on stage. We have talent behind the scenes, the kind that puts a needle and thread to fabric and creates some of the most beautiful costumes imaginable. Bessie Woomer the distaff side of the Woomer team that runs the Pine Tree Shops, is a remarkable designer and seamstress. She has turned cheesecloth into satin and silk. Bessie is a graduate of Radford College with a bachelor of science in elementary education. She taught the six grade in Norfolk, the second and fourth grades in Stafford County and has as been a child welfare supervisor for three years in Pulaski County. Bessie has designed costumes for the summer drama workshops at Mary Washington College and the Stafford County schools which include wardrobes for such productions as "Tom Sawyers", "Oliver", and "Oklahoma".

Wardrobe design and development is a team effort and involves a variety of skills ably performed by Pam Bryant, Myrna Holder, Bobbie Harris and Sharon Moretz. Some very special outfits from the turn-of-the-century were generously lent to us by Mrs. Glenn Pless, Mrs. Lynton Andrews, Miss Jean Kemp and Mrs. Jack Guynn.

Another extremely technical and difficult role behind the scenes is that of lighting director. It's red spot – swing over the blue – flood the stage – sequence that must be delivered instantly On-Que-- – and this job is being expertly rendered by Nancy Burke one of the most popular teachers at Galax High School. Another highly technical skill is drawing and painting backdrops and scenery. Priscilla Richardson from Sylvatus, a teacher at Woodlawn High School has done an outstanding job making River City, Iowa, pictorially come alive.

One of the most difficult jobs in a production of this kind is conducting and arranging the musical score. Split-second timing is uppermost in wedding the music to the story. Moods of various shades must be captured by the orchestra and transmitted to the performers and the audience. The score of Music Man is acknowledged as one of the fastest, most difficult ever written for the stage so its rendering must be in the hands of an expert. This column would hardly suffice to do justice to the skills and talents of our own Don Knox. Through his dedicated and untiring work, he has molded a stage band of remarkable versatility and musicianship. Without this band it would be difficult to do this show. Without Don Knox it would be impossible.

Every modern musical relies heavily on chorus and Music Man is no exception. Chorus used to propel the action and help move the plot. It must be a clear, harmonious blend of voices that can project the lyrical contents of the play. Directing our chorus is Lanny Johnson is who is also portraying the role of Marcellus. Lanny's versatility is clearly matched by his talents – and we're most fortunate to have him on our team.

Those of you who enjoyed nostalgia will surely want to pay close attention to the railroad scene and the actions of the vocal renderings and of Dr. Barney Jennings as he plays the conductor and if your fetish is barbershop quartet singing, you love the mellow voices of Ken Helton, Bill Moore, is Jen to a and David Barker is a harmonize their turn-of-the-century songs for your enjoyment.

Now you know that every town has its gossips, it's pick-a-little ladies and River City, Iowa, is no exception. As a matter of fact we may have the best Pick-a Little Ladies gossips ever and the numbers they are doing for the show are bound to call for encores. Featured in this cultural group are Jackie Morris, Gay Gordon, Beverly Muggler, and Kitty Gordon. Well that's it for now. In mean time, think Music Man

The Music Man by Victoria Vandegelder
Galax Gazette March 2, 1975

This is it. The houselights dim. Don Knox raises his baton. The orchestra pops to attention. The audience stirs in anticipation. And then it happens ... the thrilling sounds of musical overture begin the adventure of live theatre in Galax. Meredith Wilson's great show, Music Man, comes to life.

Please don't miss it. Be a part of this experience. Be in the audience Friday, March 21 and Saturday, March 22. General admission tickets are still available at Boaz Studio in the Galax Plaza and at the Pine Tree Shops in downtown Galax ... or, if you prefer, t the door. Again, I urge you not to miss this production. Get your tickets before they're all sold.

As opening night nears, your reporter is just as excited as the talented performers on stage and behind the scenes. It's really exciting watching Peggy Slayton put her dance choruses through their final routines. Peggy is the choreographer of the show and has done an outstanding job. She whirls, she glides, she shows them how it's done and they do it beautifully. Peggy is more than an innovator of dance routines. She motivates her players and gets the best they have to offer. My hat's off to this dedicated and talented lady.

Unsung heroes and heroines abound in theatre life. Things that are taken for granted are really quite complex and require unique skills. Makeup for the performers is such an endeavor. Under the supervision of Ginger Correll, geography I and world history teacher at Galax High School, the players are getting their faces expertly powdered and a primed. Assisting Ginger is Carol Annis, chemistry and biology teacher at GHS, and Jayne Victor, popular junior at GHS who is a talented actress in her own right, preparing for her trip to Bluefield as one of the stars of the award-winning high school play, The Flattering Word.

Closely related to the make-up process is hair styling. The hair styles must be in keeping with the turn-of-the-century mood of the play. Through the generosity of Helen Roberts and Thelma Pilkins of the new Community Beauty Shop in the Gladeville Shopping Center our players will be decked in the authentic styles of the period. Thank you, ladies. We appreciate it.

Rehearsals often foretell who the show-stoppers will be. You can feel it happen as a truly colorful and talented player performs. Star-quality it's called ... and nobody knows why it comes through but it does. As they say, you either got it or you ain't. Lois Fincher has got it. She is absolutely sparkling as she plays Eulalie McKechnie Shin, the mayor's wife. Her glowing portrayal is a delightful mix of caricature and comedy. For this reporter, Lois Fincher has been one of the show-stoppers and I know you'll agree as you watch her perform.

Teaming with Lois in the role of Mayor Shin is Bob Woomer. His acting experience and great sense of timing light up the stage. His antics are pure joy and you'll be applauding his delightful interpretation of the role. Bob is head of the Pine Tree Shops in Galax and has been a powerful influence in the development of The Galax Theatre Guild.

The opening scene of any show is critical. The performers entrusted with this responsibility literally set the pace for the scenes to come. We are fortunate to have a group of talented men to get things going. As the curtain rises we are aboard an oldtimey train wherein six traveling salesmen begin our story. Clarence Young, an outstanding performer and civic-minded member of our community, (his Geraldine performances are familiar to all), gives us still, another glimpse of his talent and versatility as he plays one of the salesmen as well as the role of the constable later in the show. Another dedicated member of the sales troupe is Dick Lyons who commutes from Radford to participate in our show. He is a highly skilled gentleman and we are, indeed, grateful for his fine portrayal. Dick is associated with our Twin County Community Hospital and we hope to see more of him in future shows.

Also cast as a salesman is Dana Mooney. This junior at Galax High School is a whirlwind of talent. He won first place recently for singing at the Bland Music Festival and he directed the award-winning GHS play, The Flattering Word. Dana is also a member of the GHS Stage Band and has been an all-around happy addition to our cast. He is an outstanding young man.

Ken Waddell, our able Administrator at Twin County Community Hospital, is trying his hand at performing for the first time as he portrays one of the salesmen. It's a whole new experience for Ken and he's doing just fine. Although he admits that acting is not his forte, he is anxious to help the theatre project succeed and is trying real hard. We're all rooting for you, Ken. Also part of the sales troupe is Dr. Don Fincher. After his practice of veterinary medicine, Don takes to acting with a vitality that makes him fun to watch. He's great in the role of Charlie Cowell, who in the play is out to expose the Music Man, Harold Hill. Don's technique is so professional it belies the fact that he has had no prior stage experience.

Completing the cast of salesmen is Steve Nuckolls, a GHS senior of great ability. Steve comes from a talented musical family. His mother, Eleanor, has been assisting Don Knox at the piano during the staging of our show. Steve, by the way, is starring in the GHS play, Flattering Word, in the role of minister and we wish him well in Bluefield.

Continuing our presentation of the cast we spotlight our teen stars of Music Man, vivacious Connie Hilliard and handsome Joe Steffen. Connie has her eye on a stage career and she has all the gifts for stardom. She'll sing and dance her way into your hearts in her role as Zanetta. Playing opposite Connie in the role of Tommy is Joe Steffen. Joe is a newcomer to Galax and as a senior in our high school has made his mark as president of the debating team. Originally from Des Plaines, Ill., this is Joe's first crack at the stage outside of his role on debating teams. He has placed high in debating tournaments in Illinois and recently at Virginia Tech. We wish him well in his stage debut.

As I've said so often there are many bright spots in a musical extravaganza and it's hard to review them all. But I must say a few words about the adorable Kendall Kegley who has the child lead as Amaryllis. Kendall is the pretty and talented daughter of Mr. and Mrs. Howard Kegley, Jr. and this is also her stage debut. I know she'll warm your hearts with her performance.

And now a word about Liza Hackler. Liza is a wonderful lady who has contributed her talents to our production. She, personally, made 40 pairs of oldtimey spats which the men wear in the show. She is the grandmother of Dana Mooney. Bless her heart for all she's contributed to the show.

In the three months that this reporter has been visiting the Music Man rehearsals, I have been most impressed by the fine pianist accompanist, Mrs. Eleanor Nuckolls of Galax. Eleanor has done an outstanding job in helping the cast with their songs and this reporters hats' off to her.

Well, as they say in the movies, "That's All, Folks". The next time we get together we'll be in the audience thinking and enjoying The Music Man

The Music Man Cast, Crew and Production Staff

CAST (In Order of appearance)

TRAVELLING SALESMEN	Clarence Young, Dick Lyons, Kenneth Waddell, Steve Nuckolls, Dana Mooney
CHARLIE COWELL	Don Fincher
CONDUCTOR	Barney Jennings
HAROLD HILL	Bill Waddell
MAYOR SHINN	Bob Womer
EWART DUNLOP	David Barker
OLIVER HICKS	Jim Tinney
JACEY SQUIRES	Ken Helton
OLIN BRITT	Bill Moore
MARCELLUS WASHBURN	Lanny Johnson
TOMMY DJILAS	Joe Steffen
MARIAN PAROO	Theresa Cardinale
MRS. PAROO	Bonnie McCormick
AMARYLLIS	Kendall Kegley
WINTHROP PAROO	Patrick Nuckolls
EULALIE MACKECKNIE SHINN	Lois Fincher
ZANEETA SHINN	Connie Hilliard
GRACIE SHINN	Ruth Ann Otey
ALMA HIX	Beverly Mugler
MAUD DUNLOP	Gay Gordon
ETHEL TOFFELMIER	Jackie Morris
MRS. SQUIRES	Kitty Gordon
CONSTABLE LOCKE	Clarence Young

CITIZENS OF RIVER CITY, IOWA AND CHORUS

Linda Burnette, Clark Fincher, Bobbie Harris, Sarah Hawks, Worth Higgins, Martha Lindsey, Andy Moretz, Sharon Moretz, Chris Morris, Kelly Morris, Allison Nunn, Emily Nunn, Mariah Nunn, Susan Nunn, Joe Otey, Clarine Pickens, Jim Pickens, Pattie Rector, Steve Rector, Press Turbyfill, Jayne Ward, Jimmy Ward, Ellen Watters, Sylvia Wilson, Heather Womer,
Bonnell Young, Clarence Young

DANCERS

Connie Hilliard, Sandie Lindsey, Beth Porter, David Nunn, Marianna Hampton, Steve Nuckolls, Teresa Beamer, Clark Williams, Donna Edwards, Jimmy Zachary, Jill Montgomery, Joe Steffen,

ORCHESTRA
Don F. Knox, Director
Holly Waddell, Tammy Wyatt, Danise Busic, Kathy Parks, Donna Sizemore, Bill McFarlin, Dana Mooney, Charles Rudy, David Lawrence, Sandra Norman, Billy Buchanan, Gary Jones

Piano Mrs. Gene Nuckolls

PRODUCTION STAFF of THE MUSIC MAN

Producer	Carol Waddell
Choreographer	Peggy Slayton
Scenic Design	Jim Galyen, Jerry Wolford , Al Victor Ann Cochran, Priscilla Richardson
Lights	Nancy Burke, Chairman. Craig Miller Tom McAllister
Properties	Carol Kegley, Chairman, Jackie Morris Shelby Morris, Bob Womer
Stage Managers	Lucille Porter, Loraine Akers
Assistants	Mariah Nunn, Peggy Slayton

Chorus Director	Lanny Johnson
Cover Design	Al Victor
Set Construction	Jerry Wolford, Chairman
	Eddie Harris, Assistant Judy Wolford, Darlene Douglas, Priscilla Richardson, Sarah Hawks, Susan Nunn, Mariah Nunn, Roy Nunn, Beth Waddell, Jeff Facemire, Jim Zachary, Teresa Cardinale, Ken Waddell, Hollis Phipps, Doug Ross, Beckey Webb, Martha Kello, Virginia Lippencott, Steve Nuckolls, Charles Rudy, Nancy Burke, Karen Cruise, Jaynie Victor, Brent Crockett Mariah Nunn
Stage Hands	Bryan Waddell, Steve Irvin, Tom Dendy, Tom McAllister, Evan Nunn, Jim Steffen, Brent Crockett, Barney Jennings
Prompters and Ticket Sales	Fran Cregger, Bea Nunn, Martha Carter, Carol Dickerson, Mariah Nunn
Technical Advisor	Millie Victor
Publicity	Victoria Vandergelder
Costumes	Bobbie Cregger Harris, Chairman
	Bessie Womer, Co-Chairman Crew: Phyllis Felts, Fran Cregger, Sharon Moretz, Carol Morris, Pam Bryant, Tina Vuurman, Bonnie McCormick, Myrna Holder, Eliza Hackler
Music Director	Don Knox
Rehearsal Pianist	Eleanor Nuckolls
Make-up	Ginger Correll, Chairman, Carol Anness, Jaynie Victor, Allison Nunn, Kyttie Miller, Julie Sprinkle, Janet Blair, Angela Edwards, Cindy Halsey, Robbie Murphy, Sarah Zachary, Lyn Bolen
Concessions	Pat and Steve Irvin, Harriet and Mike Miller, Edna and Joe Cardwell, Marie and Herb Walker,
	Linda and David Byers, Tom and Carol Lander, Tom and Judy Littrell
Ushers:	Betty Waddell, Chairman
	Rebecca Williams, Pam Harris, Toni Nunn, Janet Huffman, Cathy Walker, JoAnna Cardwell, Julie Frye
Tickets and Program	John Nunn
Curtain Puller .	Lucille Porter

Producers Comments: It started as a dream.

Carol Waddell had dreamed dreams before. As a girl growing up in Chicago, she dreamed of appearing on the stage like those she watched at the Oriental Theater. She did so, as an actress, model and in TV commercials and industrial advertisement films.

It was natural when she came to Galax that she would be interested in what the area had to offer in the way of live theater.

She found that it had a movie theater, all right, but nothing in the way of stage performances. For that, one had to travel to Roanoke, Abingdon or Winston-Salem.

She had another dream - of a local drama group which would deliver the kind of performances she had grown used to seeing in Chicago and the other metropolitan areas to which her career had taken her. That dream came true, too.

It began with a small group, meeting in homes. It became the Galax Theater Guild and, in the spring of 1975, produced its first show -Music Man," an ambitious first step for an organization that had never staged a play before. "Music Man" was such a hit that it drew sellout audiences both nights and did two encore performances a month later again to packed houses in the Galax High School auditorium.
It is estimated 175.000 people have seen a production of the Gala Theater Guild

Images from Belk's days in Galax

Left to right top to bottom

#1 Belks occupying 3 stores on Grayson Street

#2 Shoe dept: Bess Galyean fitting a customer.

#3 Ava Lee Duncan and unknown in Baby dept

4 Jack Beamer, Joe Crockett and Floyd Landreth

5 Lena Young,

#6 & 7 Ann Carico McMillian

#8 Plina Roberts (Mary Guynn's mother) #5-10 were in a Belks fashion show as the store often use Galax Citizens to model fashions. 9 Sue Beamer,

#10 Mary Margaret Beamer and Carol or Diane McFarland #11 Mary Jane Lawson in

back and Isabelle Devault in front in the service/office desk
#12, Founder's Day early 1960s.

66

Courthouse Rambles Play for the Rockefellers

Courthouse ramblers are the greatest bluegrass and old – time band run amok that nobody should ever heard of. Well, except for the Rockefellers

Galax – it's around 8:30 on a Wednesday night and Peggy Rockefeller's favorite band is tuning up.

The Courthouse ramblers are in session as about 50 witnesses sequester themselves beneath a

large canopy near the Felts Park tennis courts to get to listen to the band's first show of the 1997 old fiddlers convention.

For the next couple of hours, the seven-member mini – orchestra will use a mix of guitar, banjo, dulcimer, washboard, kazoo, standup bass, whistle and a hose with a bell on the top to produce a mutant brand of acoustic music described by guitar player Rob Mangum as bluegrass and old-time run amok.

"Mixed with barnyard humor", adds Banjoist Leon Frost.

These people play for the Rockefellers?

Well, yes, and for Lady Bird Johnson.

Being the self-described "society band" to the rich and famous has become the greatest claim to fame for this electric set of longtime friends and spouses from Virginia and North Carolina. But it's just part of the saga of the group that got together 16 years ago for a local talent night and just kept playing, a group one local fan proclaimed "the greatest band nobody's ever heard of".

That doesn't count the couple of hundred fans drawn like moths to the bug zapper when the group plays under its big yellow and white tent at the fiddlers convention. It also doesn't count the hundred and 50 or so socialites who heard the Grayson County-based ramblers play songs like "Road Kill" and "How about a Hand for the Hog" at a black-tie celebration of David and Peggy Rockefeller's 55th anniversary two years ago.

Five years ago at the invitation of textile heir and underwear King Philip Hanes, the group was the entertainment for a meeting of the American Farmland Trust in Roaring Rock (Gap) North Carolina, a place described as "a playground for the upper crust" by Mangum and a place where Pres. Lyndon Johnson's widow caught the band while visiting friends.

After playing a set, Frost was approached by a group of elderly women wanting him to give a demonstration of his spoon playing virtuosity.

I said, "well, pull up those evening dresses and cock your leg up here and we'll get into it" said Frost a Carroll County native who lives near Galax.

One of the ladies who learn to play the spoons that night was Peggy Rockefeller, the American Farmland Trust's founder who happen to be married to the billionaire former head of Chase Manhattan Bank.

A couple of years later she called the band out of the blue and invited it to New York to play for David Rockefeller's 80th birthday. The band couldn't do it because of the conflict and actually turn the Rockefellers down.

Then she asked, "how about our anniversary?" Said Frost.

Jed Clampett must've felt the same way that day he shot at food only to strike oil.. The next thing you know, the Old Courthouse Ramblers are on Rockefellers private jet and heading for the billionaires home in Tarrytown, New York.

"George Bush had flown in it the week before", said rambler Becky Ward, a singer and dulcimer player.

The band hammed it up for the black – tie affair. For their first set, the men wore overalls and women had curlers in their hair. Bassist Mark Rose brought out a rubber chicken on the Rockefellers silver platter when the group played the Mountain standard "Cluck old Hen".

The group was a hit.

These people were just like you and me, said Frost, who later performed a spoons duet with Peggy Rockefeller. They later exchange instruments – Frost came home with some of the good silver.

Aside from the tuxedoed and jeweled bedecked spectators, the show was no different from the ones this week in Galax, where, in addition to the aforementioned times, you can hear Ramblers "hits" like "Hangover Blues" and the much requested "Bill-Bill" whose touching story of a boy and his pet pig is summarized in the refrain.

"The rich kids all had puppies but I never had no dog

It was always me and Bill-Bill the ol' fat boy and his hog "

"Those people {at the Rockefeller party} all that down to ground when I sang that", Frost said

In the stomach turning favorite "Road Kill" and the line "Don't blame me for swinging at Bambi, I'm just a man trying to feed my family", is the most appetizing of the nauseating verses.

Songs like those – some original, some borrowed – have earned the Courthouse Ramblers a following. The band has made a couple of tapes and hopes to have a CD out next year, but the real treat is seeing Ramblers live.

What we lack in musical ability, we make up for an enthusiasm, said Lenora Rose, a singer and impresario of the washboard and kazoo.

The group plays fewer than a dozen times a year. That's because the band members, following the advice that many other burgeoning musicians ignored, kept their day jobs. Playing music is fun not work.

The group's current seven-member lineup is made up of three married couples – Lenora and Mark Rose of Mouth of Wilson, Becky and Edwin Ward of Galax and Bet and Rob Mangum of Piney Creek, North Carolina. – And Frost, whose wife Lisa, occasionally plays in the group as does fiddler Tim Terry and other friends and guest who sit in.

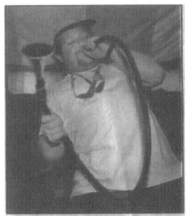

CINDY PINKSTON / *THE ROANOKE TIMES*
It looks a lot like a beer bong, but Mark Rose's contraption is really washing-machine hose with the bell of a toy horn at one end and a trumpet mouthpeice on the other.

When they formed the band in 1981, they chose the name Courthouse Ramblers because some in the group were active in saving the 1908 Grayson County Courthouse in Independence from demolition.

Their shows are rife with music, wisecracks and silly antics provided chiefly by Mark Rose, Rob Mangum and Frost, whose lively in-song banter spices up the numbers.

Rose especially, is a crazy showman who specializes in wacky instruments including a standup bass emblazoned with hard rock stickers of groups like Social Disorder, Biohazard, the Meat Puppets and Bad Brains. "I've always got an obnoxious noisemaker", he said.

The wackiest is a homemade device made from the hose of a Kenmore washer with a trumpet mouthpiece on one hand and bell on the other. It resembles a similar hose – and – funnel device used by college students to expedite the beer – drinking experience process, but sounds like, well, what a trumpet would sound like if played through the hose of a Kenmore washer.

"When I met Lenora, I wasn't a playing musician", he explained, so I cut a guys water hose off his camper and started playing it. That is, until my lips got mangled.

Now they just mangle the music. Some people will hear a song that's off the wall or funny, and they'll say we should do it, Frost said. Then we take it and slaughter it.

By Ralph Berry Jr. the Roanoke Times.

A. Glenn Pless shares Memories of Early Galax

I would like to say a few words about things that happened when Galax was young. To cover the growth and development of Galax over the past 77 years would take several hours, so this brief report will be about a few of the happenings over the early years. Some of these things I remember but many of them have been told to me.

Our community has had several names. This area was first called "Anderson's Bottoms." When the first lot sale was held Dec. 17, 1903, the circular advertising the lots gave the community the name of Cairo. The surveyor listed our community as "Mont Plan." Then our next name was Bonaparte. Some have said the name originated from the "Bones and Parts", which were used to mark some of the streets and lots. It was then suggested that the name Galax be used to honor the beautiful Galax leaves, which grow wild in our hills and mountains. When the railroad was extended from Blair to Galax, the first express shipment was Galax leaves.

A. Glenn Pless,
President.

In order for Galax to grow, it was necessary to have employment for its citizens. The first industry was the canning factory, which was located where Vaughan-Bassett Furniture Co. stands today. This was the beginning of a concentrated effort to establish industry in Galax. The efforts of our founding fathers have paid rich dividends. I wish to emphasize that industry in Galax did not just happen. It was because of the interest of local citizens, who were willing to give of their time and money to attract industry, that factories and businesses were gradually built.

I wish to pay tribute to the many citizens who believed in the future of Galax. I wish to mention a few of these men at this time.

Robert Emmett Jones moved to our community in 1904. At this time it was called Bonaparte. He became our first postmaster.

James P. Carico, one of our outstanding civic leaders, was instrumental in persuading the Washington Mills Company to build the dam and mill on New River, so the town of Fries was born. During the construction of the dam and mill, the Norfolk & Western built a rail line to Fries. Then the line was extended to Blair and from Blair to Galax. The death of Mr. Carico in 1936 was a loss to our young town.

Captain John Blair Waugh, born in 1842, enlisted in the Confederate Army at the age of 19. He commanded the 61st Regiment, which participated in the famous Battle of Missionary Ridge.

At the lot sale in 1903, he paid the high price of $250 for the lot on the southeast corner of Main and Grayson Streets, and built the Waugh Building. At that time, Grayson Street was known as Depot Street and Main Street as Mount Airy Street. He was one of the outstanding founding fathers of early Galax.

Other outstanding citizens were A. C. Anderson, A. C. Painter (both of these families still reside in the original dwellings), R. E. Jones, T. L. Felts, Dr. J. W. Bolen, J. F. Vass, W. K. Early, Dr. J. H. Witherow, B.D. Beamer, Harvey M. Todd, S. R. Dixon, McCamant Higgins, D. S. Vass, John A. Messer Sr., Dan B. Waugh, J. C. Matthews, J. H. Kapp, Dr. J. K. Caldwell, B. C. Vaughan and Taylor G. Vaughan. The list could go on and on. These are only some of the citizens who were willing to invest their time and money' in order to build a community with churches, schools and employment for its citizens.

Our town was incorporated in 1906. In 1922 our charter was changed to the town manager form of government. I. G. Vass served as our first town manager. He was followed by Harvey M. Todd, Orbin Rhudy, W. G. Andrews and Harold Snead, who presently served in this capacity.

Early Galax either had muddy or dusty streets. The muddiest spot on Main Street was in front of Skip Henderson's Jewelry Store and Floyd Williams' Ice Cream Parlor. As boys, we would go seining in the creek after a rain and catch a few water dogs along with the fish. We would bring the water dogs to town, placing them in the big mud hole. We then would place a sign on a stick, which read, "No fishing allowed." Early citizens told tall tales about the mud holes. Perhaps the tallest tale of all was told by Harry Early. He stated a man was walking down Main Street and saw a hat in a mud hole. He waded into the mud and picked up the hat; he discovered a man's head under it. He asked the man if he needed some help. The man replied, "No thanks, I'm alright, I am on horseback."

The "Great Galax Fair" originated soon after our town was started. T. L. Fells and J. P. Carico promoted the idea and a group of 90 or more citizens formed the Galax Fair Association. Shares of stock were sold at $100 per share, and no one person was permitted to own more than one share of stock. A 22 acre tract of land, now Felts Park, was purchased where a race track, exhibit building and grandstand were constructed.

Fair Week was truly the social highlight of the year. Visitors and relatives came from the surrounding area. Entire families came in covered wagons, camping on the Fair Grounds, streets or anywhere they could find space. The Siamese Twins were an attraction at the 1906 Fair. The Siamese Twins lived on farms near White Plains, N.C. and are buried there.

As a youngster, I well remember the lumber wagons pulled by teams of oxen. Cattle, sheep and even turkeys were driven from the farms to the loading pens on the railroad.

I also remember our bottom where one would have to jump from Tussock to Tussock to keep from sinking down on the black muck. Heavy rains would cause Chestnut Creek to overflow its banks, causing an untold amount of damage to homes and industry. After our big flood of 1940, we secured financial help from the federal government to widen, deepen and straighten the creek, which eliminated the overflowing problem.

In 1923 the first paved road in Carroll and Grayson counties was built from Galax to Hillsville. Part of this road is now known as Glendale Road. The farmers of the area were paid $1 per wagon load for field rock, to use as the base of the road. These rock were knapped up with sledge hammers, then crushed rock was placed on top, making an excellent base for the road. In 1924, the first paved streets were completed in our town.

Galax has been blessed with good government. Business people have been willing to give of their time, serving on the council and working on projects. The foresight of our council, several years ago in purchasing 1,300 acres of land in the fisher's Peak area, which is the watershed of Chestnut Creek, insuring our city a good free stone water supply. Good water is in short supply in many areas of our country and the lack of it will become more critical in the future.

All Galax citizens did not have a private well. The town provided two wells, one on the corner of Main and Center Streets, where the post office is located; the other well on the corner of Main and Oldtown Streets; next to the South Hotel. The Texaco Station occupies this lot at this time. Early Galax depended on these wells for water for household use and the bucket brigade used them for water to fight fires.

I well remember the ice house, which faced the alley and was back of Mrs. Maude Gardner's building. The roof was an A Frame about six feet above the ground, with a door facing the alley. The ice was stored in a hole 15 to 20' feet deep and nearly as large as the roof. When the ice in the river and creek froze thick enough, the ice was sawed into 50-100 pound pieces, then a layer of sawdust, then layers of ice until the hole was filled. This was the only ice for making ice cream and cooling food in the summer, until the mechanical ice maker was built.

As boys we would skate two-three months in the winter, which is proof that our winters back then were colder and more severe than they are now. I remember my grandfather telling me about teams and wagons crossing the river on the ice. I also remember him telling me that he wore an overcoat on July 4, while cradling wheat.

In my travels, I have not found an area blessed with such fine people, good churches, good schools and excellent climate as we have in this section. We live in the garden spot of the world.

EDITORS' NOTE: The speech above was given by Glenn Pless during the services in Felts Park last Sunday night. Many people have asked that it be published so they could save it for a souvenir.

71

Posey Martin
Chief of Police is slain by Howard Delp; Feb 21, 1935

What was undoubtedly one of the most shocking tragedies ever enacted in Galax occurred early Thursday night when Chief of Police Posey Martin was brutally murdered and Officer Frank Dotson was seriously wounded.

Chief Martin was killed by Howard Delp, 22, as the officer opened a cell door of the local jail to release Dow Leonard, Delp's cellmate. The two had been arrested late in the afternoon by Officers Martin, Dotson and J. 0. Jones on drunkenness charges and were placed in jail.

Delp is alleged to have used a large pocket knife as he struck Chief Martin a savage blow in the neck, severing the jugular vein. The two officers were rushed to the nearby Galax hospital but Chief Martin was dead on arrival there, and Dotson was in a serious condition from loss of blood, although it is thought that, barring complications, he will recover. Officer Dotson was slashed across the head and face.

Bond had been provided for Leonard and Chief Martin was completing formalities of this action when he went to the jail to release Leonard and met his death.

Just before the tragedy Chief Martin was attending a dinner given by the local Business Men's club at Bluemont hotel when he was called to his office, which is separated from the jail cells by a narrow hall, to arrange bond for Leonard. Martin and Dotson prepared the bond in the former's office. Then Officer Martin crossed the hall and opened the jail door, asking Leonard to come into the office and sign the bond. As Leonard came out of the cell, officers said, Delp followed him.

Martin pushed Delp back; it was said, declaring "no one has arranged your bond. You stay here. We have sixty dollars against you besides this."

Delp, witnesses said, escaped into the hallway where it is said he stabbed Chief Martin, who staggered through the doorway into his office saying, "Get a doctor, I'm killed," and calling Dotson, who was yet in the office. Dotson rushed out and attempted to put Delp back in the cell, when the wounds he received were inflicted by the criminal.

Chief Martin, who was 50 years of age at the time of his death, was born in the Spike Creek community in Carroll County. He was the son of the late Mr. and Mrs. Isaac Martin.

Surviving is the widow, who was, before her marriage, Miss Anna M. Wright, also of Carroll County: three daughters, Misses Euna Lee, Alene and Iris Martin and a son, Rayburn. He also leaves a brother, Will Martin, of Fancy Gap, and three sisters, Mrs. Isaiah Worrell and Mrs. J. C. Haymore, Mount Airy, N. C., and Mrs. M. B. Salmons, of Akron, Ohio.

The deceased officer had been on the local police force for about two years, assuming the office of Chief on January 1, 1933.

Persons who saw the attack included Dowe Leonard, prisoner; John Salmon, carpenter at work on the door to the police chief's office; Dewey Adams, who, it is said, was slightly cut on the shoulder by Delp while trying to assist the officers; Ernest Davis, merchant; J. G. Owens, attending an American Legion meeting in the building.. and H. B. Leonard. A. C. Leonard and R. L. Weatherman, who were arranging bond for Dowe Leonard.

After the tragedy became known excitement reigned for several hours in the town hall, where the jail is located, and a large crowd assembled on the street outside. Feeling was running high as Mayor B. D. Beamer assumed charge of the situation and organized a search. He began to swear in special officers and posses were dispatched to all sections of the nearby country. Authorities at Pulaski, Floyd, Mt. Airy, N. C., and other nearby towns were asked to watch the roads.

Late Thursday night a message was received from Hillsville stating that police there stopped an automobile at a road intersection and arrested one man. A second man in the car, believed to have been Delp, escaped.

It was later learned that the man detained in Hillsville jail is Manuel Easter, said to be a relative of Delp's by marriage.

Word of the slaying was quickly flashed to state police and local officers in nearby communities. From Pulaski, officers with sawed-off shotguns were sent to guard highway intersections at Dublin and Fort Chiswell. When first alarms were sent out it was believed Delp had escaped in an automobile bearing Tennessee license tags, but the car was later found.

A throng continued to mill about the street in front of the town hall. Mayor Beamer said late in the night that Delp, if arrested, would not be brought to Galax.

Friday and Friday night, while preparations for the funeral of Chief Martin were going forward, authorities pressed their search for his alleged slayer.

In the meantime a message was received from Sheriff Ralph Moreland, of Elizabethton, Tenn., saying authorities there were holding a suspect whose description resembled that of Delp. Nothing, however, came of this report.

Bloodhounds which were used in an attempt to pick up a trial near Hillsville Thursday night were taken to the Snake Creek section, five miles from Hillsville, Friday afternoon after a person answering Delp's description had eaten dinner at a farm house. He was said to have appeared to be in a highly nervous state. The bloodhounds were unable to follow the trail.

Saturday night, bloodhounds from Marion, it is said, struck a trail of Delp near Red Hill filling station between Hillsville and Laurel Fork, and followed it to the Fancy Gap road, leading toward Mount Airy, where the trail could not be followed further. This gave support to the theory advanced by some that the fugitive might have boarded an automobile or adopted some other means of vehicular travel when he reached the Fancy Gap road.

Announcement of the slaying and a description of the alleged killer, followed by news of the progress of the search from time to time, was broadcast from radio was broadcast from radio station WBT, Charlotte, N. C., by Grady Cole, well known radio news commentator.

Officers are still combing the section of Carroll County where Delp is said to have been sighted several times since the fatal stabbing, for traces of the fugitive.

Yesterday (Sunday) the search shifted to the Fancy Gap area of Carroll County with posses believed close on his track. Mayor B. D. Beamer said last night that Delp was believed to be hiding in the Fancy Gap section.

Residents of the section told officers engaged in the hunt that a man answering. Delp's description was seen there Saturday night. Officers who were using bloodhounds found the last definite trace of the fugitive yesterday morning at 4 o'clock when a glove, believed to have been dropped by Delp, was picked up.

Authorities said they believed the alleged murderer was either trying to reach the Mount Airy section across the North Carolina line or attempting to head back toward Galax.

It became known this morning that a man at the livestock yards in Felts park reported a man answering the description of the hunted criminal as having been at Pine Ridge filling station, about five miles this side of Mount Airy, on the Low Gap road. Local officials made hasty preparations to investigate this report.

Dowe Leonard, who was an eye witness to the knife attack on the two officers by Delp, told officers Friday that Delp had threatened, while in jail, to kill Dotson, who, while serving as a prohibition agent, according to authorities, killed Delp's father, Joe Hix Delp, in a gun battle here on May 17, 1925. The elder Delp was suspected of handling illicit liquor. In the battle Officer Guffey Coomes was slain, it is said, by Joe Hix Delp. Authorities said it was generally known that young Delp had frequently threatened to "get" Dotson.

Crowds have continued to gather about the Municipal building from time to time practically every day since the tragedy. There was high feeling here Thursday night when word was circulated that Delp was surrounded, a score or more of officers and citizens rushing to automobiles and, it is reported that the cry, "get a rope" was heard. The situation was extremely tense until it was learned that. Delp had escaped.

From the scrapbook of Sharon Martin Blevins

First Barber Shop in Galax

The Bryan family, yesterday and today, are known to Galax as barbers. The Bryan shop in Galax was first started in 1905 by "Uncle Abe" Bryan who didn't have a barber chair but who used a folding chair for shaving purposes and a straight back chair 'for the hair cut. And it could also be a folding chair or a swing. "Uncle Abe" charged 5¢ for a shave and 10¢ .for a haircut (which shows how times have changed). Then "Uncle Abe" bought two second-hand chairs and the price jumped to 25¢ for a haircut and 10¢ for a shave.

The first shop was started by "Uncle Abe" on the present location of the First National Bank building. Then it was located in the basement of the bank building and now is on East Grayson street.

It's a project that has grown from one to five chairs. "Rev. Abe" had before coming to Galax barbered at Independence, Blair, and Oldtown. He had taught school, preached in various communities, and was a great leader of his race. His son, 'Walter F. Bryan, became manager of the barber shop, and Walt, in turn, taught his four sons, (Rudolph, Richard, Walter, Jr., and Gilbert) the trade. Now Walter, Sr. and his sons, Richard and Gilbert, along with Willie Lee Goins and Raymond Brown, operate the shop. These are the words of Walter F. Bryan: "I hope that within the next fifty years that there will still be a place in Galax for the Bryan Barber Shop and that my grandsons will continue to make the shop one of the best in Galax." (Editor's Note This was intended for use during the week of the Celebration, but because of a delay on receipt of the engravings had to be held over until this week.)

Galax Gazette written sometime during the "Golden Anniversary" Celebration of Galax in 1956.

Galax Mayors

Left: top to bottom:
Ben F. Calloway
1906-1908
J. F. Vass
1909-1911
1912,1913
1916-1920
D.A. Robertson
1913-1915
1920-1922
Middle top to bottom
J. P. Carico
1928-1930
1932-1934
B.D. Beamer
1934-1940
1952-1954
Right: top to bottom
J. W. Stamey
1908-1909
R. E. Jones
1911-1912
DaCosta Woltz
1930-1932

Left: top to bottom:
W. G. Andrews
1940-1942
E. E. Chappell
1924-1928
Ross Penry
1946-1948
Mid top to bottom
Dan B Waugh
1954-1956
McCamet Higgins
1956-1968
Right top to bottom
D. Shelby Vass
1922-1924
R. L. Nelson
1942-1946
1948-1950
Dr. R.C. Bowie
1950-1952

Galax Mayors

Left to right top to Bottom:

C. M. Mitchell: 1992 to present
John B. Vaughan:1974-76
Jack Guynn:1968-72
Gene T. (Fuzzy) McKnight:1976-78
Glenn Wilson:1978-1986
Van B. McCarter:1986-92

The Vass Family

Considering the number of stores ruined by the Great Depression in the 1930s and other cyclical downturns through the years, one family owned hardware store's motto could be taken from the lyrics of disco diva Gloria Gaynor's song "I will survive."
Vass-Kapp Hardware Co. Inc. is almost as old as Galax.

The store at 10I W. Grayson St. in Galax was born in 1908 when J. Frank Vass and J.C. Matthews entered a partnership. Until 1921 the store was operated under the firm name of J.C. Matthews & Co.

In 1921 Vass bought Matthews' interest in the business and the Vass family has owned the store ever since.

After the death of J. Frank Vass on August 17, 1946, the store fell into the hands of Dennis Shelby Vass, J. Frank's son.

After his death in 1956, the store went from Dennis Shelby Vass to his son Dennis "Pete" Vass, who died in 1991.

From there, majority ownership of the store was split between Pete Vass' three daughters - Sarah Sizemore of Galax, Danise Reynolds of Galax and Cathy Vass-Skoog of Winston-Salem, N.C. Vass-Skoog said that four grandchildren also have a share of the business.

The secret of the store's success, says Vass-Skoog, is the "really good people" who work there.
Employees tend to work at the hardware store for years.

Paul Cox began working there on Nov. 19, 1940 and stayed for nearly 50 years, according to employee Roger Jennings. Jennings himself worked at Vass-Kapp from 1974 to 1986 and then came back in 1991.

The Vases' themselves have made numerous contributions to the Galax community.

J. Frank Vass served as mayor of Galax from 1916 to 1920. Pete Vass was active in the early stages of the downtown revitalization project that started in 1987, according to Vass-Skoog.

In 1994 the Vass family financed the restoration of the Rex Theater marquee and donated it to the city in memory of Pete Vass.

His daughter, Sarah Sizemore, is a pharmacist at Twin County Regional Hospital. Daughter Danise Reynolds is a teacher at Galax Elementary School. Third daughter Vass-Skoog is a certified financial planner in Winston-Salem.

Matthews Hardware on the left corner of South-West Grayson Street and South-West Main Street, which later became Vass Kapp Hardware Company. Picture taken in 1913.

By **STEPHANIE JOHNSON** Staff The Gazette

Black History in Galax , Oldtown and Local Area.

History tells us that the Black man was brought from his native homeland, first as indentured servant, and later as a slave. His new environment was completely different and he was forced to learn new jobs, develop new skills, and make many adjustments. He was needed by his owner for the cultivation of the fields, clearing the wilderness, or performing the many household chores.

Many times his new life was confusing to him and his knowledge was limited to the boundaries of his owner's plantation. His one sustaining force seems to have been his faith. The roots of early Black history seem to be deeply embedded in his religious beliefs. His life revolved about his labors and his church.

Although it is not known how or why the Black race came to the Grayson-Carroll-Galax area, it is known that the church was an essential part of their life.
The first church for Black people in this area is believed to have been in North Carolina near Sulphur Springs (near Mt. Airy). About 1870, a church was established at Pleasant Hill, near Jefferson, N. C., in an old log cabin with a huge rock chimney in the back. Another church was built in the River Hill section near Baywood. Before long there were 15 churches in the area with one common faith and belief. They were as follows:
Bethany Baptist Church at Woodlawn; Tolliver Chapel near the Blue Ridge Parkway; Mount Carmel at Ivanhoe; Mt. Zion at Independence; Redmond's Creek near Baywood; White Plains near Sparta, N. C.; Macedonia near the Blue Ridge Parkway, beyond Sparta, N. C.; Bridle Creek at Fox; Grassy Creek, N. C.; Pleasant Grove near Jefferson, N. C.; Oldtown Baptist Church (established about 1930).

The entire group of churches is organized into the New Covenant Baptist Association.

In the wars that America has fought; In the Spanish American War we know that Rev. Hilary Williams and Rev. Bill Blair (known as Uncle Willie) fought for their country. Charlie Hash of Woodlawn, James Hale, and Joe Brown were veterans of World War 1. World War II, Korea, and Vietnam called many of the area's young men, some who never returned. The late Richard Bryan, son of Mr. and Mrs. Walter Bryan was a disabled veterans of WW II.

THE BRYAN FAMILY

A business establishment that has become an institution in the history of Galax is the BRYAN BARBER SHOP. Even before the town began, the Reverend Abe H. Bryan operated a barber shop at Blair and at Oldtown, devoting one-half day to each concern. In addition to his business duties, Mr. Bryan served as a teacher and a minister. When the new town was established and there was a need for a barber shop, Mr. Bryan began one of the town's oldest business concerns. He opened his first shop on Main Street. The business, now located on Carroll Street, has moved locations several times in its history.

The Rev. Abe Bryan was married to the late Mary Bryant and to this union one son, Walter F. Bryan, was born. Before he came to Galax, Mary died and Abe married Rosa Wolfe. Their children were Knoud, Oscar, and Abe.

Walter Bryan assumed operation of the barber shop when his father died in 1926. Like his father, Walt, as he was most often called, was active in church and community affairs. He was a trustee of the Oldtown Baptist Church, a master mason, promoter of the school, and farmer. His greatest pride was his horses, and his favorite was a white horse named "Dan," which he rode to and from work.

Walter was married in 1914 to Leota Hale, who still resides at the old home place in Oldtown. At the age of 80 she is still active in church affairs and attends many senior citizen functions. Seven children were born to Walt and Leota: Rudolph, Lotis Blair, Richard (deceased), Walter, Jr., Rose Kyle, Gilbert, and Leota Saunders.

Gilbert, a small equipment operator for the Bank of Virginia and R. L. Persinger, is part owner of a shoe-repair business, and the present owner and operator of Bryan's Barbershop. Raymond (Tojo) Brown assists Gilbert in the operation of the small but thriving enterprise. Gilbert has maintained the family tradition of practicing the barber trade and assuming leadership of church, civic, and community affairs. He is Senior Warden in the Masonic Lodge, an active member of the Y's Men Club, Deacon of Oldtown Lodge.

Gilbert has seen many changes in the barber trade. He recalls his grandfather's stories of customers sitting in straight-back chairs for a shave (5 cents) or a haircut (10 cents), heating water in a pan on a potbellied stove, and using a feather duster for removing loose hair from the customer's neck.

Other businesses in Galax which are operated by Black owners are as follows:
Riteway Shoe Shop, Weldon Phipps, owner and operator. He began his trade at the age of fourteen when he worked for Earl and Ellis Melton. He opened his own business in 1974 with Gilbert Bryan as part owner. He and his wife, the former Iola Saunders, have three children.

City Body Shop, Blaine Hash and Joe Poe, owners and operators. This business is located at 106 Carroll Street and is an automotive repair shop. Blaine began working in body repair at B & L Chevrolet in the early '30's. He started work at Galax Motor Co. in 1946. Joseph Brown is the only employee.

THE SPELLER FAMILY

Speller's Cafe, Mrs. Annie Speller owner and operator. Mrs. Speller is the widow of the late George W. Speller, a long time resident of the City of Galax.

Shortly after the Great Depression a young couple, George and Annie Speller, came to Galax from Winston-Salem, N. C. The Spellers were teachers who later engaged in diverse enterprises, many of which were designed to aid the Black people of the community through greater employment opportunities. Among their many business ventures were a gas station and general store, beauty parlor, a barber shop, a cafe, a real estate office in Galax and other cities, and rental property.

Like many men of vision, Mr. Speller was able to realize all of his dreams; among , a theatre, shoe repair shop, and a factory for the employment of Black citizens. Although he was unable to accomplish all he wished to do, his efforts enriched the lives of many. Those who knew him pay him tribute when they remember him as "a friend to man."

The first Black school at Oldtown was held in a two-story frame building in 1910. The first teacher was Miss Louise Porter of South Boston. Other early teachers were Watson Willis, Frank Maxwell, Zemri Holmes, Mrs. Odessa Davis, Mrs. Luella Tidline and Mrs. Josie Early.

Black students going to high school prior to 1949 went to Christiansburg Institute or other places. After this date, Black students were bused from Galax and Grayson to Scott Memorial in Wytheville. Students from this area now attend Baywood or Fairview Elementary and Galax High School.

Rosenwald-Felts School

A Black School in the City of Galax, Virginia was a fond desire of area citizens for many years. It was not until 1924, that a group of interested citizens contacted the city officials to see what could be done toward this much needed project.

Seeing a vast need for a Black School in this area, Mr. T.L. Felts, Galax, Virginia, gave the entire land where the present school is located as well as five hundred dollars toward the building fund.

Realizing that this step was just the beginning, Mr. Felts suggested that the Rosenwald Foundation of New York City, be asked to support the effort. Mr. William Gershwin, representative for the Rosenwald Fund and state supervisor of Black Schools, was contacted.

After many months, the superintendent, Mr. J. Lee Cox, Councilmen Mr. Charles P. Warren, Mr. Emmett Cox and Mr. Shelby Vass, Sr., were informed by Mr. Gershwin that the Rosenwald Foundation would finance the school erection.

Rev. Calup Carson, Mr. William Martin, Mr. Rich Garrett, were chosen the first trustees.

Mr. James Isom, Independence, Virginia, called together the parents of this community and the first Parent Teachers Association was organized. This association launched many programs and activities to raise funds for the new school.

Finally, March 1926, a two-room school, named Rosenwald Felts, was opened for student attendance.

Mr. James Isom, Independence, Virginia, was selected to be the first principal. Teaching with him was Miss Alberta Clark. Approximately seventy-five students from Galax and Oldtown, Virginia, were enrolled.

Principals and teachers following were:
Mrs. Sears, Miss Nowlin, Mrs. Josie Early, Mrs. Odessa Davies, Miss Pace, Miss Wotten, Mr. Anderson, Miss Bowan, Mr. Hart, Mr. George Speller, Mr. Booker, Mrs. Dixon, Mrs. Seay, Mr. Hensile Millner, Mr. Forte, Mr. Henderson, Mr. John Beamer, Mr. Robert Early and Mrs. Lillie Bradley. 1968-69 faculty: Mr. J. G. Williams, Principal; Miss Volyn Dykes, Mrs. O'Leta Goins and Mr. Theodore Gibbs.
The Rosenwald-Felts Elementary School was closed in 1969 and the new Rosenwald-Felts Kindergarten was opened in 1973.

Senator Floyd Landreth

Having served for 37 years as the president of the First National Bank of Galax, the Honorable Sidney Floyd Landreth is only the bank's second president. He is just as enthusiastic about the bank's welfare now, even though he is about two months short of his 90th birthday, as ever before. Just the other day, on Tuesday, Jan. 21, Mr. Landreth presided with his usual grace and dignity over the bank's annual shareholders' meeting. There are few Galax residents who have lived here any appreciable length of time who do not know, or at least, know something about, Floyd Landreth. Mr. Landreth has lived with a lot of Galax history. In fact, he has helped make a lot of the city and region's history.

Not only in his home town , but also throughout the state, he been well known and highly respected, as a businessman, lawyer, churchman and politician. He has served as president of the Virginia Convention of Christian Churches (Disciples of Christ), and as a member of the Board of Trustees of his church's college, Lynchburg College. He is an Elder and Trustee of the First Christian Church, Galax. Generally, he has always given his church priority over his other activities.

Prominent in the affairs of the Republican party for all of his adult life, Mr. Landreth served Galax and Carroll Counties for 20 years in the Virginia State Senate, where his advice and counsel were sought by both Democrats and Republicans alike, as did five Democratic governors during whose administrations he served in the Senate.

At the Republican State Convention held in Roanoke on Saturday, June 30, 1945, Mr. Landreth was nominated as his party's candidate for Governor. During the summer and fall of 1945, Mr. Landreth waged an aggressive campaign, stumping the state against then Lt. Gov. William M. Tuck of South Boston, the Democratic nominee. Mr. Tuck was elected Governor that year, but Mr. Landreth only lost by a 1,000 vote.

Mr. Landreth was born in a log house on a farm in the Oak Grove section of Carroll County on March 27, 1885, to the Rev. James J. Landreth and Mrs. Missouri Phillippi Landreth. His father was a farmer and minister. His mother, like many farm housewives, was well versed in native herbs and plants essential to the home remedies necessary for the treatment of many ailments, and was often called upon to "help out" with the sick folks in the community where she lived.

A charter member of the Galax Rotary Club, which celebrated its 50th Anniversary last May, Mr. Landreth has been chairman of just about all of the club's committees. He has also been a sympathetic advisor to all Rotarians, especially new members. He served as president of the Rotary Club in 1926-27.

He attended what, in those days was called "Free School" at Oak Grove. School terms then lasted "as long as. the money held out," which was usually three to four months. At Oak Grove, the pupils began by learning the ABC's (alphabet), forward. and then backward. Mr. Landreth has recalled that he did pretty well on his ABC's, except for the letter, "J," which he labeled "that crooked letter." When old enough, he attended, during four summers, the Teachers' Training School at Woodlawn, and became qualified to teach at the age of 18. He taught one winter at McGee's Mill School, and the next winter at Corinth, both of which schools were in Carroll County, and, incidentally, both were within horseback-riding distance of his home. His third winter of teaching, which proved to be his last, was at Reed Island in Pulaski County. It was during the winter that he was teaching at Reed Island that the late Dexter Goad became Clerk of Carroll County Circuit Court, and young Floyd Landreth was selected, by a committee appointed, to fill the position of Deputy Clerk, in Mr. Goad's office in Hillsville.

Mr. Landreth served as Deputy Clerk for two and a half years. As an officer of the Court, he was present at the last "hanging" which was ever been carried out in Carroll County. The man who was to be hanged, had been brought before a Grand Jury, and was, apparently, indicted. Later, the man. allegedly went to the home of the man who had served as foreman of that Grand Jury, knocked on the door, and when the man opened the door, shot and killed him. It was for this crime that the man was hanged.

With money saved from his work as a teacher, and his work in the Clerk's Office, Mr. Landreth had a year of schooling at Washington and Lee University, Lexington. There were many at W&L who tried to interest him in playing football, because of his robust size. But he said he knew he had only enough funds for one year, and had to cram two years of law into that one year -- and this he did, and thus received his degree in law.

with Governor Holton

He passed the State Bar Examination before the Supreme Court, sitting in Wytheville, in 1909. Then it was back to Hillsville and Carroll County, to set up his law practice. Persons desiring the young lawyer's legal services were not overly plentiful at first, so, when the opportunity presented itself for him to add to his income, he took on the Federal Census for the 5th Congressional District of Virginia, in 1910. As Census Supervisor, the future senator needed to be located where he could use the handy railway service, in order to expedite his reports. So, on Dec. 23, 1909, with suitcase in hand, he stepped off the Mail Wagon in Galax, having come in from Carroll by that means of transportation. He had chosen Galax as the seat of his Census Supervisor work. He set up his Census office here, for the oversight of the census enumerators who worked in the various areas of the different counties in the 5th District. in the taking of the 1910 federal decennial census.

His census job was completed in record time, and Mr. Landreth stayed on in Galax. and has practiced law here ever since. On Aug. 13, 1913, in a Washington, D.C. Episcopal Church, Miss Lola Evelyn Lintecum became the bride of Sidney Floyd Landreth. Subsequently, a daughter, Katherine, was born to the couple, and, as Mrs. Katherine Franke, she presented them with a grandson, Walter (better known as "Topper"). Now, their great - grandchildren have come to be "the apple of his eye."

Always actively interested in civic and community affairs, Mr. Landreth has been especially interested in the promotion of new industry for the Galax area. Therefore, with other like-minded leaders, he was instrumental in persuading officials of Burlington Industries and Hanes Corporation, to located plants here.

With his "Bride"

State Sen. Ted Dalton of Radford (who was later twice to receive the Republican nomination for Governor and who is now judge of the United District Court for the Western District of Virginia, and another Carroll native) was among others who played major roles in that convention. He was particularly active in matters relating to the platform, etc. Virginia's present Lt. Gov. John N. Dalton of Radford (elected in November, 1973, with Gov. Mills E. Godwin Jr.) is Judge Dalton's son.

When asked in an interview some years ago if he did not approach his duties as prosecutor during the trials that followed the famous courtroom tragedy that occurred in Hillsville March 14, 1912, with a degree of trepidation, being only 27 years old at the time, Senator Landreth replied:"Yes, I did. I had good help provided by the state, but each trial took about a week. I was in the courtroom when the tragedy happened. The little room was filled with people, so you couldn't see it all. It was the most notorious case of my career, but I've worked with several murder cases."

Mr. Landreth said , "I was first appointed Commonwealth's Attorney for Carroll in March of 1912 to fill in for the man killed in the Courthouse tragedy. Then I was elected to the office for a second term.

"Answering a question about his defeats for Congress and the governorship, "How do you feel about those losses?," Mr. Landreth's answer was:"Well, if I had won the Governor's race, it would probably have ruined me, politics being the way they are in Virginia. They are bad in other places, but Virginia is worse than other places."

In answer to the question, "What do you enjoy most about banking?," Landreth, who has been president of the First National Bank of Galax since the death of Sen. T. L. Felts, whom he succeeded, in 1937, said: "Well, I started my first bank account when I was 18 with the $17.50 I was paid for one month's teaching. I've given $1.00 savings account openings to several people. One girl turned that $1.00 into $20,000 by the time she was in her twenties. Banking is not a gold mine like many people think.

"I like to counsel young folks to practice economy. But the best thing I like about it, is helping people to get their own homes. I've been president here for 34 years, and people just don't manage money as good as they should. Of course, they didn't have much to manage in those earlier days, but today they make good money. and mismanage it."

Senator Landreth is a man who apparently enjoys living. At any rate, I've always thought so during the more than 40 years that I have known him. His familiar jolly countenance, along with a seriously earnest demeanor as occasion and circumstances demand has been his trademark through the passing years. He has been, and still is, a useful, conscientious citizen of Galax, Virginia and the United States.

Many are the individuals to whom, in one way or another he has extended a helping hand. He has served well in various fields of endeavor, and thousands appreciate what he has done for God and Country! I am not hesitant to say that Galax, Carroll and Grayson Counties, and Virginia, are better places in which to live because Floyd Landreth has lived among us for all these almost 90 years.

A First National Bank Stockholders meeting January 23, 1964. Heard report of Continued growth from the President of the Bank, Floyd Landreth, with Executive Vice-President T. R. Jennings and Cashier Robert M. Webb looking on. Reporting growth of more than 2.5 million in two years.

From an article in the Galax Gazette by Munsey Poole
February 1964, Edited by Mariah K. Nunn

Galax Black and Blue Football teams. November 11, 1970

Blue team-- L to R:
First row: Harry Schaeffer, Tim Coomes, Greg Williams, Robert Maxwell, Jed Goad, Mike Shaeffer
Second Row: Joe Shaeffer, Steve Morris, Allen Vaughan, Victor Rios, Doug Bartlett, John Waugh,
Third Row: Allen Dickerson, Billy Cardwell, Taylor Vaughan, Doug Davis, Steve Vaughan, Jeff Bedwell. Not Pictured- Coach Carroll Clark.

Black Team: L-to R-
First Row: Doug Woody, Tony Moretz, Donald Houk, Lee Wensel, Allen Kyle
Second Row: Chad Rector, Mike Norman, Charles Hodge, Mark Poole, Billy Brannock, Kevin Burnett, Eddie Hanks
 Third Row: David Clontz, Mark Evans, Robin Reeves, Mike Butler, Coach Pete Cregger. Not Pictured Tommy Sturdivant, Bart Wallace and Rickey Brown

84

Galax High School Basketball January 1972

TOURNAMENT BOUND -- The Galax Maroon Tide will participate in the New River District Tournament at the VPI Coliseum in Blacks burg tonight (Thursday) against the Narrows Green Wave. L to R -- team members are Verl Brown, Dennis Stanley, Ray Billings, Donald LaRue, David Mallory, Phillip Webb, Jimmy Jones, Thomas Stanford, Tommy McKnight, Tony McMickle and Bruce Herman, and Coach Ronald Quesenberry.—Chambers

THE GALAX JUNIOR Varsity squad, with a record of 5-1, will travel to Wytheville Friday night.
L to R -- Greg Adams, Greg Boyer, David Hankley, Zack Kyle, Tony Brown, Donald Ayers, Randy Bedsaul, Claude Carson, Ed Weaver, Dennis Smith, Russ Brown, Fred Davis, Thomas Richardson, and Marshall Hamden. Kneeling is Coach Ray Bedsaul.

Last time for New River District Championship:
Galax wins the District 1977-78

Left to Right: Terry Wilson, Mark Harris, Victor Rios, Mark Quesenberry,(co-MVP)
David Cheek, Nate Robinson, Doug "Roach" Davis(co-MVP) Charles "Fuzzy" Bartlett, Mike Brown, Greg
Kyle, Bill Sutherland, Matt Hamden, Kneeling L to R: Coach Ron Quesenberry and Coach Larry Spangler

Maroon Tide Plays Christiansburg today.

Left to Right front: Coach Hager, Chicken Chappell, Bobby Pless, Co-Captains John Pless and Charles Frye, Jim
Nuckolls, and Eugene Rosenbaum, Back Row: Manager Roger Boyer, Alex Blackburn, Benny Hurd, Tommy
Hawks, Doug Pedigo, Bernard Edwards and Jerry Cook *According to Jim Nuckolls who was a Sophomore , this was in 1955*

86

GALAX HIGH SCHOOL GRADUATES
CLASS OF 1936

Front Row: Etoile Amburn, Gladys Hampton, Bonny Lynn Todd, Ruth Hawkins, Aileene Elliott, Kate Harmon, Lucille Rector

Second Row: Mr. Kyle, Principle, Miss Cassie Gardner, class sponsor; Helen Hampton, Bertha Delp, Mildred Lawrence, Nena Hale, Katy McCarty, Jama Lee McKnight

Back Row: Preston Phipps, Boyd Vass, Jack Williams, Roy Bowie, Rayburn Martin, Robert Carlan, James Cox

GHS CLASS OF 1943 HAS REUNION.

The Galax High School class of 1943 recently held a 45-year reunion at the Elks Lodge in Galax. From left to right:

Front Row: Edith Davis Higgins, Mrs. McKinley Wolfe (guest), Edith Burcham Edwards, Louise Taylor Choate, Dorothy Poe Lineberry, Thomasine Callaway Lemons, McKinley Wolfe (guest) Ruby Mabe Lindamood, Eva Frazier Diamond, Ruth Blevins Golding, Crena Kegley Frost, Juanita Smith Hampton.

Middle Row: Pauline Pennington Ramey, Thomas Matthews, Carl Rector, Mildred Waddell Martin, Theressa Cain Matzke, Eloise Roberts Vass, Mildred Martin Fever, Mary Davis Morris, Celene Young Cornette, Kathleen Moore Gentry, Beulah Isom Harris, Hilda Mitchell Fielder, Janice Cox Wensel

Back Row: J. Curtis Hall, James Carico, Verlin Gentry, Charles Chappell, Pete Vass, Ralph Pierce, Bill Weave, Charles Wright, Rex Seaver

Photo by April Wright –Gazette 2008

The Galax High School class of 1943 recently held its 65th reunion at Bogeys Restaurant. "Who would believe when we stumbled down that creaky auditorium that we would be here 65 years later and still looking pretty good" Janice Cox Wensel told her fellow GHS alumni. Pictured are (from Left to Right)

Front row: Mary Davis Morris, Carl Rector,
Second Row: Eloise Roberts Vass, Beulah Isom Harris, Edith Burcham Edwards, Janice Cox Wensel, J.C. Cox, Hilda Mitchell Fielder, Gene Nuckolls,
Third Row: Kathleen More Gentry, Ruby Mabe Lindamood, Verlin Gentry, Juanita Smithers Hampton and Harold Choate

CLASS OF 1952 Galax High School

All individuals are listed below from left to right.

Front row: Joan McCraw (later married Charles Lineberry); Jeanette Ann Blevins; Bessie Evelyn Choate, Doris Lee Mitchell, Constance Dawn Clifton, Betty Marie Stroupe. Myrna Joan Paisley.

Second row: Jimmy Delp Bowie, Thomas Lundy Murphy, John Kyle Kegley, John C. Matthews, George Graham Coulson, Franklin Edison Patton, Billy Reed Hanks, John Kelly "Buddy" Davis.

Third row: Margaret L. Stroupe, Jessie Lee Frost, Eula Mae Williams, Nancy Gail Lane, Earnestine Doris Dalton, Juanita D. Murphy,   Mary Lee Barrett, Jess Burch Higgins.

Fourth row: Robert Lee Hash, Carl Fred Davis,   William A. Cockerham,
Don Roe Williams; Jimmy Duane Sizemore, James Franklin Rhodes, Rex Litrelle Boyer, Edwin Dale Liddle.

Fifth row: Howard Rudolph Todd, Ira Wilson Green.

Galax schools did not include an eighth grade until it was added just behind the students who graduated in 1951. There would not have been a graduating class of 1952, except for students who transferred in from "feeder" schools, such as Baywood and Fairview, plus a few of us who should have graduated in 1951, but lacked sufficient credits.

Names Furnished by Jim Bowie, member of the class of 1952

Galax High School CLASS OF 1964

The Galax High School Class of 1964 held its 20-year reunion on Saturday, Aug. 11, at Cumberland Knob Park. Over one-half of the graduating class members were present with their families.

The Rev. David Roberts of Fayetteville, N.C., gave the invocation and a moment of silence was observed for the deceased members of the class.

Master of ceremonies Donnell Hall presented the following awards: member traveling the farthest distance, Jeanne Davis Porter, member with most children, Joyce Mink Setliff; member with most grandchildren, Doug and Joyce Carico Sexton, member with youngest (expected) child, Margaret Burnett Cheek.

Teachers attending the reunion, Kate Dickens, Margaret Jones and Rexene Spraker, were introduced, after which door prizes were awarded.

All members present were then introduced by Beverly Higgins Rios and each member introduced his or her family and gave a brief synopsis of activities for the past 20 years.

Class of 1964-left to right, front row: Linda Vaughan Roop, Iva Lee Wilson Hudson, Jeanne Davis Porter, Doug Sexton, Roger Golding, Barry Reynolds, Donnell Hall, Harry Delp, Gene Jones, John Hartsock, Pete Ramey and David Roberts.

Second Row: Linda Butler Jernigan, Nancy Hudson Blair, Betty Lou Fortner Amburn, (not visible), Nell Shumate, Carol Rosenbaum Johnson, Myra Smith, Lois Edwards Harmon, Carolyn Horton Farmer, Elizabeth Edwards Owen, Celene Tiller Thompson and Joyce Mink Setliff.

Third row: Becky Liddle Darby, Jean Martin Hurt, Jane Diamond Williams, Patsy Eastridge Thompkins, Hattie Bob Felts Wilson, Margaret Burnett Cheek, Beverly Higgins Rios, Gaye Carico Lineberry, Gary Lowe, Jimmie Dale Vaughan, Pam Richardson Dickenson and Don Dickenson.

Fourth Row: Jean Thomas Carico (not visible), Judy Reedy Bond, Annlynn Wingold Easton, Carlene Reeves, Glenda Glasco Purvis (not visible), Joyce Carico Sexton, Clayton Edwards, H.B. Thomas, Joe Shumate and Bobby Elliott.

Fifth Row: Larry Cornette and Glenn Burcham.
Present but not in photo: Nona Hammock Jones, Barbara Leath Sawyers, Connie Cochran Chafin, Lorretta Petty Turnstall, Ralph Boone, Judy Davis Hackler, Betty Wright Carico and Pat You

Galax High School class of 1956 Girls & Boys

Galax High Graduates-Girls—
First row: Edna Carico, Bonnie Sexton, Alice Cox, Jean Harris Cook, Libba Hawks, Phyllis Cox, Maude Frye
Second Row: Helen Belton, Wynell Bell, Shirley Murphy, Emmalene Kegley, Diane Young, Barbara Bartlett, Barbara Wood, Shirley Jennings, Jewel Bartlett,
Third Row: Jo Ann Moser, Elanore Jennings, Mildred Oakley, Doris Moser, Barbara Anders,   Shirley Carico,
Fourth Row: Pat Rorrer, Frances Funk, Ina May Goodson, Kitty Green, Mary Taylor and Shelby Mayes.

Galax High School Boys:
First Row: L-R..Roger Boyer, Alex Blackburn, Bernard Edwards, Ronald Boyer,   Charles Bolt, Leslie Nichols, Bill Murphy.
Second Row: Floyd Nuckolls, Tommy Hawks, Benny Hurd, Johnny Morris, Bill Pierce, Billy East, Larry Alley,
Third Row: Mickey Foster, Wayne Chappell, Jerry Cook, Cecil Nichols, Jim Thomas, Dick Taylor, George Jones, Allen Bedwell, Verlin Stockner,. About 11 boys were not present for this picture.

91

Class of 1972 40th Reunion

Galax High School Class of 1972 - 40th Reunion Galax, Virginia 8/11/12.

GHS Class of 1972 40th Reunion at First Christian Church in Galax, VA 08/11/2012

L to R standing: Walt Hampton (Mike), Dixie Leonard, Kay Cruise Creed, Bobby Adams, Debbie Edwards Patterson, Beth Wienberry Dix, Stephen Fayne, Judi Nelson McBride, Bobby Vaughan, Ouida Caudill Jordan, Susan Custer Higgins, Susie Burris Huffman, Pat Manuel Woods, Bobby Kane, Anita Wright Spurlin, Mike Spurlin, Brenda Crouse Harmon, Beverly Hanks Frederick.

L to R kneeling: David Hampton, Miles Compton, Tony Montgomery.

Homecoming Queen and Court 1977 Galax High School

Julie Frye of Galax was crowned Homecoming Queen during halftime ceremonies Friday night. Making up the court were Mandy Shores and Joan Milgrim. At left is her escort, Don Singletary.

Gazette Photos by Larry Chambers

One of these young ladies will be crowned as the 1977 Galax High School Homecoming Queen this Friday night. Members of the GHS Homecoming Court are from left - front row: Kaye Nobblitt, Toni Nunn, Susan Chappell, Jo Anna Cardwell Second row: Debbie Gentry, Renay Milgrim, Julie Frye, Joan Milgrim. Back row: Kathy Wilson, Cathy Walker, and Grace Largin. (not pictures: Mandy Shores)

Gazette Photo by Terry Hill

93

GHS Homecoming Court 1990

Gazette Photo by Angela Funk

. Galax homecoming court named

Galax High School will Crown its homecoming queen Friday night during halftime activities at the Shawsville game. Members of the homecoming court are (from left)

Front: Carrie Kirkland, Jessica Jo McCarter, Holly Dannelly, Christie Hawks, Stacey Musser

Back: Susan Galyen, Michele Galyean , Ashlyn Dannelly, Julie Gillespie, Lisa Cox, and Michelle Boone. Not Pictured, Chrysty Wittman

Homecoming Queen 1990
is Michele Galyean escorted by her father, Charles C. Galyean.
Maids of Honor are: Susan Galyen and Stacy Musser

Galax High School 1993 Homecoming Queen Kate McCoy and her Court

Kate McCoy was all smiles last Friday night after she was crowned the 1993 Homecoming queen during the halftime celebrations of the Maroon Tide-Floyd County football game. She was escorted by her father, Douglas McCoy.

Runner-ups were Mary Ellen Edwards and Sofia Holm

One of these Galax High school students below will be crowned Homecoming Queen Friday night at halftime in the game against Floyd County High School. Homecoming court members are : left to right--Sofia Holm, Mary Ellen Edwards, Kate McCoy, Tracy Kirby, Tonya Baumgardner, Shannon Cox, back row: Rae Alderman, Brooke Pratt, Lisa Dixon, Rachel Porter, Renee Murphy and Lauren Spivey

Galax High School Homecoming Queen and Court 1994

Brooks Frost (center left) escorted by her father, Billy Frost, was crowned Galax High School's Homecoming Queen 1994 Friday night at halftime of the Maroon Tide's 48-14 win over Auburn. Maids of Honor were April Bagatta (left) and Jaclyn Dickens (right)

Gazette Photo by Craig Worrell

1994 Homecoming Court Below are:
Back row: Mary Mitchell, Lisa Gunter, Lisa Warf, Sally Sawyers, Jaclyn Dickens, Mary Stuart Gatchel
Front Row: Brooks Frost, Becky Walls, Kelly Burnett, Fonje Hairston, Aril Baggatta and Julie Stevens.

Gazette Photo by Drew vanEsselstyr

Homecoming Queens 1969 and 1970
Galax High School

Bobbi Cochran is shown with her farther Pete Cochran after she was chosen 1969 Galax Homecoming Queen at the Galax-Blacksburg football game Friday night.

Regina McKnight and Carolyn Wagner were runner-ups

1970 Homecoming Queen 1970

Jackie Higgins, a senior at Galax High School, was selected the 1970 Homecoming Queen at the Galax – Narrows football game, winning over nine other contestants. At left is 1969 Queen Bobbi Cochran. AT right is Jackie's father, Ray Higgins.

Galax High School   Class of 1961 reunion 2011

Attending the 50-year reunion of Galax High School class of 1961 were:
Row one (from left). Catherine Padgett Anderson, Judy Davis Haynes, Mary Ellen Kyle Philen, Jane Burris and
Doris Diamond Spangler:

Row two: Nena Hash (teacher). Marilyn Lundy Tiller, Betty Ann Smith, Patsy Pugh Boren, Shirley Robinson
Smith, Helen Sparks Rippey, Carolyn Sparks Easter, Frances Guynn Newman, Margaret Spurlin Willis, Shirley
Wilson Shumate and Brenda Utt Lundy;

Row three: Larry Bartlett, Paula Burcham Stoneman, James Tiller, Betty Bowers Moxley, Charlotte Hankley
Shepherd, Carol Hale Felts, Peggy Shaw Sumner and Faye Hammock Cox.

Row four: Joan Boyer Bryant, Roger Martin, Lloyd Jones, Doris Brendle Edwards, Arthur Cox, C.B. Caudell,
Dale Higgins, Dixie Young Varanko and Ella Jane Higgins Robinson;

Row five: Edward Parks, Ronald Catron, James Higgins, Nancy Bartlett Phipps, Jerry Johnson, James Martin
and Roger Wilson.
Not pictured: Thomasine Lemons (teacher).

2006 All CLASS REUNION of Galax High School

Front L to R: Mike McMillian, Jane Burris, Maude Cornwell Frye Bledsoe, Mary Ann Spinks Dotson, Mrs. Rube Waddell, "not identified", Carolyn Hankley, Wesley Lineberry, Mrs. Ronnie Martin.

2nd Row: Ann Carico McMillian, Charlotte Hankley Shepherd, Mary Ellen Kyle Philen, Shirley Akers Rosenbaum, Sharon Chapman Felts, Darryl Quesenberry, Ted Hall, Elwood Bartlett and Ronnie Martin.

3r. Row: Peggy Parson Chappell, Frances Lowe Hampton, Frances Dixon, Gene Rosenbaum, Harold Brannock, Sambo Lawson, Jerry Cook

4th Row: Betty Dalton, C.B. Hampton, cannot see the next three, Larry Waddell, Bill Cole, Bill Collins

Leaders of Galax' first Scout troop and Scouts recall some camping trips 0f 50 years ago

Many local-area persons may not know that the Scoutmaster of the first Boy Scout troop ever organized in Galax- which was formed only two years after the Scout movement was introduced into American in 1910 by the late W. D. Boyce, Chicago publisher- is still around. He is, though- very much so, and hale and hearty. He is Mr. Lance M. Todd, of 308 West Oldtown St.

And so are a number of "boys' who were charter members of that old Troop No. 1, Galax, which was organized in 1912-- 51 years ago this year.

The roster of this first Scout troop in the area was as follows: Paul Kapp, David Bolen, McCamant Higgins, Otto Hawks, Fred Witherow, Roosevelt Robertson, Ralph Rhudy, Rob Roy Rhudy, Jim Ted Rhudy, Bruce Hawks, Lonnie McMillan, Rex Wright, Raymond Wright, John Gary Carico, Hix Weatherman, Ben Nuckolls, Robert Bolling, Byron Williams, Price Davis and Garnett Spurlin.

Mr. Todd said he was Scout-master of Troop No.1 and it was really No.1 Galax as Boy Scout troops go.

Mr. Todd and other members of the troop who are still in Galax recall some of the camping trips on which the troop used to go- among them having been treks to Rural Retreat in Wythe County, and to Mount Airy, N. C., and by "covered wagon," which conveyance was furnished by Mr. Todd, a trip in those days to either of the places mentioned was "quite a trip", and "quite an experience" for eager growing boys.

The photograph reproduced above was taken in Fries, just below the Norfolk and Western Railway station in what was then the very young town of Fries, as the troop was on its way to Rural Retreat. The journey was made from Fries by way of the old Blair's Ferry at Fries, and then by way of Speedwell, at or near which town the Scouts pitched camp for the night, continuing on to Rural Retreat the following morning.

Dr. David Bolen, long-time Galax dentist, said the Scouts entered into various forms of pastime while at Rural Retreat, including games of various kinds, the usual routine Scout-troop activities, nd rides on "local" N. & W. trains to Wytheville and back. (Dr. Bolen is a son of the late Dr. J. W. Bolen of Galax, and a nephew of the late Judge D. W. Bolen of Fancy Gap.

According to what seem to be the best efforts possible now, after half a century, at identification, the eleven persons in the above picture, including the Scoutmaster are--left to right--as follows: Byron Williams, Paul Kapp, (Dr. Kapp, also a Galax Dentist, who has practiced with Dr. Bolen through the years), McCamant Higgins (now Galax's Mayor Higgins), scoutmaster Lance M. Todd, Rex Wright, David Bolen,(the Dr. Bolen already referred to) Roosevelt Robertson, Ben Nuckolls, Ralph Rhudy, Rhudy (Col. Ralph C. Rhudy, U. S. Air Force, and son of the late Attorney and Mrs. J. Hix Rhudy, as also were Rob Roy Rhudy and Jim Ted Rhudy, also listed as charter members of the troop), and John Gary Carico.

Mr. Todd still has in his possession a collection of interesting old papers-- certificates, trip expense account records, pictures, etc.- concerning the troop. Among these is an official certificate, saying: 'This is to certify that Lance M. Todd, having met the requirements

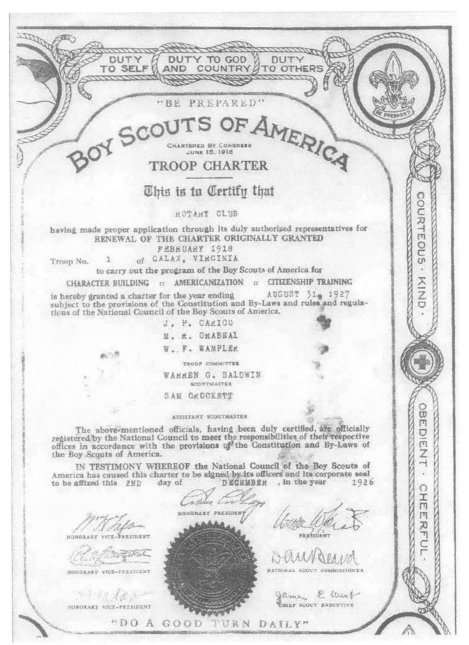

prescribed by the National Council of the Boy Scouts of America, is hereby appointed to serve as Scout Master No. 11620, Troop No. 1, Galax, Grayson County, Va., for the year ending September 30th, 1914, in accordance with the rules and regulations of the National Council. In witness whereof the seal of The Boy Scouts of America is hereunto affixed this, 29th day of October, 1913.

The certificate was signed by Dan Beard, National Scout Commissioner, and by the president of the BSA, and the National Scout.

The certificate also bears the signatures of Woodrow Wilson, honorary president, BSA, and Wm. H. Taft and Theodore Roosevelt, honorary vice-presidents.

Brownie Scout Troop 265   Held Investiture Services Oct. 17, 1977

Brownie Scout Troop 265 of the First United Methodist Church recently held investiture services. Pictured from left to right:

Front Row: Sherri Black, Wendi Roudebush, Amy Westmoreland, Stacy Butler, Cheryl Funk, Missy Vaught, Heather Douglas.

Second Row: Sarah Gillespie, Amy Zeh, Angie Braiser, Cherie Diamond, Margaret Lander, Faison Nuckolls, Allison Hemphill, Caroline Dickerson, Terri Chambers.

Third Row: Karen Hunt, Karen Pierce, Christy Roberts, Martha Bobbitt, aige Riddle, Tonya Hyatt, Beth Boniface, Absent. Susan McGrady

A few Eagle Scouts over the years.

Three Galax scouts received Eagle Scout Badges at the Court of Honor for the Carroll-Grayson District of Roanoke area council recently. They are (left to right) Elbert Hale Wampler, son of Mr. and Mrs. Wythe F. Wampler, Billy Walsh, son of Mr. and Mrs. John Walsh, and Buford Lindamood, son of Mr. and Mrs. W. B. Lindamood, all of Galax

Bernard Wampler last week became the third member of his family to attain the highest rank in Boy Scouts. The son of Mr. and Mrs. Wythe F. Wampler, his two older brothers Thornton and Elbert became Eagle Scouts a few years earlier. This was in the mid 40s.

Note of interest. The right scout above, Buford Lindamood
Is the father of the left scout below, John Lindamood

Four boys were presented with Eagle Badges at the First Methodist Church Sunday September 21, 1969. Left to right, front row: Ney Austin, scout executive for this area, John Lindamood, Jeff Bobbitt, Jerry Bobbitt and Bobby Vaughan.. Back row: Mr. and Mrs. Buford Lindamood, Mr. and Mrs. Delmer Bobbitt, Mr. and Mrs. Gene Vaughan and the Rev. Carroll Skeen, former pastor of the church

James Nuckolls watches his mother Mrs. Jim Nuckolls pin his Eagle Badge on his uniform as Dr. Tom Littrell, Scout Master watches.

James Nuckolls and Jimmy Combs received their Eagle Award badges from Scoutmaster Tom Littrell during ceremonies at the First Methodist church Sunday December 2, 1983.

Nuckolls and Combs have been members of the troop for seven years and active in the camping and hiking program. Both attended Philmont Scout Ranch earlier this year in New Mexico, and both are members of the Order of the Arrow.

Littrell said both scouts had to complete projects as part of the requirements for Eagle Scout.

Combs' project was to expand a 10x 12 platform at Camp Dickenson in to a 12 x 16 enclosed cabin. Nuckolls' project was to make a permanent Boy Scout display in the T. Jeff Matthews Museum in Galax.

Combs is a graduate of Galax High School where he played varsity foot ball. He is a freshman at Catawba College and the son of Mr. and Mrs. W. L. "Dub" Combs Jr. who just recently moved to Columbus, Ga.

Nuckolls attended Galax High School and played on the varsity basketball team last year. He is a junior at Woodberry Forest in Orange, Va., and the son of Dr. and Mrs. Jim Nuckolls.

Scoutmaster, Dr. Tom Littrell watches as Mrs. W. L. Combs, Jr. pins The Eagle scout award on the uniform of Jimmy Combs.

William Chad Austin was presented the rank of Eagle Scout during a presentation in December 1993. He is a member of the Galax Moose Lodge Boy Scout Troop 834 and a graduate of Galax High School...*below left*

Tom Pryor receives Eagle Badge from Tom Littrell Scoutmaster while his parents Robert and Susan Pryor look on....*on the right*

From left: Tom Littrell, Scoutmaster; Tim Pryor, Eagle Scout; Susan Pryor, mother; Robert Pryor, father.

I plan on collecting as many of the Galax Eagle Scout stories as possible and add them to the Eagle Scout category on www.Galaxscrapbook.com, *If you have information on any Eagle Scouts, please share them with me.*

104

Local Scout Troop 188   visits around the world

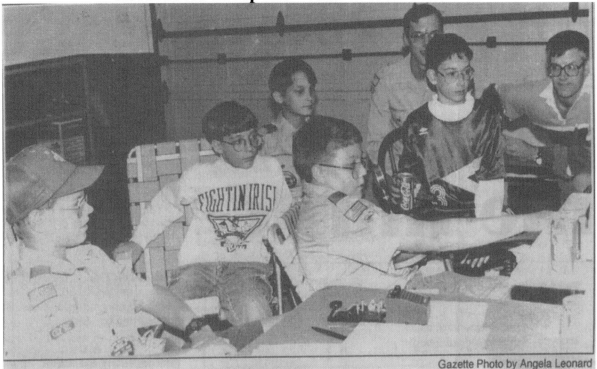

Gazette Photo by Angela Leonard

Boy Scout Troop 188 of Galax recently participated in the Scout Jamboree on the Air using a ham radio station in Pipes Gap. Participating scouts were (from left) Mac Garner, Austin Lineberry, Will Ritchie, Matt Harris, Zack Porter and Lee Morris and John Garner, assistant scout leaders.

By Angela Leonard Staff Writer
The Gazette October 29, 1993

Boy Scouts from troop 188 in Galax spent part of the day Oct 16th making friends in Mexico.
And South Africa, France, Jamaica and Barbados.
 Closer to home they visited Texas, Oregon and Reno Nevada.
All through the magic of short wave radio.
The five scouts and two assistant scout masters were participating with Girl and Boy Scouts from around the world in the Scout Jamboree on the air.

Taking advantage   of a ham radio station UD4BTF operated by Tommy Lineberry on Pipers Gap road, the scouts were able to talk with other scouts from around the world.

What About?

Frequently the Weather.

The Jamboree was in its 35th year and lasted from midnight Oct 15th to midnight Oct 17th.
In addition to talking with Boy Scouts in six countries and three states, the boys also talked with Girl Scouts in Jamaica. One of the three states visits was with the National Boy Scouts of America Station K2BSA17in Reno.

They said they enjoyed the experience and hoped to talk with a few more stations before calling it a day. At the top of their remaining list was Australia, followed by Japan, but it meant waiting another   hour or so because of the time difference.

The Gazette October 1993

GALAX GAZETTE

ROTOGRAVURE SECTION

* * *   GALAX, VIRGINIA » » » MARCH, 1937   * * *

Galax, Virginia, a Progressive, Growing Industrial Town, Ideally Located in the Picturesque Mountains of Southwest Virginia.

Left, H. W. Boaz.

H. M. Todd, Town Manager.

A. B. Gardner.

Dr. J. K. Caldwell is the sixth member of the board.

Left, Mayor B. D. Beamer.

● Nestling in an enchanting valley, on the borders of Carroll and Grayson counties, Galax, Virginia, is a prosperous industrial and commercial center, and one of the fastest-growing towns in the State. By reason of its location in the picturesque mountains of Southwest Virginia, at an altitude of 2,500 feet, with a delightful year-round climate, pure mountain water, and surrounded by a rich agricultural and grazing country, Galax possesses many attributes not common to the usual industrial towns, and is in every respect an ideal place in which to live.

● It is one of the younger towns of Virginia, having been founded in 1905, and is the second largest furniture manufacturing center in the State, in addition to having a large hosiery mill and other plants of a diversified nature. It has modern paved streets, progressive schools, handsome churches and a social environment second to none. It has adequate railway and motor freight facilities, and is located on U. S. Highways 58 and 221. The Skyline Scenic Highway, connecting the Great Smoky Mountain and Shenandoah National Parks, now under construction, will pass a few miles to the south, with which it will be connected by state highways.

● Galax wants the homeseeker and investor to investigate the many extraordinary opportunities offered by the city and the counties of Carroll and Grayson, and invites correspondence to this end. The town has a very liberal policy and sympathetic attitude to new industries, and will give all possible cooperation and assistance to investors and homeseekers.

W. G. Andrews.

J. W. Stanford.

J. Henry Brown.

Street Scene in the Business District of Galax, Virginia, One of the State's Fastest Growing Towns.

A Modern and Efficient Fire Force Gives Adequate Protection and a Low Insurance Rate to Galax.

These Firms Make ... GALAX a Great Retail Shopping Center

[The progressive retail enterprises shown on this and adjacent pages, with their large and diversified stocks, efficient service and modern merchandising methods, draw trade from a sixty-mile radius of the rich Southwest Virginia territory.]

Galax is a well rounded and self-contained community, with modern stores. None, however, presents a more congenial and inviting atmosphere than

The Jewel Box • 115 N. MAIN STREET

featuring reliable jewelry of every description. Also, an efficient repair department, where a high standard of workmanship is maintained.

Claire's Fashion Shoppe

Next to Town Hall.

Features smart Wearing Apparel for Ladies, with exclusive accessories. One of the most modern stores of its kind in Southwest Virginia, enjoying a liberal patronage from a discriminating clientele. Located on Main Street, next to Town Hall, Galax, Virginia.

Mrs. Claire Goldstein.

Joe Goldstein.

A Local Newspaper for Local Homes ... Covers Carroll and Grayson Counties Like a Blanket.

—Mike R. Crobill, Publisher.

W. L. Porter, President.

Mrs. R. T. Porter, Vice President.

R. T. Porter, Treasurer and Manager.

Sales and Display Quarters of W. L. Porter & Co., Inc., Furniture and Music, 213-215 South Main Street, Galax, Virginia.

Display room featuring bedroom suites.

W. L. PORTER & COMPANY, Inc., carries a better line of furniture, featuring solid and veneer hardwood suites in modern and period designs; also Stewart Warner Refrigerators and Radios, Westinghouse Refrigerators and Washers, R.C.A. Radios, and the best in musical instruments. The firm does an unusually heavy volume of business, drawn from a wide territory, and it requires six delivery trucks to serve its customers.

THE MERCHANTS AND FARMERS BANK of Galax was established in 1934, and has experienced a steady and consistent growth in resources every year of its existence. Today, it has a capital of $30,000.00, and surplus of $30,000.00. Its total resources are over $1,291,000.00.

The officers of this institution are Frank Adams, President;

Frank Adams,
President.

Jack M. Matthews, Vice President; John Webb, Cashier; Miss Gertrude Morton, Assistant Cashier; Mrs. Elizabeth Larue, Teller, and Miss Doris Browne, Bookkeeper.

The directors are Hubert S. White, A. G. Pless, W. A. Alderman, T. N. Woodruff, Jack M. Matthews, John Webb and Fred Adams.

The Merchants and Farmers Bank, Galax, Virginia.

Lobby, The Merchants and Farmers, Bank.

Views of the lumber yards and plant of W. K. Early & Son, Inc., Galax, Virginia.

G. B. Early, President.

Office, Store and New Warehouse.

The lumber business of the present W. K. Early & Son, Inc., was first organized in 1906, which makes it one of the pioneer firms of this section. In 1927, it was incorporated under its present title. In addition to its large lumber and building material volume, it handles coal, cement, roofing, Glidden paints, and does all classes of mill work in its plant. This company serves all Grayson and Carroll counties, parts of the nearby North Carolina territory, and is the largest of its kind between Bristol and Roanoke.

G. B. Early is President; Dr. J. L. Early, and H. E. Early, Vice Presidents, the first and last named being actively engaged in the firm's activities.

GALAX UPHOLSTERING FURNITURE COMPANY
Living Room Suites and Upholstered Chairs

Plant of Galax Upholstering Furniture Company's plant, manufacturers of well constructed, highly styled line of Living Room Suites and Upholstered Chairs.

The Cutting Room.

J. A. Messer, Sr.,
Chairman of the Board.

Lieut. Kenneth G. Messer,
President
(On leave with the Navy).

D. E. Ward,
Vice President.

M. D. Gordon,
Secretary-Treasurer.

The Sewing Room.

Styling and good construction have made the Living Room Suites and Upholstered Chairs of the Galax Upholstering Furniture Company well and favorably known throughout the nation. The company employs 75 persons and its yearly payroll is in excess of $100,000.00. The plant is modern in every respect. In addition to the officers shown above, Mrs. E. H. Chappell is Assistant Secretary.

GALAX MIRROR COMPANY, INC.

PLATE GLASS • BENT GLASS • TINTED GLASS • SHOCK MIRRORS • FRAME MIRRORS • VENETIAN MIRRORS

J. A. Messer, Jr.
President.

Main Plant Galax Mirror Company, Galax, Virginia.

Wiley Gentry,
Superintendent.

J. A. Messer, Sr.,
Founder and Chairman
of the Board.

Office Building, with section of factory in background.

Mr. J. A. Messer, Sr., the founder and present chairman of the board, is a prominent and veteran mirror and furniture manufacturer, having devoted nearly fifty years to the business. He is also Chairman of the board of the Webb Furniture Company and the Galax Upholstering Furniture Company, of his native city.

The Galax Mirror Company is one of the prosperous industries of Southwest Virginia, which has maintained a steady and consistent growth since its establishment in 1927. This increasing demand for its popular products has necessitated several additions to the original plant until now it is one of the largest in its line in the state. The company serves the furniture manufacturers of Virginia and North Carolina, and makes a popular line of mirrors which is sold in every state in the union. It also produces the well known Southern Beauty Line of Frames and Novelties.

Sectional View of New Plant.

Another View of Original Plant.

Higgins Lumber Company Plant, Galax, Virginia, one of the largest
lumber manufacturing companies in Southwest Virginia.

HIGGINS LUMBER COMPANY

MANUFACTURERS OF
WHITE PINE AND YELLOW PINE FRAMING

TELEPHONE 106

GALAX · VA ·

The Higgins Lumber Company was established in 1936, and has grown to be one of
the largest concerns of its kind in this section of country. At the local mill, 189,000
feet of lumber has been dressed and loaded in a single day. The normal output is
around six million feet monthly, but has reached as high as twelve million feet. A
large proportion of the product is sold to West Virginia wholesale lumber dealers.
Mr. McCamant Higgins is the owner of this business.

The Mill Plant.

Plant of The Galax Knitting Company, Galax, Virginia.

Right, J. T. Pollard, President.

The Very Latest in Scientific Machinery, and the Best Working Conditions
Afforded by Engineering Science, are Typical of The Galax Knitting Company.

● Manufacturing a varied line, including Men's Hose, Ladies' and Children's Seamless Hosiery, and with its own finishing and dyeing departments, the Galax Knitting Company, Inc., of Galax, Virginia, is one of the prosperous industries of Southwestern Virginia.

The company was established in 1924, and constant additions to the plant and equipment have been found necessary to meet the demand for its output. Today the company operates 425 machines and gives employment to 350 persons. Its products are sold to the jobbing trade throughout the country.

Mr. J. T. Pollard is president of the Galax Knitting Company, and Mr. H. L. Harris is Vice-President and Treasurer.

The Dyeing Room.

The Inspection Department.

Galax Has Adequate Airport Facilities

That Galax is airminded is evidenced by these individually owned planes lined up on the airfield five miles south of the city.

Galax is prepared for the expected post war development in air transportation. Situated on a hard surfaced road five miles south of the town the Galax Airport, with ample runways, modern and capacious hangar, with all the requisite service features, is ready to extend all necessary facilities to commercial and private planes. The airfield embraces an area of seventy acres.

The Galax Airport, Inc., is composed of a number of local aviation enthusiasts and business men.

Galax Airport Hangar, with adequate services for visiting planes.

Rex and Colonial Theatres

Rex Theatre, Grayson Street.

In the REX and CO-LONIAL Theatres, the Galax community has two moving picture houses showing the productions of the major producing companies. Matinee and regular showings are given each weekday by both houses, and the Rex has a Sunday program. Cecil W. Curtis is manager.

Colonial Theatre, Main Street.

Type of Trucks Serving Patrons of the Blue Ridge Transfer Company, Inc., of Galax, Virginia.

● The Blue Ridge Transfer Company, Inc., was organized in 1932 for the primary purpose of serving the furniture industry of Galax, Virginia. This it does by supplying an efficient delivery service to furniture trade in fourteen states, operating under interstate permit. On return voyages the trucks handle general freight for Galax and all southwest Virginia points and Mt. Airy, N. C. Fourteen person are employed by the company. J. W. Stanley, Jr., is President and Manager.

TWIN COUNTY MOTOR CO., INC.

One of the Most Complete Automobile Sales Agencies in Virginia

Gordon C. Felts, Owner.

TWIN COUNTY MOTOR COMPANY, Inc., of Galax, Virginia, is the Ford Sales and Service Agency for Grayson and Carroll counties; also Ford-Ferguson Tractors and a complete line of Ford-Ferguson Mounted Implements. Its plant, one of the largest and best equipped in Virginia, represents an investment of over a quarter million of dollars. In equipment, skilled personnel for every department, and efficient service, this agency takes high rank among the model Ford Agencies in the entire country. It gives every conceivable service at reasonable cost.

When peacetime reconversion comes and the new Fords arrive, Twin County Motor Company will be in a position to give its many customers in this territory a product and service unequalled in the automotive industry.

E. G. Cummings, Secretary and General Manager.

Machine Shop, Repair and Service Departments.

113

VAUGHAN-BASSETT FURNITURE COMPANY
Manufacturers of Bed Room Furniture

• The Vaughan-Bassett Furniture Company is the pioneer and also the largest plant of the Galax, Virginia, furniture industry. The company was organized in 1919, and such was the success of the venture of its inception that additions to the factory and equipment have been necessary from time to time in order to supply the constantly increasing demands for its products. The company employs about 335 persons, exclusive of the sales force of thirty-five, the latter covering every section of the United States. Permanent Exhibits are maintained in the American Furniture Mart, Chicago, and in the New York Furniture Exchange.

Mr. B. C. Vaughan, the founder, president and treasurer, has long been identified with the furniture industry of the South, and in addition to the large factory at Galax, is interested in other furniture plants in North Carolina and Tennessee. Lieut. C. W. Higgins, Jr. (on leave with the armed forces), is vice-president, and J. E. Wilson is assistant secretary.

Lieut. C. W. Higgins, Jr.,
Vice President (on leave with
the armed forces).

B. C. Vaughan,
President and Treasurer

Miss Beulah Cox,
Credit Manager.

J. E. Wilson,
Assistant Secretary.

The Vaughan-Bassett
Furniture Company,
the Pioneer
of Galax's Furniture
Industry, and one
of the Most Substantial
and Modernly-Equipped
Plants in the
Country

114

WEBB FURNITURE COMPANY
Manufacturers of Bedroom Furniture

Lieutenant Kenneth G. Messer,
President
(On leave with the U. S. Navy).

J. A. Messer, Sr.,
Chairman of the Board

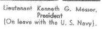

D. E. Ward,
Vice President and Manager.

The Webb Furniture Company is one of the major industries of the thriving industrial center of Galax. It manufactures a well known and popular line of medium priced Bedroom furniture, which is sold in every state of the Union.

The company's payroll amounts to over $275,000.00 annually, and its yearly purchases of lumber is around $400,000.00. Normally, 300 persons are employed.

J. A. Messer, Sr., a veteran mirror and furniture manufacturer, is Chairman of the Board; Lieutenant Kenneth G. Messer, at present on leave with the Navy, is the President, and D. E. Ward is Vice President and Manager. Other officers are S. C. Hampton, Treasurer, and Ailene Baumgardner, Secretary.

Sectional Views Showing Large,
Modern Plant of

WEBB FURNITURE COMPANY
GALAX • VIRGINIA

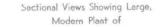

The Veneer Warehouse. Here are stored great quantities of fine veneers to be used in the manufacture of this company's well known products.

Vaughan Furniture Company 1923

Much of this history was written by John Vaughan, former chairman of Vaughan Furniture Co., for the company's 75th Anniversary in 1998.

The company's corporate office on Glendale Road in Galax

The furniture industry has been a major part of Galax's 102-year history, and Vaughan Furniture Co. has been there almost from the beginning.

John B. Vaughan

The company was founded in 1923 by Taylor G. Vaughan Sr., his brother Bunyan C. Vaughan, members of their families and friends.

The brothers were born and raised near Bassett. Their father died when they were both small children, and they were no strangers to hard work and earning their own way.

They worked hard, saved their money and managed to pay for education at National Business College in Roanoke.

Afterwards, Bunyan went to work for Bassett Furniture Co. as a bookkeeper, and Taylor went to work for R.J. Reynolds Tobacco Company in the same capacity.

B. C. VAUGHAN
President -- 1940-1955

Bassett recognized that Bunyan was a hard worker and fast learner, and soon had him learning the ins and outs of the furniture manufacturing business.

Taylor would shortly go on the road selling Bassett furniture from Western Pennsylvania to Michigan and held this position until volunteering for service with the U.S. Army in 1917 when the United States entered World War I.

Bunyan had married and begun a family in Bassett, and Taylor was engaged to J.D. Bassett's daughter.

While Taylor was still in France in late 1918 to early 1919, Bunyan and J.D. Bassett came to Galax to buy a small cabinet plant they had heard was for sale. This purchase was the beginning of Vaughan-Bassett Furniture Company.

In 1920, shortly before his marriage, Taylor moved to Galax and went to work for his brother at Vaughan-Bassett. Both families had found a home and lived and worked in Galax for the balance of their lives.

In 1923-24, Vaughan Furniture Co. was organized, financed, and built to make a line of dining room furniture to supplement Vaughan-Bassett's line of bedroom furniture.

Shortly thereafter, J.V. Webb and his wife — Bunyan and Taylor's sister, Hattie — moved their family to Galax and started Webb Furniture Co. in 1925.

Soon Galax Mirror Company was built to make mirrors and cut glass for the three furniture companies, and John Messer came from the mirror company in Bassett to run this facility.

In 1926 or thereabouts, an effort was made to merge Vaughan and Vaughan-Bassett, but this effort was soon abandoned and the two companies would remain separate and competitors.

Under the able leadership of Taylor Vaughan, the company prospered during the 1920s and managed to run at a small profit during the years from 1930-1938. Due to circumstances beyond his control, Taylor Vaughan decided to sell the business in 1938 and the plant was closed for several months.

After receiving many calls from area business people and former employees encouraging him to reopen, Taylor agreed and the company began making furniture again in 1939 with Everett C. Dodson as superintendent of the factory.

Taylor would have only a short time to supervise this new beginning before his untimely death on Feb. 28, 1940, at the age of 49.

Taylor Vaughan also served this area in the Virginia Senate from 1930 until his death.

Bunyan Vaughan offered to run Vaughan Furniture — in addition to Vaughan-Bassett — until Taylor's sons, T. George Vaughan Jr. and John Vaughan, could come into the business and were able to take control.

George came to work at Vaughan permanently in June of 1947

At this time Vaughan was considered a producer of low-cost bedroom and dining room furniture. T. George Vaughan realized that if the company was to prosper in the post-World War II era, the company needed to improve both its designs and quality.

By the time John Vaughan arrived at the company in 1954, many improvements had been made.
"Back in the 1930s we were selling bedroom suites for as little as $24.95 for a complete suite," John Vaughan wrote in 1998. "In 1954 we were selling our lowest priced suite for a whopping $69.95 and this included a double dresser, chest-of-drawers, tilting Venetian plate glass mirror, bookcase headboard and panel footboard. We also had a total of two higher priced suites at $79.95 and $89.95."

When T. George Vaughan was elected president and assumed control of the company in 1955, he immediately announced plans to expand the factory. At the time, Vaughan Furniture had about 225 employees in its plant and offices. An all-out effort was made to improve manufacturing methods and efficiency and to make the company's level of quality as good as or better than competitors in its price range.

Taylor G Vaughan Sr.

"I was given the job of setting up a quality control department and system to accomplish these goals," John Vaughan wrote. "By 1960, we were beginning to be known as a company who not only exhibited personal integrity, but integrity of product design and ever-improving quality and service."
This reputation enabled the company to further expand its plant and personnel in 1964.
"With men such as Everett Dodson in charge of production, Bobby Thomason Sr. working in quality control and sales manager Perry Frye in the process of putting together one of the best sales teams in America, Vaughan Furniture was beginning to make some waves," John Vaughan wrote.

Also about this time, a bright young graduate from North Carolina State's furniture curriculum, Press Turbyfill, became Everett Dodson's right hand man. He later became an executive with the company.

John Vaughan eventually became CEO of the company.

John and T. George Vaughan's children run the company today. Bill Vaughan was elected the company's fifth president in 1995. Taylor Vaughan was elected the company's sixth president in 2007 and today serves as chairman, president and CEO. David Vaughan is senior executive vice president.

Vaughan Furniture's successes included the purchase of Empire Furniture Corp. of Stuart in 1969, building the B.C. Vaughan Plant in 1973, purchasing half interest in Webb Furniture Enterprises in 1976, building the E.C. Dodson Plant in 1984, building the Chestnut Creek Veneer Plant in 1991 and renovating the T. George Vaughan Plant in 1996-97.

In 1998, the company's six plants — including its interest in Webb Furniture — employed more than 2,200.

"Our employees remain our greatest asset, and we consider them the best team of employees to be found anywhere," John Vaughan wrote.

Vaughan Furniture built a new office complex on Glendale Road in Galax in 1999.

A few years later, the global economy began to take its toll not only on Vaughan, but also on the entire domestic furniture industry.

Companies found it hard to compete with lower-cost bedroom furniture imported from China.
In 2003, Vaughan joined others in the domestic furniture industry — including Vaughan-Bassett and Webb — in an effort to convince the federal government to investigate the "dumping" of Chinese imports on the American market.

The companies alleged that the imports — marked down to unreasonably low prices — were a form of industrial sabotage, aimed at destabilizing the American furniture industry.

Bill Vaughan

After a lengthy investigation, the government found that Chinese manufacturers were violating international trade laws and began collecting duties on Chinese companies found to be in violation. The money was then distributed to companies like Vaughan that participated in the campaign.

Bill Vaughan said the company received about $3.3 million over two years — an amount that could not save it, but "helped us keep the factory open" for a few more years.

The company closed its T.G. Vaughan bedroom manufacturing plant off Stuart Drive — its oldest facility — in 2003. Now, it serves as the company's shipping and distribution center for the company's imported furniture products.

Bill Vaughan said imports began to hurt the company around 2002, but "really began to snowball in 2004."

The Empire Division, Johnson City closed that year, along with the T. George Vaughan Division in Stuart.

The E.C. Dodson plant on Poplar Knob Road in Galax closed in 2006. The building now houses a company from Spain that processes, packages and exports local lumber for the European construction industry.

Vaughan Furniture's 85 years of manufacturing in Galax ended in 2008, with the closing of the B.C. Vaughan plant.

Last year, Albany Industries, an upholstered furniture manufacturer, bought the B.C. Vaughan facility for a major expansion. The company invested $2.5 million in the project and plans to create 335 jobs over the next three years.

Taylor Vaughan   **David Vaughan**

118

The History of Vaughan Guynn Funeral Home

T he History of Vaughan Guynn Funeral Home dates back to 1913 when J. Crockett Guynn began stocking coffins and caskets at his country store. In 1919 Crockett Guynn joined with C.L. Smith, the undertaker for Galax, to purchase a horse-drawn hearse that was used in both Grayson and Carroll Counties until the building of hard-surface roads.

In 1923, realizing the need for updated funeral services, Mr. Guynn sent his oldest son, Gilman Guynn, to school to be trained as a licensed embalmer and funeral director. When hard-surface roads made its use practical in 1928, the Guynn's purchased the county's first motor hearse.

Gilman Guynn

Vaughan-Guynn Funeral home in Galax was established in 1936 when Gilman Guynn, Glendi Guynn, Garnett Guynn and Wayne Vaughan bought out the funeral business of C.L Smith and established the Vaughan-Guynn Funeral Home in Galax. Mr. Vaughan a native of Grayson County managed the funeral home from 1936 until his death in 1957.

Wayne Vaughan

Mr. Smith's funeral Home was above the addition to the Vass-Kapp Hardware store on West Grayson Street. The elevator is still there that was used to take coffins up to the 2nd floor. The location of the New Vaughan Guynn Funeral home was on the NW Corner of Grayson Street where The Galax Florist business is now located. The Vaughan Guynn business bought the Scott Home at 203 West Center Street where they are still located.

Jack Guynn, the only child of Gilman and Cassie Guynn, after returning home from the Marines at the end of World War II and graduating from VPI, obtained his funeral directors license and became manager of the funeral home after Mr. Vaughan's death. Avis M. Vaughan, widow of Mr. Vaughan, became active in the business and remained Secretary/Treasurer of both the Galax Funeral Home and Hillsville Funeral Home until her death in 1996. Jordan Dawes McGrady became a partner in the corporation in 1936 and ran the Hillsville Funeral Business until his death in 1994.

Jack E. "Jay" Guynn, Jr. became president of Vaughan-Guynn Funeral Home and Vaughan-Guynn-McGrady Chapel in April 1979 after the death of his father Jack. Jay still serves in this capacity today.

Vaughan Guynn Today

Scott House on Center Street

119

A DAY AT THE FURNITURE MARKET APRIL 1969

High Point Showrooms

Top Left: in the Vaughan Bassett Showroom (left to right)
James Edwards, Wyatt Exum, C.W. "Buck" Higgins and Les Alsworth

Top Right: in the Vaughan Furniture Showroom,
Mr. and Mrs. R. L. Nelson

Bottom Left: in the Vaughan Furniture Showroom
John B. Vaughan, and Perry Frye (right) talking things over with their designer

Bottom Right: In the Webb Furniture Showroom
John J. Nunn, Jack Bailey, Roy Nunn and seated, Dick Kirkman

Galax Gazette April 24th 1969-- Frye Collection.

A DAY AT THE FURNITURE MARKET APRIL 1969
High Point Showrooms

Top Left in the American Mirror Showroom:
Tom Morris 2nd from Left Frank Morris on the right with two Buyers

Top Right Galax Chair Showroom : Maurice Vaughan, left and Bill Dickerson right with a buyer

Bottom Left: In the Galax Mirror Showroom: Elwood Bartlett shows a prospect one of his catalogs.

Bottom Right : Sawyers Furniture Showroom: Hubert Watson Right, looks over cover samples with two buyers.

Galax Gazette April 24th 1969—Frye Collection

Burlington Mills leaves Galax in 1982

BURLINGTON INDUSTRIES closed its Galax Weaving Plant in 1982, ending 45 years of operation in the city.

On April 13, the Galax-Twin County area received some shocking news. On that day, Bob Sills, Galax Weaving plant manager, announced that Burlington Industries would cease plant operations in Galax.

Burlington, which had operated the plant in Galax for 45 years, said it was phasing out production at the plant as a result of market changes and the general economic climate which have reduced the demand for decorative fabrics woven at the Galax facility.

Sills said plant operations had been curtailed over the past several months due to a drop-off in demand for home furnishings.

The Galax Weaving Plant, which was built in 1937 and used as a unit of Burlington House Fabrics Division (BHFD) for the past several years, was dependent on the draperies trade, which had been hurt by the slowdown in home building, high interest rates and changing market.

"It is a difficult decision because of our long history of operations here and the continued good performance by employees," Sills said about the closing.

Galax Weaving had employed as many as 300 people during maximum operating efficiency and 275 at the time of the announcement.

The majority of employees were Carroll and Grayson county residents. Galax residents made up an estimated 25 percent of the employees.

Tony Siceloff, Group Manufacturing Director of BHFD, division of Burlington Industries, said the plant totaled about a $4 million payroll annually.

Sills, who had just been reappointed to the Galax School Board, also announced that he would remain with Burlington Industries.

I've certainly enjoyed the past ten years I've been in Galax. I really hate to leave the area," he said.

Although some Galax employees were offered jobs at other Burlington plants, the majority were not. However, on May 4 another announcement provided a boost to the area economy.

At that time, Bill Barker, plant manager at Fries Textile, announced that the plant would add a fourth shift and hire between 150-200 employees.

By creating new jobs, the Fries plant will be able to provide jobs for local people as well as some people from the Galax Weaving Plant," said Barker.

He added that the decision to add a fourth shift was "timely, because it gives us a chance to hire experienced people, and we will be lending a hand to our Burlington friends."

Following Burlington's announcement, the Galax-Carroll-Grayson Chamber of Commerce and the Galax Industrial Development Authority immediately began searching for an industry to replace Burlington in the Galax Plant. However, when 1982 ended, the plant was still vacant.

Galax Gazette 1982

TWO-WAY RADIO
Program Comes to Galax

Chairman Dr. C. W. Richardson (center) handles the "mike" of a two-way radio set up Tuesday night at the regular meeting of the Galax Lions Club. At left is Club Secretary Robert Coomes and standing is Fred Bennington, Club president. The Lions heard a brief talk by Gazette Editor Arthur Gurley on the operation of the Blue Ridge Runners CB Club and the use to which the two-way radio equipment is being put in this area by the more than 100 licensees.

The growing popularity of two-way radio communications available to businesses and individuals in this area was the subject of a talk Tuesday night at the Galax Lions Club.

Gazette Editor Arthur Gurley, treasurer of the Blue Ridge Runners CB Club, gave a brief history of the Club and its operations and demonstrated the ease with which modern, two-way radio equipment can be used.

The CB Club has some 40 charter members, having been organized last spring. In addition to the Club Members, there are more than 60 other individuals and business firms licensed to operate the two-way equipment in the immediate area.

Dan H. Rector, one of the "pioneer" Citizens Band two-way radio operators in Galax, is president of the CB Club, with John A. Messer, Jr.,. vice president and James I. Sublett, secretary.

Services of the Club members and the use of their equipment are on a strictly voluntary basis when used in community and other worthwhile projects, it was pointed out. Latest use of the Club members equipment on a. community-wide project was December 17 during the annual Community Christmas Party broadcast.

During the broadcast citizens of the area telephoned Radio Station WBOB to offer donations of cash, food and clothing for the Christmas baskets. Club members in radio- equipped cars were used to supplement the customary "pick-up" service provided by the civic clubs of the area.

Information regarding "pickups" was radioed from a portable unit at the radio station to a "base station" at Mr. Rector's home who in turn assigned the "pick-up" to one of the Club members — via radio.

The Club members also have, in the past, made their services available for relaying messages into areas not served by other means of communications; have been called on to aid in the search for a lost child in Carroll County; and have been used in other capacities.

At the request of the Civil Defense Director of the Area, Dr. E., C. Sutphin, the CB members have agreed to augment the regular CB radio communications system whenever officially requested to do so.

Equipment for the demonstration at the Lions Club meeting was made available by Galtron Inc., the area distributor for the radio equipment.

Early Days of the Galax Plaza Shopping Center in 1967

Galax Plaza Shopping Center in its earlier days. This photo from the Galax Gazette Feb 21, 1967 shows the Eastern section with a partially paved parking center, and nothing to the right of the Peoples Drug Store . Minks Motors has a position in the lower left where they are still located. This property was the Higgins Lumber Company for many years where they operated a sawmill and lumber yard. Larry Chambers took this picture while flying with Bill Halsey, a local businessman and auto dealer. Located on East Stuart Drive with Krogers and Roses still occupying space there

Removal of a Landmark, Twin County Ford showroom coming down!

Gazette Photo by Larry Chambers

Construction crews removed a landmark from Galax's main street last week when the old Twin County Motor Building was demolished. The building, which once housed the Ford -Mercury dealerships was constructed in the very early 1900s. Originally the Twin County Livery Stable, the high pitched A-frame building housed the stables which in early Galax was the main mode of transportation, many years before the Auto came to town. At the time there were probably four such businesses in Galax to provide a horse or horse and carriage to the many visitors arriving daily on the N&W Railroad passenger service. Most of these visitors were "Drummers" , traveling salesmen bringing the outside world to the area. Galax also had four or five hotels at that time to house these visitors. This old stable later had the front installed and served as the showroom for Twin County Ford. Owned and founded by T. L. Felts.

On March 22nd, 1919, Mr. J. S. Dobyns bought "1 Ford Car" from the Twin County Motor Company for $604.30. no, not a tire, the whole car !
Courtesy of John Ashby

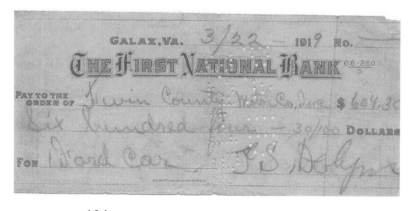

124

Dixon Lumber Company

S. R. Dixon

The story of Dixon Lumber Company, Inc. is a story of progress--from a five-horse-power Geyser steam engine saw mill operation to the present day 4,000 electrical horsepower operations at Galax and Warm Springs Mill.

Founded in the early 1920's as S. R. Dixon Lumber Shop by S. R. Dixon, the business began as a small saw mill operation employing six men. The saw mill was expanded in 1938 to include a planning operation.

The business became Dixon Lumber Company in 1941, and in 1945 the entire operation was moved from New River to Galax and manufacturing was begun at its present location on Boyer Road. With this move Dixon Lumber Company began its retail and wholesale lumber supply. By 1948 they had become one of the largest hardwood flooring manufacturers in the state.

Dixon Lumber Company became a corporation in 1949, and in the early 1950's they expanded into a dimension plant to become one of the largest wood building material manufacturers in the East.

S. R. Dixon was a very progressive man. He could be called a pioneer in the lumber business as many times he went against everyone's advice and tried new methods that to everyone's surprise worked out and led to more efficient production. In the late 1930's Dixon was the first to replace his logging mules and oxen with a crawler tractor. In the early 1950's Dixon Lumber Company was one of the first companies to utilize fork lift trucks which removed much of the burden and time consuming effort of having to handle the lumber.

Mr. Dixon gave Dixon Lumber Company the start that today has become one of the few operations that continue to process wood materials through each step--from the live tree to the finished products. Dixon Lumber Company has always been concerned with the problem of air pollution.

S. R. Dixon, the Founder and President, passed away in 1964. Upon his death, his son, Glenn W. Dixon, who had worked alongside his father and other employees from 1934, became President.

Since 1952, long before the government placed restrictions on pollution, Dixon Lumber Company began a very effective program to combat this problem. Much equipment has been purchased by Dixon's to alleviate pollution of the air. At the present time they are in complete compliance with the federal government regulations on air pollution and have installed equipment to the tune of one- half million dollars.

Galax Gazette "Look to the Future Edition"

An aerial view of the plant when it was in full production.

Penry Manufacturing
Construction of a new Plant 1964

Work begins on new building to house Penry Mfg. Co., operations in Galax.

Plant to be located on Valley St, Ground was broken Tuesday for a 25,000 square foot building to house the Penry Manufacturing Co. operations..a garment plant.

The site of the new building is on Valley street, just off Glendale Road. A contract for the construction, in the amount of $127,500, has been let to J.E. Davis and Sons, Inc., Galax contractors.

Hugh Sample, President of the Penry Mfg. Co., wielded a shovel to "break ground" at brief ceremonies, Tuesday afternoon. Also in attendance were officers and directors of the Galax Development Corp., which is erecting the structure.

Penry Manufacturing Co., has been located on Carroll street in Galax since it was organized here 15 years ago by the late Ross Penry, Fred Stern, Bob Morris and Fred Roberts.

The new location will allow for expanded operations of the company.

The building will be of block construction, faced with brick. One side will be left to provide for future expansion as needed on the 6 1/2 acre plot.

City Council Monday night voted to re-zone the tract from residential to industrial in order that the building could be built.

George Davis, of the construction company, said that with favorable weather the building should be completed In 60 days.
Oil-fired, warm air heat will be used in the 200 by 130- foot building,
In addition to space for production machines, office space also will be provided in the building.

GROUND IS BROKEN for the $127,000 building to house the expanded operations of Penry Manufacturing co., when completed. The brief ground-breaking ceremony was held Tuesday, Oct. 27, 1964, just a few hours after Galax City Council had approved re-zoning of the tract, off Valley street, from residential to industrial. Shown wielding the shovel of earth to signal the start of grading at the site is Hugh Sample, President of Penry Manufacturing Co. Left to right are: A. Glenn Pless, P resident of the Galax Development Corp., Dr. R.C. Bowie, Vice President; Joe P. Crockett, manager of Radio station WBOB, H.S. White, Jr., and George B. Davis, directors of the development corporation; and Galax City Manager W.G. Andrews. Ready to begin operating the bulldozer is Gene "Fuzzy" McKnight.

October 29, 1964 Galax Gazette Galax Va 24333

Galax Furniture and Lumber Company, the first Furniture Factory in Galax

CREW OF GALAX WORKERS ALMOST 70 YEARS AGO—
Now about 102 years ago (2013)

Pictured above is the picture, then unknown as to time or place, which appeared in the Gazette recently. The picture was brought to the office by Glenn Pless, and it was thought to have been taken in 1911. It has since become known, however, that the picture appeared in the Gazette the first time, so far as is known, in the issue of Nov. 5, 1953.

The caption used at that time reads, in part, as follows: "A CREW OF WORKERS FORTY YEARS AGO '-The workmen pictured above were employees of the old Galax Furniture and Lumber Co. and worked in the second building, which burned in 1915. The original building was destroyed by fire in 1907." So the picture was made between the two dates. . .
Tossie W. Bartlett said, just recently, that his father, Chap Bartlett, and his grandfather, John Bartlett, both were in the picture.

Mr. Bartlett, figuring from his father's age and-or his grandfather's age, arrived at the opinion that the picture was made in 1908. If so, the time would be 68 years ago, and 1908 was between 1907 and 1915.

Mr. Bartlett said the building partially pictured stood near the former Felts Transport site.

Editors note:
Mr. Howard Coleman, a California resident, is owner of this dresser and mirror manufactured by the Galax Furniture and Lumber Company. Labels on the back indicate that it was shipped to William and ?? in Glade Spring, Virginia. Mr. Coleman inquired several years ago about the history of the factory, but at the present time the dresser is not for sale. JJN

Handwritten story of the Galax Furniture and Lumber company, the first Furniture factory in Galax. Do not know who wrote it or when it was written, but I believe it to be a good history of the business. The letter was found in the papers of Pete Robinson. See next page….
Courtesy of Brenda Crouse Harmon

127

This is the true story of the
Galax Furniture and Lumber Company
1905-1913

Early in Jan. 1905 a group of Business
Men met to raise funs to Build a
Furniture Factory in Galax. With money
they raised. They built the first
Furniture Factory. They named it
Galax Furniture and Lumber Company
John B. Waugh elected Sed & Treasure
and S. E. Wilkerson as Plant Manager
They went in business making oak
Birch & pine Bed Room and Dining Room
suits also chest of Drawers and cabnets
Selling this furniture to Speigels, Sterns
and Montgomery Ward and shipped by
Norfolk & Western Rail Rood. But on
Oct 6, 1906 a great teogety accured at
12:30 P.M. The Factory whistle sounded
that the factory was on fire, Every
one did what the could to save Supplies
and stock but most of it burned.
The Company owners desided to rebuild
a new factory. New stock contifues were
issued, and a larger Factory was built

128

New officers were elected with E. W. Dodd as sec & trea and L. E. Wilkerson as Plant Supt. The new plant went in operation in the fall of 1908. With more kinds of furniture which included cupboards called tak desks, hutches and different kinds of chests along with the same kind of Bed room suits and Dining room suits.

They also bought cross ties ~~ties~~ bridge lumber and different kinds of lumber for shipment to other parts of the country. This new factory was in operation until Dec, 9, 1913 when is was again destroyed by fire but was never Rebuilt

The next furniture factory was built in 1919 when it begon operation By Bunyon c Vaughan and John D Bassett and was named Vaughan & Bassett Fur Co. and has been in production every since 1919 cept it burned in Feb 1951 but was rebuilt a year later

129

GORDON WOOLEN MILL BUILT IN 1880

By JIMMY BOBBITT

An old two-story frame building, about three and a half miles from Galax, was once a thriving little factory - a woolen mill that operated from 1881 until about 1945-46, and furnished employment for a dozen people.

This old building known to many as "Gordon's Factory" or "Gordon's Woolen Mill" is located- just off U.S. Highway 58 some 150 yards east of the New River Tavern, near the banks of Meadow Creek.

This old mill was established in 1880-81, construction began in 1880 and its opening took place in 1881, under the joint ownership of the late William M. Gordon and Sandy Reavis.

William M. Gordon came to this vicinity in 1880 from Green Hill in Surry County, N.C., near Mount Airy. There he had been employed for some time at a large woolen mill. With him from North Carolina came his wife and four children. The Gordons built their home just above and behind the old mill site.

Some years later Mr. Gordon purchased Mr. Reavis' interest in the little factory and operated it throughout the remainder of his life. The plant's name was then changed from Reavis and Gordon Woolen Mill to Gordon's Woolen Mill.

In an era when transportation links to this part of the state were few, a small industry, like this one, filled a vital need for this area.

This little building, containing very intricate machinery-for that day and time - converted wool into blankets, Tart, linsey (woolen cloth used for women's dresses) and jean cloth a dark colored woolen cloth used for men's pants.

Meadow creek on whose banks it was located, provided the power for the little industry. An 11 foot diameter "overshot" water wheel and water race was used to harness the creek's power. In later years a turbine wheel replaced the old "overshot" wheel.

Sheep raisers over a wide territory hauled their freshly sheared wool to the factory by wagon. These sheepmen would trade their wool for cloth, blankets, etc., or wait for their wool to be "worked up" into blankets or cloth.

The little company also sent out agents to purchase wool for the use of the factory.

Manufactured products, such as blankets and cloth, were shipped to various points - among these was Chatham Manufacturing Company, in Elkin, North Carolina.

The Gordon Mill was in operation under Mr. Gordon's management until he passed away on September 3, 1925, at the age of 78 years.

In 1926 the mill and the residential property was sold to Mr. Gordon's widow (who was his second wife), Mrs. Martha Gordon.

Somewhat later Mrs. Gordon sold the property to one of her step-sons, Elijah Gordon, who operated the woolen mill for about twenty years. Under the management of Elijah Gordon, yarn was the principal product manufactured by the little industry.

As the demand for yarn diminished, he operation of the factory was halted and the plant closed, since it was no longer profitable to continue production.

Elijah Gordon made chairs in the old building for a short while after the wool processing ended.

The building was then used for a storehouse and the idle machinery inside was dismantled and removed.

Mrs. Thomas A. Melton, daughter of William M. Gordon, who resides at Route 2, Galax, told of a raging flood that struck the Reavistown area in 1900- a flood that threatened the little factory as well as its contents.

The turbulent waters of Meadow Creek carried a number of buildings into nearby New River. Among these was a store house owned by her father and the late Frank Williams.

Bolts of cloth from the shelves of the store were seen floating in the turbulent waters of the creek and river. Some of these floating bolts of cloth became entangled in trees and saplings along the water's edge. Mrs. Melton said there were plenty of people trying to get what they could of the floating or entangled merchandise in the water.

The raging waters threatened the little factory as the water crept up to the first floor. The wool, cloth, etc. that was stored on the first floor was moved to the second floor as a precautionary measure. The goods were safe there.

All that remains of the Gordon Woolen Mill is the old building which is used as a storehouse by Elijah Gordon, who still lives in the old home place near the mill.

The old building, showing the effects of age, is empty, no noise from the machinery is heard - no production is made - no employees go there to work but the old Gordon Mill is a part of our heritage - a forerunner of our large scale textile manufacturing plants in this area.
Galax Gazette March 29, 1966

Christmas Dinner at Harris–Marshall

Harris-Marshall has a in-house meal with management serving the employees. Henry Harris the President serves a Christmas Dinner December 1963

Henry Harris came to Galax to work at Pollard Hoisery Mills and later left to start his own business with Mr. Marshall from NY City. They built the modern brick factory at the top of Shaw Street now owned by Vaughan Bassett Furniture. Harris – Marshall had an office in NY City in the famous Empire State Building. These pictures are from a Gazette feature article on the business as they served a Christmas Dinner to the employees.

Shown are Harry Cook left and Howard "Bull" Kegley and Joyce Sexton on the right. Below is Layton Harris. The two bottom photos show other factory employees enjoying the dinner.

HARRY COOK demonstrates the s-t-r-e-t-c-h.

JOYCE SEXTON is more interested in the photographer than what Howard Kegley is distributing.

LATON HARRIS dishes out a helping of ham.

FRIDAY, DECEMBER 27, 1963   B-1

WATCH THOSE CALORIES, Girls!

HAVE a hunk of turkey!

Gazette Photos by Ruth Tucker

132

Galax Gazette "a new look"

New high-speed printing equipment

Modern unit permits printing in color as well as black and white during regular press run

Historic moment – – Mrs. Author Gurley, co-publisher of the Galax Gazette, presses the control button to start the new Thatcher offset press installed as part of the improvement program underway at the Gazette. At left is foreman Roy B. Lineberry and at right is Kenny Langley. Thatcher press technician.

A new dimension – color – is made possible for the Galax Gazette through the completion of the installation of a new Thatcher web fed rotary offset press.

The installation of this modern equipment for producing a newspaper puts the Gazette and a select – but growing – field of newspapers that are keeping abreast of the many advances in the art of printing. Naturally as with any new machinery there will be several adjustments to be made before the full capabilities of the new equipment will become evident.

However an examination of the various sections of the days issue of the Gazette will reveal considerable improvements over the printing quality of issues printed on the 50-year-old machine the new equipment replaces. There will also be evidence of improvement in the various sections of today's issues with sections A and AA showing the results of the experience that Gazette crew gained in the printing of sections B and C.

The improvement program representing a considerable outlay of capital is evidence of the Gazette's confidence in the continued growth of Galax and the Twin Counties.

"The installation of these modern facilities is evidence of our faith in the future growth of the area", editor publisher Author Gurley, said today.

"The new equipment utilizes basic principles of photography for the reproduction of images of type and illustrations in a manner considerably different from that previously used," he said.

Once the "bugs are ironed out we will be able to produce newspaper comparable to that producing cities many times the size of Galax".

In section B of today's paper are several stories and pictures relating to the new method of producing the Gazette.

The new press was obtained through Insco sales and leasing company in Kansas City the national distributor. The press is made by the Thatcher company at Boeing Field near Seattle Washington.

The basic frame of the press is made of a special extruded aluminum perfected by Alcoa especially for Thatcher.

"A special camera and other photographic equipment were obtained by Graphico Incorporated in Richmond

A factory- trained director installed equipment and a specialist in offset printing is to remain in Galax several days to instruct Galax personnel in the finer points of the method.

Today's issue contains spot color-- the first time that color has been printed the same time as the usual black without the necessity of running the paper a second time through a press.

The Thatcher press permits the use of several colors of ink to be "spotted" on any or all of four pages being printed.

The press prints eight pages all-black at one time turning them out already folded.

A special 10 hp electric motor with electronic controls provides for the operation of the press at speeds up to 18,000 eight- page papers a hour – – nine times as fast as the old press.
Normal operating speed of the press will be about 12,000 papers an hour, at least for the next several months.

133

Businesses from 1949 Phone Book

Doctors & Dentists (13)
Dr. V. O. Choate, Dr. Joseph Coats, Dr. Virgil Cox, Dr. W.P. Davis, Dr. B. F. Eckles, Dr. R.S. Kyle, Dr. Z.G. Phipps, Dr. JB. Spinks, Drs Bolen & Kapp, Dr. R.J. Gardner, W Oldtown St, Dr. C.L. Hampton, Dr. R.L. Jones,

Cab companies (5)
Sexton's Taxi, Silver Top Cabs, Veteran's Cabs, White Top Cabs, Wright Taxi,

Restaurants (9)
Maggie Austin's Lunch, E Oldtown, Bus Center Grill, W. Center, Galax Café, Main, Goodson's Café 116 Grayson, Hampton's Grill, 118 N Main (across from Bluemont Hotel), Herb's Bakery, 116 E Grayson, Steve's Ideal Café, N Main, Virginia Street Lunch, E. Virginia, Bluemont Hotel, N Main,

Automobile Companies, New. (9)
Blue Ridge Sales, 510 S. Main, White Chev. Sales, S Main, Felts Pontiac, E. Stuart Dr., Galax Motor, W Grayson, McCann Motor Sales, 108 W Oldtown, Porter Auto, 303 W Oldtown St., Gwyn Porter Auto Sales, 300 S. Main, St Lo Motor Co., East Oldtown St., Twin County Motor Sales, 306 N Main,

Beauty Shops (10)
Elsie's , Jefferson St., Frankey's Shop, 2021/2 S Main, Kathryn's Shop, W Oldtown, Mattie Reeds Shop, S. Main, Modernette Shop, Main, Skyline Shop, Main, Stylette Shop, 101-1/2 W Grayson, Vanity Shop, 106-1/2 W Oldtown ST., Vogue Shop, S. Main, Waverite Shop, Main

Dry Cleaners (4)
Todd's Cleaners, W Oldtown, Rhodes Cleaners, W Grayson, Williams, W. Grayson, Galax Laundry and Cleaners, Webster St.

Dept & Retail Stores (6)
A & Z Stores, Belks Dept Stores, W. Grayson, Globman's Dept. 119 S Main, Harris Dept Store, W Grayson, Newton's Dept Store, N Main, Dan B. Waugh & Co., 103 E Grayson , Frank Osborne's Men Shop, S Main, J.H. Witherow Mans Shop, S Main, Claire's Fashion Shop, N Main, Perelman's Store, S Main, Truitt's Clothing Store, S. Main, Galax Decorating Shop

Furniture Stores (5)
Pless Furn, E Grayson, W.L. Porter 213 S Main, , Vass-Kapp Hdw. & Furn, 100 S Main, .E. Jones & Sons, 102 N Main, Harris Furniture, 121 W Grayson,

Manufactures (11)
Carroll Furn., Galax Furn., Heirloom Furn., La-Flora Upholstering, Price Furn., Reavis Shop, W. Oldtown St, Sawyers Furn., Vaughan Bassett Furn., Vaughan Furn., Webb Furn., Bluefield Church Furn., Galax Mirror Co., E Grayson Street

Grocers (12)
Big Chief Markets, 106 N Main, H A Halls, Hillcrest, Huwals Frozen Foods, Oldtown St,
Ideal Market, 117 S Main , McKnight's Grocery, Morton's West Galax, N & H Reliable, Norman's Store Webster, Phipps-Pugh, W Oldtown St, Pinions Grocery, Givens St, White Oak Station, N Main, Galax Mercantile, E Grayson,

Knitting Mills, (4)
Galax Knitting, Virginia St, Harris Marshall, Shaw St, Old Dominion, Oldtown St, Penry Mfg. 108 E. Oldtown

Service Stations (20)
Atlantic Service 110 W. Center, Auto Fountain 301 W. Oldtown, Carroll County Hillsville Hwy, Cassell Station, Hillsville Hwy, Center Station, Main, Childers Station, Hillsville Hwy,
Fairview Station, Hwy 89, Harrell Station, 506 N Main, Higgins Oil, Oldtown , Hillcrest Station, 89 South, Jennings Station, RFD 3, Martin Elvin Station, Hillsville Hwy, Park View Station, S Main, Gwynn Porter Motors tation, N. Main, Pure Oil Station 204 S. Main, Shell Station, Hwy 89, Stuart Drive Esso, W. Oldtown, Texas Station , Main & Oldtown, White Oak Station, 507 N. Main, Wolf-Glade, RDF 3.

Kennys
New Drive in opens in Galax

A new concept in drive-in restaurants was inaugurated in Galax this week when Kenny's open the doors of the new ultramodern restaurant on Route 89 S., Monday, November 25.

With a dining room seating 65 and serving line that can handle 16 customers a minute the new concept in restaurants is a combination of drive-in and cafeteria. As in an assembly line, the tray moves along one side of a sneeze guard as a customer moves along the other side he points to the items he wants.

William Kennedy, President and founder of the 11-year-old chain began incorporating dining rooms and patios in his drive ends when he noticed his grandchildren smearing mustard on the upholstery of his new car.

(Under the picture) Kenny executive, Howard Garland, gives pointers to employees a Kenny's new drive in a cafeteria and Galax. Left to right are Claudine Kane, Mabel Widener, and Catherine Dylan.

General manager of the Roanoke based Kenny Corporation, Dick Cregger, says that the variety of food served is part of the new concept. Drive-ins usually offer only three or four items because most of their customers are just passing through town.

"But we'll serve at least 21 different items" Cregger said. "We want the people of Galax to come back often".

Galax residents Charles Crouse manager and Elmer Lake Coleman, assistant manager have been with the Kenny Corporation for months. They received their management training in Radford and Pulaski.

Among Galax firms furnishing materials and services to construct the stone, brick and tinted glass building is the Brown Furniture Company. They installed the multicolor canopy over the serving line which sets the mood for the bright décor of tangerine and blue chairs, yellow tables and futuristic globe chandeliers.

MUSTARD ON upholstery led to colorful dining

20 Galax area residents will man the serving counter and electric broiler. Trained by Howard Garland, Kenny area supervisor, they are Claudine Cain, Catherine Dillon, Gertrude Linville, Elizabeth Pearman, Nannie Poole, Sue Weddle, Mabel Widener, Eddie Lee Powers, Mattie May flick, Ila Faye Payne, Villa Jones, James Hurley Hash and Dennis Darnell Cruise.

A formal opening when free Cokes and specials will be offered, will be observed in early December.

Located next to the pilot gas station on Route 89 S. Kenny's will be open from 10 AM to 11 PM Sunday through Thursday at 10 AM to midnight Friday and Saturday.

The new Kenny's will have takeout service which includes macaroni salad, coleslaw, chicken salad, potato salad as well as regular specialties of fried chicken and the broiled chicken dinners. **Galax Gazette November 28, 1968**

Aerial View of the 1962 Galax Fair

Galax Fair: Early Kemp of the Galax Gazette staff took a helicopter ride Wednesday...and came back with this picture of the Felts Park Fairgrounds. His pilot was James Bailey of Newark Maryland., whose helicopter is one of the features of the Fair this year. August 23, 1962

4000th TELEPHONE

The 4000th telephone served by the Galax Exchange of the Inter-Mountain Telephone Co., was installed a few days ago in the home of Miss Gaye Cox on West Stuart Drive. There are now more than six and half times as many telephones here as there were in 1941 when E. P. Cullop, Galax Exchange manager, came to Galax. Mr. Cullop recalled that when he came here there were only 605 telephones on the Galax exchange--now there are 4000. Inter-Mountain installer, Tommy Nichols, is shown with Miss "J. D." Guynn, niece of Miss Cox, holding the Princess-type instrument installed in her bedroom . - -Boaz Studio Photo.

Blair, VA

as it looked 60 (110 now) years ago. The Village that Moved to Galax

This picture probably made about 1900, looks like a very beautiful country Estate, which it was then and is again now. Three things stand out in the picture. They are in matter of importance, the T.L. Felts home, the store building of J.B. Waugh and Son and the rail siding that had two names before the village moved to Galax.

At the time that this picture was made, the N. & W. depot called Blair and the Post office soon to be established was called Ethel Felts, having been named for the wife of the builder of the village, the late T. L. Felts.

It would be most interesting to 'have a picture story of the development the change and the final moving that took place in the next decade, the first ten years of the 20th century.

When the branch line of the N. & W. was on the planning board, it was thought that the original plan meant to go on to Mount Airy and eventually to Wilmington, N. C. But in those days there were folks that were in favor of the railroads and those who held different views on what they considered the intruders of the area.

And so it was, that at the turn of the century the railroad stopped, of Blair where strong men hauled in great piles of hewn cross ties (see stacks in the picture) and merchants from here to Sparta, Mouth of Wilson, Independence and of course the immediate area, hauled their merchandise from the depot to their stores by wagon over bad winter roads.

Before the line was finally built on to Galax, there were many changes in the picture. Just across the, rood from the several poultry. Houses and lots, several business establishments were built to thrive a few short years.

Beginning at the left side of the picture near where the tenant houses can almost be seen, was Crystal Drug Company, owned by Dr. J. K. Caldwell, Dr. S. M. Robinson and Dr. J. Lewis Early.

Next to the drug store was the hardware store of (Sam) Jackson and (S. B.) Kinder and beside these was the establishment of H. P. Cox and Son.

Not long after this picture a as mode, a small hotel was built in the upper left corner of the picture. It was called the Call-Inn. At another spot near-by another business, Lindsey and Muse come into being.

137

It is noteworthy here to say that the depot agent at the time was E A. Anderson, and that Young Walter M. Jones of R. E. Jones and Son just back from a sojourn in the great west in 1903 to clerk for J. B. Waugh and Son in the large wooden building shown down by the depot.

During the first six years of the present century, the master of the Felts Estate was influential in getting the railroad built on into Galax, then began the exodus of Blair, later called Cliffview, to the new town of Galax.

Crystal Drug moved to Main Street and later to East Stuart Drive. J. B. Waugh and Son moved and built at the present location, now operating as Waugh's Warehouse.

The old turning of the "Y" at Blair or Cliffside was ripped up and a new one built down by Felts Park.. As Galax mushroomed into a thriving town, the business section of Cliffside began to fade away and the Felts Estate began to take on its former appearance and to become a dairy and livestock farm.

The writer is indebted to Mr. Walter M. Jones for this brief recreation of the story of the railroad terminal of Blair and of the Post Office of Ethel Felts, the name of which was changed to Cliffside.

Galax Gazette Feb 20th 1961
The picture below was made before the T L Felts home was built. In the picture above the home "Cliffside" shows to be just above the depot on the right side of the picture. Not sure of the date or the source of this photo, probably from the Matthews Museum and about 1900
Beginning at the left side of the picture near where the tenant houses can almost be seen, was Crystal Drug Company, owned by Dr. J. K. Caldwell, Dr. S. M. Robinson and Dr. J. Lewis Early.

Two Old Grandstands in Felts Park

Below top : This is the first Grandstand in Felts Park, It was located about where the Rec. center is now. The occasion might have been a horse race, or maybe a performance for the Fair. Not sure of when it was replaced by the new structure. The second Grandstand was is in the center of the park just North of the tennis courts. This image shows the Annual Fiddlers Convention filling the seats

Then in Feb. 15th, 1972, it was also removed.
The Galax Volunteer Fire Department disposed of the Grandstand in Felts Park last Wednesday night to make room for a new stadium which is planned for the Park this year. In the photo on the left, Galax City Councilmen, L to R- - City Manager Harold Snead, Gene T. (Fuzzy) McKnight, Horace Cochran, Jimmy Ballard, and John Vaughan look on as Vice-Mayor William Waddell ignited the fire as a large crowd gathered to watch the event.

139

Merchants and Farmers Bank Replaces Bluemont Hotel

Landmark to be Razed—The Bluemont Hotel, corner of Center and Main, is to be torn down to make room for a new building to house the Merchants and Farmers Bank of Galax. Fred Adams, Galax Postmaster and President of the Bank, purchased the property from the Ellis Caldwell estate for $75,000. Center of civic and communities activity since it was built more than 40 years ago, the Bluemont will be closed to business after Saturday.

VANTAGE POINT - Workmen tearing down the old Bluemont Hotel had a fine vantage point from which to watch the Fourth of July Parade.

William R Innes hne

Below: Rubble Now—This area formerly was occupied by the Bluemont Hotel Clubroom and Annex. The old landmark is being torn down to make way for a modern bank building to be occupied by the Merchants and Farmers Bank of Galax.

GALAX, VIRGINIA -- THURSDAY, JUNE 27, 1963

Sumner photo

Digging a Hole—A break in the weather last week enabled workmen to begin work on the excavation for the new Merchants and Farmers Bank building on North Main Street at Center Street **photo by McMillian**
Fingers in the sky— Steel girders point to the sky as the new Merchants and Farmers Bank bulding takes shape.In the background is the First Baptist Church.

140

"I remember the Bluemont Hotel in the 50s as being an elegant place to have a Sunday dinner, white tablecloths and napkins with fine china and silver.

Editors Note:
The local furniture executives were entertained there in the fall with a Rabbit and Squirrel hunt with the game being cooked by the hotel and served to a large crowd of the furnitrure men, this affair was sponsored by a Finishing Material company that did business with these factories. A fine dinner and afterwards, games and other entertainment that lasted into the late hours of the evening." **John Nunn**

Editor's note: The deck provided local and visiting dignitaries with an excellent location to view parades that passed by on Main Street. The grand staircase in the lobby provided an excellent location for large group photographs. The hotel annex was located at the back right corner between the hotel and the Baptist Church. This small conference room was used for club meetings, private luncheons and dinners, and by local dance teachers and their students. JNAlley

Probably the most interesting lot in Galax

This lot, 112 North Main Street was the site of the first building in Galax.

The land office for the sale of the lots in the town of Galax was located on this lot, with the local jail later built on the alley behind.

The company pictured here was the first department store, the Galax Department Store. Two men from Bristol opened here in 1910, and went bankrupt in 1913.

The next business to occupy this building was the Dan B Waugh Company. After a few years in this location, they moved next door to J B Waugh and Company on East Grayson Street. Then Glen Pless and others opened the Pless Furniture And Electric Company and stayed here for a few years. Pless relocated also on East Grayson Street, where the City Offices are now located.

The A and Z company was located on the South East Corner of Oldtown and South Main Street and had a fire that destroyed the building. They then moved up the street into the building pictured above and remained there until moving into their new building on South Main where the Corner Stone Church is now located.

The white building in the picture above to the right, was the Galax Drug Store built by Dr. Caldwell, who had his offices in the rear of the building. There have been many businesses to occupy this lot space over the years.

Gazebo On Main Street

Today, we have the Gazebo occupying this space, along with the small park maintained by a local group. Carter Bank owns this lot and the condemned building to the right. Glad it was not turned into a parking lot.

Goodson's Fire, January 1961.

Goodson's Cafe, Economy Dept. Store gutted, damage expected to exceed $100,000
Ice-coated firemen from, Galax, Hillsville and Independence fought a courageous, night long battle against flames and sub-freezing weather last (Wednesday) night to contain a blaze that threatened, for a time, a considerable portion of the downtown business section.

Two buildings on West Grayson Street---occupied by Goodson's Cafe and Economy Dept. Store---were completely gutted. A quantity of tires stored on the second floor of the structure was a total loss as well as a considerable amount of groceries and food-stuff in a storeroom to the rear of the Economy Dept. store. The tires were the property of Parks Auto Supply and the groceries belonged to Big Chief Market.

Unofficial estimate of the loss of the two buildings was $80,000 to $100,000. Replacement of the structures was estimated to cost "more than $100,000."

Troy Hunt, of Big Chief Market, estimated their loss in groceries and a large, walk-in-cooler at "$3,000 to $4,000." Arlie Harrison, co-owner of the Economy Department Store, estimated their damages to stock and fixtures at $23,000 to $25,000. Troy Goodson, owner of Goodson's Cafe, estimated his loss would "run close to $35,000." The cafe was remodeled a few years ago and a considerable amount of new equipment was installed at that time.

Look at the Ice cycles hanging from the awning, a terrible day

Graham H. Parks, owner of Parks Auto Supply, estimated "between 800 and 900 tires" were stored on the second floor of the cafe building. These, with a quantity of powered garden cultivators, appliances, anti-freeze and an aluminum boat, were estimated to cost about $5,000" by Mr. Parks.

The flames, fed by the rubber tires and other flammable goods were still going strong late this (Thursday) morning, with huge columns of black smoke pouring out from the buildings. The fire was reported to Police Dispatcher Harold Williams at 9:08 p.m. Wednesday. A second siren call was sounded to summon all additional help possible and the Independence and Hillsville firemen were radioed for assistance.

A truck and a half dozen or so firemen from these two departments responded. The Pulaski Volunteer Firemen radioed they would come if needed, but were told the blaze apparently had been brought under control.
All off-duty policemen in Galax were summoned to aid in handling traffic and curious spectators who braved the 15-20 degree cold to watch the activity. (As a sidelight, Dispatcher Williams reported that "I've received 62 telephone calls in two hours about the fire." The flood of calls hampered him in his radio work in helping the firemen combat the blaze. One fireman, Joe Anderson, suffered an injured foot and was hospitalized at Waddell Hospital and x-rays were to be made this morning. His injury was considered not too serious.

The sub-freezing temperatures soon turned the streets around the buildings into sheets of ice, as firemen poured water onto the flames. When the roof burned through, flames shot skyward and rained sparks onto adjacent buildings several hundred feet away. The rear of the first National Bank building, just across an alley from the

Economy Department, began "smoking" from time to time from the intense heat, and firemen kept it doused with water. The same was true of the Waugh Building which flanks the Goodson Building on the West.

Firemen mounted the roof-adjacent buildings to pour water over the rooftops and sides to confine the blaze to the two structures destroyed. Several bottles of liquid petroleum stored at the rear of the Goodson Building were quickly dis-connected and hauled away, preventing a possible explosion had the flames got to them. A fuel oil tank was kept covered with a coating of water and ice.

Water and spray hitting the firemen's coats and hats quickly turned to ice, adding several pounds to their weight and hampering them in their movements. The slippery footing also made their work extremely hazardous and was blamed for the slip and fall that injured Firemen Anderson's foot.

Late this morning the interior of the Economy Department Store and the storeroom of the Big Chief Market were burning fiercely as continued attempt to "water it down". The burning tires that fell through the burned out floors are attributed as the cause of the stubbornness of the flames to resist efforts to quench them.

Sheets of ice on the walls and icicles are mute evidence of the intense cold that hampered the work of the firemen last night. This view of the front of the Goodson's Café and Economy Department Store on West Grayson street. In the background is the First National Bank building which firemen kept from bursting into flames by dousing water on it during the height of the blaze.

The streets and alleys around the West Grayson block were roped off and traffic detoured to other streets. State Patrolmen in the area joined with the Galax City Police in helping to handle the hundreds of cars and persons

who converged on the downtown section. With their husbands and fathers battling the flames, the Volunteer Firemen's Ladies Auxiliary also went into action, under the leadership of Miss Rebecca Wilson, President. They prepared hot coffee and sandwiches for the fire fighters. Snow and sleet began falling in downtown Galax about 5 o'clock this morning (and was continuing at press time), but this precipitation was too late to be of much assistance in the battle against the flames.

The Wednesday night blaze was the first big fire in the downtown section since January, 1954, when a building on South Main Street housing Robby's Army Store and upstairs apartments was destroyed. Other major fires suffered here included the destruction of the Vaughan-Bassett Furniture plant in February 1951, and the burning of nearly the whole South Main street block between Grayson and Oldtown streets in the 1920's.

The Galax Gazette

Sawyers Furniture Company
Fire Destroys Plant Early Tuesday Morning.

Interim operations and re-building of plant subject of conference.

Officials of Sawyers Furniture Company Inc., officers of the Galax development Corporation, and officials of the City of Galax were in conference late Wednesday at attempting to work out some plan for interim operation of the burned-out furniture plant.

Also on the agenda for discussion was a rebuilding of the manufacturing establishment, which is located at the Western corporate limits of the city.

Hubert H Watson, President of Sawyers, asked the Gazette to convey "our deep gratitude and heartfelt thanks to the volunteer fireman from Galax Fries and Hillsville and to all others whose splendid work kept the loss from being greater than it was".

Mr. Watson said arrangements would be made, if possible and as quickly as possible, to take care of " our customers and our employees".

More than 200 employees are affected by the loss of the furniture plant. The hope is to provide some sort of interim operations to provide employment for highly skilled key personnel as many others as possible and at the same time to provide for the filling of customers orders. The firm manufactures one of the top lines of upholstered furniture in the country. A. Glenn Pless, President of the Galax Development Corporation, was among those in conference with the Sawyers officials late Wednesday. We certainly will do everything within our power to assist them to continue their operations, Mr. Pless said and we certainly hope to work out one some sort of arrangement for the rebuilding of the plant as quickly as possible.

Mr. Watson said that as soon as something definite was worked out this information would be passed on to the firm's employees and to the general public.

He added that an accurate estimate of loss in the fire cannot be determined until we have done a lot of checking, however, there is no question but the damage would be very heavy. He said that the loss would only partially recovered by insurance.

The cause of the fire is not known. The destroyed building covered some 100,000 ft. square in two stories and a basement. The fire was discovered by Mrs. Hubert Watson at about 3 AM Tuesday. She and Mr. Watson and Mrs. C. F. Sawyers are co- owners of the plant.

Mrs. Watson said the fire apparently started near the loading truck bay were a truck loaded with cotton had been parked for the night. Shorted wires that started the truck horn to blowing cause Mrs. Watson to awaken apparently.

The Watson home is located adjacent to the plant and volunteer Firemen from Galax, Fries and Hillsville poured water on the house to prevent the flames for spreading to it.

However, by the time the firemen had arrived at the scene, about a half mile west of the Galax Corporate limits, the flames had such headway in the plant that they could not be contained or extinguished. The firemen did manage to prevent the fire from spreading to the office building and also saved the finishing building and the boiler room.

High winds fanned the flames eastward, burning the grass in a large area of pasture across the surfaced road from the plant. Flying embers also set several bushfires nearby

The Sawyers Plant before the Fire

The New Sawyers back in operation

Galax Gazette: April 15, 1965

The Vaughan Memorial Library Becomes a Reality

By Cindy Lawson

The Vaughan Memorial Library had its beginning about 34 years ago, through the efforts of the Galax Business and Professional Woman's Club.

During the past 19 years or more, the Appalachian Power Company had been providing the present library space, in its building on South Main Street, free of charge.

In Sept., 1970, the large B. C. Vaughan home, and spacious grounds on West Stuart Drive, were donated to the City of Galax by the heirs, the late Mrs. C. W. Higgins, and Mrs. Wyatt P. Exum.

During the last two years, the Vaughan property has been undergoing remodeling into development as a Public Memorial Library facility. Additional items of furniture and equipment were ordered during Dec.1973 and delivery has been promised by April 29. The work is nearly complete, and it is anticipated that everything will be moved into the new facility by the latter part of May.

NEW VAUGHAN MEMORIAL LIBRARY.

Over the many years, faithful and dedicated individuals, and civic organizations, have kept the hope alive for a modern facility in which our community can take pride. There are many pressing needs and opportunities for every citizen of our city to share, in making this dream a reality.

The effort to establish this library stands as a tribute to local accomplishments. Except for $357 annual state aid, the library facility is being provided for and operated by local funds.

There are many people connected with the establishment of the library, who deserve special recognition. First of all, there are members of the present Board of Trustees. All of these people are appointed by the City Council, and serve on a volunteer basis.

They are: R. Tyler Price, Chairman, Mrs. Avis Vaughan, Secretary and Treasurer, A. Glenn Pless, W. G. Davis, Mrs. Wyatt Exum, and Russell T. Farnsworth.

There are also the present librarians, R. V. Redman, and Mrs. R.L. Williams, and Miss Donna Brown, Area Public Library Consultant at Marion, who is providing valuable information for setting up and operating a library facility.

Johnny Lemon's Memories of Early Galax

Good afternoon. My name is Johnny Lemons. I was born in Galax, Virginia on July 18, 1925. I grew up here and have lived in Galax all my life. I'm going to try to tell you changes that have taken place during my lifetime in downtown.

Beginning on the East side of Main Street, corner of Main and Stuart Drive (Route 58), Coulson's Grocery Store and Service Station was located. Next door, on Main Street, there was a brick house owned by the Bowers family. The next house, which is still standing, was occupied by Dr. David Bolen and his family. The house on corner of Main and Virginia Street was owned by the Carlan family who also owned a drugstore downtown. Across Virginia Street on the corner was a lot, with a beautiful sunken garden, owned by the T. G. Vaughan family. Across the alley was a vacant lot where Dr. R. C. Bowie built his office and apartments.

Where the Snead Building is now, a large brick house stood and was known as the Baker house. Next the Phipps home was located where the Motel 8 is now. These two houses occupied this entire block from Webster Street to Washington Street. Across Washington Street the W. K. Early home was located. The Early family owned the W. K. Early Lumber Company which was just one block behind their home.

Where the telephone company is now, was a Texaco Service Station owned by Sam Griggs. Prior to the old Post Office, now Macado's, there was a large white building that was a hotel -- having a long, inviting porch across the front with rocking chairs, where people would sit and visit.

Across Center Street from the hotel, was the First National Bank building. It later became occupied as City Hall (housing City offices), and now is the Social Services offices. The building back of this building and on Center Street was the Galax Fire Department, housed on the first floor. On the second floor were the Police Department, Court Room, and jail. On the third floor was the Firemen's Legion Hall where the firemen sponsored a square dance every Saturday night

Next to the bank, going South on Main Street, was Claire's Fashion Shoppe (now The Framer's Daughter). Then the next building was the Royal Cafe, later Newton's Department Store, and now Adams-Heath Engineering. I think a vacant lot was next where the Colonial Theater was built sometime in the 30s. Then Arlie's Boot Shop (now Donald Walker Associates). Steel's Jewelers was in the next building, later The Jewel Box and now Lemons' Jewelry. Steve's Grill was next, now called The City Grill.

DeHaven's Shoe Store (now the Crisis Center) was the next building, then Phipps' Barber Shop which is now Virginia Link. A & P Grocery was next, then Kroger's Grocery, and then a shoe repair shop. Later Roses 5 & 100 Store occupied all three of these locations, which is now an Art Supply Store. On the corner of Main and Grayson Street was Bolen's Drug Store where The Smoke House is now.

Going East on Grayson Street and behind Bolen's Drug Store

Peoples State bank to the left, behind Bolens Drug Store

was a state bank, which went broke in the 30s, closing during the Depression years. Bolen Drug Store then expanded, occupying where the bank used to be. The next building was the Parsons building for Joe Parsons' law offices. Before the Parsons building was built, the lot was empty and local people sold produce. Across the alley was a Street Car Diner, then the City built a two level parking building, torn down later and is now a City parking lot. The building which is now the machine shop was built by Mr. Zabreski who published The Galax Gazette. Kyle and Williams Insurance occupied the next small building beside the Gazette.

Across the street on the corner of Grayson and Carroll Street was the U. S. Post Office (in the 1920s and 1930s). This was the second location of the Post Office -- the first location being on Main Street below Vass Kapp's Hardware and next to Roy's Diamond Center. Then the Post Office was moved to its new location (now Macado's), the building was occupied by Rex Sage's Auto Supply, followed by several other businesses and now the Red Door Gifts, Unlimited.

Where the Adam's CPA office is now was Bowers' Restaurant followed by several other restaurants and offices. Where the Rex Theater and the Municipal Building are, were empty lots until the Theater was built and one half of the Municipal Building was Pless Furniture Store and the other half of the building being added later. Matthews Hardware #2, followed by H&R Block in one half of the building and a beauty parlor in the other half. This building is now occupied by Hair Classics. The next building was Dan B. Waugh's Men's Store – now Chapter's Book Store.

The corner building (corner of Main and Grayson) was Roses 5 and 10¢ Store. When Roses moved to Main Street, Dan B. Waugh expanded, occupying both the spaces where the Chapter's Book Store and the consignment shop are now. Following Dan B. Waugh's Ready to Wear, The Fashion Shop owned and operated by Dot Cock preceded the two stores now there (Chapter's Book Store and The Double Takes Consignment Shop).

Going South on Main Street -- and below Dan B. Waugh's Building - was Threatt's Dry Cleaners in one part of the building and Parson's and Murphy's Barber Shop, which had the only public bath in Galax, in the other part of that building. This space is occupied by Barr's Fiddle Shop today.

Across the alley from the Fiddle Shop was Goodson's Restaurant which later moved to Grayson Street, then an ice cream parlor, followed by the Corner Gift Shop and Babyland Boutique is there now. The next store was Barr Topman 5 and 100 Store, later Wilson's Sporting Goods and now Bonaparte Antique Shop. Next was Witherow's Men's Store, later The Men's Store was owned and operated by John Cock and now Shapes' Beauty Salon. Chappell's Meat Market and Grocery Store was next, later Ted's Market. Globman's expanded and added this building to their store which extended to the corner. Cones & Coffee and The Antique Apple (antique mall). But in the earlier days before the Globman's building was constructed, there was a livery stable located on the corner owned by the Bishop family.

East on Oldtown Street was the Boaz Studio (photography), Welsh's Feed Store and now an apartment building. Across from Globman's on the corner of Main Street and Oldtown Street was an empty lot until 1947 when Lydge Alderman built Peoples Drug Store, operated by Jack Schooley, later bought and operated by a pharmacist by the name of Wingold. Family Hair Care is now occupying this building. Where Roberts Gift Gallery is now was originally a movie theater, followed by a pool room. Next door to that was Pop's Greek Restaurant known as Snappy Lunch, and a variety of businesses have been there until The City Gallery of Fine Art which is now located in the building. The next building where Nester's Clock Shop is located became the second location of the Merchants and Farmer's Bank. When the bank moved to the corner of Center Street and Main Street, Galax Office Supply moved from Grayson Street to this building. Matthews Hardware #1 was next, then Porter Furniture Company where the Stringbean store is now.

There was a grocery store next to Porter's, and later Porter Furniture Company expanded, occupying that space also. Next was Amburn's Grocery (now a gift shop) then there was a pool hall in the adjoining building (now empty). Pennington's Grocery was next where there is now an antique and gift shop. Y. B. Hall had a feed store and grocery in the next 2 spaces, today the first space is empty and the second space is a Marriage and Therapy office. Next was known as the Dalton Building, which was a men's clothing store, later an auto parts store. A small building beside the Dalton Building was a variety shop, later torn down and the A and Z store was built next to the Dalton Building. From the A and Z store to Felts Park were all private homes. On the West side of Main Street going North there were private homes also, down to Blevins Building Supply which was White Chevrolet Sales originally. On the Corner of Main and Calhoun Streets (next to Blevins) was an Exxon Service Center. Across Calhoun and on the corner of Main was a vacant lot. Pure Oil Station was located where Frost's Insurance Agency is now. In the very early days a hotel was located on the lot where Roberts' Citgo is now.

Across Oldtown Street from Roberts' Citgo was a building that Kroger's Grocery Store moved to from Main Street, then it was Green's Auto Supply, later Robby's Army-Navy Store, now empty. Across the alley from the Army-Navy Store was a building built by Henry Brown in 1929, and located on the corner of Oldtown Street and Main Street. Carlan's Drug Store was located in this building, following in later years by Flipp Reece Men's Store, and now Bearly a Memory. Next was Mick or Mack Grocery later occupied by Truitt's Ready to Wear and now Carol's Consignment Shop.

Where the Chinese Restaurant is now was divided, one side occupied by an auto supply store and the other side by the Post Herald Newspaper. The space was later combined and Carlan's Drug Store moved to that location. Carlan's closed and Western Auto moved in. The next store was Perelman's Ladies Ready to Wear, later occupied by a book store and today Creative Threads and Dana's Boutique. Next was Henderson's Jewelry Store, afterwards occupied by Hank's Insurance office, now Marie's Variety and Gifts. A pool room was next to the alley, and later Henderson's Jewelry moved to that space. This store is now owned by UCT #720.

Across the alley was Lineberry's Jewelry Store, and next was the original Galax Post Office. When the Post Office moved to Grayson Street the space was occupied by a barber shop. Richard Vaught bought Lineberry's Jewelry and the barber shop space and combined the two spaces for Lineberry's Jewelry Store. Roy's Diamond Center is now located there. The next space was occupied by the Corinthian Beauty Shop which is now a dress shop. Vass Kapp Hardware was the next building that extended to the corner of Main and Grayson Streets and is now the antique mall A Place in Time.

Going west on Grayson Street next to the Vass Kapp building was Burgess' Furniture Store which became a part of the Vass Kapp Hardware Store later. The next 3 buildings combined was Belk's Department Store which is now divided into The Proper Choice shop, Doug Vaught's office, Wachovia Investments office and the Trophy Shop. The Trophy Shop was previously occupied by R. E. Jones Furniture when Belk's closed. L. S. NET (local Internet service provider) building was originally a bowling alley. Fine Lines Gift Shop was known as the Mountain Loan building. In the back of the Mountain Loan building was the Galax Gazette newspaper printing company. In the empty building where Innovative Systems was located was a grocery store operated by Joe and Grover Moore. Galax Education Center was Pontiac automobile dealership. The corner building now empty was originally a grocery and feed store operated by Mr. Weaver and later occupied by Home Finance Company then later a health supply store.

Across the street on the corner of Jefferson Street and Grayson Street where the Galax Florist and the bakery shop Sweetie Pies is now was Vaughan Guynn Funeral Home.

Grayson Commons was previously White Chevrolet Sales followed by Galax Motor Company followed by Western Auto and now Grayson Commons. Goodson's Restaurant moved from Main Street to the building next to Grayson Commons building and next to it was Harris' Department Store. Goodson's and Harris' building burned in the 50s. This space is now a parking lot and there is a stage on the back side of the lot which can be used for community activities as needed. (*Goodson's burned in January of 1961 Editor note*)

Vaughan Guynn Funeral Home

Across the alley from the stage and parking lot is the First National Bank building which also faces Main Street. There was a side entrance to this bank building on Grayson Street which provided space for Bryan's Barber Shop in the basement level, an Insurance office on the main level and a telephone switchboard of the Inter Mountain Telephone Company was located on the top level. This building is not occupied now.

North on Main Street and next to the National Bank Building was Jones Furniture Store and Funeral Home. This space is now occupied by H&R Block. The next building was occupied by Fulton and Vass Hardware followed by

150

Perkins Auto Supply, after that Parks Auto Supply and now The Treasure Box. The next building was a grocery store, the Big Chief Market, now Modernette Beauty Shop. A barber shop was next, and then the first location for Pless Furniture Stores was in the next building. These two spaces were combined for Hampton's Real Estate and Auction Company and now Kimberly's Florist Gallery.

The next building was the A and Z Store built in the 30s. This building has been torn down and a small park is there now. Next to the A and Z Store was a printing company owned and operated by Maude Gamer. Next was a Western Union office. When that office moved to a space in the Bluemont Hotel, Hampton's Restaurant occupied the building. Next a service station was located on the corner of Main Street and Center Street. The printing office, the Western Union office and the service station is now occupied by Mountain National Bank and parking lot. Behind the original service station space, B&G Paint Store was built in later years, now empty. The next building was the Galax Hospital which is now an apartment building.

Across the street on the other corner of Main and Center Streets the Bluemont Hotel was built sometime in the 20s. The last location of the Merchants and Farmers Bank replaced the Bluemont Hotel Building and now Wachovia Bank is located there.

Next was the second location of the First Baptist Church built in 1928, now occupied by Rooftop of Virginia. A private home was on the corner lot, which now is an insurance office. Across the street and on the corner of Washington and Main Street the First Christian Church was located.

Dr. Bowie's home and chiropractic office was located next, now occupied by Caudle's Law offices. Next to that was the First Virginia Bank building now closed.
Twin County Motor Company was next located on the corner of Main and Webster Street. This space now provides parking for Twin County Tire which also occupies part of the original Twin County building.

Across Webster Street and on the corner of Webster and Main Street is the Gordon Felts house, now owned by Dr. and Mrs. Luague. Next is the Kapp house, and still owned by the Kapp family, which is located on the corner of Main and Virginia Street.
Across Virginia Street on the corner is a house that was owned by a Dixon family now the Mount Rogers Powerhouse Clubhouse. The next house was owned by the Brown family now empty.

The Welsh House corner of Virginia and Main Street, a Sears & Roebuck house

A Sinclair Service Station was located on corner of Main Street and Stuart Drive, and is now the location of Martin's Cleaners.

I have tried to recall these facts as best I can remember from my childhood. I'm sure there are other businesses or changes that took place in some of the buildings or spaces, either before the 30s or even after the 30s that I have not remembered exactly as they were, but I hope you enjoy reading this and that it will help you think of early Galax days and the many changes that have taken place and maybe even do some research on your own.
I'm happy I was born in Galax and have always lived here. It's a great place to live and Galax, Virginia, my hometown, will always be a part of me.

Thank you for the opportunity of sharing these memories with you.
These "Memories" are from Sharon Plichta, where they were collected for the 50th reunion in 2007 of the class of 1957

Gray Anderson's
Memories of Galax High School
Football Team 1922
Undefeated

Editor Galax Gazette
Galax, Virginia
Sept. 11th 1964

Dear Sir:

A recent statement in your paper indicated you welcomed some old pictures, and since it is now the football season, I am enclosing a picture of the Galax High football team for the year 1922, as shown on the football. Not all of the players are shown in the picture. However, the lineman shown seated left to right are: Dr. John Bolen, Guy Hawks (captain), Judge Jack Matthews, Bergen Branscome, Ernest Cox, Dan Anderson, Hurley Cox, Glenn Pless and Payne Gentry. In the back field standing left to right are: Grey Anderson, J. C. Lindsey, Earl Nuckolls and Olen Ward (deceased).

If my memory serves me correct, football first began at Galax High School with a team composed of such players as John Gary Carrico, Dr. Bill Dobyns, the Lineberry brothers, Lloyd and Everett, Raymond Wright and as always, a Hawks. I believe Bruce was on that team and Mike and Allen. (Allen Crabill was the quarterback for the team). There are others, I am sure, and know that you can be supplied this information from former players, as well as the years they played.

Also, there was Ralph Todd and Joe Todd. It has been said that Ralph was the hardest running fullback to ever play for Galax High.

It is my recollection that these first teams did not fare too well in the win column; nevertheless, it is interesting and should be pointed out that when they went on a trip, such as to Pulaski, they would play one or two teams on successive days, so that no doubt, took a great deal of physical strength to play on successive days, which is never heard of today in present football circles.

There was another era of football at Galax High around the early twenties, in which a number of fine football player's performed for Galax, and they were Cliff Kyle, Dannie Busic (now deceased), Raleigh Hampton, Burr Lyons, Fred Witherow, another Hawks....Otto, who it was said, could tackle with the force of a ton of bricks, Pat Dodd (Bob's brother) also played with these athletes before moving to Kingsport, Tennessee. Delmar Kanode and Kyle McMillan (deceased) were other players. I know there are several other players, not here mentioned, who played during this area, and the information as to their names, etc., can be supplied by some of the players with whom they played, at Galax High School.

I think the next era of football fortunes beginning with 1922 through 1924 was one of the best. We finally got a coach. (Remember we had to personally furnish all of our equipment with the exception of our football pants, which were handed down from year to year, and there was at most during those years, about 15 pairs, so once you were lucky enough to get a pair, you had to play pretty good and regular because very seldom were there any substitutes put in the game. A look at the picture gives you an idea of the homemade hip pads, etc.) But getting back to our coach, Paul Sutherland, brother of Judge Horace Sutherland (deceased) agreed to coach. I don't think he ever received any pay. He had formerly played a rugged end for Washington and Lee University, and in coaching our ends, his style was to the effect (a crashing end) in which Paul taught the end when the play was coming around his end, the end was instructed to knock down everybody who was in front of the ball carrier, and as Paul would say, "My tackle then will stop the play." (I felt for those ends)

As I recall the 1922 football year, Galax High School went undefeated and the team scored 208 points against the opposition. Marion and Radford were defeated, so was Austinville, 66 to 0, and Fries 88 to 0. In the Fries game, an incident occurred, which I shall always remember. We were leading 88 to O with about two minutes remaining in the game. Fries had possession of the ball, and as they came up to the line of scrimmage, Bill Bolton, their quarterback, admonished his team to get in there and fight, stating, t he game was not over by any means."
Other football players not in the picture were John Reid Smith, 'Bull Dog" Bobbitt and Preacher Semones (whom everyone considered, along with "Bull Dog ", to be the finest linesman ever to play for the Maroon Tide. Johnnie Reavis was another end.

While over the years we have had some fine and great high school players, including Jules Ward of Duke, and Earl Nuckolls as a full back, I considered John Reid Smith, pound for pound, one of the all-time greats of Galax High School.

With this era ending in the 1924 football year, any old timer can and will tell you about Paul Sutherland and the late B.C. Vaughan taking 12 or 13 Galax High School players over to Johnson City, Tennessee, and beating the East Tennessee outfit. This is enough about those years. Someone else will have to bring you up to date, in that I entered V.P.I. in the fall of 1924. It is my understanding, however, that our Galax High School teams did not fare so well in East Tennessee thereafter, and I'm referring to a game with Kingsport, Tennessee, but you will have to ask Bill James or Bull Kegley about that. I think they were there, and pretty well know all about it.

Gray Anderson
Room 308 Hartford Bldg.
1011 E. Colonial Drive
Orlando FL
Sept 11th, 1964

note: Gray Anderson was a lawyer and involved in the WWII Japanese war trials...

Munsey Poole's Echoes From the Past
Cliffside, Herds of Sheep and Turkey Drives

MORE SHOULD BE SAID ABOUT CLIFFVIEW since it had so much to do with the beginning of Galax. By reason of the name of the Felts estate, the area was also called "Cliffside". Dominating the Cliffside community landscape - or the town, as it was considered by many in 1904 - is the stately mansion, which formerly was the residence of the late State Senator Thomas L. Felts. There was a time when the community was called also "Ethelfelts". It was for Mr. Felts' wife, the late Ethel Housman Felts, that the name, "Ethelfelts," was identified with the community that is now Cliffview.

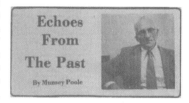

Echoes From The Past
By Munsey Poole

Now, 73 years later, "Cliffside" is the home of Mr. and Mrs. Hubert S. White Jr.

Until recent years, much of what is known as Cliffview was owned by members of the Felts family, from whose hands it has now passed - since the death of Senator Felts in 1936, and that of his son, Gordon C. Felts, much more recently.

There was a newspaper published at Blair. It was the Blair Enterprise. Quoted from the editorial column of the May 25, 1904, issue of the Enterprise are the following few paragraphs:
"GALAX is already putting on the appearance of a new town, and right here we wish to remark that any town should have an organization, in a business way if no other, which will improve or beautify it. One improvement more we would suggest in the new town is water works, which, with the natural advantages, can be put in with a very small outlay.

"The business men of the town can well afford to do this, first, for their own protection, and next. for the amount they will save on insurance. Another advantage will be that the people wishing to come to Galax to invest their capital, will do so more quickly if they have ample protection from fire.

"We have the interest of the town at heart, and offer this as a suggestion with the belief that the amount required to accomplish this will be money well spent."

(The late F. W. Farmer, who in later years was associated with the former Galax Post-Herald, was listed in the Enterprise masthead as "Editor.")

POSSIBLY SOME PRESENT PIONEER citizens of the city can recall having witnessed a "sight not soon forgotten" when they saw Chap Hampton or the Carr brothers drive large herds of sheep through town to the livestock pens on the railroad. Dogs of almost unbelievable intelligence would keep the flocks moving over the prescribed route, keep the sheep off private lawns, turn them at the proper corners, and guide them around horse-drawn or ox-drawn wagons. Seldom would one of the animals stray and have to be forced back into the drive.

Another interesting and rather spectacular feat often witnessed in Galax, in those early days of the town's life, was a turkey drive.

Using dogs also for this purpose, dealers would drive huge flocks or turkeys into and through town, from various rural collection points where the turkeys had been brought to market by the farmers who had raised them.

Often the turkey drives were made in constant dread of snow, because when snow began to fall in any appreciable amount, the turkeys would take to the trees along the way, and when they did this the job of rounding them up became a major problem.

Winters in those years were rough hereabouts, and flowing ice was a menace during much of the winter season to operation of the ferry boats which provided about the only means of crossing New River. Oxen were the only draft animals, and the "covered wagon," with full equipment, it seems, was about the only reliable mode of transportation.

Before the time when improved highways first began to make their appearance, Galax often held first place on the entire N&W Railway in the shipment of livestock. And Grayson County is said to have led, at that time, all counties in the United States in the percentage of purebred sires in the production of beef.

First child born in Galax is visitor at Gazette office

By Ida Dean Cock

One Saturday morning a most charming lady came into the office and announced herself as the first child born in Galax.

She was Mrs. George A. Craighead, the former Miss Blanche Gallimore.

Mrs. Craighead had been prompted by news of our Golden Jubilee celebration to tell us of this interesting fact.

She was born August 31, 1904 in the house on N. Main St. where Dr. Paul Kapp lives now and she was delivered by Dr. John W Bolen.

Mrs. Craighead's parents were Edgar Gallimore now living at Pismo Beach California and Mrs. Bertie Cox Gallimore, deceased. She has one brother, Roy, who also lives at Pismo Beach and a sister Mrs. Imogene Mullins, San-Luis Obispo, California. *(editor's note: The Gallimores built several houses in Galax)*

Her paternal grandparents were Billy and Surilda Gallimore, who lived in and near Galax for a number of years. Maternal grandparents were L.W. and Alice Cox, who lived near Elkhorn in the Pipers Gap section.

After attending school at Radford State Normal College, Radford, she roomed with Miss Lavie Cornett, Mrs. Craighead taught school at Pine Grove, atop the beautiful Blue Ridge Mountains.

Mrs. Craighead met her husband, who is a native of Floyd County in West Virginia, and they were married at Welch, West Virginia in 1924. They have one daughter, Mrs. Virginia Carroll Hedgecock, Roanoke . Mrs. Craighead pointed out that memories of her childhood lead to her daughter's name.

Mr. and Mrs. Craighead were employed in the coal fields of West Virginia for many years. In May of this year they moved to Roanoke. In Roanoke, Mrs. Craighead is employed as a secretary at the R and S Building Corporation.

We moved around a lot when I was very young, said Mrs. Craighead, and I can't remember very much about Galax in its young days. She went on to explain, however, that she had been reared in the knowledge that she was the first child of Galax, and this combined with other relations had kept the progressive little city dear and her memories.

Mr. Mrs. Craighead are making plans to be present for the Jubilee festivities and she says that her father is coming from California to help Galax celebrated his 50 years of progress.

Ida Dean Cock, daughter of Mr. and Mrs. Payton Cock, graduated from Radford Collage, now Radford University. Her Mother, Dot Cock, worked for Claire Goldstein in her shop, Claire's Fashion Shop next to the City Hall building on North Main Street. After Claire retired, Dot bought the business from Claire, and later moved it to the J.B. Waugh Building on the corner of East Grayson and South Main Street. Then it was renamed "The Fashion Shop", now the home of Chapters Book store. Ida Dean and her husband Yates Forbes took over the business from Dot and ran it for several years. Then, after selling the business, they moved to be with their children in Indiana.

Galax Flood of 1940
Galax and Twin Counties area suffer from devastating floodwaters.

Damage wrought by floodwaters of Chestnut Creek and New River very heavy, no lives are lost.

Galax citizens awoke Wednesday morning to find a swirling flood that had come during the night to the low-lying sections of Galax and areas in the surrounding countryside adjacent to new River and the larger creeks etc. to such an extent that some the older citizens say the flood tide was the highest and most destructive of any that had visited the section since 1878. The only flood that is ever visited this vicinity since the founding of Galax comparable with

the one that came Tuesday night was the one that wrought so much damage in Galax and sections during the summer of 1916 during war, some say of the old-timers.

Rain that had fallen intermittently throughout this section since Sunday gradually increased in volume of downpour, until, by shortly after dark Tuesday night, it had almost reached deluge proportions by 4 or 5 o'clock yesterday morning Chestnut Creek that runs through the low-lying sections of the East side of Galax had overflowed its banks and was rising in such proportions that many of the citizens of that section had to flee from their homes for safety. So narrow was the escape of so many that there was no time to snatch even enough clothing to protect themselves from elements before they were compelled to seek safety on higher ground.

One instance of the narrowness of escape from the swirling waters was that in connection with the family of Vivian Sexton whose house which stood near Chestnut Creek, near the intersection of Pipers gap and Low Gap roads, just south of town, was swept from its foundation and carried approximately 150 yards downstream. All members of the family were sleeping soundly, and none were aware of the perilous positions which they were in until a small son of Mr. and Mrs. Sexton was awakened by popping or cracking sound and turned on the light to find the water almost up to the level of his bed. He had once awakened the other members of the family, and so great was the haste in which they were forced to desert their home that no articles of clothing other than barely enough to wear out into the falling rain, could be taken with them, and Mr. Sexton could not find his shoes in floodwaters already within his house. According to reports, no sooner had the family step from the porch of their home that the house was swept from its foundations.

A few other instances of a somewhat similar nature had been reported although this was the only one definitely confirmed in which a house was actually washed away with those living within having so narrow and escape

The local Red Cross organization is busy providing shelter food and clothing for those who were forced to leave their homes and refugees are being housed temporarily in the old Galax Hospital building on W. Center St.

Traffic in the Galax was practically at a standstill throughout the day yesterday as the Galax-Independence highway was flooded between New River Bridge and Riverside Camp, make it impossible for vehicular traffic to pass that way, and the bridge across Chestnut Creek on the Hillsville highway at the entrance to Galax was totally submerged until almost noon, and then it was considered unsafe for cars to attempt to pass over. Some traffic was being routed in the Galax yesterday from the direction of Woodlawn and Hillsville, by way of Cliffside and the Fries Hill Road. Throughout traffic to Hillsville however was disrupted because of the washing out of a bridge a short distance east of the golf links near the home of A.G. Pless.

Traffic to Hillsville was being routed by way of the Pipers Gap Road via the Blue Ridge Parkway to Fancy Gap and then back to Hillsville such was the condition of the highway in the Fancy Gap section that only one-way traffic was possible in a part of the vicinity it was reported. It was also said that travel towards Mount Airy over the Low Gap Road was also blocked to the heavy rainfall.

The extent of damage to stocks of furniture, lumber etc. in the Vaugahn Furniture Company factory, the Vaughan-Bassett factory, the Webb factory, the Galax Furniture Company factory and W.K. Early and Son, lumber dealers is unknown but is thought to have been as heavy as the lower portions of those plants were flooded. The Galax Knitting Company plant is said to have been the only industrial plant that was not reached by the floodwaters.

Enormous damage was wrought to hay and grain crops while Chestnut Creek and other streams in this section and along the river, not to speak of the possible destruction of livestock and other property.

At the crest of flooding yesterday crowning around 10 o'clock, the river at the site of the serge, a few miles west of Galax on the Galax-Independence highway, was said to have reached a height of approximate 28 feet above the normal waterline. From the bridge, where hundreds of persons from Galax and section went to view the yellow raging torrent during Wednesday, could be seen haystacks, wheat and straw stacks, and trees, as well as almost all kinds of debris fed into the flooding river by swollen tributary streams swiftly floating down the river on the crest of the flood tide.

Outstanding among instances of property loss was that of the large newly- constructed lumber storage house belonging to Steve Dixon, just across the highway from the Dixon mill and lumber shop a short distance west of the new River Bridge, where the building was swept away by the flood, together with between 50,000 and 100,000 board feet of lumber that was stored within.

Much difficulty was experienced by many persons just in the morning and reaching their work, especially those who lived on the east side of the creek in Galax, or those who lived out of town and had streams to cross in order to reach here.

During a large portion of Wednesday, Galax was without electric power, and telephone service between here and most neighboring towns and communities was also disrupted by the flood. Practically no incoming mail reached the local post office yesterday, and the little outgoing mail was dispatched at the local office, due to washed out bridges, flooded highways, etc. Reports reached here yesterday shortly afternoon that New River was uncrossable at Jacksons Ferry Bridge near Popular Camp, due to flooded approaches to the bridge.

Galax had no train service Wednesday, due to damage to the N&W tracks here and elsewhere caused by the floodwaters. It is understood that the train on the Pulaski branch of the N & W line did not come further than Ivanhoe.

Whenever people gathered here yesterday almost the sole topic of conversation was the flood and the damage wrought by it.

A number of persons in Galax and sections were concerned for some time yesterday for sons and daughters who are members of the Blue Ridge Disciples of Christ Young People's conference being held this week at Camp Pot Rock, near Hebron on Crooked Creek. It was learned, however that those in the camp were removed to safety, before the floodwaters too deeply engulfed the campsite. Members of the Boy Scout Troop number 59 Galax are in camp this week at Fairystone and State Park, near Bassett, but nothing regard to rainfall conditions there has been learned.
Galax Gazette.... 8-15-40

First Presbyterian Church of Galax

The history of the Galax Presbyterian Church begins with the organization of a Sunday School at Oldtown, Virginia in Grayson County in 1860. At that time, Carroll County had not been set apart from Grayson and Oldtown was then the county seat for the entire territory. Among the families who came to Oldtown was the McCamants, the father having come to Wytheville from Pennsylvania and later to Oldtown, where he was a practicing attorney . Virginia McCamant, a daughter of Attorney McCamant, who later married Rev. C. M. Howard, an evangelist, was born and reared at Oldtown . She was educated at Wytheville and Greensboro, N. C. While at school in Wytheville, she was converted and joined the Presbyterian Church. She graduated at the age of 16 and came back to her home at Oldtown.

SUNDAY SCHOOL

In 1860 Mrs. Howard organized a Sunday School which was held in one room of the Court House . The nearest Presbyterian Church was at Hillsville 18 miles distant. Rev. Lee C. Brown of Hillsville, Rev. J. D. Thomas of Wytheville and others rode horseback the long country miles to preach at this remote school. In a short time the founder had a band of followers with no church building. The war came and about ruined any hopes for a church. People were poor and had no means with which to build.

$1,000 .00

The very determined Mrs. Howard had one desire "We must have a church ! Col . William Dickinson gave a lot upon which the church was to be built. The People of Oldtown and vicinity gave what they could for the building and then Mrs. Howard decided to visit an aunt in Brooklyn, N. Y. , who was a member of Henry Ward Beecher's Church and appeal to him for help. Bravely she carried out her plan.

The great preacher heard her story and said , "You must come to my services tomorrow morning and tell my congregation just what you have told me . I am sure they will help you." Supported by her faith in her cause, she faced that huge assemblage and presented her case.

The congregation raised one thousand dollars and this young 18 year old girl who had such an eloquent plea for the religious needs of her home community returned to Oldtown triumphant. The building was erected in 1871.

CHURCH ORGANIZED

"By· order of Abingdon Presbytery Revs. William V. Wilson and Lee C. Brown were appointed to organize a church at Grayson Old Court House. Accordingly on the 12th day of November 1871. the said committee attended and the few members there expressing a willingness and desire, they were fully organized into a church consisting of the following members: Mr. Thomas H. Rogers, Mrs. Sallie Rogers, Mrs. Clorinda Rogers, Miss Virginia McClorinda Rogers, Miss Virginia McCamant, Mr. Mumford Patton, Mrs. Bettie Patton, Mrs. Catharine Patton, Dr. Charles Witherow, Mrs. Sarah Witherow, Col. John Dickerson, Mrs. Margaret Dickerson. Dr. Charles Witherow and Mr. Mumford Patton, elected as prescribed, were duly set apart by ordination and installation to the office of Ruling Elders. Mr. Thomas Rogers was set apart to the office of Deacon."

The church grew slowly, there being only about 12 active members at the start. Several years later under the pastorate of Rev. Meben, Dr. Dinwittie and others the membership grew to approximately 50.

About 1906 Galax came into existence and it soon became evident that Galax would be a flourishing town and the center of activity. The property at Oldtown was sold after Mrs. Howard suggested and urged the congregation to sell the old church so the proceeds might be used to erect a new church to complete her life work by building this new church.

MOVED TO GALAX

The Land Improvement Company donated the lot. It was through Mrs. Howard's efforts and the help of a few loyal members and friends that the present church was erected. It was dedicated August 7, 1905 by Rev. George Gilmerand and Rev. R. D. Carson the 1st resident pastor. Mrs. Howard was present at this dedication, the only time she was able to be in the church. The ruling elders at that time were Mumford Patton and Dr. A. R. Grubb. In 1907 W. K. Early became an elder. Dr. Grubb held this office 43 years.

In 1907 Mrs. Howard died and just before her death she gave Rev. Mr. Carson $20 in gold coins, saying she would die happy if the church that she had worked for and prayed for so long could be out of debt. Rev. Carson took the money to Mr. Will Early, who sent him back to Mrs. Howard with the word that the debt was paid. He and a few' others made up the amount needed. Rev. Carson wrote: "I was away when Mrs. Howard died, but the Galax church owes its life to her and to Mr. Will Early more than to any other two people." At this time the church still carried the name of Grayson Presbyterian Church.

After the church was moved to Galax and Rev. Carson served as first pastor there followed several years at which time there was no regular pastor. Rev. George Gilmer, Supt., of Home Missions, preached at intervals and sent many others to help out, among whom were Rev. Luther Beattle and Rev. Mr. Morton. Rev. J. McConnell was called but remained for only two years. He was followed by Rev. S. H. McBride in 1909 for four years. Rev. Gray for one year, who was succeeded by Rev. James McChesney. Rev. McChesney was stricken with a serious illness after the close of the World War and again there was a period without a pastor.

FAITHFUL WORKERS

No history would be complete without emphasizing the work of these faithful servants of God who served this mission church so well along, with Mr. & Mrs. W. K. Early, A. C. Painter and Dr. A. R. Grubb who worked with untiring efforts to keep this small church going in its early years at Galax.

REV. SIDNEY MCCARTY

In 1924 Rev. Sidney McCarty was called to the work. His 17 years as pastor of the church were fruitful years in which the membership grew. Soon conditions permitted the church to become self-supported and independent and was no longer a Home Mission Church. The church was brick veneered and a Sunday School was added to the building and many modern improvements made. A Hammond Organ was presented to the church by Mr. Randell Knisley. The Ruling Elders under Mr. McCarty were Mr. W. K. Early, B. G. Witherow, B. D. Beamer , E. B. Crabill, C. L. Baumgardner and Dr. B. F. Eckles. Deacons, J. W. Witherow, Mike R. Crabill, P. V. Dalton, D. S Vass, Will Grubb and J. S. James. In 1941 Rev. McCarty resigned after accepting a call to Roanoke and it was several months before another pastor was secured

REV. WEIGLEIN - REV. MURRAY

In 1942 Rev. D. R. Weiglein was called and remained pastor of this church for six years. It was during his pastorate that a building fund was started which enabled the new Sunday school addition to be completed. Rev. Weiglein resigned in April 1948 and our present pastor, Rev. George Murray III came the following October I, 1948.

For many years it has been a burning desire of every Galax Presbyterian to erect a building to adequately house the Sunday School. A kitchen, pastor's study, rest rooms and a Social Assembly Hall large enough for all fellowship gatherings were badly needed.

The church group has been small, the years have passed on and many of the faithful workers have gone to their eternal home, but God has and is blessing the work of this church. Faith, patience and untiring efforts find the First Presbyterian Church of Galax modern in every way.

The new Sunday School building dedicated this week is rapidly being equipped for a fast growing attendance. This addition cost approximately $31,000. The church organization together with members of the congregation have shared in making this much needed church addition a reality. A very small indebtedness remains.. The Sunday School administration has for many years been in the capable hands of Mr. E. G. Cummings who also served on the building committee.

MISSIONARY SOCIETY FORMED ABOUT 1907

The Virginia Howard Missionary Society was organized about 1907 by Mrs. W. K. Early and Mrs. R. B. Couch, Sr. Among its members were Mrs. J. K. Caldwell, Mrs. R. S. Baldwin, Mrs. J. S. James, Mrs. J. H. Witherow, Mrs. E. B. Crabill, Mrs. A. R. Grubb, Mrs. McCamant Higgins and Mrs. Clate Higgons.

The group was small but did excellent work for the glory of the Master's Kingdom.

This group grew and about the year 1921 The Woman's Auxiliary of the Galax Presbyterian Church carne into existence from what was known as The Virginia Howard Missionary Society. Mrs. J. S. James, in a very earnest manner, brought before this Society the wonderful work of the Auxiliary and it was she who organized and worked until this group became a regular Auxiliary, recognized in all branches of the church up to the General Assembly. As president she faithfully led this group through the "infant years".

The first few years there were no circles, no secretaries of the different causes, no regular Bible study, no mission study class. Today there are three active circles with regular monthly meetings of The Women of the Church. We have a Secretary appointed for all the causes, two Bible study classes and two mission study classes each year.

The work started by this very small group in 1907 took root and from that time until the present our ladies have done a good work.

Especially near and dear to their hearts has been the Foster Falls School. Their faithful, earnest prayers and generous help have carried out the idea of specific Home Mission Service.

(Editor's Note) The history of the First Presbyterian Church was compiled by Mrs. Joe Nick Felts whose family has been closely associated with the church since its organization. If there are errors or omissions, Mrs. Felts would be grateful if they are called to her attention, as an effort is being made to have a permanent record, complete in every detail.)

(This article appeared in The Post Herald, Galax Virginia, Thursday, April 23, 1953)

History of the First Baptist Church

The following was furnished by The Dixon and Garner Families

The organizational meeting of the Baptist Church of Galax was held on April 30, 1905. The work was established in Galax with the assistance of Baptist people in Fries, Pulaski and Wytheville. The original church membership consisted of twenty charter members and Rev. W. L. Richardson was called as pastor. There are no existing written records of church activities from the organization date until January 5, 1907, at which time Rev. W. J. Banks is recorded as pastor. Lost records must tell the story of the beginning of a church building. The minutes of a meeting on April 27, 1907, state that the most important subject before the conference was to complete the church at once." The location of the building was Block 17, lot 2, Oldtown Street. This building still stands and is now occupied by the Friends Church. During these years it was the custom of many churches to call a pastor for only one year, especially in rural areas, as they were unable to support full-lime pastors and this was the case of Galax Baptist Church. On January 2, 1909, Rev. W. E. Lankford was called to succeed Rev. Banks, but there is no record of his acceptance. Among the earliest pastors of the church were Rev. J. I. Spaulding, Rev. Sam N. Hurst, Rev. R. K. Johnson, Rev. E. S. Vaughan, and Rev. C. E. Anderson. Some years found the church without a pastor. Many of the written records from this period are not available.

In January of 1915, Rev. C. E. Anderson was called to be pastor of the church and in February of the same year a committee was appointed to canvas the membership to take subscriptions on his salary. Rev. Anderson was asked to serve a second year as pastor in 1916.

The growth of the congregation is reflected in the appointment of a committee in July, 1926, to make recommendations for a new location and plans for a new church building. In March, 1927, the committee recommended that the new building be erected on Main Street and property was donated by Mr. E. B. Lenox for the new site. . Henry Brown, B. C. Vaughan, and E. B. Lenox served as the building committee and the project was completed in May, 1928, at a cost of $65,000.00. The plaque on the front of the building named the church as the First Baptist Church of Galax, indicating that the name was changed at this time or sometime prior to the new construction.

In January, 1937, Rev. Herbert R. Carlton, of Kenova, West Virginia, was called as pastor. Rev. & Mrs. Carlton moved to Galax, with their two children, a son Herb, Jr., and a daughter Carolyn. Rev. Carlton's ministry was the occasion for many steps forward by the church. In 1938, a Hammond Organ and chimes were given to the church by Mrs. E. B. Lenox in memory of her husband E. B. Lenox. During these years Mrs. Thelma Hampton was music director and Mrs. Gussie Rudolph was organist. In 1940, growth in the church's educational ministries necessitated plans for the construction of an educational building. This building was not to be complete, however, until 1951. In the year 1943, six Life Deacons were appointed: Gene Carico, C. E. Kanode, C. A. Collier, Dr. J. M. Powell, E. M. Lindsey and B. C. Vaughan. The rotating system of deacons was also instituted at this time. Another major step in the church's growth was the employment, in 1945, of its first full-time educational director, Miss Hope Blanchard. First Baptist Church has, from its organization, been evangelistic in nature and mission-oriented in its programs. Rev. Carlton, during his ministry, also served on the Baptist Board of Missions and Education for the Virginia Baptist General Association for two terms, 1942-1945 and 1945-1948.

May, 1946, Mrs. Ruby Porter had a beautiful scene of the Jordon River painted on the back wall of the baptistery.

Mrs. Carlton was very active in the ministry of the church, serving as Superintendent of the Youth Sunday School and Training Union Departments, as well as with all church ministries and activities.

In September, 1947, a mission was formed on the south end of Galax on Highway 89. in October, 1947, the

161

church bought a lot for the mission at the price of $900.00. In May, 1948, funds were transferred for the mission to the newly organized and several letters were granted to persons helping to organize it. On October 19, 1949, the church on Main Street took as its goal the completion of the new educational building by October I, 1950. The new structure was built at a cost of $75,000.00 and was occupied in May of 1951.

In April, 1952, Rev. Carlton submitted his resignation as pastor of First Baptist Church to accept a position as Secretary for Eagle Eyrie, to make plans for construction and holding assemblies.

In November, 1952, the church extended a call to Rev. Robert F. Cochran, Jr., pastor of First Baptist Church, Piedmont, South Carolina, to become the pastor. He accepted and Rev. Cochran, his wife Jo and three Sons came to Galax. Rev. Cochran began his ministry January 11, 1953, and served First Baptist Church of Galax until December, 1957. Some statistics given on his fourth anniversary were: 400 additional members in four years, debt reduced from $86,000.00 to $30,000.00, and church budget increased from $22,000.00 to $67,000.00. The church library was started in 1954, with Harold Stevens elected church librarian. On May 9, 1954, the church voted to purchase the Giersch property next door to its building, consisting of a lot and two buildings, for $80,000.00. The congregation's involvement in missions was expressed again in 1954, as it assisted in the development and constitution of the Calvary Baptist Church in Galax.
On August 21, 1955, First Baptist held its first Homecoming and celebrated its 50th Anniversary.

In January, 1956, the church again reached out in a mission project and worship services were begun in the brickyard section of the city. A very strategic ministry of communication was initiated in 1957 as the church bulletin, called "The First Baptist" was mailed to the home of each member. This weekly mailing is now entitled "The Forerunner" and serves a vital need in our church family life. In June, 1958, the church purchased the C. W. Higgins, Jr., property on Lafayette Street for $25,000.00 to serve as a parsonage.

In November, 1957, Rev. Cochran resigned as pastor to become pastor at Bon Aire Baptist Church, Richmond, VA.

January 15, 1958, Rev. J. P. Gulley was called to serve as interim pastor for three months. Following Rev. Gulley, Dr. Joe Hough, Jr., served as interim pastor until Rev. Claxton Hall, pastor at Pilot Mountain, North Carolina, was called to become full-lime pastor of Galax First Baptist Church. Rev. Hall, along with his wife Alice Lea and small daughter Jeannie (age 3\12), began his ministry August 3, 1958. Their son Dwayne was born after the family came to Galax.

During Rev. Hall's ministry, First Baptist Church reached out again in a mission project. In 1961 the church voted to purchase the property on the corner of Jefferson and Washington Streets for the expansion needs of the church on Main Street.

In September, 1961, the church voted to organize and maintain a mission on Givens Street and provide adequate facilities and personnel. A house on Givens Street was purchased for that purpose.

Rev. Hall's ministry continued until May, 1962.

On August 19, 1962, the church voted to call Rev. James C. Pickens, pastor of West Broadway Baptist Church, Louisville, Kentucky to serve as its pastor. Rev. Pickens, his wife Clarine, and their son, James, came to Galax October 7, 1962, and Rev. Pickens served First Baptist until 1976 and gave leadership to the church during a very strategic period in its life and ministry.

A gift of a piano for the sanctuary as a memorial to Mr. & Mrs. S. R. Dixon was given by the family. Also, a wooden arch was installed above the baptistery in the sanctuary in memory of Mrs. Mae Burge, given by her husband N. F. Burge.

During the ministry of Rev. Pickens, it became evident that additional space was needed for the church to continue to grow and meet the needs of its ministries. A long range planning committee was formed and in 1964 the recommendation was made that the church buy 12.39 acres of land for $28,467.00 on the new Hillsville Highway to be used as the site for a new church plant. The contract was awarded to J. E. Davis & Sons of Galax at the cost or $850,000.00. On August 25, 1968, groundbreaking for the new project was held and the congregation moved to its new facilities in 1970. Dedication services were held on May 16, 1971. A Grandfather clock, built by Rev. Carlton, was placed in the church parlor in memory of his wife, Mrs. Annie Carlton.

Several new staff ministers came to First Baptist during Rev. Pickens' ministry. In 1970, Hilton Moore was employed as youth and education director. The music ministry of the church grew in 1974 as Lanny Johnson was employed as choir director, Mrs. Ruth Winsette as organists, and initiated a program of graded choirs. In 1976, the church employed Richard Rudolph as minister of music. The music ministry took another step forward in September of that same year when a set of hand bells were donated to the church by Mr. C.W. Higgins in memory of his wife, Mrs. Margaret V. Higgins and the hand bell choir program began. Rev. & Mrs. Pickens were very involved in community service while in Galax. Mrs. Clarine Pickens taught at Galax High School and served tirelessly in church, school and community activities. The Pickens' ministry at First Baptist came to an end in March of 1976.

In May, 1977, Dr. Kenneth Hemphill was called to serve as pastor. Dr. Hemphill, his wife Paula and two daughters Kristina (2 years old) and Rachael (3 months), moved to Galax in May, 1977. A number of significant events took place during Dr. Hemphill's ministry. In 1977 a child's playground was "fenced and equipped, a program for senior citizens was started, mother's day out program began and in October a note-burning ceremony was held to signify the early retirement of the church's debt. Also, the Good Samaritan Booth at the annual Fiddlers' Convention was started. The youth lounge of the church was equipped in this same year, thus providing the young people with an excellent facility for learning and recreation.

In 1978, the church purchased a grand piano for the sanctuary and called Miss Cindy Morris as minister of music .Rev Michael Curry was called to serve as associate pastor in April of the same year. A church van was also purchased in 1978. During the 1979 church year, a multi-purpose church bus was purchased. Joe Northcut served during the summer months of this year as music intern. In September of 1980, Cindy Morris resigned to further her education in music and Carolyn Davis was hired as interim music director. During 1980, the church began a homebound tape ministry and installed storm windows to conserve energy expenditures.

February, 1981, Rev. Paul Northern became minister of music. Dr. Hemphill and family left Galax in 1981 to accept pastorate of First Baptist Church in Norfolk, Virginia.

In 1981 Dr. William L. Palmer of Morristown, Tennessee, was called to be the new pastor and he and his wife, Ellen, moved to Galax. In July of the same year, the church council was established to help facilitate better communications and planning among the many ministries and organizations in the church family.

A wonderful addition to the music ministry and worship services of the church was made in 1982, as the congregation installed a Rogers Organ in the sanctuary. A dedication service for the new organ was held on May 2, 1982. Rev. Mike Curry was associate minister, Rev. Paul Northern was the minister of music, Ms. Laura Wright was church organist, and Keith Chapman was guest organist for the dedication.

Two new staff ministers came to First Baptist in 1983. Jerry Malloy was employed as minister of music and Doug Brown as minister of youth and education. During the same year, a memorial board was placed in the church by Mrs. E.J. Richardson. Jr., and Mrs. Pamela Dickerson in memory of their husband and father, E. J.

Richardson.

In 1984, Dr. Palmer resigned his pastorate at First Baptist to become President of Harrison-Chilhowie Baptist Academy in Tennessee.

Dr. Don Reid was called to serve as pastor in 1984. During the years that Dr. Reid was pastor, he emphasized the logo "First Baptist Church, a Sharing Community," the church had adopted a few years before his arrival. He was always showing love, concern, and care for his congregation, the community, and missions.

During his tenure Dr. Reid headed a mission team from First Baptist Church to Southern India, which was a second trip for Dr. Reid, and a third was planned for 1986. Also, a group of about thirty five Galax First Baptist Church members went on a mission trip to Outer Banks.

On March 6, 1988, Dr. Leon H. Hollingsworth, interim pastor, announced that Rev. Carroll Golden would be the new pastor of First Baptist Church starting on Easter Sunday, April 3, 1988. He came to Galax during the week of March 21, 1988, returning to Tennessee to preach until Easter Sunday. Stephen Burnett came as minister of music on August 28, 1988. Bruce Minett, youth and educational minister, left on July 26, 1989. Joe Whisnant came on June 8, 1989, and was hired as youth and educational director.

A Ladies Bible Group was started on October 3, 1988, by Mitzi, our minister's wife and lots of interest was shown. On January 30, 1989, the Bible studies were very well attended by the community with many other churches represented. In 1990, Mitzi organized a Precept Studies by Kay Arthur which was also well attended.

The Baptist Free Medical Clinic opened July II, 1992. This service to the community was a dream of Dr. Ohlen Wilson (originally from the Galax area) to come back home and help those in need. Dr. Wilson was organizer and director, being assisted by his wife, Martha, a registered nurse.

The Baptist Free Medical Clinic was located in the east wing of the First Baptist Church, Galax, Virginia, and functioned as a free clinic. Volunteers from the community, including physicians, nurses, and W.M.U. members, worked in the clinic. It was a non-profit corporation, composed of nine members of the church and Dr. Robert Pryor was chairman. Mrs. Glennis Morris was secretary and manager. The Baptist Free Medical Clinic is functioning today as "a clinic without walls," which means volunteer doctors accept patients, who qualify as to need, in their offices.

Dr. Golden and his wife, Mitzi, started many programs to further our church's ministries. In December, 1995, Dr. Carroll Golden resigned as pastor of First Baptist Church and they are now (2004) serving as missionaries in Costa Rica.

1996 -Stephen Burnette, minister of music, resigned. John Garner served as interim until Chris Bridges became minister of music in the June of 1999.

Dr. Lawrence Childs, a retired minister residing in Hillsville, Virginia, was called in July, 1996, to serve as interim pastor and served until December, 1997. Dr. Childs was not only a retired minister, but had served as Director of Churches in Missions, Charlotte, North Carolina, and had served in several churches as interim before coming to Galax.

Dr. Childs was a very effective preacher, preaching sermons on diversity, love for each other, harmony. compassion, and forgiveness. During his tenure as interim Betsy Rector Wright was the first lady to be ordained to the ministry on August 30, 1997. On July 13, 1997, Thomasine Calloway Lemons was the first lady to be ordained as deacon in the First Baptist Church of Galax, Virginia.

Rev. Slayton accepted the call to become pastor on October 29, 1997. Rev. Slayton, his wife Helen, and son Jonathan came to us from Green Run Baptist Church in Virginia Beach, Virginia.

In 1996 a brick entrance way to the church was built, being donated by Mrs. Ruby M. Lindamood in memory of her parents, Roby and Pearl Mabe.

During 1999 a bus ministry began. The church vans brought children (primarily Hispanic) living in the area to Sunday School and church and to Wednesday evening activities. A Hispanic Research Committee was organized to consider the possibility of employing a full time Hispanic Pastor at First Baptist Church. Rev. Ricardo Alvarado was called to this position, October, 2000. January 1, 2001, Rev. Alvarado and his wife, Maria, and three children, Ricardo, Jr., Eugenia, and Rebecca, moved to Galax from Costa Rica.

Rev. Slayton accepted a call from Powhatan Baptist Church in the fall of 2001. He stated that he and Helen wished to be closer to their aging parents and be available to help with their care.

Rev. Gene Strickland, his wife Renee, and two daughters Jeona and Rachel, moved to Galax in December, 2002, and Rev. Strickland began his ministry as Senior Pastor of Galax First Baptist Church on January 12, 2003.

During the two years of this ministry he has played an important role in the many different church, school, and community activities, including the Galax Ministerial Association, the New River Baptist Association, and Southern Baptist Convention, organizing and conducting mission trips to Mexico and to Bluefield College to refurbish a building to be used for a missionary in residence program.

With Rev. Strickland's emphasis on evangelism the ROCC ministry (Reaching Our Community for Christ) was formed. This ministry has held many events, such as: honoring departing and returning reserve service units, and Friday night in-house Billy Graham movies for the community.

As Rev. Strickland continues his ministry at Galax First Baptist Church we look forward to future spiritual growth.

First Baptist Church on North Main Street

Memories by Duane E. Ward Sr. of the First Methodist Church

(shared during the 100th birthday celebration of the First Methodist Church)

One thing I want to get straight is that I am not the oldest member of this church. I noticed that there are three of them who are still members here who joined about 4 years after I did and I joined in 1920. I went to see two of them yesterday, Nita Sue Carico and Irene Nuckolls Alderman. I didn't get to see the other one.

There has been a lot of changes that have taken place since that period of time... a lot of things that we have to get used to as we go along. I remember Galax way back and I will be able to tell you some things that took place then that I remember. Some may be repetitious.

I know that when I was first growing up and in the first maps I saw, there was no Galax listed. There were three places listed in this vicinity at that time. There was Chestnut Yard, Old Town and Ward's Mill. Now Ward's Mill was located just beyond Milo Cockerham's. You know where he lives in the country here. My father and his two brothers were here at the first sale of property in Galax. So I am an old-timer and I have a cousin back here (sitting in a pew in the church) who is an old-timer too. They bought property here and we have been here ever since, so we have seen a lot come and go. Back in those days there was a lot of activity in Galax, (you wouldn't call it activity), but there used to be a string of wagons come into Galax from the South side Monday through Friday. Some were drawn by horses, some by mules and some by oxen and they were carrying cross-ties. I know as kids we used to get on a coupling pole and ride out to the edge of town and get on another one coming in. We spent a lot of time going back and forth.

Things have moved along pretty fast since that period of time. We went through a lot of different things that have taken place since then. We had a lot of Christian churches in Galax at that time, and most of them are still here today. In addition to that, the churches all got together and built what we called a Tabernacle which was a wooden building. They built it at the foot of the Galax school hill. I don't know how many people it would seat; probably 100-125 people. No floor, sawdust on the ground and homemade benches. But all the churches together would get the services together and get a man come in to preach and lead the music and it was a very active situation that took place in the summertime. They worked together. But they used it for other activities too as they had a variety of shows and boxing events. It was a very active place for the people in the town, but eventually the building was torn down.

Going back to the building of the church here, I remember well the old church was located right where this one is today. There is a picture of it here in the Annex. That church was right where this one is located now. It had a pipe organ; I guess the only pipe organ they had ever had in Galax at that time. Someone had to pump it in order to get it to operate. There used to be a man who sat right next to the preacher and when they got ready to sing songs, he would go in the back and pump the organ. But it was very effective. At that time we had two stoves for heaters. And during that time it was decided to put in a heating system and they started digging back behind the choir directory and the back of the church fell in. I read where someone was killed during this, but I don't remember that phase of it. They started on it and it got so bad that they decided they would have to tear the church down. So when they did, they built this building we have now and since that time we have had an awful lot of additions. But, we haven't had the people to fill them up. Seems like a lot of other things we overbuilt. Because, at one time, I can well remember here the men's class had 125 people here for our Sunday session. Now, if you go back and look at your membership today you see this and wonder what has happened. But that is what was going on at that time.

M.E.Church South, Galax Va.

I always like to come here and I like to hear Frances Crowder sing. She sings my favorite song, "Life's Railway to Heaven." It was sung at my Grandfather's funeral, my father's and I want it. And she does a good job.

A lot of things happened in Galax during that time. One thing that was very active here was the Galax Fair. People used to come here in covered wagons and would sleep in their wagons for a week's time and attend the fair. They had a carnival that would come in here by rail. They had horse racing and a lot of activities for it. And the ones of us that remember the time, remember that it was always in September and everything was dusty because there was no pavement at that time. It was something to look forward to.

Another thing that happened during that time that is very clear in my memory was that the first automobile I saw was a Ford car. I don't know what model it was but it had to be in the early 20's. It had a copper type radiator and had headlights that had to be lit by hand and a horn on the side that you had to mash. At that time if you got to church or anywhere else, you walked. You didn't have any parking problem at all. There were a few other automobiles in town at that time, but that is the one I remember. It belonged to Mr. M. T. Blessing. He had a home right in front where you go into the Fairgrounds now. And his wife, I remember when his wife, who was a member of this church, passed away. You've been told this before, but they tolled the bell for her. They would toll the bell the number of tolls for the age of the person involved. And if you knew somebody who had been sick you knew pretty well who passed away. I don't know when they quit that but I remember very well when that was going on here.

Another thing that was going on in Galax was Revival meetings in addition to what they had in the Tabernacle. I can remember in this church where some stranger to us would come in here to hold a Revival meeting. This church was filled to capacity and they would put loud speakers in the basement to take care of the crowd. You don't hear of that anymore, do you?

When they built the new church they went in debt like the Methodist always do and it took some time to get much of a headway to pay it off. But, so far along in the deal, Mr. Taylor Vaughan made the church a proposition. Whatever you raise to pay on this debt, I will match it. It sounded like a good proposition. Well, Mr. Messer (John A. Messer, Sr.) had moved to Galax at that time and was a member of this church. He made a counter-proposition. He told the church whatever you get I'll match that and then Mr. Vaughan can match both of them. So they paid the debt off. There has been a lot of building take place since that time. You have a lot of extra rooms and I don't know whether you are in debt now or not, but I know the Methodist like to stay that way.

167

First Methodist Church before Sunday room classes built.

We had a lot of people involved in the church here that a lot of people remember did a lot to build it up. I remember Aunt Sally Sutherland, Aunt Laura Jackson, Beulah Cox and Ruby Branscome. And I know there are lots of others. I can remember in those days that Mrs. Paul Kapp was my Sunday school teacher. Each Christmas she would have the whole class come to her home for Sunday dinner, which we all enjoyed very much. But, there are a lot of people spent a lot of time working with a bunch of ornery kids to try to keep us going.

I can remember what was the largest funeral ever held in this church. There was a strike in West Virginia and the Felts-Baldwin Detective Agency was hired to protect the mine property. A lot of people from here went out to help restore order. Three people from here were killed: T. L. Felts' two brothers and Mr. Hagens, a local policeman. The church here was before this building and this funeral brought in a big crowd. The church was full inside and packed all the way around the outside. This was the largest funeral attendance at this church that I have ever seen and I have attended a lot of funerals here.

I know that the church has had quite a bit of influence in this community. I know that my Father and his brothers were here at Galax at the first sale and bought lots and built homes on them and have been (at least part of them) all the way through the life of the church. I am in the second generation and have part of the third generation here and more of them coming. So, we have been very much involved in this church and have received lots of benefits from it.

We have had a lot of good preachers here. I remember Preacher Bunts (I guess he probably served here two different terms) and he was a fine minister. During the time he spent here his wife passed away and she was to be buried at Emory and Henry College at their cemetery. There was quite a bunch of people that went from here to there for the funeral and that was in the 20's. I remember driving with my Father and Mother to this funeral. We had to cross Jackson's Ferry to get there and Mr. Jackson owned and operated that Ferry and knew what was going on, so all the cars that were going to the funeral were taken across the river, all going over and coming back, free of charge; which was a nice gesture from him. There were a lot of people involved in it.

I don't know how much I can add to what you've already been told about it, but I do know that the church has had quite an influence in the lives of the people here and has done a world of good and has been very important to this community. I'm glad to see it going along as well as it is. I think you have right now one of the best newsletters you send out and the most informative that we have had for a long time. I go to a Methodist Church in Florida, but I'm still quite interested in this church and what is within this church. It is my pleasure to be here this morning and I am more than anxious to hear this good song form Frances Crowder who is going to sing my favorite song.

Note: Duane Emery Ward Sr. was the son of Marvin Marville Ward and Mary Maude Cox Ward. He was born on 28 August 1913 and passed away on 17 April 2006.

GALAX FIRST CHRISTIAN CHURCH CELEBRATES 100 YEARS

THE 100-YEAR HISTORY OF FIRST CHRISTIAN CHURCH OF GALAX IS TIGHTLY ENTWINED WITH THAT OF THE CITY ITSELF.
GALAX JUST CELEBRATED ITS CENTENNIAL IN 2006, AND THE CHURCH IS GETTING READY TO HONOR THAT SAME MILESTONE THIS WEEKEND.
ONE OF GALAX'S FOUNDERS, T.L. FELTS, WAS INTEGRAL IN PROVIDING A HOME FOR THE DISCIPLES OF CHRIST CONGREGATION IN THE EARLY 20TH CENTURY.

B.F. Callaway — Galax's first mayor — was the first man to preach from the pulpit in 1909, though not as the church's first official pastor.

State Sen. S. Floyd Landreth was an influential member of the church and Galax community.
"Galax and this church kind of grew up side-by-side," said pastor Casey McKenna. "It's amazing to think that this church was formed before the first cars. So much has happened in the past century, and the church has stood through all that."
First Christian is planning a two-day celebration of its rich history this weekend, with visits from pastors past, music, food and fellowship.

McKenna said the church members have pulled together to get things ready and give the building off Jefferson Street a facelift.

This photo shows the Congregation of First Christen Church of Galax in the 1920s, standing outside the original church building. This church was on N Main street, where the parking lot of Wachovia Bank is now located.

Ground was broken for this church in 1907 and the Church opened in 1908

Getting Started

According to a history prepared for the centennial, First Christian Church of Galax was born around the time the town first took off as a major trading stop on the Norfolk & Western Railroad.
During a meeting of Christian Church delegates in 1904, those attending talked about how the Galax community was growing by leaps and bounds and had 25 Disciples of Christ members living there.
The delegation decided then to start a new congregation in Galax.

A committee was chosen, comprised of J.H. Cooley, S.C. Edwards and William Gallimore, and undertook forming the new church. In 1905, T.L. Felts bought a lot at the corner of Main and Washington streets in downtown Galax for the church for $100. Ground was broken in 1907, and the church was completed around 1910.

Felts bought the original bell from a church in Crockett. Alec Redd took a wagon to pick it up, and it took two days to make the trip. It is the only bell ever used by First Christian Church, and was moved to the current church when it opened in 1957.

C.W. Martin rang the bell for many years, in both the old and new churches.
The site of the original church on North Main is now Wachovia Bank, next to Twin County Tire.
Mayor Callaway was a trustee and elder of the church during its formation. He was followed briefly by Rev. Burnette — first name unknown — and then by the first official pastor, Conley Greer. He served from 1911 to 13.

The next pastors were S.P. Miller (1913-17), Arthur Wake (1918-20) and Gray Russell (1920).

Hard Times & Revival
In 1920, the church fell on hard times and closed, according to a history written in 1974 by late church member Ruth Cooper.
After a city-wide revival in 1922, Cooper said the remaining Disciples of Christ members — about 25 people — began a drive to reopen their church.

That November, First Christian Church reorganized and called E. Roy Gentry as its new pastor. Cooper said the church flourished under his guidance.
Gentry was followed by Warren Baldwin (1924-26) and A. C. Meadows (1926-42).
During Meadows' term as pastor, the church grew and was renovated to make room for the growing congregation. During this time, the parsonage was built and there was remodeling to add classrooms.
W.P. Taylor served as pastor from 1945 to 52. During this time, the church bought its first organ and the idea of building a new church sprang up.
McKenna said that in the 1950s, the church experienced another surge in membership. "There was a point that if another person had joined, they'd have had to knock down a wall to make room."
Cooper wrote that the next pastor, R.A. Ferguson (1952-54), made the push the church needed to start building a new facility.

Ground was broken for the new church off Jefferson Street on April 5, 1953.
She said several members loaned money for the new building.
The next pastor, Dr. H.O. Wilson (1954-57), was there for the dedication of the new building in November 1957.

That same year, First Christian hosted a state convention.
Wilson helped the women of the church change from the Ladies Aid & Missionary Society to the Christian Women's Fellowship, which is still active.

Pastor William E. Cunningham (1958-66) helped the church grow in membership once again.
Under the direction of C. Oral Lowe (1967-75), the pastor's children donated 100 hymnals to the church. A house was purchased and the property used for a new parking lot.

The sanctuary and pews were refurbished and special Crimson ornaments were made for the sanctuary Christmas tree under the supervision of pastor Dr. Larry Patterson (1976-80).

Robert C. Johnson (1984-90) came to First Christian after several interim pastors. During this time, the church started a clown ministry and puppet ministry for children.

The church also bought adjacent property for future expansion.
Randy L. Johnson was pastor during 1990-99. The picnic shelter was built during his tenure, the fellowship hall was refurbished, church offices were relocated and the church began planning for an elevator.
After interim pastor Jim Compton, Carl Bean served as pastor in 2000-06. He helped start the food bank and oversaw the elevator installation and renovations to the kitchen.

The Church Today
McKenna has served as pastor since 2006, and one of his biggest contributions has been preparing for this year's centennial.
First Christian has about 130 members on the books today.

The pastor was pleased to find that his new church has always been dedicated to preserving its history. "We've held on to so many things for people to see, all the way back to the original church."
Church member Hilda Walters said First Christian has preserved artifacts and archives of its history in a heritage room upstairs behind the sanctuary.

In the center of the museum-like room stand the original chairs and communion table from the first church.
Walters said they will be taken down to the sanctuary for the centennial services this weekend.
"We have communion every Sunday," she said. "It's a central part of our worship service."
A glass display holds copies of "Famous Recipes from Old Virginia" cookbooks that have been sold by the church's Christian Women's Fellowship since 1915.

Draped over a wooden rack is a nearly century-old quilt a project of the early church's youth group. They sold quilt squares for 10 cents apiece to raise money.
(A note says that T.L. Felts gave a whole dollar for his square.)

Galax First Christian Church is active in the community. On Mondays at 6 p.m., it hosts a "soul feed" program, which is a food bank and short worship service.
"We have 10 people, up to 75," Walters said.

At Thanksgiving, the church gets names of needy families from the Department of Social Services and members deliver hot meals to them. Last year, the church delivered 200 meals.

First Christian offers classrooms for community music classes, holds a "songfest" musical event for local churches and is host church for the annual Holy Week services in Galax that bring several congregations together.

The church's charitable work includes hosting parties for residents of the Southwest Virginia Training Center and supporting Ronald McDonald Houses in Roanoke and Winston-Salem, N.C.
McKenna said the centennial celebration puts things in perspective.

"This church has been serving and caring for the community for 100 years. Imagine where the spirit is going to take us in the next 100 years."

Brian Funk, Staff Writer, Gazette. September 27, 2007

Galax Industry

By Ottie Padgett

By 1914, Galax had a Board of Trade, and in a brochure prepared by Wightman D. Roberts, the board said then it was seeking industry and population growth.
Also, the board claimed the title for Galax as the "largest 10year-old town in Virginia. "

"Galax is, in this year of 1914, ten years old with a population of 2,500. It is not an old southern town rejuvenated, but an out and out, spic and span, brand new and flourishing young city spreading in all directions upon the easy slopes of her Blue Ridge counties of Grayson and Carroll in Southern Virginia. It is just a beautiful little city, that's what it is - 2,500 feet up in the matchless blue skies of the Blue Ridge Mountains, which with many a curve and undulation, trail away in billowy perspectives into the "Old North State (North Carolina)," Roberts wrote.

The brochure went on to say Galax is "a direct product of the yield of these two rich, but sparsely populated, counties ... It is the market place and shipping point for both, situated on the North Carolina Extension of the Norfolk & Western Railroad, 52 miles south of Pulaski, and 110 miles from Roanoke, Virginia. It also serves in the same capacity for the bordering counties of Alleghany and Ashe in North Carolina.

Commercial Records

"The gross amount of this commerce is shown concretely by the records of the railroad's tonnage at Galax. For July 1914, the outgoing freight amounted to 19,427,777 pounds, while the receipts (incoming freight) amounted to 3,875,414 pounds."

As far back as 1914, the Galax Board of Trade recognized the value of homegrown products such as "fine crops of hay, corn, oats, buckwheat and vegetables ... and fine forests of poplar, oak, pine, hickory, ash and chestnut, which have brought into being the flourishing woodworking plants at Galax and assure them many years of successful operation."

Galax, by 1915; according to the brochure was "an important manufacturing town," with a furniture factory whose products were distributed throughout the United States and abroad; three planing and interior finish mills, two flooring mills, a chair factory and a bottling plant.

The late H. Prince Burnett, who later became a prominent lawyer and businessman, was editor of the GALAX POSTHERALD (one of the newspapers from which The Gazette evolved) in 1914. His contribution to the brochure was a story titled "Ideal Manufacturing Conditions."

In it, Burnett said, "After a manufacturer has secured a suitable location, the great question - the greatest of all items in the debit column is the cost of production, and this item, to a great extent - resolves itself into the cost of labor.

"As to the location, don't let that worry you. The citizens of Galax have bought sites for two industries during the present year - one for a chair factory, which is now in operation, and one for a large merchant mill, which is nearing completion. These two industries represent an expenditure by the owners of approximately $40,000.

"If you are seeking a location for a sound manufacturing proposition and will come to Galax, you can omit the building site from your estimated cost of plant and equipment. This will be donated by the citizens. There are acres and acres of perfectly level building sites fronting on the Norfolk & Western Railway in the town Galax.

"As to the cost of labor, do not believe that there is another section in the United States that can compete with us. Naturally you will enquire, is the labor of an inferior grade, or do you expect to underpay them? Neither! You would have to travel far to find a stronger, a straighter and sturdier people than found in Carroll and Grayson counties.

"Galax, which is on the border of these two counties, is composed mainly of their people. Most of its people who work in the factories own small farms in one or the other of the two counties, and they can raise for themselves nearly everything consumed at their tables which they would otherwise have to buy; and those who are not thus fortunate can buy the necessities of life at a savings of at least 20 percent under prices in the larger cities. This is due to the fact that Galax is the center of a great agricultural and fruit growing district and is the largest produce market of any town its size in the state, if not the largest in the south, and its people can buy from the producer and thus save the middleman's profit. Many own their homes, and clean and comfortable cottages, including a garden, can be rented at prices ranging at from $5 to $10 per month.

"These facts make it possible for our people to work for you at this great saving on your cost of production, and at the same time they will have lived better and will have saved more than their less fortunate brothers who do not have the advantages which I have enumerated above.

Clean and Wholesome

"The employer of labor demands that his employees shall lead clean and wholesome lives, and one of the greatest questions confronting him today is the best solution to this perplexing problem. The solution is, come to Galax-not only for the sake of yourselves and families for reasons explained elsewhere in this booklet, but where you can employ young men and women who are of strong mind and body; men and women who are not contaminated by the vices of the city; men and women who can give the service you have the right to demand and who will give you the value received for your payroll. "

The caption above the pictures of the Galax Board of Trade in the 1914 brochure is "Galax - where all your constructive work will yield it's just compensation."

Board of Trade members in 1914 were Thomas L. Felts, president of The People's State Bank; Charles Waugh, manager of J. B. Waugh & Son; E. W. Dodd, manager of Galax Furniture and Lumber Co.; R. J. Cornett, cashier of The People's State Bank and Board of Trade secretary; Capt. J. B. Waugh, president of The First National Bank of Galax and president of the Board of Trade; C. A. Collier, cashier of The First National Bank; B. D. Beamer, the town of Galax's treasurer and recorder and manage of Dalton Produce Co.; D. A. Robertson, mayor of Galax and manager of Galax Buggy Co.; and Prof. G. F. Carr, superintendent of Galax Public Schools.

(Editor's note: The brochure, from which the above information was gleaned, was made available to The Gazette by Mrs. Rufus Beamer, Rt. 1 Fancy Gap. The Gazette is grateful to Mrs. Beamer for her contribution. She said the brochure's original owner was R. L. Jenkins a relative. Interestingly enough, the brochure listed the 1910 populations at 775 for Galax, 1,775 for Fries, 431 for Troutdale, approximately 200 for Independence, and 288 for Hillsville.)

Blair Village

Before there was a Galax, there had been a settlement a mile north on Chestnut Creek for more than 100 years that was named for John Blair, who built a forge there about 1770. It had developed into a "small, flourishing trading center" by 1900.

Advertisements in the "Blair Enterprise," indicated some of the business establishments there by May 25, 1904, were. Blair Hardware Co., J. B. Waugh & Son, Sunnyside Inn across from the Norfolk & Western Railway depot (Mrs. J. H. Capp, proprietor), and Crystal Drug Co.

The community is now known as Cliffview. As far back as 1902, Cliffview was highlighted by the stately mansion, "Cliffside," constructed in 1902 by State Senator Thomas L. Felts for his wife, Ethel Houseman Felts. At one time; during an existence of a post office, the postal address of the office's service area was "Ethelfelts." Cliffside is now the home of Mr. and Mrs. Hubert S. White Jr.

Because Blair was not geographically located to allow for future expansion and growth, and because Chestnut Yards, located another two miles downstream on Chestnut Creek was so inaccessible to reach by roads, people induced Norfolk & Western (N&W) to extend its line to the present site of the city of Galax.

After the railroad was extended in 1904 to Bonaparte's Anderson's Bottom, most of Blair's businessmen followed. A year later, the town of Galax was chartered by the Virginia General Assembly.

No one seems to be certain why the young settlement, with the advent of the railroad extension from Blair, was first called Bonaparte. The named was short lived, however. Soon after the railroad line was extended, the name was changed to Galax to honor the Galax plant which grows best in a 75-mile stretch of mountainous terrain from Galax, Va. to Spruce Pine, N.C. The plant has commercial value and is used in the manufacture of wreaths and floral arrangements. Ironically, Galax leaves were the first express freight to be shipped over the new railroad line extension.

Move to Galax

Dr. J. W. Bolen was the first to move his business into Galax. He moved his office, or little drug store, from Blair without dismantling it. Three days were required to move it because roads had to be widened and holes along the way filled.
Next came F. H. Martin with his harness shop. Martin was followed from Blair by Blair Hardware, which became Galax Hardware Co.; J. B. Waugh & Son (later Waugh's Department Store), Blair Grocery Co., and Blair Bank (later the People's State Bank).

Galax quickly became an important shipping point for the N&W. Wagons pulled by oxen, horses and mules loaded with crossties for railroad construction and tanbark, needed for its chemical qualities, could be seen headed for the lumber yards in Galax. Also coming in for export by rail were herds of cattle and flocks of sheep and turkeys driven by dogs accompanied by their masters on horseback.

Barrels of berries, chestnuts and chinquapins were brought to the Galax depot for shipment. Much of the area's produce was taken to a cannery located , about where the Vaughan-Bassett Furniture plant is now located.

Manufacturing began in the town soon after the arrival of the railroad extension from Blair. Captain J. B. Waugh, S. E. Wilkerson and Creed Hanks established a furniture factory with the idea of exporting the area's plentiful forest products into finished commercial items instead of rough crossties and lumber. Their factory was located where the Wonderknit Corporation's plant on Virginia Street now stands. Fire destroyed the young business in 1907 and it was never rebuilt. (*editor's note: it was rebuilt*)

Other early industries of the town that furnished employment included a handle factory, operated by W. P. Swartz for the manufacture of ax, pick and mattock handles; a chair factory for the manufacture of split-bottom chairs, and a flour mill, established by Charles Bryant and E. F. Perkins.

The flour mill was later operated by the late Fred Adams. It is no longer operated as a flour mill; however the building still stands on East Oldtown Street and is used by Guynn Enterprises in connection with its business operations as a retail outlet.

With the advent of the railroad extension, salesmen, commonly referred to as "drummers," began to come into Galax. C. H. South built a row of flats on the corner of Main and Oldtown Streets to accommodate them.

Many factors induced the industrial and commercial growth of Galax. Not to be excluded are the influences of local government and the environments of its churches and public education systems.

After WWI

Galax experienced no large scale industrial growth until after World War I. Soon after the conflict, Mayor J. F. Vass and other civic leaders met with John D. Bassett and Bunyan C. "B.C." Vaughan, noted industrialists from Henry County, who were engaged in the manufacture of furniture, and the result of that meeting was the establishment of the Vaughan-Bassett Furniture Company. B. C. Vaughan came to Galax as president of the newly formed company.

His brother, Taylor G. Vaughan, a World War I officer, was placed in charge of sales. E. B. Lennox was production manager and Thomas B. Stanley, who later became governor of Virginia and a 5th District Congressman , was secretary-treasurer. The new business, which began production in 1919, prospered.
It continues to operate, although its Galax plant burned in February 1951 and was rebuilt a year later.

B. C. Vaughan could very well be considered the father of Galax's furniture industry.

Taylor G. Vaughan proposed the organization of a new furniture factory in 1923. Two years later, through local stock subscriptions, it became a reality. From the Vaughan Furniture plant, the business grew into a multi-factory corporation now headed by his sons, George Vaughan and John Vaughan.

J. V. Webb approached Galax businessmen about forming yet another furniture plant. The group made a direct contribution of $5,000 toward the enterprise, and in 1924 Webb Furniture Co. began business. It continues to operate and provides employment for scores of persons at two plants.

Galax Furniture Co., Inc. was established in 1925 by C. L. Smith. John Messer Sr. gained control of the corporation in 1943 and merged it with Webb Furniture.

Messer came to Galax in 1927 and started a mirror plant in a shed. From it evolved a string of manufacturing investments, some of which remained in Galax.

The textile industry in Galax began when a High Point, N.C. resident with the surname of Robbins agreed to start a hosiery mill provided Galax citizens would underwrite the purchase of stock equal to one-third of initial investment. The money was "dug up" and J. T. Pollard was sent into the area to organize The Galax Knitting Co. The plant, which began operations in 1924, was located where the Wonderknit's plant is now operating.

Carnation Plant

Probably no other plant opening in Galax caused as much public attention as the opening of Carnation's milk processing plant on May 10, 1937. Its opening was designated as "COW Day." The featured speaker was Virginia Governor George C. Perry of Russell County. Other invited guests for the grand opening included the area's FFA members and their faculty sponsors. One of the FFA members who attended the grand opening was Wayne Larrowe of the Woodlawn High School Chapter in Carroll County. Larrowe was the plant's last superintendent. It was closed about five years ago.

(Editor's note: Should anyone desire more information on the plant's opening, he or she need only to contact Bill Creasy, a Gladeville community resident in Carroll County. Professor Creasy, now 93, was Woodlawn chapter's FFA advisor then. Creasy was instrumental in getting Carnation to locate in Galax and sponsor a subsequent dairy-breeding program in the area for FFA members.)

Probably no other endeavor contributed to the improvements of economic conditions of farmers in Carroll and Grayson counties, as well as adjacent counties, as did the establishment of the Carnation milk processing plant.

Burlington Industries opened its Galax Weaving Plant in 1937. The plant has expanded substantially since then.

Then there was Sawyers Furniture Co., established in 1945 by C. F. Sawyer. It survived until about a decade ago.

Harris-Marshall Hosiery Mills, Inc. began operations in Galax in 1945.

About 1946, Ross Penry came to Galax from Martinsville and joined with Hubert White Sr., Waldo Price and others in forming The Old Dominion Knitting Co. The venture developed into the Penry Manufacturing Co.

Dixon Lumber Co. evolved from a sawmill business in the early 1920s, owned by S. R. Dixon and approximately six employees.

W. K. Early & Co., Inc., now a Bailey Lumber Co. outlet, was one of Galax's oldest businesses. It was established in 1906, perhaps earlier.

There are other manufacturing and commercial enterprises established in Galax that have contributed to the city's growth. Many of them developed and established employment sites since World War II. To identify them, without overlooking some, would be extremely difficult.

The rapid industrial and commercial development has brought greater employment and prosperity to the entire area. Shopping centers in Galax have sprung up during the past 15 years. Much of this growth could not have taken place without the efforts of those along the way during the past 75 years who desired the town, and later the city, to grow. Galax's growth didn't just happen. It grew because someone wanted it to grow.

To The Future

Frank M. Heaster wrote in the 1956 Galax souvenir booklet these words: "So until the 100th anniversary rolls around, I would wish for all Galax, present and past, residents 50 more years of happiness and prosperity, and challenge the youngsters of today to make the 100th anniversary a mountain compared to the molehill of this celebration of 1956.

"What the future of Galax, the nation, and the world holds cannot be seen. As Omar Khayyam in the Rubaiyat wrote ... 'There was the Door to which I found no key; There was the Veil through which I could not see.' Perhaps the future is as Pinero wrote ... 'only the past entered through another gate.'

.. If that is true, surely the year 2006, the 100th year of the City's life, will find Galax exceedingly more prosperous, and, I hope, as friendly, as neighborly, and as warm-hearted as it is in this year, 1956."

The following is an industrial directory of the Galax area, taken from the Virginia Division of Industrial Directory and supplied by the Chamber of Commerce in 1981:

American Mirror Company, Inc., E. Stuart Dr., Thomas H. Morris, Chairman of the Board; Frank E. Morris, President.
Cardinal Stone Company, Rt. 2, Sam T. Brown Jr., Owner.

Chestnut Creek Corporation, Shaw Street, John J. Nunn, President.

Commonwealth Finishing Corp., 204 Shaw Street, John Morris, President.

Consolidated Glass and Mirror Corp.,. Edmonds Road, Bobby N. Frost, President.

Dixon Lumber Company, 152 Boyer Road, Glenn Dixon, President.

Encore Furniture Industries, Rt. 2, William Archer, President.

The Gazette, 108 West Stuart Drive, Robert S. Tucker, Gen. Mgr.

Galax Apparel Corp., Shaw Street, Ted Hale, Plant Manager.

Galax Weaving Plant, East Oldtown Street, Robert Sills, Plant Manager.

Gazette Press, Inc., 510 South Main Street, Roy B. Lineberry, President.

Hanes Corp. Knitwear Division, 1002 Glendale Road, Mackey McDonald, Director of Manufacturing.

K and W Machine Products, Route 4, Bob Kegley, Owner.

Lindeman Corporation, East Stuart Drive, Ronnie Sikes, Manager.

Maurice Vaughan Furniture Company, Hillsville Hwy., F. Maurice Vaughan, President.

New Galax Mirror Corporation, East Grayson Street, Edward G. Burcham, President.

Patton Ready Mix Concrete, Inc., 115 Railroad Avenue, Joseph L. Patton, Manager.

Penry Manufacturing Company, Inc., Valley Street, Cecil Mashburn, Manager.

SAMCO, 206 Carroll Street, Hugh Sample, Owner

Vaughan Furniture Company, Inc., Railroad Avenue, John B. Vaughan, President.

B. C. Vaughan Furniture Company, Bill Kinney, Superintendent.

Vaughan-Bassett Furniture Company, Railroad Avenue, C. W. Higgins Jr., President.

Webb Furniture Corporation, Railroad Avenue, D. E. Ward Jr., President.

Wonderknit Corporation, 206 Virginia Street, Tony Patti, Plant Manager.

75th Anniversary Edition The Galax Gazette1906-1981

By Ottie Padgett

Pioneers, Ghosts, Bonaparte and Galax

By Ed Cox

One of the earliest settlers of this area was Flower Swift, who settled and built his cabin near the present camp of the Kiwanis Club camp on New River, west of Oldtown, and his land extended up to the present town of Oldtown.

One of his daughters married Major George Currin, who had migrated from North Carolina and he purchased a tract of land off the Buchanan survey, which included all the land now where the City of Galax is located.

He built his home on the lot where Dr. Virgil Cox's house now stands and raised his family. One of his daughters married Thompson Roberts, who had come from North Carolina, and they in turn became the owner of the farm of his father-in-law, who also raised a large family at the old home place.

His youngest son, Thomas F. Roberts, owned the home place when the Railway was extended up to its present site and the town of Galax was started.

The country surrounding Galax was settled principally by people of the Quaker faith, a majority of them coming up across the Blue Ridge from North Carolina after the battle of the Alamance in 1771 , and the only wagon road across the mountain at that time was the Good Spur Gap road that reached the summit of the mountain at the old Morris Cemetery, near the present Fancy Gap Methodist Church, This road, being the first built, extended north, passing near Good Hope church and on by the present Poor Farm in Carroll County and on north crossing the river at or near Jackson's Ferry and on connecting with the road leading east to west at Fort Chiswell in Wythe County.

It was stated that the stage coaches were used over this road when the weather would permit; it is also stated that a couple of yoke of oxen were kept at the foot of the mountain to assist the emigrants up and over the mountain.

A little later a road branched off this road near the Poor Farm and extended west through Grayson county to the Washington county line. This was perhaps the first through-road built through the county and this road passed through the present city of Galax, crossing the creek near the present bridge on Route 58, following closely the present Stuart Drive, around the town and on out through West Galax, crossing Meadow Creek near Reavistown, on through Baywood, Cox's ford on New River, over Brush Mountain and on west to Washington county.

After Grayson county was cut off from Wythe county about 1792, other roads crossing the mountain were built, one from Pipers Gap to the County Seat of Grayson which was located at the present town of Oldtown, this road followed closely the present Piper's Gap Highway and crossed Chestnut Creek near the present Carroll Furniture plant and followed on the creek bank down to the present filtering plant, then crossing the hill passing in front of Brother Anderson's and the A. C. Painter home and West Galax on to Oldtown.

Also a road was established across the Low Gap and on through the Fairview section to Oldtown. Earlier than the two last mentioned, a trail led from the mountain across the Coal Creek and Wards Mill Creek valleys and joined up with the road going west at the present Country Club. Chestnut Yards was so inaccessible to reach by roads that it did not help the surrounding country very much; finally the people induced the N&W to extend their trains up to Blair where it would be more accessible to wagon traffic but the people soon realized that there was not sufficient room to accommodate the business that had begun to pour in from all directions, whereupon they induced the N & W to extend the line up to the present site of the City of Galax.

J. P. Carico, a native of Stevens Creek community and a trader of horses and mules in the South, was perhaps the most successful promoter of enterprises this section has produced. While staying in Winston-Salem on a trip south with horses, he contacted Colonel Fries, who was a successful textile manufacturer, and induced him to build a mill.

After he had helped establish this industry at Fries, and the N & W had agreed to extend their Railway up to the present City of Galax, he, along with J. B. Waugh and perhaps others formed a land company and purchased all the land between the Creek and the present highway on the west side of the creek up to the Anderson property, and proceeded to lay out the town.

They secured an engineer from Lynchburg, Mr. DeMot, to whom was given the task of laying out the town which was destined to grow to a city of the second class in a period of fifty years.

'Good Ground Goin' to Waste!'

When the task of laying out the town was finished, a day was set for the opening of lot sales and a large crowd gathered for this opening sale. The most frequent expression heard from the crowd that day was "Why all these wide streets and sidewalks. The town will never grow to where it needs streets for cars will be needed; it's just a waste of good ground."

When the crowd found that they could buy lots on the main part of town for $100 to $250 for corner lots and could buy lots a couple of blocks back for $50 they shook their heads and said it was entirely too much and many went home with the money in their pockets that they had brought with them for the purchasing lots.

But there are only a few of us left now to see just how wrong we were on that day, to know the prices that are being offered for the crowded condition of these wide streets now with automobiles, a thing that was hid from our thinking at that time.

But business people who saw the advantage of doing business at a point near a railway station began moving in and setting up business; also those who saw the advantage of having in a town where they would have more conveniences also began building homes here.

Among those moving up from Blair were J. B. Waugh & Co., Blair Grocery Co., William (Billy) Dalton, also the Bolens, Kapps, and others. The Ward brothers came in from the Pipers Gap or Wards Mill section, Jim Reavis and R. E. Jones from Reavistown, J. H. Witherow from Oldtown, and many others. Among the business firms that came to the town at the beginning and have continued under the same firm name to the present time are W. K. Early & Son, R. E. Jones & Son, J. C. Matthews & Co., Vass-Kapp Hardware Co., and Bolen Drug Co.

Logs, Crossties and Tan Bark

At this time the country surrounding Galax contained a large percent of original forests of hardwoods, poplar and pine timber and the marketing of this timber became the main industry of the country around the town; this Industry encouraging the building and grading of better roads, although the roads remained dirt roads for many years.

The farmers in this section used oxen largely for farming and hauling to town, and during this period, Galax could boast of more Ox teams in town any day than any other known town.

J. P. Carico bought the E. P. Givens farm on the east side of the creek and moved there in 1904, and his son James K. Carico, was born there on January 30, 1905, and would be in the running for the first child born in Galax.

This trail was known as the Quaker Trail and the Quakers built a meeting house and laid out a burying ground on a high hill overlooking the Wards Mill Creek. This meeting was first called Mt. Pleasant but was later changed to Chestnut Creek and the burying ground is known as the Old Quaker Graveyard. The land for this meeting house and graveyard was given by Joshua Hanks and William Riddick and the deed was recorded soon after the County of Grayson was established, about 1792.

Joshua Hanks had title to about 1,000 acres of land on both sides of the Mill Creek and built his cabin not far from the meeting house and graveyard. The marker to his grave states that he was born in 1760 and his wife's name was Ruth. He must have moved to this location soon after his marriage and built his cabin.

"And What of Nancy Hanks?"

Joshua Hanks' brother whose name was Thomas (as I remember it) was on his way with his family to find a home in the West and came to his brother, Joshua, with his family, and spent considerable time there before deciding to go on farther west; and while he was staying with his brother his daughter gave birth to a girl who was named Nancy. This child went on with the family farther West where they stopped for some time in what is now West Virginia, where she married Thomas Lincoln and became the mother of Abraham Lincoln.

This tradition had been handed down through three generations when it was told to me and I have talked to others Who have passed on now, that had been told the same story.
After checking all the circumstances and dates, I find nothing that would prevent this story from being possible and in all very probably as authentic as any that has been told and written through the years.

Blair's Forge on Chestnut Creek

About the year 1770, John Blair built a forge just below Blair station on Chestnut Creek for the purpose of smelting and making iron out of the iron ore in that section. The iron bars from this forge were fashioned into shape by the use of a trip hammer; this hammer was powered from a dam built across the creek. After about five years he turned the operation of the forge over to his son, who operated it for many years.
The plateau surrounding the present town consisting of some four or five counties in these early periods was all rural country, with not a single industry to employ the labor outside of the farm, even in most cases to the clothing for the family. The young men who sought to better their circumstances, went where they could find work, and some earned and bought property and settled there.

Town Emerges from a Swamp

This rural condition remained until the Railway extended into this community. The N&W Railway had decided to extend the branch line from the main line at Pulaski, Virginia, up New River and Chestnut Creek and on across the mountain to connect with the Railway at Mt. Airy, N.C., so as to give them a more direct route from the coal fields to the South, but they had only succeeded in getting trains running as far as Chestnut Yards when they secured a lease on the line from Roanoke to Winston-Salem that gave them the southern outlet, when they then abandoned the building of this branch line.

Mr. Carico in addition to managing the land company, helped to establish the First National Bank and became its president for a time; he also helped in establishing the Galax Fair Association and was for a long was also Mayor of the town for one or two terms.

J. B. Waugh moved his business and home to Galax and built the home where Mrs. Charles P. Waugh now resides, and his son, Dan B. Waugh, is now in business on the same corner occupied by his father.

R. E. Jones was one of the first comers to Galax and established early the business of R. E. Jones & Son which is now carried on by his son, Walter, and grandson, Walter, Jr. He was also the first Postmaster in Galax and was also one of its first Mayors.

B. F. Calloway, a native of this section, and an attorney, came to make his home in town early and engineered the getting of the first charter for the town and became its first Mayor. He had charge of the land company for some time but finally moved to Salem, Virginia, where he resides at this time and is nearing his ninetieth birthday.

Much of the land where the town now is at its beginning was grown up in bushes along the branches and wet places in the lower bottom, and one particular place known as the bog or sink hole where no bottom could be found, was located near the W. K. Early & Son lumber yard and the Esso bulk stations. There have been many tales spun about his particular spot but the oldest one known was "That a boy was plowing near this spot when his horse or mule became frightened and bolted, running into this bog and sank out of sight, plow and all, and was never seen afterward."

It is well authenticated by older people that this bog could not be successfully navigated without carefully hopping from one tussock or stool to another and that a fence rail could be pushed down out of sight end-wise with the hands, the black watery muck was so fluid.

When the Railway was constructed to its present site, a canal was cut from this bog to the creek that lowered the water so that buildings are being erected on the place where this treacherous bog once existed.

It was believed by the people interested in laying out the town that the business street would be what is now known as Center Street, so it was called Main Street and the street running north and south that is now Main Street was named Mt. Airy Street

The names were changed and the street named Main in the beginning was changed to Center Street, and the Street name Mt. Airy was changed to Main Street as it is today.

The town was first called Bonaparte but the name did not seem to ring just right and it was seen that it would not be popular, so the name of Galax was decided on as this is the name given to an evergreen, that grows along the Blue Ridge adjacent to the town and is gathered and shipped to all parts of the country.

About Ghosts and Murderers. Other old stories told about happenings near the present town of Galax are interesting.

This one concerns a haunted turn in the Old Pipers Gap Turnpike near where the road crosses the creek near the Carroll Furniture Company.

Near this turn in the road is a graveyard and this graveyard seemed to be the favorite staying place for this haunt which appeared in the form of a small dog that would wait for a lone rider that might have to pass that during the late hours of the night and proceed to jump on the horse behind the rider and accompany him to a point near the ford of the creek when it would leap off and disappear as mysteriously as it had appeared.

In the hill just east of the Carroll Furniture Company plant is a hollow where in the early days a family of Negroes lived, and in this cabin a Negro man was murdered, and as might be expected this locality became haunted. Travelers who had to pass along the road near this point late in the night, could see a bright light moving around in this hollow and a little bell would start tingling and follow them until they were well out of the vicinity of this tragedy. There were men in the community beyond this point who were allergic to haunts that could not be induced to go to Oldtown for a doctor at night because of having to pass this place.

Far and Few Between

At the time the town was being laid out there were no more than three dwellings in sight of the place on the west side of the creek and only two that I can think of on the east side of the creek.

The land purchased by the land company contained no roads or houses and there was nothing in the way to obstruct the laying out of the town, which accounts for its orderly appearance at the present time.

Until the laying out of the town of Galax, Oldtown had been the center of the surrounding country, from the time the county was cut off from the county of Wythe, about 1792, and all roads led to Oldtown.

About the First Courthouse
 The land for the site of the first court house of Grayson County was furnished by Flower Swift and Clark Nuckolls. There were two courthouses built for the county. The last one is still standing and after the courthouse was moved to Independence, the building was occupied by William Waugh and used as a home and hotel. The little brick building across the street on the corner was built and used as the clerk's office but just when this building was erected I do not know but it must be one of the oldest buildings standing in the county. After the court was moved to Independence this building has been used for the post office, until just recently when it was discontinued.

This Is Charles Bolt's Galax

Blue Mountains and Green Meadows

Galax is a mountain town, the Appalachian trail runs down Main Street, and yet it is located in what is actually a high (2,500 feet) valley-like plateau which runs south all the way from the Potomac deep into North Carolina.

It is gentle country, marked by rolling swells of grassy hills and by neat, extremely well-kept farms along the eastern edges, where the country tilts upwards to form a great ridge and then plunges steeply down to the floor of the Piedmont, it is a ruggedly beautiful country.

The Blue Ridge Parkway threads down that crest. The Parkway, only seven miles from Galax, marks the dividing line between the rocky, wooded mountain shoulder and the softer grass-lands of the magnificent mountain valley.

The local people are justly proud of the friendly, progressive city of Galax which nestles in this picturesque setting. To those unfamiliar with this section, it may seem far from civilization, but to those who live here and love it, Galax is the center of the universe.

A Green Leaf Becomes the Name of a City...

It's not exactly easy pickin's, and one won't make a fortune at it. It takes some mountain climbing, too. But one can work in the shade, and quit when he gets ready.

So a lot of mountain families still "galack" for their groceries along the southern crest of the Blue Ridge Mountains. When they turn the children and the old folks loose at it, too, the shiny leaf of the Galax plant pays a fair share of their sustenance.

For picking the Galax leaf is a Southern Appalachian monopoly, and the florist trade still offers a ready market for the wavy-edged, heart-shaped leaves.

So the enterprise which gave Galax its name fifty years ago still sends Virginians and North Carolinians out over the slopes with tow- sacks trailing when the season is right.

Cities like Boston, Chicago, Philadelphia, and New York take them by the thousands, and many others find their way into the florist markets throughout the world.

The Galax leaf thrives in cool, moist soil in the shade, where the root of the herb sends up five or six leaves, each appearing separately above the ground on its own long stem. In summer the leaves are bright green, and in winter they turn a golden bronze.

The leaves can be picked any time of year except from about mid-March through May.
Galax grows best in a seventy-five mile stretch from Galax roughly to Spruce Pine, North Carolina, according to T. N. Woodruff, Low Gap, a merchant and farmer, who started his present business of shipping Galax leaves In 1907.

Every city in the United States and Canada large enough to have a florist has done business with the firm of W. M. Woodruff's Son and Company.

"Galacking" is only an incidental business now to fast growing Galax. But the folks keep a sentimental interest in the expeditions that gave Galax its name. The younger ones probably don't even know the place was first called "Bonaparte" when one or two houses appeared before 1905; and even the old ones don't know why. But the title lasted only a few months, according to City Manager W. G. Andrews.

It changed, he says, after an official of the Norfolk and Western Railway, J. W. Cook, saw a wagon load of Galax leaves sitting on the tracks In town.
"Why don't they call the place Galax?" he said. And so it was.

In 1920, There Was One Sidewalk. ..

Galax may well be said to have its actual beginning in so far as any particular date is concerned, on December 17, 1905, when the first lot sale was held. Because of the railroad being extended, December 3, 1903, people began to move here from Blair and Carroll and Grayson Counties.

Among the most prominent in the activities, that resulted in the founding of Galax, and the busy, growing second class city that we know today, were the late former mayor, J. P. Carico, the late former mayor, R. E. Jones, the late Senator T. L. Felts and the late Captain John B. Waugh. Others were instrumental in the beginning of Galax, but these four may be considered as having been the most active.

The first house in Galax was built by Billy Gallimore. The house is located on the corner of North Main and Virginia Streets. It is now the residence of Dr.and Mrs. Paul H. Kapp and has been occupied by the Kapp family since 1905.

The late Dr. J. W. Bolen was the first to move his business here from elsewhere. He moved his office, or little drug store, from Blair without tearing it down. It took three yoke of Oxen to move his office. Three days were required to move it because the roads had to be widened and holes had to be filled.

Good Government Brought Progress to Galax••

When Galax was incorporated in 1906, there was a Mayor and Council Government. Under this government the clerk and treasurer were appointed.

Ben F. Calloway was mayor when the first Town Charter was issued.

The first council was: Elbert F. Wright, carpenter and builder, Dr. J. K. Caldwell, E. C. Williams, a jeweler, M. L Bishop, livery stable proprietor, J. H. Kapp, hardware merchant, and Dr. J. W. Bolen, physician and druggist.

Ex-Mayor Ben F. Calloway, about eighty-seven, now lives at Salem, Virginia. He remembers that Galax quickly became a busy shipping point for cross ties, acid wood, livestock and poultry, and tan bark after some of the leading citizens persuaded the Norfolk and Western Railway to extend its line.

Calloway, first a lawyer and then a minister, is the only surviving stockholder of the land development company which gave Galax its start. He assisted in drawing up the town's charter and went to Richmond to help get the General Assembly to approve it.

Calloway carried on his law practice in addition to his municipal duties. He had had a reasonably good practice," handling both criminal and civil cases in the wide territory around Galax.

The mayors following Calloway in succession were: J. W. Stamey (1908), J. F. Vass (1909), R. E. Jones (1911), 1. F. Vass (1912), D. A. Robertson (1915), I. F. Vass (1916), D. A. Robertson (1920), DaCosta Woltz (1930), J. P. Carico (1932), B. D. Beamer (1934), W. G. Andrews (1941), R L. Nelson (1942), Ross P. Penry (1946), Dr. R. C. Bowie (1950), B, D. Beamer (1952), and Dan B. Waugh (1954).

In 1922 the town charter was amended to adopt the Town Manager form of Government and I. G. Vass, who had acted as Clerk of the Town, was made the first Town Manager. There have been only four Town Managers in Galax during its history. They are: I. G. Vass, H. M. Todd, Orrin Rhudy, and W. G. Andrews.

The manager acted as clerk to the council as well as Commissioner of Revenue. He had complete charge of the business of the city under the supervision of the city council.

The new charter went into effect September 1, 1954. After the extension of the corporate limits the population was 5,237, which classed Galax as a second class city under the Virginia law. This gives the city its own government independent from the county government.

Additional councilmen were elected in June, 1955, the first election as a second class city. Councilman Dan Waugh was chosen by the councilmen to act as Mayor and has no power other than presiding over the council, although he does have a voting privilege on the council.

The school system was also changed when Galax became a second class city. Three people (men or women) are appointed by the town council and have control of all the operations of the schools.

The school board, Mrs. Don Dickenson, Mr. O. L. Parsons, and Mr. Duane Ward, appoints the Superintendent of the City Schools. This person may be a high school principal. L. W. Hillman is the present Superintendent of Schools and Principal of Galax High School. Bryan Collins is principal of the Grade School.

First School Building in Galax

'In Youth We Learn"... Galax and Its Schools .

When Galax was laid off, the promoters set aside about ten acres of a beautiful pine grove or public school purposes. Within two years money was raised through box suppers, home-talent shows, and private subscriptions to build an elementary and high school building. It was wooden structure with four classrooms on the first floor and an auditorium on the second, all of which were heated by wood burning stoves. This building was replaced in 1925 by the present auditorium and classrooms. G. F Carr was the first principal of the school. He held this position for seven years before he became superintendent of schools in Grayson County.

By 1908, Galax had a population of six hundred and very inadequate school facilities. A new brick building was begun, consisting of eight classrooms, a music room, and an office. This building was used until 1936 when it was burned, being replaced the following year by the present modern building used now for the lower grades.

In 1955 a separate high school building was constructed and equipped at a cost of more than three hundred thousand dollars. This building is presently occupied by high school students who enjoy the new equipment, the cleanliness and cheerfulness of the walls and matching tile floors, adequate sanitary drinking fountains, and a modern heating and ventilating system.

When the auditorium, gymnasium, cafeteria, laboratory, and stadium have been completed, Galax can well boast of the progress it has made toward giving its children the proper facilities to become outstanding young men and women.

Students were given the opportunity to study music, expression, and were from the beginning. However, in recent years these subjects have not been a part of the school itself.

Here is a complete list of the principals of Galax High School in succession: G. F. Carr, S. W. Brown, Ned Hunger, S, G. Wright, J. A. Livesey, B. M. Cox, Miss Jessie Bruce (now Mrs. Lee Beamer), W. J. B. Truitt, Heath A. Melton, Stanley T. Godbey, Wythe F. Wampler, Roy Kyle, Fred Wygal, Paul Cox, and Leslie W. Hillman.

Along with Virginia as a whole, Galax shares in a difficult school problem, but far-sighted and efficient leadership, supported by an intelligent citizenry, will solve this problem, just as other perplexing situations have been solved in the community and section.

Wheels and Machines Caused a Village to Become a City

Galax has been fortunate in escaping the inherent weaknesses of absentee ownership. With the exception of the Carnation Company's milk condensing plant and the Burlington Mills weaving plant, all of the city's industries are home owned.

Lumber Helped Bring Prosperity to Early Galax

With the same two exceptions, the Galax industries began modestly, most of them on a borrowed shoestring and grew with the town.

B. C. Vaughan may well be considered the father of the furniture industry in Galax, with the Vaughan Bassett Industry as the parent organization. Mr. Vaughan and J. D. Bassett, organizer of the largest furniture industries in the world, met with a group of citizens in the old Masonic Hall over Vass-Kapp Hardware Company and formulated plans for what proved to be the first successful industry in Galax. Later Mr. Vaughan was joined by his brother, T. G. Vaughan, when he was released from the armed forces after the first World War. In 1925, T. G. Vaughan organized his own factory, the Vaughan Furniture Company largely owned by local capital, which is presently operated by his sons, George and John Vaughan.

The Vaughan Furniture Company, Incorporated, manufactures a popular line of medium-priced bedroom, dining room, and dinette suites, which are sold all over the United States. Its large and substantial plant is equipped with the most modern machinery, and the working conditions in this factory are the very best. This plant has recently increased its facilities about one third.

The Vaughan-Bassett Furniture Company, established in 1919, was the pioneer and also the largest plant of the Galax furniture industry. It burned February 27, 1951, but was rebuilt in 1952.

John Messer came to Galax in 1927 with little except a gleam in his eye for assets. The Mirror plant which he started in a shed a quarter of a century ago has silvered more mirrors than any other plant in the United States.

On top of that, John Messer has since added a second mirror plant (located in Mount Airy), and three furniture factories (all in Galax) to his string of investments.

The Galax Mirror Company was founded in 1927, and is the parent company of the Messer Industries. One of the great furniture manufacturing enterprises of the south. The mirror plant serves furniture manufacturers in the southern states and produces a popular line of mirrors which is sold in every state in the Union. J. A. Messer, Jr., is president of the plant.

The Webb Furniture Company is one of the major industries of the thriving Industrial center of Galax. It manufactures a well known and popular line of medium priced bedroom furniture, which is sold in every state in the Union. The company is important to Galax by providing one of its largest payrolls, in addition to the purchase of several million feet of local lumber annually. It was founded in 1925 and is a unit of the Messer Industries.

The Galax Furniture Company, Inc., was founded in 1925 with C. L. Smith as its owner. In October of 1943, the company was purchased by John A. Messer, Sr., becoming, with the purchase, a unit in the Messer Industries group of factories. With this change of ownership, the plant has been thoroughly modernized in every respect and has enjoyed an increase in production each year thereafter. The company has enjoyed over these years a fine reputation for manufacturing a better grade of popular priced upholstered furniture.

The fifth division to be added to the Messer Industries was the Carroll Furniture Company. It began operations in 1946 and manufactures a quality grade of bedroom furniture, sold in the National Market, with some going to export.

In January, 1955, the Webb Furniture Company and the Carroll Furniture Company were consolidated under the name of the Webb Furniture Corporation.

Probably no other factor has contributed as much to the improvement of economic conditions of the farmers of Grayson and Carroll, and adjacent counties of this area, as the Carnation Company since it was established at Galax in May, 1937. Farmers in the Galax area realizing that they have a dependable market for all the milk they can produce, have made much progress toward becoming better established in dairying.

The Galax Weaving Plant, a unit of Burlington Mills Corporation, is a modern, efficient textile plant affording employment opportunities for hundreds of Galax, and Carroll and Grayson county people. Several additions to the original plant, erected in 1936, have been necessary. Each addition has brought an increase in the number of employees, making it one of the most modern, scientifically equipped plants for the production of drapery, upholstery, cloth and slip covers in the United States. The company endeavors to provide steady employment, fair wages, excellent working conditions, and a number of employee benefits to its people.

Harris-Marshall Hosiery Mills, Inc., which began operations in 1945, is another prosperous industry of Galax. The plant of the company is modern in every detail, with equipment representing the latest development in machinery designed for efficient and economical production of men's hosiery. Working conditions In the plant are ideal. H. L Harris, president, treasurer and manager, has over twenty-five years experience in the manufacture of hosiery.

Sawyers Furniture Company manufactures living room furniture. Their product has been distributed in many states throughout the United States with excellent acceptance. It was established in 1945 by C.F. Sawyer and expanded in 1950.

The Penry Manufacturing Company, organized in 1944 under the name of the Old Dominion, expanded in 1950. Ross P. Penry, president and general manager, is well known to the textile industries of the South. Mr. Penry whose Christian attitude has meant much to the Galax community, offers prayer every morning with its employees. The company manufactures polo, "T" and sport shirts.

Galax continues to grow Industrially. In 1954, the Wonderknit Corporation located in the old Galax Weaving plant. Today, the company is one of the City's top employers, manufacturing shirts of every description that go throughout the nation for sale. Wonderknit has become an important cog in the economy of Galax.

The R and H Hosiery Co. was formed only months ago and now occupies a site on Oldtown street adding to the industrial picture of Galax.

The famous brand name "Hanes" is now part of Galax. Early in 1955 the Hanes company (headquarters, Winston Salem, N. C.) began the local manufacture of many items in the Eades Building on South Main. This year the Hanes firm has opened a second plant on West Grayson street. Hanes definitely has come to Galax.

The Churches of Galax .•••••. From Whence Comes Our Strength

The history of a city's churches indicates well the trends of that city's development toward a well-rounded life for its citizens. The moral and spiritual growth of its people are of even greater importance than Its physical and mental growth.

Galax points with pride to the zealous growth and expansion of its churches. This nation, under God, was founded upon religious principles of love for God and respect for the rights of one's fellow man; hence, our city gratefully acknowledges this dependence upon God's merciful care and leadership. It is these principles of religious piety and love of country over which patriotically Old Glory protecting flutters in the breeze.

Major denominations represented by the churches of Galax are the Christian (Disciples of Christ), Baptist, Methodist, Presbyterian, Friends (Quakers), Brethren, and Protestant Episcopal. Handsome edifices of worship are maintained by all of these organizations.

The history of Methodism in Galax is practically synonymous with that of the city itself, the first Methodist Church having been erected on West Center Street where the present large and commodious First Methodist Church now stands. The congregation moved here from nearby Oldtown soon after the beginning of Galax as a town. The present church edifice was erected in 1926. Various improvements have been wrought from time to time since, including acquisition of a handsome and modernly convenient parsonage.

Also early in the history of the city came to Galax the Baptists as a group. Their first church home was established on West Oldtown Street. Later in the 20's, the neat and vastly modern structure that is now the First Baptist Church on North Main Street was constructed. Great improvement has been made since, in the way of additions to the church plant, and otherwise.

In the days of Galax the Presbyterians maintained their church home at Oldtown, where they were housed in a handsome frame building. Later, as an outgrowth of this beginning, the present brick structure on West Center Street that is now the First Presbyterian Church was erected. In this congregation also came the need for expansion as the years passed, and suitable additions were made.

Many years ago also the Disciples of Christ organized here and constructed a frame building on Washington Street, near North Main. In due time this congregation too felt the need for more room, and the need, transferred into constructive action, took the form of the magnificent structure that is now the First Christian Church, pointing its tall spire heavenward from a commanding eminence that overlooks a large portion of the city, from its site on West Stuart Drive. This is Galax's newest downtown church building among those of the major beliefs.

The Friends (Quakers) purchased the former Baptist building on West Oldtown Street when the Baptists moved to their new location. The Friends have added many improvements through the years, and now form an active, if small, church organization. The Friends Church building is the oldest house of divine worship in the city.

One of the newer churches in the city is the handsome stone structure that houses the congregation of the First Church of the Brethren on Givens Street. Here an active and dynamic church program is promoted by a zealous band of believers. The building was erected through a program of donated labor in a concerted "spare time" effort.

In recent years the Pentecostal Holiness denomination has erected a church on an eminence of ground in the western heights overlooking the city. There, also an active program of religious promotion is being carried forward.

St. Andrew's Episcopal Church is the city's latest addition among its church organizations. Only In recent months has this small, but determined, flock reached a status whereby it can have the services of a full-time rector. This church is housed in what was formerly the Presbyterian Church at Oldtown, but is definitely a part of the larger Galax area. An improvement project has been earried forward.

A Primitive Baptist Church has also been a part of the church life of the city for many years. This church building stands on MacArthur Street.

Galax Becomes a City

Galax Post Herald Thursday December 3, 1953

Galax became a city Monday afternoon, November 30, 1953, approximately fifty years after the town was laid out. In one of his last official acts before his retirement December 1st, Judge John S. Draper signed the necessary papers to make Galax a city. As a city, Galax will assess and collect taxes for the city and the state. Residents in the corporate limits will no longer pay county taxes.

Before taxes are levied for Galax next year the city will have to reassess all property within the corporate limits. Until this assessment is made, it is impossible to predict the local tax burden but officials expect that the new city taxes will be less than the combined county and town taxes paid this year.   "

Town Attorney H. Prince Burnett is now busy preparing a charter for the new city of Galax to be approved by the Council and the General Assembly. He hopes to have the charter approved by February, 1954. Meanwhile Galax Will operate under the same officials and charter that it did as a town.

H Prince Burnette

New School Board May Be Appointed

Several changes will be effected in the government of the city of Galax when the new charter is approved. One, according to unofficial opinions of city officials, may be made sooner. As a city, Galax will have a separate school board. Officials told the Post Herald that the Council may appoint a school board before the charter is approved. These officials approve a separate school board and believe that the Council needs relief from the many details of the school administration.

Now that the Galax School system is outside county jurisdiction these officials believe that the new city school board should be appointed as soon as possible. It is the thinking of these officials that a three man school board would be best, the members to be appointed by the. Council outside of its membership.

Other changes under the city form of government include the election of a Treasurer and Commissioner of Revenue

Also to be appointed will be a school superintendent. The new charter will determine when and how these new officials will be elected or appointed. Until that time the present town officials will conduct the affairs of the city.

Next June Galax will elect eight new councilmen, two from each of the four wards of the city. To be determined by the charter is how the Mayor will be elected. The thinking now prevalent among officials is to have the mayor elected , by the council from its membership.

Dr. Bedsaul's "Early Memories of Galax"

Dr. Bedsaul, author of the most interesting article published below, is the son of Mrs. P. Reece Bedsaul, Galax, and the late Mr. Bedsaul, and was born and reared near Galax, on RFD No. 3. At the present time, he is coroner of Floyd County, and he and Mrs. Bedsaul, the former Miss Rosamond Vaughan, of Spring Valley, are prominent citizens of the Floyd county-seat town. Early in his medical career, Dr. Bedsaul practiced for brief period in Galax, Fries and Elk Creek. —Editor

Galax Native, Now a Floyd Physician Writes of "EARLY MEMORIES OF GALAX"

I have grown up with Galax and have seen this city develop from a tiny crossroads village to the thriving metropolis it is today. The first couple of stores and half a dozen dwellings were scattered along a dirt road, leading in from Hillsville, Woodlawn and Wolf Glade, threading southward along the foothills on the west side of Chestnut Creek, then dividing into two roads, one leading up towards Pipers Gap and Mount Airy, and the other via the Glades to Low Gap. This road became Main Street.

Another road winding among the Carroll County hills and knobs (out my way) descended Spivey Hill, crossed Chestnut Creek , extended west across Main Street and up the hill to lose itself into roads leading to Old Town Street. There were no wagon bridges across Chestnut Creek and all vehicular traffic, pulled by oxen and horses, from the east side splashed through open fords. There was a swinging bridge for pedestrians down by the Caldwell home on the Hillsville road. A wobbly footlog served that purpose on our road.

The twin county village of Galax had an ideal location in the heart of a rich farming area. A wide expanse of fertile creek bottoms spread out to the east on the Carroll side. These bottoms merged into rolling hills and knobs. The most prominent of these was Wards knob, towering higher than all other land in the area, and bearing a crest of green trees above pasture fields on the steep slopes. The Grayson side climbed more abruptly from a foothill plateau, with Fries Hill meeting the horizon on the northwest and a rolling hill, beyond a branch on the southwest end of the village. This hill, which later became known as School House Hill, was covered by a dense forest of towering pines. My first visit to Galax was to this forest. I accompanied my parents and some neighbors, in a covered wagon, to hear Governor Montague speak.

My young mind was intrigued by the stories my people told me about the early Galax community. My own ancestors migrated from Old Town and acquired lands along Chestnut Creek. One of my great grandfathers, at one time, owned much of the land upon which East Galax now stands. Then, there was the exciting story of the two bell-making blacksmiths who operated a shop towards Wolf Glade, out on the Hillsville road. These men had a secret silver mine (in the Galax area) where Bedsaul Branch emptied into Chestnut Creek. They carried the ore to their shop in buckskin sacks. Their days were spent in making bells; their nights in smelting the ore and making counterfeit coins. Before daybreak, the molds and ore were carefully hidden and the smiths again hammered away upon their bells.

Government agents finally grew suspicious and when the counterfeiters were about to get cornered, they buried their "money" molds and skipped out, carrying the knowledge of the location of the secret deposit of silver with them.
Prospectors have searched ever since, but nobody has ever been able to rediscover it. The mouths of the various branches have shifted back and forth as these streams meander across the bottoms along Chestnut Creek. This mine seems almost big a secret as that of "Death Valley's Scotty's".

Galax came near not being Galax at all. Some of the founding fathers wanted to call it "Bonaparte." Others finally won out in their decision to call it Galax, after the evergreen "coltsfoot" leaves which grew abundantly in this area of the Blue Ridge Mountains.

Galax did not remain a village long. The founding fathers, with foresight and faith, laid out adequate streets and alleys, and new buildings began to spring up all over the place. More stores, two hotels, two working plants,

189

blacksmith shop and dwellings crowded out into the meadows and fields in every direction. Lumber from near-by Virgin forests and bricks from Wards' Brick Yard at the foot of Wards Knob furnished abundant building supplies. Even the towering pines on Schoolhouse Hill were felled and found their way into new Galax homes.

The growth of this town was speeded up considerably by the coming of the railroad. The Norfolk & Western had built a spur line from Pulaski up New River, and had reached Blair (Cliffview). It was a red letter day when the railroad was extended up to Galax. Young and old, alike, lined the tracks to hear the mellow roar of the locomotive whistle, and to see it steam into town. Almost overnight, farmers began to haul in crossties and tanbark to the new shipping center. The many packs of "ties and bark" in the railroad yards looked like a small town within themselves. Strings of heavily laden wagons rattled along dirt roads as oxen and horses strained to move the farmers products of forest and farm to market. But little could done to improve the roads with axle deep mud, across the Chestnut Creek bottoms in Winter and after heavy rains.

However the increase in traffic caused the building of wagon bridges across the Creek. I remember "ours" quite well. It was a clumsy humpbacked, wooden affair with a steep ramp ascending from the ground level, on each end of this center section. Old 'Muck" and "Baldy" would moan and wheeze as they struggled against the ox bows and yoke to pull the heavy load up the steep incline. When the hard pull was over, and the going was easy along the level span, the oxen would become frightened and pull against each other until their feet trod almost the same path.

All this, plus the groaning of Ole bridge timbers and rumbling of wagon wheels over the board floor were rather exciting to the barefoot, overall-clad boy sitting upon four bundles of oats in a burlap sack and perched high upon the load of bark. If one could look straight ahead instead of peering downward upon the rolling waters of Chestnut Creek, far below, the going was much easier. Then the scene would change. The wagon pitched forward and rushed upon the cattle down the steep ramp on the other side. The wagon tongue pushed so heavily against the ring in the ox yoke that the poor, blowing animals seemed to fear that their heads would be pulled off. The lad had to almost stand with one foot upon the brake leaver and make the wood rubber blocks sigh against the rear wheels of the wagon as he guided his crude craft to a safe landing down onto the road again. After a few more minutes of pulling and jerking against the single rope line that was snared about the horns of the lead ox and after a lot of clucking and yelling of "Haw" and "Gee" and "get up Buck!", the wagon made its way among the piles of ties, ricks of bark, and empty freight cars to reach the weighing scales.

There, one was greeted by familiar odors of sap, bark, new lumber and coal smoke puffing from the freight engine shifting the cars. The coming of the railroad to Galax not only brought in raw materials but also started the town booming as a manufacturing center. The first ones were a canning factory and a furniture factory. The canning factory was a wooden structure ivory in color, sprawled out a along the east side of the railroad tracks. It was a series of rooms, breezeways and sheds connected end to end. The furniture factory was located farther down to the north, between the tracks and Chestnut Creek. It was a large brick structure.

I have heard interesting memories of some of the early citizens and first business houses in Galax. There was J. P. Carico, often referred to as the "Father of Galax". He lived in a pretty farmhouse on the Carroll side of the Creek, just where the foothills of Wards Knob and Spivey Hill met the level bottom land. He was a pleasant, friendly man who was public spirited and always looking for a chance to boost his town.

Just across the railroad tracks, and near the Depot and beginning of Grayson Street, was W. K. Early. He was a dealer in building materials and fuel.

Then, J. C. Mathews had a hardware store in a frame building on the north side of Grayson Street. This friendly little man moved about quickly as he helped farmers select tools and farm equipment.

On the other side of Grayson Street, a little farther up and about the present location of the Rex Theater, was the first bank. Just above this little brick building, was a rambling produce store operated by M. T. Blessing. This fellow was round faced and fat. He looked much like Santa Claus with the whiskers shaved off. He was always busy, crating eggs and shifting squawking chickens from one coop to another.

Across the street and just above the present Gazette office, was Bill Dalton's dry goods store. He was another fat man. Much of his loafing time was spent sitting in front of his store and conversing with farmers as they drove by, and around to the wagon yard behind his store. Little's blacksmith shop was located about the center of the hitching ground. The ringing of his anvil served to break the monotony of the neighing of horses, lowing of oxen, the occasional braying of a hungry mule and the clang of bells and puffing of locomotives down in the rail road yards.

One of the most colorful characters of early Galax was Captain J. B. Waugh. I can almost see him now, a large man, sitting in front of his brick store on the corner of Main and Grayson Streets. He sat erect in his chair, wore a derby and tapped his cane against the sidewalk as he whiled away his time. The old gentleman was every inch a stalwart Confederate soldier.

R. E. Jones was a furniture dealer on Main Street. This man, with a booming voice and always wearing a derby hat was also referred to as "the Daddy of Galax".

Lute Bishop operated a livery stable on the Northeast corner of Main and Old Town streets, where Globman's now stands. He was not only a good businessman but also a good Christian layman who concerned himself about the souls of men. Diagonally across from the livery stable on the corner now occupied by the Texaco Service Station, was a large, rambling boarding house with a high porch across the lower side. This hotel was a favorite hangout for the horse traders.

Another livery stable was located where Twin County Motor Company now stands. This establishment was owned by Thomas L. Felts. Mr. Felts was an influential businessman and a leader in the progressive growth of Galax. He was a handsome man who drove the prettiest horses and buggies in town. Stories about this man's experiences as a brave detective excited us youngsters of that day. Mr. Felts was our hero, a sort of living "Dick Tracy."

Dr. Pless was a pioneer dentist in Galax. Doctors Caldwell, Bishop and Bolen were early physicians of the town. Their saddle horses were the pride of the community. As I continue to reminisce about early Galax, many old friends pass by in review, S. E. Wilkinson (connected with the early furniture factory), C. A. Collier, cashier of the bank down on Grayson Street and then in what is now the Municipal Building, Swift and Charlie Waugh (congenial clerks in the J.B. Waugh Store), "Doc" Jim Witherow (in his drug store where the First National Bank now stands), Vass & Kapp (in their hardware store across Main Street from Waugh's), the three Ward Bothers (in three brick houses, beyond the branch, across from Schoolhouse Hill on South Main, the first homes with running water. It flowed by gravity from springs on the side of Wards Knob). Mr. Rhudy and Mr. Calloway (early lawyers In Galax), Anderson, Painters, Todd's, Roberts's, Dobyns, Harps, Reavis's, Browns, Stanford's, and many, many more along with their wives, have left their mark on Galax and have helped to make it the beautiful and progressive city it is today.

Galax started having fairs before it was even a town. The first one was held on September 19, 20 and 21, 1905. I have always felt that this first one was about the best. It left an indelible impression upon my mind. There were hundreds of people walking all over the grounds. Nearly every man wore a mustache and many sported beards. Many heads were adorned by derbies. The Ladies wore long tight skirts. Some had on bustles as big as hats and hats as big as parasols.

We children were dressed up too. The little girls wore pigtails and ribbons of all colors. The boys were decked out in fancy ruffled shirts (called blouses) and tight knee britches with lower legs decorated by rows of buttons (like on coat sleeves). Yelling and shouting from the barkers at the side shows and concession stands could be heard above the hum of voices as neighbor greeted neighbor. The mellow, but mechanical music of the hobby horses, punctuated by the irregular popping exhaust from the one-cylinder gasoline engines, could be heard on one side while the band would be playing in front of the grandstand.

Horses, buggies, hacks, bicycles, and wagons were on the move. Neighing horses entering through the gates and descending the hill towards the grandstand would be answered by others hitched along the blind fence over to the south, and out on the hitching grounds across Main Street at the foot of Schoolhouse Hill. The bell in the tower just inside the race track would clang and the horse racing was on. The roar of a lion in the big tent sent chills up and down our spines. A stroll through the exhibit hall (under the grandstand) and a visit to the stock pens, then we were ready for another visit to the lemonade stand. Some found seats up in the grandstand, some of us sat out on the grassy knoll under the shade of the oak trees. This fair even had a moving picture show. It was located in a darkened tent. The hand-cranked and gas lit contraption cast a weird flicker upon a sheet. The scene depicted in a cigar-shaped craft. Year by year, the Great Galax Fair grew in size, more exhibits, better balloon ascensions, better farm machinery, steam-tractors, sawmills and gasoline farm engines, were on display. Fireworks made the nights quite entertaining. The loud booms, with popping of fiery balls high in the air, showers of colored stars and sparks which reflected a weird glow over the crowd, pin wheels and patriotic figures in flame kept us excited. Horse traders (like the Roberts Boys and the Bartletts) were much in evidence at the fairs. All kinds Of 'horse flesh" was paraded up and down Main Street with a mighty clatter of hoofs as these animals trotted, pranced and loped at the commands of their owners. There were good, bad and 'indifferent animals on display; the fiery Western ponies, the slow draft horses and mules, and the plugs. More emphasis seemed to be placed upon the raw boned, bellowed, string-haltered, and sweenied nags. It took more salesmanship to sell this type of animal. The riders would "tap up" his steed and encourage him to muster all his reserve energy to prance and to remain on his feet long enough to effect a sale.

Fourth of July celebrations were gala affairs in the early days of Galax. We assembled at the fair grounds where the hot weather made us frequent the lemonade and ice cream stands. Many loads of watermelons were also in evidence.

The Confederate soldiers had pulled their aging, gray uniforms out of the moth balls, and were properly attired for the occasion. They would line up and march to the music of the bands. Nearly all of them wore long white beards. Some stood quite erect and marched with a sprint in their steps; others stooped and limped along as best they could. All would liven up "Dixie". Then, public speaking was in order. I remember one occasion when these old soldiers were being called upon for war stories. One by one, they arose all over the grandstand to tell their battle stories of Bull Run, Chickamauga, Cedar Run, Seven Pines, Fredericksburg and Manassas.

The master of ceremonies happened to spy one lone Yankee in the audience, " I see we have one soldier here today who fought with the North". He announced, "Mr. Ingersoll, suppose you tell about your war experiences in the Civil War." The old fellow arose, looked about the crowd and answered, "I've been listening to all these other fellows' stories about the battles they took part in, but all I can say is, that I was right there, too."

There was more patriotic music and games, and contests for the children. I well remember a foot race I took part in. I ran neck-and-neck with the fastest for about twenty yards. My feet tangled and I hit the dirt, taking half a dozen down with me in the pile-up. When it was all over and we brushed off the dirt, Ray Bedsaul growled at me, "If it hadn't been for you, I'd a won that race."

The festivities usually ran smoothly until about three o' clock in the afternoon. Then, almost without warning, the rain would pour down in sheets. It was a mad scramble to find shelter. Those who were caught too far from the grandstand clamored into top buggies and covered wagons and watched all the flag and red, white and blue bunting get soaked and plastered down around the stands.

Galax continued to grow in rather normal fashion with the addition of new faces, more homes, more factories and places of business, more churches, new and larger school. The tempo of traffic stepped up with larger number Of horses, buggies, and wagons clattering about the streets. The furniture factory and a business block or two were wiped out by fire. Chestnut Creek got up high enough a time or two to threaten the bridges and a few homes down on the edge of the bottoms. Everything seemed to be rocking along rather smoothly. Very little had happened to disturb the tranquility of the town.

Then it happened!

E. Lane Whitley and W. H. Bolling appeared in town, driving sputtering and smelly automobiles. These gasoline-propelled vehicles put the whole town into a panic. Every horse in the community was scared into fits; by the very sight, sound or odor of an automobile. Teams bolted, snorted and tried to run away. Conditions became so critical that Galax authorities had to adopt drastic rules and regulations to control the driving of automobiles in the town in order to safeguard the lives and limbs of the driving public.

The livery stable men felt the automobile fad was only a passing fancy, and soon would fade out of the picture. It did not work that way. Some men in Galax got the Ford agency and Model "T" touring cars with brass radiators began to run all over the streets. Horses finally accepted them and a new age was born.

A few general stores put in hand-operated gasoline pumps to supply fuel to the automobile owners. Do you remember the first "jitney" in the Galax area? It was a Model "T" touring car driven by Mr. Lundy. This old gentleman wore a long white beard. He was afflicted with paralysis agitans (palsy), and the shaking of his head and his hands upon the steering wheel almost kept time with the chuckling motor as he bumped along over the pebbles on Main Street. He was quite busy because everybody wanted to know what it was like to ride in an automobile. That didn't apply to me however, I had already been honored by a ride in the W. H. Bolling car, two blocks up Grayson Street.

Automobiles created quite a problem for us boys at Galax High School. Those who were fortunate enough to own them were always getting fined for exceeding the fifteen-miles-per hour speed limit; those of us who didn't own cars were almost socially ostracized, because the girls had but little interest in boys who could not take them out motoring."

About the time automobiles were fully accepted, aero planes began to come to the Galax Fairs. The first one was a flimsy, motorized kite contraption and it had the appearance of bed sheets tightly stretched over quilting frames. It sat in the center of the race track. Each day about two o'clock in the afternoon, we were asked to move back across the track to give the craft more room to fly. It needed more than room to make it air worthy. The second plane was shipped in by freight train, assembled on the grounds and actually flew. From then on, they flew in and out at will. Just a few years passed until some of the Galax men owned their own planes.

The Galax streets were paved in the early twenties, new factories were scattered up and down Chestnut Creek, the wooden bridges gave way to modern steel spans, the Creek bed was dredged deeper to protect the town from floods. residences and filling stations lined the highways in every direction The town built its own radio broadcasting station, and radio and television antenna sprang up from nearly every house-top as the "electronic age" became a reality to this new city of over 5,000 souls.

Galax is celebrating its fiftieth Anniversary on August 2-11, this year. I plan to be back in the old home town for this "Golden Jubilee" to meet old friends, and travel again over the familiar streets where I once (as a lad) peddled almost everything produced upon a small truck farm, everything from wild strawberries to rutabagas. I feel that I shall be welcome. I haven't been around Galax very much for the last few years, and I do not know all the present driving regulations on the streets of this fair city but I shall feel free to drive an automobile most anywhere because I still carry a "Driving Permit Card, issued by the Galax authorities. I know it is valid because it bears the signature of I. G. Vass, the first Town Manager of Galax.

Courtesy of the Galax Gazette April 1956

The Galax Story, after 75 years

Seventy-five years is but a moment in the span of history, but for Galax it has meant the growth from a few scattered farms, interspersed with brush fields, woodlands, bogs, and swamps, into a thriving and progressive industrial city. Three quarters of a century has meant a growth in population from only a few families to a small city inhabited by slightly over six thousand people. Another forty thousand people reside in the adjoining counties of Grayson and Carroll, within easy driving distance to Galax for shopping at modern stores, or for employment at diverse businesses and industries.

The history of Galax cannot be complete without the inclusion of the histories of Carroll and Grayson counties, for the city lies astride the line dividing the two counties. Political divisions separate the city and the counties from each other, but, in reality, the growth and prosperity of the entire area has been due to the close relationship of the counties and the city. Perhaps this is why the area is called the "Twin Counties."

Although the history of Galax is synonymous with that of the counties, time and space will permit only a portion of that history to be included in this publication. Reliable information about the pioneer settlers who moved into the New River Valley is scarce. It is known that among them were the Quakers who came from North Carolina after the Battle of Alamance in 1771. The Scotch-Irish immigrants also pushed westward from the Virginia Tidewater and settled in the highlands, an area which reminded them of their native homeland. Many early settlers were also of English heritage.

One of the early settlers was Major George Currin, great-grandfather of Dan and Fred Roberts, who had migrated from North Carolina. He had purchased a large tract of land from the old Buckhannon survey, which included all the land where the City of Galax is now located.

Over a hundred years before the town of Galax was founded, a settlement was established on Chestnut Creek in the region now known as Cliffview. This village was called Blair in honor of John Blair, who built a forge there about 1770. Blair had developed into a small but flourishing trading center by 1900. Advertisements in the Blair Enterprise of May 25, 1904, indicated some of the business establishments to be as follows: Blair Hardware Co., J. B. Waugh and Son, Sunny Side Inn, Mrs. J. H. Kapp, proprietor (opposite N & W depot), Crystal Drug Co.

The Cliffview community was dominated by the stately mansion "Cliffside" built in 1902 by State Senator Thomas L. Felts for his wife, Ethel Houseman Felts. At one time the little community was called Ethelfelts in her honor. "Cliffside" is now the home of Mr. and Mrs. Hubert S. White, Jr.

The community of Blair was not geographically located to allow for future expansion and growth, so when the N & W Railroad agreed to extend its line to the new town of Galax, most of the Blair businessmen followed.

In 1792 Grayson County was formed from Wythe, and Oldtown became the first county seat. Flower Swift and Clark Nuckolls " donated land for the first county courthouse, a post office and a jail. The first Grayson County Courthouse was built at Oldtown in 1794. A second courthouse which is still standing was built in 1838. About 1850, after the formation of Carroll County, the county seat of Grayson was moved to Independence.

As the twentieth century began, the area that is now Galax was still farm land. The William Roberts place was just above Stuart Drive and just west of the N & W railroad crossing. The Tom Roberts (Fred and Dan Roberts' father) house stood about where Dr. Cox's house now stands on Stuart Drive. A little farther west in the "big curve" of Stuart Drive was the Hugh Roberts' house.

This building, which is still standing, is the large white house near the Vaughan Memorial Library. The A. C. Anderson and the A. C. Painter houses located just off Anderson Street, both still serve as residences for members of the families. John Barger Caldwell, father of Dr. J. K. Caldwell lived about where the A. B. Todd residence on East Stuart Drive is now located. About 1870, for the sum of $1,500.00, he acquired several acres of land on the east side of Chestnut Creek (including the land where the present Twin County Community Hospital is located).

Mr. Caldwell's farm was bordered on the south by the E. C. Givens' farm in the vicinity of the present Burlington Mills location. Much of this land on both sides of Chestnut Creek was marsh land and had to be drained.

A TOWN IS BORN

Just before the turn of the century, a Grayson County man, J. P. Carico, persuaded Washington Mills to build a dam and locate a plant on the New River. The milltown which sprang up was called Fries. Mr. Carico then conceived the idea that the N & W Railroad should extend its line from Blair into a new town yet to be built a few miles up Chestnut Creek. He joined with Capt John B. Waugh, R. E. Jones, and a few other investors in forming a real estate company to acquire the site for the new town. After about 375 acres of land west of Chestnut Creek was purchased two engineers, named Arnold and DeMott from Lynchburg, were employed to lay the land off into streets and lots. In the fall of 1903 the first lots were auctioned off. The price of the lots ranged from $25.00 for a 50 foot lot on a side street to $250.00 for a corner lot on Main Street. It is interesting to note that what is now Main Street was first called Mt. Airy Street and that Grayson Street was thought of as Main Street or Depot Street.

Fred Roberts recalls that Mr. A. C. Painter bought all the lots on both sides of Center Street from where the Methodist Church is now located to Main Street for $25.00 each. Dan Waugh remembers that his father, Capt. John Waugh, bought the corner lot at Grayson and Main, where he later built his store, for $250.00.

Dan Roberts tells the story of how John Caldwell, who had a reputation for plowing the straightest furrow of anyone around, brought a bull-tongued plow and plowed a furrow from stake to stake to lay off the streets.

No one seems to be certain why the young town was first called Bonaparte, but the name lasted only a short time. Soon after the railroad came in 1904, the name was changed to Galax, after the beautiful green leaves used in floral arrangements, which grew in abundance in the area. J. W. Cook, an official of the railroad is said to have suggested calling the town Galax. Another story goes that Mrs. Kirsley, who sold insurance in the area, suggested the name Galax because she thought the leaves were so beautiful. At any rate, Galax leaves were the first express freight to be shipped over the new line. Both the railroad station and the town were known as Galax.

In 1906 a charter was formed, a mayor-council form of government was established and Galax was incorporated into a town. By then practically all of the businesses had left Blair and Oldtown and established themselves in Galax.

Ben F. Calloway, who had come to Galax from Independence to serve as secretary for the land development company, was selected to be the town's first mayor. He assisted in drawing up the town charter and went to Richmond to present it to the General Assembly for approval.

The young town literally sprang up over night. Some of the pioneers in the business life of the new town are pictured.

Marvin, Monroe and Frazier Ward operated a mill on the Pipers Gap Road about where' the Milo Cockerham residence is now located. In 1903 the Ward Brothers bought a lot on Main Street and shortly thereafter constructed a two-story frame building. The lower floor was "gents" furnishings and general merchandise. On the second floor Monroe Ward operated the first moving picture theater in Galax. Their business had been in operation only a short time when this building and many of the other buildings on the east side of Main Street, in the block between Grayson and Center Streets, were destroyed by fire. A bucket brigade from the town's two wells at the Waugh Hotel and the South Hotel (corner of Main and Oldtown Streets where the Texaco station is now) succeeded in saving the west side of Main Street ..

Galax quickly became an important shipping point for the N & W Railroad. The dirt (often very muddy) streets of the little town usually bustled with a variety of activities. Wagons pulled by oxen and loaded with cross- ties or tan bark could be seen headed for the lumber yards; herds of cattle, sheep, or even turkeys being driven by herd dogs, accompanied by their masters on horseback, was not uncommon. Barrels of apples, berries, chestnuts and chinquapins filled the depot platform, waiting to be shipped to northern markets. Much of the farmers' produce was taken to the old cannery, located about where Vaughan-Bassett Furniture Co. now stands. Fred Roberts remembered that he was fired from his job in the cannery for cutting green beans with his pocket knife rather than breaking them as he had been instructed to do.

Manufacturing began in the town soon after the arrival of the railroad when Capt. John Waugh, S. E. Wilkerson and Creed Hanks established a furniture factory with the idea of exporting the plentiful forest resources as finished products instead of rough lumber. Their factory was located about where the Wonderknit Corporation now stands on Virginia Street. Fire destroyed the young business in 1907 and it was never rebuilt. (*editor's note: it was rebuilt and again destroyed y fire in 1917*)

Other early industries of this town were as follows: a handle factory, operated by W. P. Swartz for the manufacture of ax handles and pick handles, a chair factory, for the manufacture of split-bottom chairs, a flour mill, established by Charles Bryant and E. F. Perkins. This business later came to be known as Adams Flour Mill and was operated by Fred Adams. The business is no longer in operation, but the building still stands on E. Oldtown Street. (*Now Guynn Furniture*)

Soon after the town's beginning, the "Great Galax Fair" was originated. J. P. Carico and T. L. Felts promoted the idea and a group of about 90 citizens formed the Galax Fair Association. Shares of stock were sold at $100.00 per share and no person was permitted to own more than one share. A 22-acre tract of land, now Felts Park, was purchased, a race track, grandstand, and exhibit building was constructed and the "Fairgrounds" was ready for business.

Fair Week was truly the social highlight of the year. Visitors from all over flooded the little town as the whole family came with team and covered wagon to camp on the grounds, on the streets, or anywhere else they could find space. Townspeople opened their doors to friends, relatives and visitors as all enjoyed a few days of fun and frolic.

The arrival of the train when the Fair moved in was quite a spectacle. Practically everyone went down to the depot to see the midway shows, rides and wild animals be unloaded from the train and moved to the Fairgrounds.

It was a time when proud farmers could exhibit their produce and fine livestock. Housewives displayed their most beautiful articles of sewing, knitting and quilting. Tasty pies, cakes, cookies, jellies and preserves were also part of the exhibit. In addition to the midway shows and exhibits, the fair goers enjoyed harness races, fireworks and "free acts". But mostly, people enjoyed associating with each other and visiting friends they may not have seen or heard from since the fair the previous year.

During the winter months, the young town was practically isolated. The railroad served as its link to the outside world. Mail and passenger service to Roanoke was provided on a daily basis. It was possible to leave Galax at noon and arrive in Roanoke about 6 P.M. Anyone wanting to make the round trip could do so by leaving Roanoke about 4 A.M., and if the train made connections in Pulaski, could arrive in Galax around noon. Roads leading into Galax were hardly more than trails and were impossible driving most of the winter months.

An attempt was made by the late R. A. Anderson to do something about the town's isolated situation, through the medium of Blue Ridge Bus Lines, which he operated to Mt. Airy, N. C. and Pulaski, Va. This materially helped the mail service. Bad roads were, however, such a constant drag on bus equipment that operating losses wrecked the company before the routes were developed sufficiently to make economical operation of the buses possible.

The Good Spur Gap Road crossed the mountain near the present Fancy Gap Methodist Church, extended north by the county farm in Carroll County and connected with a road leading east and west at Fort Chiswell. A little later a road branching off the Good Spur road at the county home in Carroll County was built. This road passed through Galax along what is now Stuart Drive and extended on through Grayson County to the Washington County line. Another road crossed the mountain, followed the Piper's Gap Road, crossed Chestnut Creek about where Webb Furniture Plant No. 2 now stands, ran north by the old filtering plant, turned west about where Long Street is now, passed by the Anderson farm and extended to Oldtown. There were no bridges across Chestnut Creek and the creek had to be "forded." Swinging bridges were built for pedestrian traffic. When the creek was "up," travelers were forced to camp on the east side until the waters receded.

About the first thing an old timer recalls of early Galax history was the muddy streets and roads. Many of them will tell you of seeing oxen mired to their bellies in the mud on Main Street. Early residents tried to top each other's tall tales about the town's mighty mud holes. Perhaps the topper is the tale told by Harry Early about a man, while walking down Main Street, saw a hat in a mud hole. When he picked the hat up, he discovered a man underneath. When the man was asked if he needed help, he replied, "No thanks, I'm all right, I'm on horseback."

Galax residents continued to fight the mud until about 1923 when the town got its first paved street. Senator T. L. Felts had been instrumental in securing passage of the Robertson act which aided Carroll County to build a paved highway from Hillsville, to Galax.

Pictures show that Galax had telephones early in its history, but we have been unable to determine how this service was provided.

An early attempt to provide electricity to the town was made when a citizen's group headed by W.I. Harp undertook to build a dam and construct a municipal light plant on Chestnut Creek. High costs and construction set-backs when the creek flooded discouraged the promoters and the project was abandoned. Appalachian Power Company began supplying electricity to Galax March 4, 1926.

Industry and Manufacturing

Galax experienced no large scale industrial growth until after World War I. Soon after the war, Mayor J. F. Vass and other civic leaders met with John D. Bassett, head of Virginia's foremost furniture empire, and Bunyan C. Vaughan, also a noted industrialist. The result of that meeting was the founding of Vaughan-Bassett Furniture Company. B. C. Vaughan came to Galax as president of the newly formed company, and his brother, Taylor. G. Vaughan, was placed in charge of sales. E. B. Lennox was production manager and Thomas B. Stanley, who served as Governor of Virginia 1954-58, as secretary-treasurer. The new business, which began production in 1919, prospered and before long, T. G. Vaughan proposed the organization of a new furniture factory. Galax citizens subscribed to stock, and in 1923 Vaughan Furniture Company became a reality.

The textile industry began in Galax when a Mr. Robbins from High Point, N. C., agreed to start a hosiery mill here if Galax citizens would purchase stock equal to 1/3 the initial investment. The money was "dug up" and J. T. Pollard was sent here to organize The Galax Knitting Company. The plant which began operation in 1924 was located where The Wonderknit Corporation is today.

Galax Furniture Company, Inc. was established in 1925 by C. L. Smith. In 1943 John Messer, Sr. gained control of the company and about 1960 it was merged with Webb Furniture Company.

John Messer, Sr. could be considered the Horatio Alger of the Galax story. He came to town in 1927 with a shine on his pants and a gleam in his eye. Within twenty-five years he parlayed his meager assets into the controlling interest in two mirror plants and three furniture plants. The unofficial conglomeration was known as Messer Industries. Messer's inauspicious beginning was a shack behind Webb Furniture Company where he started a small mirror factory. This soon expanded into The Galax Mirror Company with its products marketed all over the United States. This business is now called The New Galax Mirror Company, and Webb Furniture Company is a division of The Congoleum Company.

The Carnation Company, processor and distributor of evaporated milk, began production May 10, 1937. Formal opening ceremonies were held July 23, 1937 in Felts Park on "Cow Day," and Governor George C. Perry delivered the principal address.

Burlington Industries opened the Galax Weaving Plant in 1937. The plant has expanded substantially and today it is one of the city's larger industrial firms. Robert Sills is the present plant manager

Sawyers Furniture Company, manufacturers of upholstered furniture, was established in 1945 by C. F. Sawyer. Hubert H. Watson is president and general manager of the company.

Henry L. Harris, a textile graduate of North Carolina State University, joined the staff of Galax Knitting Company in 1945. Later and C. W. Marshall formed the Harris-Marshall Hosiery Mills, Inc.

About 1946 Ross Penry came to Galax from Martinsville. He joined Hubert White, Waldo Price, and others in forming The Old Dominion Knitting Company. The business has developed into the present day Penry Manufacturing Company.

Dixon Lumber Company, Inc. originated from a saw mill business in the early 1920's by S. R. Dixon, with approximately six men. Later in 1938 the name was changed to S. R. Dixon Lumber Shop with sawmill and planing mill. In 1941, the name was changed to Dixon Lumber and moved to its present location, with sawmill and planing mill and retail lumber supply. In 1945, it began the manufacture of hardwood flooring, and in 1948 began manufacture of drawer sides which has expanded into its present dimension plant. In 1949, it was incorporated into Dixon Lumber Co., Inc. as it now operates with 250 employees.

Mr. S. R. Dixon, the founder and president, passed away in 1964. Upon his death, his son, Glenn W. Dixon, who had worked alongside his father and other employees from 1934, became president. The policy has been one of promoting and protecting the welfare of the employees in the best interest of the company. This assures a sound business which will provide the highest degree of security for all.

The Wonderknit Corporation, established in 1952 for the manufacture of knitwear, is one of the city's largest industries.

Hanes Knitting Company employs more people than any other industry in the city. Galax citizens raised over a million dollars in just thirty days to provide the local effort needed to convince the Hanes Corporation to locate a plant here in 1955.

Bluefield Church Furniture Company was established in 1956 on Oldtown Street in the old Galax Chair Co. It later moved to its present location on Shaw Street.

American Mirror Company, Inc. broke ground in May of 1957 and began operation the latter part of that same year. Full production was begun in 1958

Square Building Supply, Inc. opened for business in January, 1962, as Square Wholesale Building and Supply Corporation. The manager at that time was Boddie Melton, who, except for one year when Bill Clary took over, was manager until April of 1967 when the present manager, Don Lyon, took over. In 1963 the business name was changed to Square Building Supply, Inc. The business has always been located at its present location on Railroad Avenue.

Galax Chair Company, Inc. founded by Bill Woods in 1958, is now a subsidiary of Vaughan Furniture Company.

Joines Body Shop, makers of aluminum truck covers, was started in 1959 by "Whitey" Joines.

Chestnut Creek Corporation, manufacturers of upholstered furniture, was established in 1971. John Nunn operates this recent addition to Galax industry.

B. C. Vaughan Furniture, established in 1974, is owned and operated by George and John Vaughan. The plant is located near Chestnut Creek just north of Cliffview.

This rapid industrial development has brought greater employment and prosperity to the entire area. New retail business have expanded. Shopping Centers have sprung up and the small rural town has grown into a thriving little city.

Much of the industrial growth of the city could not have taken place without the help of the Galax Development Corporation. This corporation was chartered in 1957. Harvey M. Todd was Secretary for many years, Warren B. Giersch, Vice-President, and A. Glenn Pless, President. This Corporation is still in existence and Charles Waugh is now President. Directors of Galax Development Corporation are: Roland Alderman, Walter G. Andrews, Dr. R. C.

Bowie, George Ben Davis, Jack Guynn, Gene T. McKnight, A. Glenn Pless, Robert T. Porter, John W. Sutherland, Dan B. Waugh, Charles Waugh, Robert Webb, H. S. White, Jr. This corporation, together with the Small Business Association, helped to finance the Bluefield Church Furniture Company building, Penry Manufacturing Company (original building and the addition later), Sawyers Furniture Company, which was rebuilt after a fire destroyed it, and the Wonderknit Company.

The Hanes Company came to Galax in 1955 and began operations in the Albert Eads building on South Main Street across from White Chevrolet Company. In 1960 they wanted to expand. They made the town a proposition that if the town would raise $1,000,000.00 by subscription, they would build a large plant in Galax. To handle this venture, the Carroll-Grayson Development Corporation was chartered and raised more than the amount specified, within a period of 30 days. They now have a plant consisting of 10 acres, all on one floor. Raw cotton goes in one side of the mill and comes out a boxed product on the other side. Hanes paid back the note holders long before the notes were due.

Galax's industry did not just happen. It is here because of interested citizens who were willing to give of their time and money, even from the very beginnings of Galax.

W. K. Early and Company, Inc., one of the oldest businesses in Galax, began operation in 1906. Over the years it has grown until it is one of the largest lumber and building material companies between Roanoke and Bristol. It is one of the few businesses that is still owned and operated by the family of the original owners.

Blue Ridge Transfer Co., Inc. was organized in 1932, by J. W. Stanley, for the primary purpose of serving the furniture industry in Galax and Virginia. It now operates in nineteen states and the District of Columbia, in the movement of general freight from the principal cities of the east and from Atlanta, Georgia, to all Southwest Virginia. The company maintains other terminals in Stanleytown and Roanoke, Virginia. J. W. Stanley is president and Jack Stanley, Jr., Secretary and Assistant General Manager.

GOVERNMENT, SCHOOLS and CHURCHES

The town of Galax was incorporated in 1906 with a mayor-council form of government. Ben F. Calloway was the first mayor and the first council was: Elbert F. Wright, Dr. J. K. Caldwell, E. C. Williams, M. L. Bishop, J. H. Kapp and Dr. J. W. Bolen.

The mayors following Mr. Calloway in succession were as follows: J. W. Stamey (1908), J. F. Vass (1909), R. E. Jones (1911), J. F. Vass (1912), D. A. Robertson (1920), DaCosta Woltz (1930), J. P. Carrico (1932), B. D. Beamer (1934), W. G. Andrews (1941), R. L. Nelson (1942), Ross P. Penry (1946), Dr. R. C. Bowie (1950), B. D. Beamer (1952), Dan B. Vaughan (1954), McCamant Higgins (1956), Jack Guynn (1968) and John Vaughan (1974).

In 1922 the charter was changed to a Town Manager form of government and I.G. Vass became the first Town Manager. Other Town Managers have been Harvey M. Todd, Orrin Rhudy, W. G. Andrews and Harold Snead who presently serves in this capacity.

The town became a second class city in 1954 with its own government independent of the county. Councilmen select one of their own members to act as mayor. The Mayor has no power other than presiding over council, although he does have a voting privilege on the council. The present City Council consists of: John Vaughan, Mayor, S. J. Johnson, Vice-Mayor, Horace Cochran, Gene T. McKnight, Jim Ballard, L. A. Kyle and Glenn Wilson. Newly elected Councilmen scheduled to take office July 1, 1976 are Michael Coomes, Herb Walker and Ed Diamond.

Citizens of Galax who have served in the House of Delegates of the General Assembly of Virginia are as follows: Thomas L. Felts, 1926-28; Miss Vinnie Caldwell, 1928-30; H. Prince Burnett, 1937-39; Dr. Robert C. Bowie, 1943-45; Floyd Williams, 1949-51; Dr. Virgil J. Cox, 1962-64.

Citizens of Galax who have served in the Senate of the General Assembly of Virginia are as follows: Thomas L. Felts, 1928-32; Taylor G. Vaughan, 1932-40; Bunyan C. Vaughan, 1940-42; Floyd S. Landreth, 1944- 46.

Installation of the town's first water and sewer systems occurred in 1916. A spring and a well on the Capt. John B. Waugh property, now the home of Mrs. Charles Waugh, served as the source of supply for the town's first water system. The first water reservoir, which still serves the city, was constructed on the nearby hill. A filtering plant, located near the city warehouse, to purify the water was constructed at the same time. Beginning in 1949, under the direction of Town Manager W. G. Andrews, plans were made for modernizing the sewage and water plants. A new sewage treatment plant was completed in 1955, and a new water plant, which increased water storage capacity from 300,000 gallons to 1,500,000 gallons, was finished in 1956.

At present, the Galax City Police Department consists of Chief Nelson Lineberry, 16 male officers, 1 female officer and 1 female office clerk, who is also an officer and 4 dispatchers.

Galax's first jail was a "little frame shack" that stood near where the Bank of Virginia now stands. When the prisoners "sobered up," they usually kicked off a couple of boards and went home.

Some of Galax's former police chiefs were as follows: C. L. Dotson, Troy Higgins, Walt Anderson, Posey Martin, Joe Snow, Jack Higgins, Hugh Turner, Harold Williams, Brad Dickens, and Harold Detter.

Chief Posey Martin is the only town or city policeman to be killed in the line of duty. This occurred in 1935 when a prisoner, Howard Delp, stabbed officer Frank Dotson and Chief Martin while escaping from jail. Officer Dotson was severely wounded, but Chief Martin was unable to survive his injuries. The manhunt which followed was the largest this area had seen since the Allen Tragedy in Carroll County. Chief Martin's son, Rayburn, is presently employed by Burlington Industries.

In 1925 McGuffy Coomes (father of the late Robert L. Coomes), a Federal Revenue Agent, was slain while manning a roadblock in an attempt to capture "moonshiners" hauling illegal whiskey. The incident took place on Stuart Drive in a barn behind what is now Martins Cleaners.

In the early 1900's the first fire fighting in Galax was done by "bucket brigade." Church bells and factory whistles were used to sound the alarm and everyone grabbed a bucket and turned out to assist. The first town-owned equipment consisted of two carts with hose reels, which required 5 men to pull the hose and 5 men to hold each cart.

The first Volunteer Fire Department was established in 1912. The first fire truck was a Model T. Ford, customized by firemen to haul hose and ladder. The first Fire House was located on Center Street where the City Council Chambers are now located

The present Fire House is on West Grayson Street and is known as the Walter G. Andrews Municipal Fire Station, named for the former Town Manager who devoted several years to serving the town and city. The station was built with the future in mind. There is suitable office space and living quarters if the City ever needs a paid Fire Department. The department is now adequately equipped with a 50 ft. ladder truck, 3 pumper trucks, a tank truck, a utility truck, a Panel reserve truck, an ambulance, a pick-up truck and a brush truck.

The 36 members of the Galax Volunteer Fire Department are as follows: Joe Crockett, Chief; Richard Dalton, Assistant Chief; F. H. Anderson, Capt. Co. No.1; Mac Higgins, Lt. Co. No.1; Bill Morton, Secretary-Treasurer; Carroll Clark, Chaplain; Harvey Hennis, Capt. Co. No.2; Charles Burnette, Lt. Co. No.2; R. V. Morris, Trustee; Bays Roberts, Trustee; James Talley, Trustee; Winfred Boaz, John Bryant, Clarence Burnette, Duard Burnette, Mike Coomes, Ulyss Cruise, Larry Diamond, Royce Easter, Ralph Gatchel, Bill Gurley, Roy Hale, B. C. Hankley, James Holderfield, Mike Holderfield, Jeff Morris, obert Morris, Jr., Gale Perry, Bob Reavis, Willie Richardson, Ralph Sexton, Bolen Shepherd, Dewey Sturdivant, G. W. Todd, L. M. Todd" Glenn Wilson and Bud Wright.

Galax's First School

The first school in Galax was in 1904 over what is now Jones Furniture Store. At that time the first floor was a grocery store and the past office, both operated by R. E. Jones, the town's first postmaster. Mr. Jones also operated an undertaking business on the second floor and the little school was in the back of the building, Mrs. Mike Nuckolls was the teacher and the students were Platt Harp, Lela Beasley Jones, Callie Beasley Spraker, Grace Bishop Roberts, Dan Roberts, Fred Roberts, Walter Jones, Luther Jones, Clyde Harp Carico, Eugene Carico and Harry Carrico.

When Galax was laid off, the promoters set aside ten acres of a beautiful pine grove, called "Piney Woods", for public school purposes. Within two years an elementary and high school building known as the "academy" was constructed. Mr. A. C. Painter was instrumental in raising funds for the new school. He served as president of the Galax High School Corporation and Professor G. F. Carr, principal of the school, was Secretary and Treasurer. In addition to the sale of stock, funds were raised through "box suppers", plays and talent shows. The building was a two story wooden structure with four classrooms on the first floor and an auditorium on the second, all of which were heated by wood burning stoves.

A new brick building was constructed in 1908 to accommodate the fast growing community and another building was added in 1925.

Another of the numerous fires which seemed to plague Galax struck again in 1936. This time the target was the school building which had been constructed in 1908, but the other building was only slightly damaged. The following year the building was reconstructed and it is still serving the community. It was remodeled and expanded in 1971.

A separate high school was constructed on "Knowledge Knoll" in 1955 and today the Galax City Schools have an educational program equal to any small city in the state.

William G. Davis is Superintendent of Schools and members of the Board of Education are: Dr. E. H. Robinson, chairman; John Nunn, vice chairman; Roy Kyle; Lucille Porter; and Ed Barker.

This was written for the 75th Anniversary of Galax in 1981

Galax Grew with the USA

It was the year British troops fired on and killed five persons in front of the Boston customs house. The Townshend duties had already been imposed on glass, tea, silk, lead, paper and paint imports from England, and the Quartering Act had met with resistance from American colonists. In this year, 1770, all but the tea tax had been repealed, and the Quartering Act was allowed to die. Only minor irritations remained, and a period of fairly good relations with England existed. But it was only the calm before the storm.

In this year, also, John Blair built a forge on Chestnut Creek in Southwest Virginia, the beginning of Blair village. In just a few years, Galax would take about half the businesses from Blair village, but that's getting ahead of the story.

Here in what would much later be known as the Twin County area, the irritations of the British must have seemed far away to Blair, who set up his forge to smelt iron ore and make iron from it. He powered his trip hammer by a dam on the creek as Quakers came up from North Carolina to settle the area and the Scotch-Irish came out of the Tidewater area to make this their home.

While the Boston Tea Party was being carried out by angry New England colonists, while the colonies declared and won their independence, this area was being settled. George Washington was President when, in 1792, Grayson County was formed from Wythe County, with Oldtown established as the county seat.

When Flower Swift and Clark Nuckolls were donating land in 1794 for a Grayson courthouse, the U.S. was having a troubled year. Sectional conflicts had begun, soldiers were beginning to fight Indians in the Ohio Valley and the Whiskey Rebellion of Pennsylvania farmers against a tax on liquor and stills was taking place. But good things were happening, too. Eli Whitney patented his cotton gin and the U.S. got its first steam engine.

Moving on up in years, past the War of 1812, past the Mexican War and the Westward expansion, past the War Between the States, we come to the year 1870. Reconstruction was taking place, women were beginning their attempts to gain the vote. And John Barger Caldwell, one of Galax's early pioneers, bought several acres on the east side of Chestnut Creek, including the site of the present Twin County Community Hospital, for $1500. Much of the land on both sides of the creek was marshland.

Settlers continued to pour into the area, and we move on up to the turn of the century. We find the U.S. prospering, industrialism taking place and the American League in baseball being denied recognition by the National League. At the time William. McKinley was nominated by the Republicans for a second term as President, the Galax area was still farmland, There were few Houses: the William Roberts place was just above Stuart Drive. The Tom Roberts house was on Stuart Drive, as was the Hugh Roberts home.

The homes of A.C. Anderson and A.C Painter were just off Anderson Street, and John Barger Caldwell's home was on East Stuart Drive. But, of course, there were no streets and no street names at that time.

Anderson Home   Painter Home   Caldwell Home

In the first years of the 1900's, in the years when President McKinley was re-elected and assassinated, when Teddy Roosevelt assumed the Presidency, when coal strikes were being settled and the first post-season college football classic (The Rose Bowl) was started, back in this area, Norfolk and Western Railroad was being persuaded to extend its line from Blair village to a yet to-be-built town. J. P. Carico, who had persuaded Col. Fries to build a mill and a dam on the New, and John B. Waugh, R.E. Jones and others were forming a real estate company to buy , land for the new town. They bought 375 acres west of Chestnut Creek and hired Lynchburg engineers Arnold and DeMott to lay it off in orderly, neat streets.

On the same day that Orville Wright became the first person to fly a heavier-than-air machine by staying aloft for 12 seconds at Kitty Hawk.

N.C. - Dec. 17, 1903 - the first lots were being sold in Galax. In the auction, lots sold for $25 for a 50-foot lot on a side street to $250 for a corner lot on the main street. And lots of people went away shaking their heads at the exorbitant prices, it's said.

At that time, the main street was called Center Street and what is now Main Street was called Mt. Airy Street. A.C. Painter reportedly bought all the lots on both sides of Center street from where the Methodist Church is now, to Main for $25 each. One lot was bought by the Ward Brothers, who built a two story building. On the first floor was general merchandise, and above was the first moving picture theater in Bonaparte, as the town was called. The building was later destroyed by fire and the name was soon changed to Galax.

In 1904, when the U.S. got the Panama Canal Zone, when President Roosevelt sent a message around the world in 12 minutes by cable, N & W completed the railroad spur into the town we know as Galax. The town was named after the Galax leaves gathered here and transported round the world to be used in floral arrangements, but the stories of how it came to be named such differ. In one, J. W. Cook, an official of the railroad, suggested it; and in another, a Mrs., Kirsley, an insurance saleslady; thought the leaves were beautiful and suggested the town be named after them. But, however the origin, the name was adopted.

The following year, when Theodore Roosevelt was inaugurated for his first full term in office and when an epidemic of yellow fever killed 400 in New Orleans, Galax held its first Great Galax Fair. Ninety citizens formed a fair association with shares of stock costing $100 each and limited to two per person. Twenty- two acres of land where Felts Park is now were bought, and a race track, grandstand and exhibit building were constructed. Visitors came from all over by horse and wagon or covered wagon and camped on the grounds or stayed in homes or hotels to see the Fair.

The arrival of the train bringing the midway shows, rides and wild animals drew crowds to watch them unload and move to the Fairgrounds. Farmers exhibited their produce and livestock, while their wives took their sewing, quilting, cakes jams and jellies. There were fireworks, and people who enjoyed visiting with each other.

In 1906, when suffragette Susan B. Anthony died, when the most damaging earthquake in U.S. history hit San Francisco and was followed by a fire, killing about 700 and doing $400 million in damage, and when Tommy Burns defeated Marvin Hart for the heavyweight boxing championship, the Charter of Galax was formed and a mayor-council government established. When Galax was incorporated, about half the businesses of Blair village moved to Galax.

Ben F. Calloway of Independence, who had come to Galax as secretary of the land development company, was elected the first mayor.

The young town sprang up overnight. Pioneer businesses included Bolen Drug Store, Galax Drug Company, R.E. Jones's Store, Galax Hardware, Crystal Drug Store and Witherow's Store. Marvin, Monroe and Frazier Ward operated a mill on Piper's Gap Road, and a cannery was built where Vaughan Bassett Furniture Company is now.

Industry also came to Galax after the railroad when John Waugh, S.E. Wilkerson and Creed Hanks established a furniture factory to make use of the forest resources instead of shipping them out as rough lumber. Located where Wonderknit is now, the factory burned in 1907 and was never rebuilt. (*Editors Note: it was rebuilt and burned again later)*

In the early 1900's, fires were fought by bucket brigade. The church bells and factory whistles would sound the alarm, and people would grab buckets and go help. The town then bought two carts with hose reels that required five men to pull the hose and five to hold each cart.

In 1912, when New Mexico became the 45th state and Arizona the 48th, Galax set up its first volunteer' fire department with a Model T, which Ford had recently introduced for $850, customized by the firemen to haul a hose and ladder. The first firehouse was on Center Street where the city council chambers are now located.

In the years following Galax's formation, while the U.S. faced serious financial problems, while realistic art was getting its start, Galax, with its muddy streets, bustled with activities. There were wagons pulled by oxen and loaded with crossties or tan bark headed for the lumber yards, herds of cattle, sheep or turkeys driven through the major downtown streets, barrels e of apples, berries, chestnuts and chinquapins waiting on the depot platform to be shipped north.

But, other than the . railroad, Galax was isolated during most of the n winter months because of . the terrible conditions of its
roads. The railroad provided mail and passenger service to Roanoke daily, but roads into Galax were little more than trails and were impossible to travel in winter.

At one point, R.A. Anderson operated Blue Ridge Bus Lines to Mt. Airy and Pulaski, but the bad roads caused operating losses that wrecked the company before routes were developed enough to make the operation economical.

Early roads were the Good Spur Gap Road near Fancy Gap, which connected with the road going east and west at Fort Chiswell. A branch off Good Spur Road, built by the county farm, passed through Galax along what is now Stuart Drive and went through Grayson County and on to Washington County.

Another road crossed the mountain, followed Piper's Gap Road, and crossed Chestnut Creek about where Webb Furniture No. 2 is now and turned west where Long Street is now and went on to Oldtown.

There were no bridges across Chestnut Creek, so it had to be forded. Swinging bridges allowed people to walk across, but when
re the water was up, they had to camp on the east side until the water went down.

Galax got its first paved road, from Hillsville to Galax, in 1923, the year rumors of President Warren G. Harding's administration began to include graft and theft, and the year Harding himself died.

The year before, 1922, was the year poet T.S. Eliot published his most famous work, "The Wasteland," and the year a meteorite weighing 20 tons fell near Blackstone, Va., creating a crater 400 feet square.

It is also the year Galax's charter was changed to a town-manager form of government and I.G. Vass was made the first town manager. Galax has continued to change as the 20th century moves on. In place of the swampy bogs where Galax first was formed, there are industries and homes because, after the bad flood of Chestnut Creek in 1940, work to widen, deepen and straighten the creek eliminated most of the swamp and flood danger. The early streets had been so muddy as to be the brunt of jokes. A man saw a hat in the mud, the story goes, and lifted it up to find another man under it. He asked the man if he needed help, and the reply was, "No, I'm all right. I'm on horseback." Now, Galax has sidewalks, paved streets and modern roads connecting it to the outside world.

The fair is gone, but yearly the Galax Old Fiddlers Convention draws thousands to Galax, camping and filling every available motel space. The circus doesn't come in on the train - which has a limited run into the city but the carnival still comes on July 4, and there are crafts . festivals, theater productions and flea markets to entertain the people. The bus line does not exist anymore, but , most people own their own vehicles, and many make use of air travel from airports not far away,
Because of modern conveniences and luxuries,' most people in Galax saw on television the attempted assassination of President Reagan and the Pope, most do their washing in their own homes in automatic washers, and life is relatively easy compared to life when Galax was first established. Continuing into the 1970s, Galax celebrates its 75th anniversary by reviewing its humble origins and looking to its promising future.

Editors Note: *This is how the Old Fiddles Convention looked from the air just before darkness fell across Felts Park Saturday night, August 9th, 1969. A short time afterwards there was not a single parking place available anywhere in the park. Crown estimation varied and reached all the way to 20,000. It was undoubtedly ht largest crown to ever assemble in Galax. Galax Gazette, Tuesday August 12, 1969*

By Sally Harris News Editor
75th Anniversary Commemorative Edition
1906-1981

Cecil Lewis Martin

Cecil Lewis Martin (known as C. L.) was born on 25 December 1927 in Barren Springs Virginia. His parents, O. C. and Norma Martin moved their family to Galax in 1937. Their first home was on Pipers Gap Road (name was later changed to Anderson Road) before moving to 209 Calhoun Street. Part of their home was devoted to their florist business.

After C. L. attended Galax schools he spent the rest of his life doing what he loved best. He worked with his parents and family to build a florist and greenhouse business that would become a great asset to the Galax area and surrounding communities. He took great pride and pleasure in growing plants from seedlings to products ready to sell. Martin's Flowers and Greenhouses were household words from 1943 to the mid 1970s. The family was very proud of their accomplishments and their part in the growth of the twin counties area.

On a snowy winter day in 1948 C. L. drove to Fox Virginia to marry his sweetheart Lucille Hash. They enjoyed many years together.

The history included in this book represent many years of research, memories and talks with countless residents of the area. We are all truly fortunate that his brother Roger has allowed C. L.'s lifetime project to be shared with readers today and generations to come. We are also fortunate that C. L.'s kind spirit and love of Galax will forever be treasured.

Editor's note:
I lived several houses west of the Martins on Calhoun Street. The Nunn family resided at 209 Calhoun from 1931 to 1947 before we moved to another house in town.

I can clearly remember walking down to the Martins' home to visit with C. L. and mess around in the dirt in the greenhouse. My friend with the green thumb was a gentle soul who always took the time to show me what he was doing with the flowers. He even tried to get me interested in his other interest.... building model airplanes.

I never realized that C. L. loved history or that he was writing this excellent record of early Galax. His brother Roger indicated that Munsey Webb and his love of local railroad history probably influenced C. L.'s desire to study, research and record the history of Galax. From flowers to history, we are indeed fortunate that C. L. called Galax home and that he shared his passions with us.
JJN, May 2013

Early Development and Growth of Galax, Virginia, 1903 - 1950
Researched and written by C.L. Martin

Grayson County, Virginia, was formed from Wythe County and part of Smith County in Southwest Virginia in the upper New River Plateau by the Act of the Commonwealth of Virginia Legislature on November 7, 1792. One such pioneer of the upper New River settlement was William Bourne, who was a determined candidate running for the Virginia Legislature to secure the New county of Grayson, being defeated by William Grayson, a Montgomery County Senator, who extended his assistance to William Bourne in attaining the title of Grayson, which the people of the area named the new county Grayson in his honor, having 438 square miles of land area.

The first Grayson County seat was established in a large log born located on William Bourne's property in the Knob Fork area of Elk Creek, May 21, 1793, forming a court committee appointing their first officers to be on the Grayson Court such as: William Bourne, Clerk of Court, Flower Swift, Minitree Jones, Nathaniel Frisbie were appointed Magistrate of Grayson Court, Phillip Gaines appointed Sheriff. Governor Harry Lee of the Commonwealth of Virginia appointed Flower Swift, Enoch Osbourne, Nathaniel Frisbie, Nathaniel Pope, Matthew Dickey, Lewis Hale as Justices of Peace of Grayson Court.

Governor Harry Lee and the pursuant to the act of the General Assembly of the Commonwealth of Virginia passed January 22, 1794, to move the Grayson Courthouse seat to Greenville, Grayson County, VA (Oldtown). Flower Swift, Charles Nuckolls has strong influence in the new Grayson County Court Seat, having purchased large land tracts on the upper New River of the Greenville area. They donated a 100 acre land tract for the purpose of surveying, laying out lots, streets, roads, public buildings, dwellings, businesses, churches, and courthouse, naming the village the new village Greenville, Grayson County, Virginia. The Greenville Courthouse seat building was constructed of logs and sawed timbers in 1794, known as Rose's Cabin.

As Grayson County grew in population and the Greenville Community expanded, the Grayson Court Committee decided that they needed a larger second courthouse and the record office constructed of brick, built in 1888 to serve the peoples of Grayson County.

The wagon roads that connected the settlements to Grayson County Courthouse at Greenville were Furnace Road, Baywood Road, Fishers Gap Road, Meadow Creek Road, Piper's Gap Road, Wards Gap Road, Low Gap Road, Good Spur Road, Ingspur Road, Greenbrier Road, The roads were kept up by each individual landowner depending an which road passed through his property, checked by Court appointed overseer. The Greenville area settlers possessed knowledge of many trades that stimulated their economy that brought on monies to pay for their much needed goods. They established their farms and businesses via the early transportation of freight wagons and buggies hauling passengers, freight, mercantile supplies to their stores and farms.

The site of the Buchanan Land Grant was located on both sides of lower Chestnut Creek tributary (in present Carroll-Grayson Counties, Anderson Bottoms (Galax) which had rich soils for farming and an abundance of heavy timber resource. The Buchanan Land Grant was surveyed November 29, 1749, by John Buchanan who was the son-in-law of James Patton. The Buchanan Land Grant contained 684 acres purchased by George H. Currin of Grayson County from Andrew Boyd of Wythe County on December 1, 1806. George H. Currin was one of the earlier settlers of the lower Chestnut Creek tributary, having served as a member of the Grayson County Courthouse at Greenville (Oldtown). He sold 259 acres of the Buchanan Land Grant to James Anderson, 65 acres to Amos Ballard, leaving himself a 360 acre land tract. George H. Currin, James Anderson, Amos Ballard of Anderson Bottoms were associated with other settlers from lower and upper Chestnut Creek tributary and the Baywood areas such as the Blairs, Dickeys, Williams, Leonards, Bedsauls, Carlans,

Reeces, Lundys, Farmers, Frosts, Clonchs, Hollands. Allens, McCoys, Mckensies, Wilkinsons, Nobletts, Fannings, Swifts, Ballards, Larrows, Mullins, Hiatts, Reddicks, Howells, Johnsons, Wilsons, Cooleys, Coxe's, Davises, Hanks, Wards, Lineberrys, Robinsons, Jennings, Reavises, Nuckolls, Jones, Patton, Roberts, Waughs, Bartletts, Hamptons, McCamants, Witherows, Higgins. Most of the early settlers were of Quaker, Scot-Irish, and English ancestry. George H. Currin of Anderson Bottoms on the Chestnut Creek tributary had served several years on the Grayson County Court seat, was commissioned to help establish Carroll County Court seat. Many people who lived in the upper and lower sections of Grayson County became discouraged by the time and distance necessary to travel to the Grayson County seat location at Greenville (Oldtown).

In 1842, Carroll County was formed from Grayson County by an Act of the Commonwealth of Virginia Legislature in accord with the Honorable John M. Gregory, Esq., acting as the Governor of the Commonwealth of Virginia, signing an executive order to cut off a portion of eastern Grayson, western Patrick Counties naming the new county Carroll in honor of Charles Carroll, a signer of the Declaration of Independence. John Carroll, who had lived earlier in eastern Virginia, campaigned for a seat in the Commonwealth of Virginia Legislature on the promise to submit a bill to form a separate county. He was elected fulfilling his promise to submit a bill against John Blair whose lobbying efforts were dedicated to killing the bill.

Carroll County had 445 square miles of land area. Hillsville in Carroll County, Virginia, was established as the County Courthouse seat on June 6, 1842. The Honorable John M. Gregory, Esq., acting as Governor of the Commonwealth of Virginia, commissioned Joshua Hanks, John Blair, Benjamin Cooley, John Cocke, William Lindsey, John Mitchell, George H. Currin, William Raines, William Hall, and John Vaughan as Justices,

John Carroll, born in Ireland, came from Lynchburg in the 1830's buying a large farm on Big Reed Island in Grayson County. He later moved his holdings to Fairview, east of Hillsville, VA. He was a slaveholder, one of the wealthiest men in Grayson County. He ran for the Virginia Legislature in 1841 defeating John Blair of Grayson County in a bitter contest. He was responsible for the legislation dividing Grayson and creating a new Carroll County in 1842.

They were duly sworn in to organize a Carroll County government and elect county officials. The justices met at the home of James Stafford at Hillsville, Carroll County, Virginia, taking action on several matters. William Lindsey was elected Clerk of the Carroll County Court. A. D. Fulton, Benjamin Cooley, Richard T. Matthews, Archibald Stuart, Samuel McCamant, William F. Cooke, Madison Carter, and Joseph C. Spalding were sworn in by Thomas McCade, a Justice of the Peace of Floyd County. Each man was admitted as attorneys-at-law to practice in Carroll County Court.

Independence Village

There were three factions in Grayson County trying to decide on the location of the Grayson County seat. The people of Elk Creek and the present Greenville Courthouse were having a dispute over where a new courthouse should be located. The people of Elk Creek wanted the county seat in the Elk Creek valley. The commissioners met at the home of Hardin Cox on June 22, 1843. Several sites were considered and the final decision being William Hale's farm in the Elk Creek Valley. An independent group formed out of this dispute which offered a location to satisfy both sides. They had identified a valley below Point Lookout Mountain.

In 1849, the Virginia General Assembly in Richmond, Virginia, appointed a panel of Commissioners composed of one representative from the counties of Smyth, Wythe, and Washington to select a new location for the Grayson County seat. Meeting at the home of Colonel James Dickey, the Commissioners were faced with the two dominant factions pulling for the Elk Creek Valley and Greenville sites. Colonel Dickey sought to solve the problem and asked a third group about their preference. This group's answer was "We are 'independents' - we are not taking sides". As the Elk Creek Valley and the Greenville proponents continued in deadlock, Colonel James Dickey proposed locating a county seat "where the independent people lived" which was names the village of Independence, Grayson County, Virginia. The Grayson County Court seat was moved from Greenville to Independence in 1850. The first Grayson Court at Independence convened in April of 1851.

Commerce and Trade

The village of Greenville's post office name was changed to Nuckollsville, Grayson County, Virginia, in 1851, and to Oldtown in 1852, The Oldtown area had developed into farm lands producing sufficient agricultural crops such as vegetables, fruits, hay, oats, buckwheat, wheat, corn, and other miscellaneous crops, The area was also rich in livestock and great pains were taken with the raising of beef cattle, sheep, turkeys, and poultry. The area was heavy in timber growth with oak, pine, poplar, and chestnut. As the Oldtown Community became more established, the population grew. The late 1870's found the citizens securing more farm land and establishing businesses.

The Greenville area was linked by the Meadow Creek Road, Reavistown Road, Healing Spring Road, Ballard's Branch Road and Dickinson's Ferry Road. At Reavistown Village, Sandy and John Reavis and Jerry Jennings built the Reavis Mill in 1854 which produced flour and corn meal. J. C. Reavis and William Gordon later built a grist mill and a sawmill on Meadow Creek below the Reavis Mill which produced corn meal and lumber. In 1881, William Gordon built the Gordon Woolen Mill on Meadow Creek which manufactured wool cloth and was later operated by H. E. Gordon. George Phillips established a wood working shop on Meadow Creek which made stairways, spindles, and spokes for wagons and buggies. R. E. Jones and Lath Hampton operated a sawmill at the mouth of Meadow Creek on New River. R. E. Jones also had a General Store at the same location. The Oldtown Post Office was located in the Old Greenville Courthouse Tax and Records' Office. Previously, mail had been picked up at Wytheville, Va., Chestnut Yard at the Norfolk & Western Railway Stations and then at the Blair Station, A. R. Grubb was Postmaster of the Oldtown Post Office.

J. B. and W. P. Waugh established the Waugh Brothers General Store at Oldtown. They were wool buyers. John B. Waugh was the President of the Framers Fire Insurance Company at Oldtown and Independence. W. P. Waugh leased the Old Greenville Grayson Courthouse and turned it into a boarding house and hotel. Reavis and Gordon operated a general store. R. . Jones and J. C. Reavis operated a foundry and machine shop. H. Williams and A. Jennings operated a distillery. M. H. and T. S. Patton operated a flour mill on Oglesby Branch in the Oldtown area. Dr. C. A. Witherow, Dr. T. B. Witherow operated the Witherow's Drug Store in Oldtown. Doctors serving the Oldtown and Reavistown areas were: Dr. B. S. Cooper, Dr. W. B. Durphy, Dr. C. A. Witherow, Dr. T. B. Witherow, and Dr. Alex Grubb who was also a dentist. Doctors serving the Baywoad area were Dr. W.P. Collins and Dr. Stanley Young.

The people of the Oldtown area had a strong spiritual devotion and established churches at Oldtown on the Methodist and Presbyterian faith. The Primitive Baptist Churches were located at the crossroads in Baywood and on Meadow Creek (established in 1792). They also had a school named the Oldtown Academy. Warrick Murphy was head "Schoolmaster" in 1890.

Thomas Blair of Scottish descent from Pennsylvania, settled on the Lower Chestnut Creek in mid 1782. He had a son named John Blair who was born in Pennsylvania in 1772. Thomas Blair and Colonel Matthew Dickey had obtained a large acreage of land which was later known as the 'Gosson Lead" and rich in copper sulphate and iron pyrites minerals. Colonel Matthew Dickey and Thomas Blair formed a partnership in 1788. They constructed a stone shaft type Furnace (Bloomery) and Ironworks at the mouth of Mill Creek which emptied into Chestnut Creek. Just below the future site of the Blair Community on Chestnut Creek located in the County of Grayson (later it was Carroll

County). Colonel Dickey sold his partnership in the Blair & Dickey Furnace and Ironworks to Thomas Blair in 1794. Thomas Blair acquired the Blair & Dickey Furnace Ironworks which included the forge and 854 acre land tract.

Thomas Blair also had an interest in the Point Hope Furnace and Ironworks at Peach Bottom operated by William Bourne and Son, and an interest in the Poplar Camp Furnace and Ironworks at Poplar Camp in Wythe County. Thomas Blair departed life in late 1805. His will was probated in 1806, leaving his real estate and personal properties to his widow and son, John Blair, on lower Chestnut Creek. John Blair's family lived at the Blair home place at Blair (Cliffview). He became very prominent in the Blair Community due to his business dealings. John Blair was one of Grayson County's most influential men from his service on the Grayson County Clerk at Greenville (Oldtown) Grayson County, Virginia, and in the Commonwealth of Virginia Legislature. With his lobbying efforts, he attempted to kill the bill presented by John Carroll of eastern Virginia to form and separate lower Carroll County form Grayson County in the Legislature in June of 1842. The Community of Blair was placed in Carroll County in 1842 which was formed from Grayson and Patrick Counties. John Blair was commissioned by the Honorable John M. Gregory, Esq., acting Governor of the Commonwealth of Virginia, to serve as a Justice to organize the Carroll County Court and elect county officials on June 6,1842. John Blair departed life in 1853 at the age of eighty-one years old.

Commerce and trade began to develop on the Lower Chestnut Creek and Crooked Creek in the Iron Ridge area of Carroll County in the New River plateau with the beginning of the "copper boom" in the early 1840's. Northern investors were buying and leasing mineral tracts in free, opening copper mines along the tributaries of Chestnut and Crooked Creeks mining copper sulphate and pyhrrotite ores manufacturing copper bar. Following the reconstruction years after the Civil War, the Community of Blair began to develop having roads linked up to Oldtown, Anderson Bottoms, Ward Gap, and the Hillsville Pike. The entire area of Blair, Iron Ridge, Anderson Bottoms, and Oldtown was developing in agricultural farms which produced hay, oats, buckwheat, wheat, corn, fruits, livestock such as cattle, sheep, hogs, and poultry. The area had a large virgin timber resource such as oak, chestnut, pine, maple, poplar, ash, and birch the area saw-miller and timber man were processing. S.S. Clayton and J. F. Clayton of Baltimore, Maryland, were buying land and mineral tracts in the Iron Ridge area in the 1870's organizing the New York-Virginia Mineral Co. This business created a future for new developments in the Iron Ridge and Blair Area. The Norfolk & Western Railroad Co. had completed their North Carolina Branch Line from the Ivanhoe Junction to the Huey Junction in November 1891, opened for rail traffic.

The people of Blair Community began planning the future developments. The area citizens felt that Blair's location was superior to Chestnut Yard as it boasted wagon roads connections on the North, East, South and West with better outlet than Chestnut Yard. Merchants were establishing their stores and homes. The N & W Railway Company became interested in the Blair Community because it possessed more room for rail sidings to make-up trains for the return to Pulaski, Virginia. In 1889, the Norfolk & Western Railroad Company had purchased the right-of-ways from the Huey Branch Junction at Gossan Mine to Blair from property owners Martin Sizemore, Rachael Hollyfield, Catherine Roberts and Emily Carter in order to build the North Carolina Extension. The citizens and merchants of Blair approached Joseph H. Sands, manager of the N & W Railway Company's Roanoke office, in Roanoke, Virginia, about constructing the three miles of North Carolina Branch Line from the Huey Branch Junction to Blair. The citizens received assurance that this track would be built by the Norfolk & Western Railroad Construction Division of the Norfolk & Western Railway Co. building the three mile track in late 1896. Blair facilities contained a two rail siding, a double loop, the main track, an engine turntable, and a freight/passenger station. E. A. Anderson was appointed Station Agent for Norfolk & Western Railway Company at Blair, Virginia.

The following merchants established businesses in Blair:

Dr. J. W. Bolen ....   Dr. J. W. Bolen's Drug Store and Medical Office
F. H. Martin.................   F. H. Martin's Harness & Buggy Shop General Store
Sam Jackson, Sam Kinzer, & J. H. Kapp ..... Blair Hardware Company
H. P. Cox.. ....H. P. Cox & Son General Store
Dr. J. W. Caldwell & Dr. S. M. Robinson....Crystal Drug Company & Medical Office
W. Billy Dalton ....   W. Billy Dalton General Store
W. W. Blair...... ....   Blair Grocery Company managed by C. W. Caldwell
L. E. Lindsey & W. E. Lindsey   Lindsey's General Store
Abe H. Bryan....................   Bryan Barbershop
John B. Waugh.................   John B. Waugh & Son General Store (including Blair Banking)
Mrs. J. H. Kapp........... ...   Sunnyside Inn Hotel & Millinery Shop
Lee Frost, J. W. Russell. W. E. Lindsey. ....Lumber, Cross-ties & Tanning Bark Dealers

Doctors serving the Blair and Anderson Bottoms areas were Dr. J. W. Bolen, Dr. J. K. Caldwell, Dr. S. M. Robinson, and Dr. J. Lewis Early. .Jim Evans and E. F. Ward, Sr. formed a partnership to establish a printing and newspaper business in 1903. The newspaper was named the "f" and Nandow Farmer was the editor.

Thomas Lafayette Felts - "Cliffside"

Tom Felts, as he was familiarly called by his friends, was born in Carroll County in the area of the Crooked Creek tributary at Woodlawn, VA. In 1871. As a young man working on his father's farm (Creed Felts) through his sheer grit and determination, educated himself looking into the horizon many miles from his native Carroll County, planning his future destiny ahead by his personal investment in himself, working his way through college. At the age of 21 years of age, Tom Felts entered into a partnership interest with W.B. Baldwin, Dr., Ernest G. Baldwin, Billy Baldwin in organizing the Baldwin-Felts Detective Agency in 1894, opening Baldwin-Felts Detective Agency offices in Roanoke, VA; Bluefield, W.Va., Beckley, W.Va. The Governor of the Commonwealth State of West Virginia, M.O. Dawson and the Federal Government of the United States appointed Thomas Lafayette Felts of the Baldwin-Felts Detective Agency to protect the White Oak Railway Co., the Norfolk & Western Railway Co,, operating in the state of West Virginia in 1902, and to protect coal mining industry facilities in the county areas of Mercer, Tazewell, Clinch Valley, McDowell, Raleigh, Fayette, Kanawha, Tug River, and Thacker Coal districts in West Virginia, Southwest Virginia, during the lawless years of coal mining, railroad construction in the Appalachian-Alleghenies areas, which was often referred to as "the Last Frontier".

When John L. Lewis was organizing to begin his push to unionize the railroads and coal industries, Tom Felts during his early adventure of protecting the railroad, coal mining industries in the wild and underdeveloped maintain regions of West Virginia, Kentucky, Southwest Virginia, when civilization was almost unknown in certain areas along the state boundary lines, enduring many hardships, exposures, and privations. These areas were never too stormy nor danger too great to deter Tom Felts when duty called. Tom Felts of the Baldwin-Felts Detective Agency of Roanoke, VA., Beckley, W.VA., Bluefield, West Va., operated their offices in the coal regions during the railroad, coal mine developments, furnishing protection to construction forces, freight, passenger train crews as well as the properties of railroad and coal mining industries, The train conductors, engineers, always stated from time to time, they would have not attempted to operate rail services over their rail lines if they had not been protection afforded them by the Baldwin-Felts Detective Agency.

211

Tom Felts of Baldwin-Felts Detective Agency briefly considered expanding his detective agency into other states as their reputation grew in law enforcement. Felts established his first residential home in Pulaski, Va., building his second home in Bluefield, W.Va. gaining his wealth by purchasing real estate properties, buying iron, coal, railroad stock interests. Thomas L. Felts purchased his first land tracts in Carroll County in the present Galax, Blair areas on the Chestnut Creek tributary, buying his first large tract from Charlie & Sallie Sutherland located at one point at Blair, Va., On the East side of Chestnut Creek tributary joining the property line of J. Barger Caldwell, B. P. Givens, taking in the Mill Creek tributary, following Ward's Gap Road (Present Country Club Lane) joining the Melton tract at one point on Bishop's Knob Road. Thomas Felts, his father Creed Felts purchased a block of lots December 17, 1903, on West Webster, West- Virginia Streets along North-Main Street from the Grayson Land Co. at Anderson Bottoms, named Bonaparte, Va. Creed Felts built his home on the corner of West Virginia and North Jefferson Streets, Tom Felts and his father, Creed Felts, established their Felts Delivery stables on the corner of West Webster, North Main Streets, managed by Creed Felts, renting buggies, wagons, teams of horses, riding horses to local and traveling people arriving by the Norfolk & Western passenger train.

The citizens of Blair, Va. Began purchasing their lots at Anderson Bottoms, (renamed Bonaparte, VA. January 17, 1904) establishing their homes and businesses from 1902 to 1907, selling their real estate properties at Blair, Virginia, to Thomas L. Felts of Bluefield, W.VA., who began the construction of his large home at Blair, Virginia, in 1906, naming it "Cliffside". When completed in 1908, he established his farming development raising purebred cattle herds and raising show horse stock. Mr. Felts had the foresight to interest, endeavor and encourage other farmers in the Grayson and Carroll area to improve their farming standard and livestock raising. In all his undertakings in his business foresight, he was thorough and progressive in his ventures.

Cliffside Farm became a showplace as well as an experimental station in the changing of agricultural technology of farming and livestock raising for the farmers of local and distance areas. Tom Felts and local business people organized the First National Bank of Galax, opening for banking service July 11, 1907, being a strong important financial institution, extended his help in establishing the articles of the Galax Fair Association, being a strong organizer in the development of the Town of Galax, Virginia, in banking, commercial developments, education, transportation, roads, agriculture, industrial developments. Tom Felts served on the board of directors of the Mountain Trust Bank, Roanoke, Virginia, as a trustee of Lynchburg College at Lynchburg, Virginia.

In 1915 Tom Felts and E. L. Whitley organized the partnership of Twin County Motor Company. He donated land and monies to establish the Rosenwald-Felts School because he was born in humble surroundings he was able to appreciate the conditions of people of humble circumstances with who he came in contact with, one of his first works, when he had reached a position of substantial development in his own business life. He gave his attention to the needs of those less fortunate. His life had been filled with interesting episodes in which he played the role of benefactor to the poor. Thomas L. Felts served in the Commonwealth of Virginia legislature House of Delegates, being a Republican nominee for the Congressional seat in Congress in 1921. Fighting for good roads, gaining good response for his efforts, always being in the forefront of developments of commerce, industries, always looking forward with his keen vision and foresight. Tom Felts always had been a progressive person in all of his ideas and undertakings. Managing his Cliffside Farms, raising and feeding his large stock of purebred Aberdeen Angus Cattle, which were always prize winners at the Great Galax Agriculture-al Fairs for years.

Under the direction of Thomas L. Felts, the Baldwin-Felts Detective Agency dissolved the operation in May 1938. In his remaining years, he maintained his Cliffside home at Cliffview, and his home in Bluefield, West Virginia. Thomas LaFayette Felts departed life September 8, 1940, leaving many memories to the people of Galax and the surrounding areas. They will always remember him for his many acts of kindness. Those who knew him will tell you that he was a friend to everyone.

The Development of the Town of Galax, Virginia
1903-1950 Year of Development
The start of Galax Coverage

Grayson Land Company - Establishing the "Town of Galax, Virginia."

In the late 1890's, southwest Virginia was developing along the New River Plateau from Pulaski to Blair, Virginia. Due to the ore mining and timber resources with the building of the Cripple Creek Extension and North Carolina branch line, changes were taking place at Blair and Oldtown as more people were moving into these areas to establish homes, businesses, and farms. Blair, Virginia was located on the Norfolk& Western Railway Company's line following Chestnut Creek tributary with twelve thriving businesses. However, the area was hindered from future growth due to the terrain and topography of the land to build a railroad facility or development of an industrial town.

In 1903, a group of citizens from the three areas, Oldtown, Blair, Anderson Bottoms, called for a group meeting to discuss the possibilities of locating a new town. Anderson Bottoms was located on both sides of the Chestnut Creek tributary with level bottom land that was suited for the layout of a small town. Eight families lived on farms in Anderson Bottom and surrounding area. The families were the William Roberts, Tom Roberts, Hugh Roberts, A. C. Anderson, A. C. Painter, Charlie Anderson, John B. Caldwell, and James P. Givens. The citizen's group organized the Grayson Land Company which was chartered under the laws of the Commonwealth of Virginia in 1903 by selling stock and bond shares in the area's future developments. J. . Waugh was president, J. P. Carico was Vice-President, B. . Calloway was Treasurer-Secretary of the Grayson Land Company.

The Grayson Land Company of Anderson Bottoms purchased 375 acre land tract from Tommie F. Roberts in 1903. Contracted C. L. Demott of the Lynchburg engineering firm of Arnold & Demott to survey the 375 acre tract laying out streets, roads, residential, business, industrial building lots, sewer lines, storm drains, water storage resources, and electric power resources. Arnold Demott Engineering Firm drafted a plat map showing all lots, lot numbers, and streets. J. H. Dingee, Manager of the Virginia Land Company had purchased rail right-of-ways and properties for the Norfolk & Western Railroad Company, 333 Walnut Street, Philadelphia, Penn. On August 1, 1889, Mr. Dingee purchased for the Norfolk & Western Railroad Company several acres of land and rights -of-ways from S.C. Anderson and Hugh T. Roberts at Anderson Bottoms to construct a double track for the N & W freight rail cars descending the steep mountain rail grades of the North Carolina Rail Extension to the VA-NC State line. The New River Plateau Railway Company's engineering division surveyed the following right-of-ways purchased by the Virginia Land Company for the Norfolk & Western Railway Company which began at Blair, VA to Anderson Bottoms from the following persons: Thomas Bartlett, Floyd Leonard, Charlie Sutherland, Betty Anderson, James Anderson heirs, Hardin Reavis, C. C. Trimble, Livina Trimble, E. Trimble, James Mooney, and Samuel Callaway.

The Directors of the Grayson Land Company of Anderson Bottoms, J. B. Waugh, J. P. Carico, B. F. Calloway met with Joseph H. Sands, Manager of the Norfolk & Western Construction Division, Roanoke, Virginia, discussing the possibilities and potential of constructing 2.37 tenths miles of the North Carolina Branch Line from mile post #50 at Blair, Virginia, to mile post #52 at Anderson Bottoms. Joseph H. Sands and the railway representatives assured members of the Grayson Land Company that they would build the 2.37 tenths miles of rail line as they had completed the studies and rail survey between 1889 and 1892 in preparation for the North Carolina Extension from Ivanhoe Junction to the VA-NC State Line.

The Grayson Land Company held its first lot auction on December 17, 1903, selling lots at $25.00 to $250.00 each. R. E. Jones of the Oldtown area purchased a lot on the West side of North Main Street December 17,1903, from the Grayson Land Company on which he built the first store building at Anderson Bottoms in 1904, before the North Carolina Branch Line was completed from Blair, Virginia, to Anderson Bottoms. Virginia. The size of the Jones Store Building measured twenty-five feet wide by forty feet long, being a two-story building. R. E. Jones was appointed postmaster as of January 4, 1904 of the Bonaparte Post Office, officially opening January 14,

1904. The Jones General Store stocked small amounts of groceries, notions, produce, flour, shoes, and clothing. Walter M. Jones, Jr. assisted his father in the management of the store. One by one the people of Bonaparte began frequenting Mr. Jones' store, picking up their mail, purchasing their needed items.

Rural post offices in the outlying area of Bonaparte, Virginia, in 1904 were located in Carroll and Grayson Counties. On the Carroll side, the post offices were: Ward's Mill, Coal Creek, Pipers Gap, Blair, Chestnut Yard, Monarat, Gambetta, and Grayson. On the Grayson side, the post offices were Oldtown, Reavistown, Hampton, Collins Mill, Coxs Ford, Creela, and Davis.

Meanwhile, the Grayson Land Company of Bonaparte, Virginia, was selling lots every day for the construction of dwellings and business establishments. Floyd S. Landreth, a young practicing attorney, became a permanent resident of Bonaparte, opening his law office in the Grayson Land Company's building on the west side of North Main Street. The Norfolk & Western Railway Company's construction division under the management of Joseph Sands began construction on the 2.37 tenth rail miles of the North Carolina Branch line form Blair to the rail engine turntable site a Bonaparte in September 1904. The rail engine turn-table sire was located just above the present site of Webb Furniture plant.

The Norfolk and Western Railway Company completed their construction of the railroad and facilities as the engine turntable, stock pen, sidings, and temporary freight and passenger station December 5, 1904. E. A. Anderson who had served as station agent at Blair, Virginia, in earlier years, was moved to Bonaparte to become station agent. The Norfolk & Western Railway Company moved the passenger freight station from Blair to Bonaparte (Galax) in 1905. Mr. J.W. Cook, Superintendent of the Cripple Creek Division (which was later named the Radford Division) suggested to the local citizens that the name of Bonaparte should be changed to Galax. Mr. Cook's suggestion was based on the large abundant growth of Galax leaves growing in the deep terrains of the mountain area. Mr. R. E. Jones took a petition from the people of the Bonaparte area to the Federal Postal Department in Washington, D. C., suggesting that they change the name of Bonaparte, Virginia, to Galax, Virginia, on January 2, 1905, Mr. R. E. Jones received approval of the name change and was appointed postmaster. Walter Jones Sr., was appointed assistant postmaster. R. E. Jones appointed the rural mail carriers, E. F. Ward, Sr., Warrick Murphy, and Ben Landreth to deliver mail from the Galax Post Office out to the surrounding areas.

With shipping facilities made available by building the Norfolk & Western Railway Company's line into Galax, the town soon developed into a market for produce shipping eggs, poultry, turkeys, ham and butter to other industrial areas. Most of the early merchants were produce buyers. Prior to the building of good roads, Galax held first place in having rail transportation for shipment of live turkeys, poultry and livestock. Many merchants would buy chestnuts, chinquapins, animal hides, bees wax, feathers, ginseng, Seneca roots, and tallow shipping via Norfolk & Western Railroad Company.

Galax Market Report - July 5, 1905 Weekly

Quotations

Loaf Bread - $.03
Gallon milk - $.09
Butter- choice grade - $.10 per lb.
Chickens - hens - $.06 per lb.
Spring Line - .10 to $.111/2 per lb.
Turkeys - no demand
Crossties - 8" x 6" X 7" x 7" - $.22 to $.40 each
Animal hides (dry) - $.10 to $.11 per lb. (green) - $.04 to $.05 per lb.
Eggs - dozen - no quotation
Fertilizers - 14% phosphate - $14.50 per ton
                Virginia-Carolina 12% Acid Phosphate - $13.50 per ton

Produce :
   Bacon shoulders - $.01 to $.02 per lb.
   Beans (white) - no demand
   Beans (mixed) - no demand
   Hams - $.111 per lb. -sides $.08 to $.09 per lb.
   C.R. (cattle rib) sides - Western Bulk - $.09 per lb.
   Bees Was - $.25 lb.
   Feathers - Prime (Scarce) $.45 to $.50 per lb.
   Flour (extra) - $3.00 per 100 lbs.
   Ginseng - $5.00 to $6.00 per lb.
   Virginia Lard - $.08 to $.09 per lb.
   Flour (family size) $3.00 per 100 lbs.
   Seneca Root - $.40 per lb.
   Tallow - $.03 per lb.

Dried Fruit:
   Evaporated apples - $.03 per lb.

Seeds:
   Clover - Mammoth - $8.25 per bushel Timothy -
   $2.00 per bushel
   Clover - *Red* - $7,75 to $8.00 per bushel Orchard Grass -
   $1.90 per bushel
   Oats - $.40 to $.50 per bushel

Employee Labor Wages - $1.00 to $1.50 per day
A gallon of gas was $.04: Gold per ounce - $20.67; silver per ounce - $.57
Average income was $456.00
New home - $1,500 to $3,395.00
New car - $800.00

In the mid-summer of 1905, the Norfolk & Western Railway Company's combination passenger and freight train pulled by a Mogul J-3 steam locomotive engine had their first wreck in Galax. The freight train ran into back of another freight train which knocked the caboose off the main track just below the Galax Depot Station in the area of East Webster Street.

Galax Academy School

On July 12, 1905, all citizens interested in building a school in the village of Galax for the insuring years were requested to meet at the office of the Grayson Land Company at 10:00 a.m. for the purpose of electing local trustees to select a school board committee. R. E. Jones saw a need to develop an education system for the 15 to 20 school age children in the area. A group of citizens nominated A. C. Painter, J. Pike Carico, E. P. Wright, R. E. Jones and Ben F. Calloway to the Building Committee. J. P. Carico was named committee chairman and A. C. Painter was elected secretary. They formed a joint stock company which issued stock certificates at $25.00 each. R. E. Jones made arrangements for the children to attend school on the second floor of the R. E. Jones Store and Mrs. Mike Nuckolls became the first teacher. The school remained above Mr. Jones' store until the Academy School was finished. The students attending the first school on the second floor of Mr. R. E. Jones store: Platt Harp, Lela Beasley, Collie Beasley, Grace Bishop, Dan Roberts, Fred Roberts, Walter Jones, Luther Jones, Clyde Harp, Eugene Carico and Harry Carico. When the Grayson Land Company surveyed the future town of Galax, they set aside 10 acres called "Piney Woods" to be used for their public school grounds. The School Committee made a contract with Gallimore and Rider (builders) to give them a turn-key cost of $3,600 at this date in 1905 (they had only sold $1,800 worth of stock shares.) Gallimore and Rider had begun construction of the school and the stock shares had slowed in sales, but the construction went on. Since there were no banks in Galax, the Building Committee, [E. F. Wright, J. P. Carico, R. E. Jones, A.C. Painter] rode on horseback to Fries, Virginia, to borrow the needed $1,800 to finish the construction of Academy School. They signed a note payable to the Washington Bank and Trust Company which was founded in Fries, Virginia, on July 23, 1902. The Bank was located in the Washington Mill Commissary & Store. F. H. Fries was President, W. F. Shaffer was Vice-president, and G. L. Glenn was the cashier.

The Academy School taught elementary and high school classes. The school building had four classrooms on the first floor and an auditorium on the second floor. The construction was of wood and the building was heated by wood stoves. A. C. Painter and R. E. Jones furnished the wood for the heating stoves. The teachers were Miss Roberta Brewer of Baywood, Rose and Lucille Carr, Miss Grace Caldwell of Galax, Mrs. R. E. Cox of Coal Creek, and G. F. Carr served as the first school principal in 1906. The first graduating class of the Galax Academy School was three girls and two boys.

On Saturday, August 12, 1906, the citizens of Galax attended a drama play held at the Galax Academy School. The star performers were Warrick Murphy, Mrs. Lelia Waugh, Mrs. Mary Anderson, R. E. Cox, and Ben Calloway was quite a success. The program was well presented. The auditorium was seated to its full capacity and the Fries band furnished excellent music for the occasion. The door receipts amounted to $72.00 which went toward paying for the recently purchased piano.

Town Charter

In January 1906, the industrious people of Galax called for a public meeting, inviting all citizens of the Galax area to attend the meeting at the Galax Academy Auditorium. The purpose of the meeting was for the formation and development of plans for a town government and to obtain a town charter of incorporation under the Commonwealth of Virginia. Ben F. Calloway, an attorney and the Secretary of the Grayson Land Company, had begun drawing up plans earlier for town charter and a mayor-Council government. Persons in attendance at the meeting were Ben F. Callaway, W. F. Murphy, Dr. J. W. Bolen, Dr. J. K. Caldwell, M. L. Bishop, J. P. Carico, S. L. Welch, R.. E. Jones, E. G. Williams, J. H. Kapp, and E. F. Wright. W. F. Murphy was nominated recorder. Individuals nominated for council were M. L. Bishop, E. F. Wright, E. C. Williams, Dr. J. K. Caldwell, J. H. Kapp, and Dr. J. W. Bolen. Ben F. Calloway was nominated for Mayor: W. I. Harp was nominated to serve as first town of Galax Policeman. Galax received its Charter of Incorporation June 6, 1906, from the Commonwealth of Virginia as the Town of Galax, Virginia.

The first Town Offices were located in the Grayson Land Company's building on the West side of North Main Street, having their Galax Jailhouse located back of the Grayson Land building at the Alley way. The Town of Galax, Virginia, constructed their first municipal brick building at the corner of East Grayson and Carroll Streets, having their Council Chamber Office and jail facilities. E.F. Ward sold his interest in the Blair Enterprise Newspaper and Printing Business established in Blair, Virginia, in 1901, sold to Rufus Cox of Coal Creek, Virginia, in 1904 farming a partnership interest with Jim Evans, establishing the Galax Post Herald.

Andy L. Williams, R. H. Eversole, and Greek Wright organized and established the Blue Ridge Printing Company in 1906, providing job printing such as stationary, invoice billings, posters and miscellaneous printing. Their printing operation was located on the North side of West Grayson Street in the West end of the Galax Drug Company's building. Rufus E. Cox and Jim Evans sold their Galax Post Herald newsprint business to Andy L. Williams, R. H. Eversole and Greek Wright of the Blue Ridge Printing Company in 1908. Combining both businesses, publishing the Galax Post Herald weekly becoming an asset to the town of Galax and the area communities. The Galax Post Herald newspaper was managed by Andy L. Williams, R. . Eversole and edited by Nandow Farmer.

Mr. H. Price Burnett, an attorney from Floyd, Virginia, opened his law office in Galax, serving as an attorney in the Circuit Court system of Carroll and Grayson counties. Attorney H. Price Burnett purchased the business and stock of the Blue Ridge Printing Company and the Galax Post Herald in 1912. He employed Andy L. Williams and R. H. Eversole as publishers and Nandow Farmer as editor of the Galax Post Herald newspaper and manager of the job printing business.

The town of Galax had a devastating fire in 1913 that destroyed the following businesses on West Grayson Street: F. S. Dobyn's Delivery Stables, Galax Produce Market, J. W. Poole's General Store, Hightower's Studio, and the Novelty 5 & 10 Store. Attorney H. Price moved to Blue Ridge Printing Company and the Galax Post Herald newsprint business to the corner of North Main and West Center Streets establishing his print business in the Robert P and Ellis C. Caldwell wood frame building opposite the Waugh Hotel, where Robert P. Caldwell had operated a clothing and shoe store.

. Dobyn's relocated his delivery stables to the corner of West Oldtown and Monroe Streets. Prince Burnett purchased and installed his new printing equipment having the first linotype setting machine in the area. After a period of years of job printing and publishing the Galax Post Herald, Attorney Burnett sold the Blue Ridge Printing Company and Galax Post Herald Newspaper to Mrs. Lydia Crabill and son Mike Crabill of Galax in 1919. E. G. Crabill was station agent for the depot station of the Norfolk & Western Railway Company in the Town of Galax. The Crabill family was selling subscriptions to the Galax Post Herald at $.70 per year, or $.40 for six months. Mrs. Lydia Crabill and son Mike employed Hattie Rose, Nettie Weatherman, and Nandow Farmer in their operations of the Blue Ridge Printing Company and Galax Post Herald newsprint. The Crabill's moved their Blue Ridge Printing Company - Galax Post Herald Newspaper business to the West Side of South Main Street in 1922, when Dr. J. K. Caldwell and the Caldwell family began the construction of the Bluemont Hotel, managed by Bob Caldwell in 1923.

Attorney Prince Burnett of Galax purchased the Grayson Gazette Newspaper of Independence, Virginia, in 1920 from Willard S. Barbery, moving the newspaper business to Galax, locating the newspaper business in the back section of the Mountain Loan Company's building on the South side of West Grayson Street, publishing the newspaper under the title leading names the Grayson-Carroll Gazette edited at various times by F. L. Cox, Heath A. Melton, R. L. Branscome, and Mrs. Victor Wilson. Carroll Gazette was managed by Mr. & Mrs. Ray A. Smith from 1927 to 1931, when the newspaper business was sold to H. B. Zabriskie, an experienced newspaper publisher from Altoona, Penn. Under his management, changing the newsprint title of the Grayson-Carroll Gazette to the Galax Gazette newspaper.

Mr. C. H. South built the Central Hotel at the corner of West Oldtown and South Main Street in late 1904. The hotel served three meals each day and the cost of a hotel room was $1.50 per night. In November of 1905, Mr. South's Central Hotel and the R.L. Roupe building on the West side of South Main Street was destroyed by fire. The Central Hotel was insured in the amount of $1,700 on both the structure and the furnishings. The R.L. Roupe building was insured for $400. Mr. A. E. Disher who operated a grocery store in the R. L. Roupe Building, only carried $250 of insurance on his merchandise and stock. Mr. C. H. South's net loss was not over $600, Mr. A. E. Disher's net loss amounted to $350, and Mr. R. . Roupe's net loss amounted to $500. Mr. South rebuilt the Central Hotel and continued to operate it for several more years.

In 1914, Mr. Oscar C. Higgins leased the Central Hotel from E. H. South and changed the name to the New Galax Inn. Mrs. Lelia B. Waugh, widow of the late W.P. Waugh, had operated the Waugh Hotel and Boarding House in the Old Courthouse in Oldtown, moved to Galax and built the Waugh Hotel on the corner of East Center and North Main Street in late 1904. The Waugh Hotel was later operated by Lee and Della Baker and the hotel served three meals a day. Mr. W. I. Harp built the Red Star Hotel and Boarding House on South Main Street in late 1904 and the hotel was destroyed by fire in 1907. R. A. Holdbrook operated Holdbrook's General Store on the corner of Oldtown and South Main Streets, selling to Vass-Hawks, who operated the Vass-Hawke General Store.

In 1905, Houseman and Kyle operated a lumber and building supply building on Norfolk & Western's siding next to the N & W stock pen selling different types of finished lumber, doors, windows, and moldings. They received rail carloads arriving each day by the Norfolk & Western railway Company. They sold their building supply business in 1906 to W. K. Early who established the W. K. Early & Son Building Supply planning mill on Depot Avenue. Reavis Brothers Lumber Company which was owned by Charlie and James Reavis operated a planing mill and building supply store on the corner of West Oldtown and Monroe Streets. Gillespie Brothers Planing Mill owned by T. Gillespie and W. Gillespie was located on the corner of East Oldtown and Carroll Streets and purchased from J. O. Spears. W. H. Taylor Building Supply Store owned by W. Harrison Taylor was located on South Main Street. Galax was experiencing a building boom which supported the business of each of the preceding building supply dealers. W. Billy Dalton established the W. Dalton General Store on the North side of East Grayson Street. Mrs. J.W. Bolen established her millinery shop on the East side of South Main Street.

Banking and Industry

The Blair Bank was organized in the fall of 1904 at Blair, Virginia, by J. B. Waugh, W. K. Early, and W. W. Blair, J. B. Waugh served as the bank's president, Dr. S. M. Robinson was the Vice-President and C. W.. Caldwell was the cashier. The board of directors included: Dr. S. W. Robinson, J. B Waugh, C. L. Hanks, W. K. Early, and W. W. Blair. The Blair Bank of Blair, Virginia, moved to West Grayson Street in Galax in 1906.

Galax had no manufacturing plants for a stable payroll, the people began developing plans for future industrial businesses in manufacturing. On August 1, 1906, a joint stock company was organized issuing stock to build the Galax Canning Company which was built on the West side of Chestnut Creek on Railroad Avenue. [in the present area of the Vaughan-Bassett property] People from Carroll, Grayson, and Galax were purchasing stock shares in the venture. C.A Dickenson was president and F. Williams was secretary-treasurer. The cost of building the canning plant and installing equipment was $12,500, A Mr. McKensie from Philadelphia, Pennsylvania, promoted the building of the canning plant.

A group of Galax citizens called a meeting to discuss the possibilities of organizing a joint stock company to raise funds to develop Galax's first furniture plant. They sold stock shares in the new venture. The new furniture plant was named Galax Furniture and Lumber Company with John B. Waugh being elected president of the firm and W. K. Early was elected secretary-treasurer and S. E. Wilkinson, general manager. Construction of the new furniture plant began while Norfolk & Western Railway Company built rail siding to the plant. The Galax Furniture and Lumber Company located opposite of Vaughan Furniture Company plant [later land tract of the Galax Weaving Company] went into manufacturing furniture in midsummer of 1906. The plant made birch and oak bedroom suites and dining room furniture which they sold to the mail order houses of Spiegel, Montgomery-Ward, and Stern. Shipments were made by the Norfolk & Western Railway Company to the distant markets.

S. W. Swartz opened H. P. Swartz Manufacturing Company producing hickory handles for tools made out of kiln or air-dried oak and poplar. Mr. Swartz's company was located on Railroad Avenue and Piper's Gap Road. John B. Waugh built his brick building, the J. B. Waugh & Son store on the corner of North Main and East Grayson Streets in 1906.

The First National Bank was established on the corner of Center and North Main Streets with an opening date of July 11, 1907. [Today the building is used for the Social Services Offices.] Officers of the bank were Thomas L. Felts, President; J. P. Carico, Vice-president; and C. A. Collier, Cashier. Members of the Board of Directors were Thomas L. Felts, J. P. Carico, Creed Felts, A. C. Painter, W. D. Beasley, Dr. Jim H. Witherow, and S. Floyd Landreth having a capital stock of $25,000.

The Galax Telephone Exchange went into service in 1907. The office was located upstairs in the First National Bank on the corner of East Center and North Main Streets. Mrs. Pearl Newman was the first exchange operator.

On October 6,1907, a great tragedy occurred at 12:10 p.m. The factory whistle sounded out an alarm that the Galax Furniture and Lumber Company was on fire. Galax did not have a fire department at this time, but everyone did what they could to save the lumber stock and other supplies. Unfortunately, it was not enough - The Galax Furniture and Lumber Company was destroyed. After the loss of this company's plant, the owners decided to construct a new furniture plant and new stock certificates were issued. The new officers were elected with E. W. Dodd, Secretary-treasurer, and S. E. Wilkerson, plant superintendent. The new Galax Furniture and Lumber Company began operation in the fall of 1908 with production of furniture, roll-top desk, office furniture, and oak finished cabinets.

Mrs. J. W. Stamey opened a millinery shop on the West side of South Jefferson Street. A Mr. Edwards and Mr. T. M. Scott organized the Edwards and Scott Stove Manufacturing Company. The foundry and machine shop was purchased from R. E. Jones and James C. Reavis. The stove company manufactured wood and coal stoves and it was located on the East side of Chestnut Creek at the corner of Webster Street. The Galax Buggy Manufacturing Company built their manufacturing plant on East Oldtown and the corner of Carroll Street. They sold new buggies at $45.00 and used buggies at $15.00 to $25.00. The company was managed by D. A. Robinson.

Mr. J. K. Caldwell of Galax made a contract with the Town of Galax agreeing to furnish a team of horses and wagon at his own expense to remove the droppings of the residential privies and haul to the J. Barger Caldwell farm located on the East side of Galax. The agreement was to clean the privies the first and third week of each month. He charged $.25 to clean each privy. The contract was signed by W. F. Murphy the town's recorder and B. F. Calloway, the Mayor of Galax, in June 1906. George Tucker worked for Dr. J. K. Caldwell, cleaning the privies, hauling the waste on his "honey wagon" to the J. Barger Caldwell farm.

The Blair Grocery Company was established at Blair, Virginia, in 1896; moved to East Grayson Street, Galax, in 1907, W. W. Blair, President; W. C. Robinson, Manager; J. W. Hortenstine, Secretary and Treasurer.

219

Galax Fair Association

Mr. Thomas L. Felts, J. Pike Carico, and other Galax citizens organized the Galax Fair Association on September 12, 1907. A joint stock company was formed to issue stock certificates and Jim P. Carico was named president with Rufus Cox as Secretary. The Galax Fair Association purchased 22 acres of land off south Main Street from S. F. Welsh to build the fairgrounds. W. I. Harp was granted the contract to build the race track, grandstand, and exhibit building. Mr. E. W. Wright was foreman of all the fairground construction. In the early spring of 1908, Mr. C. M. Bryant, general manager of the Galax Fair Association, made a report on the building and construction progress of the fairground. His report stated that the race track was almost completed, the fence around the fairground was finished, the foundations had been laid for the grandstand and exhibit building, and construction was underway on the Grandstand.

The first Galax Agricultural Fair was September 19-21,1908. The arrival of the Norfolk & Western Railway Company's train with the fair equipment was quite a spectacle. Practically everyone in Galax went down to the Galax Depot to see the midway shows, rides, and wild animals being unloaded from the rail cars and moved to the Galax Fairgrounds. People traveled to the fair by buggies, wagons, and the Norfolk & Western passenger train to attend the first fair. Farmers could display and exhibit their grains, turkeys, poultry, sheep, hogs, horses, beef stock and milk cows, mules, and oxen. wheeling and dealing by the horse and mule traders were common to the event. The women displayed their articles of sewing, knitting, quilting, baked goods, jellies, and canned vegetables. On the midway were shows, games, and rides. From the grandstand, people enjoyed the free act shows, "the original dancing bear", horse racing and band music.

Later, the Galax Fair was renamed the 'Great Galax Agriculture Fair". The Galax Fair Association deeded the fairground tract to the Town of Galax in the mid-thirties. Thomas L. Felts had served the Galax Fair association many years. The fairground was named Felts Park in honor of Mr. Thomas L. Felts.

As the growth of the farming and livestock industry expanded in Carroll and Grayson Counties, the farmers would drive their live stock herds of beef cattle, sheep, hogs and turkeys to the Norfolk & Western livestock pens located on Depot Avenue where they loaded the live stock on cattle freight rail cars and crating the turkeys in shipping coops for shipping. The farmers sold their livestock to the meat packers and other buyers whose purchases were shipped via the Norfolk & Western Railway Company. Mr. Chap Hampton, the Carr brothers, and other sheep raisers pooled their lamb stocks for market shipments to load six Norfolk& Western stock cars with lambs for shipment to the eastern Virginia Lamb markets in the summer of 1907. Brothers, Marvin M. and Monroe L. Ward, of Ward's Mill Community operated a large flour and corn milling business on Ward's Mill Creek on the Piper's Gap Road. Their father was also instrumental in the milling operation in addition to his operation of a general store and sawmill.

When the Grayson Land Company held their lot auction at Anderson Bottoms on December 17,1903, the Ward brothers purchased building lots on Main Street to build their businesses and houses. They built their two-storied, frame store building on the East side of North Main Street in 1906. The first floor of the Ward's store was stocked with gentlemen's merchandise such as notions, men's clothing, shoes and other miscellaneous items and named the Gentlemen's Clothing Store. On the second story of the store, they opened the first movie theater in the Galax area. The Ward Brothers' Store had only been in business a few months when it was destroyed by fire.

In 1907, the Ward Brothers opened a second industry in Galax which was the Ward Brothers' Brick Manufacturing Plant with a brickyard on the east side of Chestnut Creek between the properties of J. J. Joines and E. P. Givens. The brick plant produced brick by the thousands for residential, public, business and industrial construction. The brothers rebuilt their Ward Building in 1908 and reopened their Gentlemen's Clothing Store. They leased a space in the back of their building to W. I. Harp of the W. I. Harp and Company who manufactured chain drive belts. The Ward brothers continued to diversify their business interests by opening a plumbing and heating shop in the rear of their store, establishing a spring fed gravity water system on the East side of Chestnut Creek in the Spivey Hill area to supply water to the Galax residential area acting. They also acted as sales agents for McCormick farm equipment and operated a large apple orchard on the east side of Chestnut Creek.

J. W. Stanley succeeded Ben F. Calloway as mayor in 1908 and councilmen were M. T. Blessing, Charlie P. Waugh, S. F. Welsh, L. L. Joines, E. W. Dodd, and J. F. Vass. J. O. Speas established a steam power roller, saw, and planing mill on the South side of East Oldtown Street in 1908 producing flour, cornmeal, stock feeds, and all types of sawmill lumber. They sold the roller mill operations to C. M. Bryant of Bridle Creek in 1911 and the planing mill to Gillespie Brothers.

Galax

Galax was a mountain town located in Southwest Virginia in the Blue Ridge Mountains at an elevation of 2,200 feet above sea level with a town proper of 2 square miles. Although it was located in the mountain terrain of the New River plateau with soft rolling hills giving the area a feeling of gentleness. The topography of the Blue Ridge Mountains plunges dramatically to the floor of the piedmont of North Carolina. The Town of Galax was divided by the borderline of Carroll and Grayson Counties with part of the town proper located in each county.

Since the early pioneer days of the New River Settlement and in the formation of Grayson and Carroll Counties, the people knew that unity and trust was necessary for survival. Cooperative and responsive government had been the hallmark of the New River area. Although the three governing bodies work in harmony to achieve their mutual goals, the people of Galax had strong spiritual and educational value expectations for their community. They established schools for the younger generation to provide them with better education to improve their standard of living and to serve in the development of a strong and growing community. A strong spiritual devotion led to the settling of many denominations in the Galax area such as the Christians (disciples), Missionary Baptist, Quakers, Primitive Baptist, Methodist, and Presbyterians. Listed below are the first established churches and their locations:

First Baptist Church - built in 1905; dedicated in 1906; located on the corner of West Oldtown and Jefferson Streets

First Presbyterian Church - built in 1905; dedicated in 1906; located at the corner Of West Center and Jefferson Streets

First Methodist Church - built in 1901; dedicated in 1910; located on the corner of West Center and Monroe Streets

Christian Church (Disciples) - built in 1906; dedicated in 1909; located at the corner of Washington and North Main Streets

Galax Primitive Baptist Church - dedicated May 10, 1913; located at the corner of Painter and McArthur Streets; (First Primitive Baptist Church was established on Meadow Creek in 1792)

Asbury Methodist Church - located on the Hillsville Pike

Quaker Meeting House - located on Piper's Gap Road in the Ward's Mill Area

Galax High School Corporation

The Galax High School Corporation was organized on October 28, 1907, for the purpose of constructing a brick high school building on the Piney Woods school tract. The Building Committee of A. C. Painter, R. E. Jones, J. .P. Carico, and G. F. Carr called a meeting of the local citizens in the Galax Academy Auditorium. Those in attendance were: Thomas L. Felts, J. B. Waugh, E. R. and Lon McMillan, Dr. A. G. Pless, Sr., B. F. Calloway, W. W. Clay, Dr. J. K. Caldwell, Rufus E. Cox, J. H. Witherow, W. G. Lowe, E F. Ward, S. F. Welsh, L. L. Joines, E. F. Wright, M. L. Bishop. C. H. Martin, M. L. Henderson, W. H. Taylor, J. H. Vass, J. S. James, E. L. Williams, W. R Smith, M. L. Ward, W.H. Potts, T.F. Roberts, A.W. Woltz , W.I. Harp, E.B. Watson, M.T. Blessing, W.H. Hightower, C .L. Hanks, B. D. Beamer, A. L. Fields, W. .E. Swartz, H. P. Swartz, Isaac Ramey, Creed, Felts, A. C. Anderson, R. K. Johnson, P. L. Vass, E. Y. Leftwich, J. H. Kapp, E. P. Givens, R. A Holbrook, S. H. Goodson, S. C. Hopper, J. C. Matthews, Walter M. Jones, Sr.; W. R. Ballard, M. M. Blair, Dr. J. W. Bolen, B. F. Nuckolls, W. F. Murphy, Marvin Ward, C. W. Hanks, E. A. Grubb, George Hounshell, and J. W. Stamey. The Building Committee organized the Galax High School Corporation, a joint stock venture, which raised funds and issued stock certificate shares for the building fund.

The committee also elected A. 0. Painter as President and G. F. Carr as secretary of the corporation. A plan was developed to build a modern brick building that was equipped with all the requirements stated by the Virginia Board of Education. The brick building would be two stories with four classrooms on each level, a large hallway and a basement with a gravity force heating system. The cost was not to be less than $7,000 or greater than $10,000. The group in attendance raised over $5,000 which was donated to the Galax High School Corporation. The corporation borrowed the other $5,000 from the State of Virginia's Literary Fund for a total of $10,000 in operating funds. The building contract was let to E. F. Wright and W. H. Taylor for construction of the Galax High School building and the Ward Brothers furnished locally made brick for the school's construction. The school construction was completed on January 28, 1909.

G. F. Carr and J. A. Livesay were principals of the Galax High School and the Galax Academy. The Galax School System had nine trained teachers offering seven grades in elementary teaching and four years of high school instruction.

J. F. Vass succeeded J. W. Stamey [due to his health in 1909]. Councilmen were: James C. Reavis, M. T. Blessing, Charlie P. Waugh, S. F. Welsh, L. L. Joines, and E. W. Dodd.

Progress on the Early 1900's

The Town of Galax had developed into an agriculture, banking, commercial, industrial and transportation center. The citizens of the Town of Galax were proud of the early progress. The population had grown to 775 persons in 1910. S. Floyd Landreth supervised the United States Census Report for Galax in 1910. The citizens were skilled in many trades to support the town and rural activities of the economy. The farmers in the rural areas of Carroll and Grayson Counties were producing vegetables, hay, oats, buckwheat, wheat, corn grains, and fruits while raising livestock such as sheep, beef cattle, hogs, turkeys, and poultry for local and distant markets.

Several timber and sawmill operations were cutting chestnut, oak, pine, hickory, and poplar for the local furniture and building suppliers, L. A. Hausman, W. H. Bolling, Charlie P. Waugh, J. W. Russell, and Charlie Muse were timber dealers who shipped lumber out of the area. Cross-tie and tanning bark dealers such as B. D. Beamer. W. E. Lindsey, C.

H. South, W. H. Bolling, J. W. Russell, and Charlie P. Waugh also shipped their products out of town. An uninterrupted line of timber wagons traveled back and forth from the counties of Carroll, Grayson, and the North Carolina counties of Ashe and Allegheny hauling their cut lumber, cross-ties, and tanning bark to Galax.

The Town of Galax was located on the North branch line of the Cripple Creek Extension of the Norfolk & Western Railway Company, a 110 mile distance from Roanoke, Virginia. The gross amount of livestock, farm grains, poultry, lumber, cross-ties, tanning bark, mining props, furniture and other products amounted to 19,472 tons of out-going freight and 3,876 tons of incoming freight in the year of 1910. B. D. Beamer's Store had a special sale on Log Cabin syrup and buckwheat flour and J. W. Poole and Company Store has a special on hog feed and chicken feed the same week in 1910.

In the same year. Norfolk & Western Railway Company ran their passenger train services for the people of Galax and the surrounding area to Pulaski for connections to Bristol, Radford, Roanoke, and all points north and south. The passenger train would leave Galax at 6:05 a.m. arriving in Pulaski, Virginia, at 9:15 a.m. The travelers from Galax who were headed to Roanoke on business or shopping would arrive back in Galax at 10:10 p.m. the someday. The passengers would be met at the Galax Passenger Station by the buggy services of the Felts Delivery Stables located at the corner of West Webster and North Main Streets; M.L. Bishop Delivery Stables located at the corner of East Oldtown and South Main Streets; or F. S. Dobyns Delivery Stables located on the corner of West Grayson and North Jefferson Streets. The delivery drivers would pick up the local people, drummers, or business salesmen and take them to their homes or hotels. After a night's stay at the Waugh Hotel, Central Hotel or Harris Hotel, the drummers would rent a buggy and horses for their business trip into Carroll and Grayson Counties to sell their wares to the general stores. Some drummers would travel for days before returning to Galax to board the passenger train for Pulaski to make train connections North, South, East and West.

Norfolk & Western Railway Company

Schedule in effect May 25th 1910 Daily Passenger Services

Arrive in Galax - 11:05 am - Leaves Galax - 12;01 pm Arrive in Fries -
9:55 a.m.. - Leaves Fries - 1:02 p.m. Arrive in Ivanhoe - 9:22 a.m. -
Leaves Ivanhoe - 1:41 p.m. Leaves Pulaski 7:55 a.m. - Arrives in Pulaski -
3:10 p.m.

Daily Passenger Services - Except Sunday

Leave Galax - 6:05 a.m. - Arrive in Galax 10:10 p.m. Leave Fries -
7:12 a.m. - Arrive in Fries 9:02 p.m. Leave Ivanhoe - 7:49 a.m. - Arrive
in Ivanhoe - 8:30 p.m. Arrive in Pulaski - 9:15 p.m. - Leave Pulaski -
7:00 p.m.

Prior to the automobiles, bus lines, and hard surface roads, the Norfolk & Western's passenger train trip from Galax to Pulaski through the New River Plateau, a distance of fifty-two miles over the North Carolina Branch Line to Ivanhoe Junction of the Cripple Creek Extension of the Norfolk & Western Railroad Company to Pulaski; which is seldom forgotten. The Railroad track was unbelievably rough and crooked, but the train crew of the N & W's passenger train made up hospitality for the like of efficiency in their railroad operation. The sociability of the setback games with Conductor Moore's was close chaperoning to see that no gambling took place. Butch White was super in his salesmanship in peddling his bananas, candy, trinkets to the passengers and kids. Brakeman Jake Kegley's comments and thoughts were items of interest about the local, state, national affairs, that drew passenger's attention to compensate for the fact it took approximately three hours to make the fifty-two mile run. There was always considerable kidding among the N & W's train crew on claim, besides blowing the whistle for the on-coming passenger station stops, that they would blow their whistle for every house along the New River Plateau tracks.

Carroll, Grayson Counties were dry territory, except for moon-shiners, a large amount of the incoming railway express shipments was government tax liquor purchased from distributors in Roanoke, VA. Naturally there was a great deal of curiosity as to who was receiving the package and baggage express shipments. The employees of the Railway Express Company had quite a time sorting the express in the express car and placing it in the express room of the Galax Depot station which in a manner of satisfaction to both the Railway Express Agency employees and the curious on-lookers.

The curious crowd always approved Mr. Bill Weatherman, an employee of the Railway Express Agency, who had a delivery contact for the agency as a sole 'licensed dragman" who delivered all types of package express to the local merchant homes in Galax; and delivery of the U.S. Mail to the Galax Post Office. When Mr. Bill Weatherman got ready to load his express wagon, he would call on his horse "Old Bob", who would back the express wagon into a loading position at the loading dock of the Railway Express Office without any help from Mr. Weatherman.

Dr. J. W. Bolen, earlier resident of Briar, Virginia, moved his medical office to Galax in 1904 establishing his medical practice and residence on North Main Street. He built the J. W. Bolen boarding house and medical offices on South Main Street beside the Harris Hotel, having two medical offices, renting one office to Dr. J. K. Caldwell. Mrs. J. W. Bolen opened her millinery shop in the Bolen building. In 1910 he began constructing a brick building on the corner of East Grayson and North Main Streets, opening the Bolen Drug Co. and Medical Office

The people of Galax were looking forward to the coming on the Great Galax Fair to be held the week of September 14th thru the 21, featuring a large wild west show, free acts, carnival on the midway, hack cart racing, fireworks, being promised by G. F. Carr, Secretary of the Galax Fair Association. The Galax Department Store was opened on West side of North Main Street in 1910 by E. M. Coffman and S. Stein of Bristol, Va., having a lady's and men's clothing line and misc. merchandise. They filed for bankruptcy October 13, 1913, being unable to meet their financial obligations. Judge A. A. Campbell of Wytheville, VA had the Galax Department Store business placed in the hands of a receiver for the benefit of the creditors. Judge A. A. Campbell appointed Attorney J. H. Rudy of Galax as a temporary receiver on October 28, 1913. E. M. Coffman, S. Stein partners doing business under the firm name of the Galax Department Store. They made an agreement to Attorney J. H. Rudy as trustee for the benefits of all creditors, all debts due them are payable by Attorney J. Rudy, who authorized J. H. Smith to receive payments and receipt.

The store was closed to invoice stock of merchandise. The store will reopen Saturday morning, and remain open until all goods are disposed of - signed by attorney J. H. Rudy as trustee. In 1914 Dan B. Waugh purchased the Galax Department Store and remaining stock, renaming the store the Dan B. Waugh's Fashion Shop.

Local news from April of 1910 highlighted the following topics: Miss Maiden, Miss Cox, Miss Bryant, Miss Allison, and Professor J. A. Livesay attended the Teacher's Meeting at Radford College in Radford, Virginia, on Thursday, Friday and Saturday. They reported a good time on the Monday morning of their return. Misses Allison, Cox, Maiden, and Bryant told the school gathering of the many things that they saw and heard. It was felt that the meeting would benefit the teachers and help the school as a whole. Miss Bettie May Early, Milliner for the Hillsville Mercantile Company, returned by train to Galax after a buying trip to Baltimore, Maryland. A bazaar was held at the Galax Academy School Auditorium by Elizabeth Scott as the hostess to the Ladies Booklovers Club. C. M. Bryant in 1910 (?) began construction on his modern roller mill, the Bryant Flour Mill located on East Oldtown Street producing flour, corn, meal, and livestock feed.

The mill managed by E. D. Perkins; R. E,. Jones succeeded J. F. Vass as Mayor of Galax in 1910. Councilmen were: Charlie P. Waugh, W. W. Blair, W. K. Early, S. B. Kinzer, James C. Reavis, L. L. Joines. C. T. Higgins, Police Sergeant for the Town of Galax, was stationed in the Mayor's office on East Grayson Street on Monday and Tuesday, October 27 and 28,1911, for the purpose of collecting the town taxes for the past year of 1910. Walter M. Jones, Sr., was the Town of Galax Treasurer. W. I. Harp opened the second movie theater on South Main Street in the Town of Galax, named the Harp Theater, selling the theater business to Claude Hackler, when modernizing the theater, named it the Grand Theater. In later years the name changed to the Market Theater.

In the winter of 1911, fire destroyed the following businesses located on the East side of South Main Street: Harris Hotel, Dr. D. W. Bolen's Boarding House, Mrs. J. W. Bolen's Millinery Shop, damaging M. L. Bishop Delivery Stables.

The Medical Community

Doctors serving the people of Blair, Oldtown, and the Galax area were as follows: Dr. J. S. Hopkins, Dr. B. C. Cooper, Dr. W. R. Murphy, Dr. J. H, Witherow, Dr. C. A. Witherow., Dr. B. S. Dobyns, Dr. J. W. Bolen, Dr. J. K. Caldwell, Dr. Glenn Phipps, Dr. John Phipps, Dr. J. G. Bishop, Dr. S. . Draper, Dr. S. M. Robinson, Dr. Lewis Early, Dr. W. P. Davis, Dr. W. R. Collins, and Dr. Staley Young. Dentist included Dr. A. G. Pless, Sr., Sr. Luther Jones, and Dr. A R. Grubb. The Medical and dental practices were well represented in the area. The excellent medical care provided by the local doctors in the three communities during the development of the Town of Galax was augmented by the recommendation of the fine old mountain tonics. The practicing doctors coupled their medical training with the mountain tonics "Good for what ails you" to help the local citizens. The medical professionals were deeply appreciated in the mountain town of Galax.

The Nuckoll's Spring, a popular resort, located on the Healing Springs Road was a picnic area which attracted crowds for hayrides and parties in the summers. Visitors from many states were impressed by the wonderful healing power of the Lithia-Bromo-Arsenic Water. It is hard to believe that "chugging" a glass of arsenic-laced water could actually be good for you. Attendants of the healing springs claimed that the Lithia-Bromo-Arsenic Water helped relieve anything from eczema, stomach ulcers, skin disorders, rheumatism, liver problems to dropsy. Other reliable medicine for the cure of rheumatism or stomach, kidney, and liver trouble was "Dr. Greens̄ Refined Sarsaparilla or a sedative cough remedy called "Chamberlains Cough Remedy" sold by Galax Drug, Bolen Drug, Dalton Drug or Crystal Drug Stores. The Nuckoll's Healing Springs Resort was commonly known for many years as healing waters. The result of the waters was so great that it gained a reputation from the many visitors. People arrive in town by the Norfolk and Western Passenger Train and rent a buggy and horse from Felts, Dobyn's, or Bishop's Delivery Stables for their trip to the Nuckolls' Healing Springs. The visitors would camp on the forest grounds, stay at different farmhouses, or return to Galax to stay at the Waugh or Central Hotels. Many physicians were pleased with the results and effects of the waters and often prescribed the water to their patients. The Reverend B. F. Nuckolls owned the farm where the healing springs was located and he shipped the healing water in large quantities to other locations. Reverend Nuckolls established the Nuckolls' Healing Springs Resort in 1898.

Reverend B. F. Nuckolls established the Nuckolls Springs Bottling Works in a modern brick building at the corner of East Oldtown and Carroll Streets, to bottle his Healing Springs Lithia-Bromo-Arsenic water, and to manufacture soft drinks. The Rev. Nuckolls plans were to build and open a new hotel at Nuckolls Springs on Healing Springs Road by the season of 1915, besides the Hotel itself, a number of cottages would be erected for those who wish to escape the summer heat of larger cities of lower altitude, by vacationing in a grove of fine oak trees at the Healing

Springs Resort.

Local news from Thursday, July 10, 1912 - a reception was given at "Fairview" at the home of Dr. and Mrs. J. H. Witherow in honor of the Ladies Social Club. Those that had the honor of Dr. and Mrs. Witherow's hospitality were Dr. and Mrs. J. W. Bolen, Mr. J. K. Caldwell, Mrs. B. S. Dobyns, Mr. And Mrs. J. H. Kapp, Mr. W. K. Early, Mrs. R. L. Humphrey, Mr. And Mrs. E. L. Whitley, Mrs. J. S. James, Mr. And Mrs. W. W. Blair, Mr. And Mrs. A. L. Williams, Mrs. W. P. Giersh, Mrs. Lucy Kriete, Mr. And Mrs. W.C. Roberson, Mrs. C. L. Lindsey, and Dr. and Mrs. A. G. Pless, Sr.

In 1912, S. F. Vass succeeded R. E. Jones as Mayor of the Town of Galax with Councilmen James C. Reavis, W.K. Early, G. F. Carr, Charles P. Waugh, R. E. Jones, and D. A. Robertson.

The Galax Volunteer Fire Department

After the Town of Galax had gone through several divesting fires which destroyed the Central Hotel, R. L. Roupe's building, the Ward Brothers' building, the Red Star Hotel, and the Galax Furniture and Lumber Company, Harris Hotel, Dr. D. W Bolen's Boarding House, Mrs. J. W. Bolen's Millinery Shop, and M. L. Bishop Delivery Stables, the town council, mayor. And the citizens of Galax called a meeting. The meeting was held at the Galax Academy School Auditorium to discuss and organize a town water system and a volunteer fire department. The current water resources were two hand pump wells located at the Central Hotel and at the Waugh Hotel, The citizens of the residential areas who had built their own homes, owned their own hand pump wells and sewer septic tanks and privets. The first fire fighting in Galax was done by the "people's bucket brigade" when the church bells sounded the fire alarm.

The Galax Volunteer Fire Department was organized in 1912 and Edd D. Perkins was nominated as Fire Chief. The department had sixteen volunteer members who were divided into fire companies of eight men. The Fire Department equipment consisted of two pull carts, called hand pumpers, with a water storage tank on each cart. The pumper hoses were connected at the well pumper head. The firemen would split into pairs to operate the well head to pump water to the storage tank on the carts. It took a fire company of eight men to pull each pumper, pump the water, and hose a fire.

The local government and business leaders continuously looked for other business ventures. The time had come for this group of leaders to concentrate on developing a water storage system and water works plant for the present day and future community's fire protection of property. The town government started exploring the possibilities of building concrete catch basins in the steep terrain of the end of Gilmer Street where there were several natural spring heads. A pump house was built, electrical power pumps were installed after receiving Appalachian Power Service, and a filtration concrete basin to hold several hundred gallons of water. At the top of the hill (near the current Waugh Street), a concrete reservoir holding tank for several thousand gallons of water was constructed. The water was pumped from the pump house to the holding tank on a daily basis. From the reservoir, water lines were laid along the streets supplying homes and fire hydrants in 1914. Galax continued to operate this water system for several years; meanwhile, the local merchants were changing from frame wood buildings to brick construction.

Mrs. E. Lane Whitley advertised in the Galax Post Herald the loss of her "tan automobile veil". A petition was prepared by the citizens of the Town of Galax, asking an ordinance be passed requiring dog owners to muzzle their dogs. The Waugh Hotel was put on the reality market July 11, 1912. Mrs. Lelia Waugh had decided to sell due to her health condition. The property consists of a 23 room hotel with six lots fronting on the corners of East Center and North Main Streets, with garden, barn, wood house and other out buildings. The property was well known and centrally located; terms to suit the purchaser; for price and information write J. P. Carico, Galax. The Galax High School fall term will open September 9, 1912, Wright and Payne principals. South Bros, Purchased W. G. Lowe's Store on East side of N. Main Street buying wool, poultry, produce, cross-ties in exchange of merchandise. In July 1912 the Norfolk & Western Railway Co. let a contract to build 55 miles of rail line of the Virginia-Carolina Railroad from Green Cove, Va. to Todd, N.C. which 12 miles of rail line pass through the Western end of Grayson County. G. C. Williams opened an electric shop on East side of North Main Street next to the Ward's building selling Westinghouse home lighting plants and supplies.

The V. S. Walker & Co. were closing out their entire line of Johnson & Woods farm machinery at cost. "Does your eyes need help" Consult Rev. W. D. Mitchell, Optician who is expected to arrive in Galax Thursday, August 1, 1912, by the N & W's passenger train to fit eye glasses at the Waugh Hotel. For an appointment, call Rev. J. S .Neel.

The Edwards Chair Co. began manufacturing double cane seat chairs in the summer of 1913. The citizens of the Town of Galax, Carroll. Grayson counties area were stunned to hear of the loss of the Galax Furniture & Lumber Co. located at the corner of East Virginia Street, Railroad Avenue destroyed by fire December 9, 1913. Losing the Galax Furniture & Lumber Co.

Manufacturing plant meant a severe loss of employment to the people of the area, and a loss of business by the local business merchants, saw mill operations. Some employees were employed by the Galax Chair Manufacturing Co.

E. R. and Lon McMillan moved their McMillan Produce Co. to the M. T. Blessing building, located on East Grayson Street next to J.B. Waugh & Son Store in 1914, later years selling their produce business to C. H. Smith and B. D. Beamer operating under the name of Smith-Reamer Produce Store.

During the rough winter of early 1914, transportation travel such as wagons, T-models, and Hup-mobiles came to a halt due to the deep snows and drifting. After ten days of being completely paralyzed, a wagoner arrived in Galax from Cherry Lane, N.C. He had been on the road three days coming to Galax. He said the folks up at Cherry Lane had gotten tired of sitting around in the dark: they persuaded him to come to Galax to get kerosene oil to light their lamps. He got his oil barrel filled at the Blair Grocery Co. located on East Grayson and Depot Avenue. W. C. Roberson was the only kerosene bulk dealer in Galax.

The March term of the Carroll County Court opened March 9, 1914, with Judge A. A. Campbell of Wytheville, presiding. The following gentlemen were in attendance serving an the grand jury: G. W. Alford, W. R. Bishop, W. A. Alderman, Floyd E. Lineberry, C. C. Phillips, W. T. Cooley, S. F. Welsh, L. A. Lineberry, F. C. Dalton, John W. Kinzer, J. B. Hall, and G. M. Hurst. Joshua A. Marshall was acquitted by the Grand Jury on the charge of retailing whiskey without a license. This was a clear case of guilty, which Judge A. A. Campbell gave the jury a severe lecture for their mistaken decision of acquittal. Bird Snow was fined $50.00 and costs upon a plea of guilty for illicit distilling. J. R. Greenwood was fined the same amount under the same plea. The courts time was consumed with the case of the Commonwealth of Virginia against one other case who was charged with retailing liquor without a license. The Grand Jury will probably render a verdict today. There are no cases of importance to be decided at the term of court and the time will be consumed in disposing of the revenue cases. The following citizens of Galax in attendance of March Court Term were: Attorneys Floyd Landreth, Hicks Rhudy, H. Prince Burnett. Others in attendance were: W. K. Early ??

On Thursday, July 11, 1912, one of the most delightful events of the year in Galax was the Confederate

Veterans Reunion being promoted by the United Daughters of the Confederacy. Invitations were extended to all surviving veterans of Carroll, Grayson Counties. One hundred and twelve of the aged veterans gather at Hotel Waugh on the corners of East Center, North Main Streets at 10:00 a.m. to join a street parade walk or riding, headed by the uniform Galax Brass marching Band, which began the parade at 11:15 a.m. from the Waugh Hotel down Main Street heading to the fairgrounds. The day was beautiful for all the Veterans who were marching along Main Street followed by a number of decorated floats and some automobiles. After reaching the fairgrounds, the Veterans, their wives and widows were assembled in the large decorated hall under the grandstand building where the Daughter's of the Confederacy served the Veterans their lunch. Following the lunch, the Veterans moved to the seats on the grandstand to listen to the opening remarks by the Mayor of Galax, Mr. R. E. Jones, Rev. J. S. W. Neal, the Methodist Minister, and E. T. Kirby. At one-thirty p.m. the Honorable E. L. Nuckolls of Fayetteville, W.Va., the son of a confederate soldier, delivered a toughing eulogy on the services rendered by the confederate veterans of the Civil War.

The Edwards Brothers, A. M. Edwards, J. N. Edwards began construction of their Edwards Chair Company building in the summer of 1912 to manufacture and produce double cane chairs that were built for service. Round, made of selected mountain hickory, kiln dried and glues at posts, warranted not to get 'rickety". Varnish guaranteed against all kinds of weather, will not "run" or become 'spotted" nor "discolored". Back post have perfect bend, and slats tenanted in past. K. S. Boyer was plant superintendent and manager. The Edward's Chair Company was located on the corner of East Oldtown and Depot Streets being the second furniture manufacturing plant to open in the Town of Galax., Va.

A party was given at the home of Captain and Mrs. John B. Waugh Saturday evening from 8:30 till 11:30 p.m. in honor of their house guests: Mrs. Chatham, Miss Perkins, Miss Noel, and Miss Guynn. The reception hall, library, parlor, dining room were joined together making an ideal place for entertaining. The guests of honor formed a receiving line. Miss Susie Waugh served punch in the reception hall. The punch bowl was placed at the foot of the winding stairway decorated in a mass of pink rhododendron and Galax leaves. Card tables were placed and progressive rook was enjoyed. Later- in the evening the guest enjoyed dancing in the dining room and parlor. Other people in attendance besides the guests of honor were Misses Mattie Payne Copenhaven, Louise Ferebee, Bessie Thompson, Alice Cardwell, Blanche Carico, Margaret Bolling, Susie Waugh, Helen Humphrey, Lynn Nuckolls, Mabel David, Eva Sue Sutherland, Carrie Neel, and Leona Humphrey. Messrs. J. E. Abshire, Harry Early, Harry Carico, Swift Waugh, Trent Neel, Charles Waugh, Dan Waugh, Richard Waugh, and Dr. Hege.

J. Barger Caldwell, father of Dr. J. K. Caldwell, R. P. Caldwell, Vinnie Caldwell, E. C. Caldwell, passed away at his son Archie Caldwell's home at Columbia, California, July 4th, 1912. He owned a farm in the Galax community. J. Barger help lay off lot lines when the first lots were sold at Anderson Bottoms, December 3, 1903. Mr. J. Barger Caldwell was buried at the Caldwell off Givens Street. Miss Vinnie Caldwell returned to Galax in 1912 when Galax was expanding in its early growth. She became active in the advancement of the town of Galax and the Carroll and Grayson area. Anna Caldwell was thrown off her buggy suffering a dislocated elbow.

The Blair Hardware Co. was established at Blair, Virginia, in the late 1890's by Sam B. Kinzer, and J. H. Kapp. J. C. Matthews moved his family from Cap, Va. To Anderson Bottoms becoming an employee of the Blair Hardware Company at Blair, Virginia, when the town of Galax was established. Sam Kinzer, Sam Jackson, J. H. Kapp moved their hardware business to Galax, renaming the business Galax Hardware Company located on the West side of North Main Street. J. C. Matthews became associated with J. F. Vass, J. H. Vass of Cap, VA in prior years operating family hardware business at Cap, Virginia. J. C. Matthews, J. F. Vass established the J. C. Matthews & Co. Store and warehouse on the corner of East Grayson, Depot Avenue, opposite of the N & W's freight and passenger station in 1904. The stockholders in the J. C. Matthews Hardware Store were: L. J. Todd, John A. Faddis, Charlie Dobyn's , B. D. Beamer. In 1911, the stockholders of the J. C. Matthews Company began construction of a modern brick stare at the corner of West Grayson and North Main Streets, opening the new J. C. Matthews & Company store in 1912. J. H. Kapp sold his interest in the Galax Hardware Company February 6, 1913, joining J. F. Vass, J. . Vass, J. . Matthews in the J. C. Matthews & Company. Sam B. Kinzer, and Sam Jackson, owners of Galax Hardware Company's stores located on the West side of North Main Street and South side of East Grayson Street, formed a partnership with M. L. Harrison of Wytheville; W. K. Early and G. D. Brown of Galax reorganizing their hardware company, Inc. opening Bluegrass Hardware Stores in Wytheville, Rural Retreat, Pulaski, and Galax. M. L. Harrison, President, W. K. Early, Vice-President, Sam B. Kinzer, Secretary-Treasurer and General Manager. G. O. Brown, was manager of the Galax Bluegrass Hardware Store. Mr. J. C. Matthews operated the J. C. Matthews & Company in partnership with J. F. Vass, J. H. Vass, J. H. Kapp, L. J. Todd, John H. Faddis, Charlie Dobyns, B. D. Beamer. For a period of years before selling his interest in the J. C. Matthews & Company and purchasing the Vass-Hawks Hardware Company in 1921, owned by J. H. Vass, C. W. Hawks located on the East side of south Main Street.

        J. C. Matthews changed the name title to J. C. Matthews Hardware Company. J. Edd Matthews joined his father in the management of the South Main J.C. Matthews Hardware Company store. J. C. Matthews opened the second J. C. Matthews Hardware Company store on East Grayson Street in the M. T. Blessings building managed by his sons T. Jeff Matthews and Walter Matthews. In 1921 J. F. Vass, J. P. Kapp, stockholders, established the Vass-Kapp Hardware Company on the corner of West Grayson and North Main Streets, establishing a warehouse on the corner of East Grayson and Depot Avenue.

        Louie Perelman opened the L. Perelman Fashion Shop on West side of South Main Street, The Women's Civic Betterment Club was organized March 16, 1914, to work together to build up the town's schools, promote legislation for better roads, guard the public's health, keep our hometown clean, beautiful, appealing and attractive to out of town visitors, creating an interest to them on becoming a resident of the Town of Galax, Virginia. It was the duty of every local woman in the town of Galax to identify herself with the movement of the Women's Civic Betterment Club owning it to her children to have eight months of free school education. If you want to see the debt paid on our school and have better public health, join the Women's Civic Betterment Club of Galax, Virginia.

        The Women's Civic Betterment Club of Galax began their work by campaigning for redemption of five lots, formerly a part of the Galax School property that could be used as a playground: presently owned by H. H. Todd, Dr. A. G. Pless, Sr. who have generously given option of the lots to the Galax High School Corp. Believing in encouragement, support of all the citizens, the women have undertaken their first task. Their first need was to increase their membership. Their next meeting was held in the Masonic Meeting Hall located over the J. C. Matthews & Company on the corner of West Grayson and North Main Streets, Thursday, November 6,1914, at 3:00 p.m. Mrs. Lelia R. Crabill, president, Mrs. J. H. Kapp, secretary, Mrs. J. K. Caldwell, Treasurer. Galax, along with other Virginia School systems shared in different school problems, but their foresight and efficient leadership support by all the intelligent citizens of Galax always solved their problems of their perplexing situation of their past and improve their town of Galax's education system in the future.

        The people of the town of Galax and the surrounding community gather along the N W tracks at the Galax Depot to see the "Great Hogg Circus" equipment being unloaded, being set-up in clear bottom opposite of the Galax Depot for a big three day event.

        The Galax Post Office was moved from the R. E. Jones Store to the lower level of the J.C. Matthews & Company store in 1912. Mr. R. E. Jones and son, Walter M. Jones, began construction of a modern brick building for their R. E. Jones & Son Furniture Store and Funeral Home located on the West side of North Main Street.

Development of Electric Power

The Appalachian Power Company was constructing and completing their Buck and Billesby Power Dams in 1912. The Appalachian Power Company's representatives were in Galax May 13,1912, mapping the streets and power pole lines for domestic and industrial electric power services. Mr. A. McMillian of the Appalachian Power Company met with the citizens and town officials at the Mayor's office chambers on East Grayson Street explaining their electric services. The Town of Galax's Mayor and Council approved the agreement with the Appalachian Power Company franchise for a period of thirty years to construct and maintain and operate its poles, posts, conduits, manholes, ducts, cable wires and all other necessary overhead and underground apparatus through streets, alleys, highway and other public roads within the town proper of Galax located partly in Carroll and Grayson Counties of the Commonwealth of Virginia. The Appalachian Power Company projected date to begin supplying electric power services to the town of Galax was October 30,1913.

An interesting balloon ascension was given by the Galax Hardware Company on North Main Street on July 4th when the balloon prizes were turn loose in front of their store. One of the balloon prizes was found by W. M. Roseberry of Galax rural route entitling him to $1.00 in merchandise.

D. A. Robertson succeeded J. F. Vass as the mayor of Galax in 1914. Elected Councilmen were: R. E. Jones, W. K. Early, J. F, Vass, B. D. Beamer, James C. Reavis, and Charlie Waugh. The public could purchase their smoking and chewing pleasures such as Ram's Horn Chewing tobacco or Union Leader pipe and cigarette tobacco for smoking from the Bolen Drug Store, Galax Drug Store, Crystal Drug Store, or Dalton Drug Store. B. D. Beamer became town Treasurer in 1914. The Twin County Real Estate Agency of Galax was reorganized, doing business under the title of Blue Ridge Land Company. The elected officers were J. H. Rhudy as President H. Prince Burnett, Secretary-Treasurer; Joel Harmon, General Manager and Salesman. Another organized firm was the Galax Real Estate Agency & Insurance Company located over the J. C. Matthews & Company on the corner of West Grayson and North Main Streets, The Peoples State Bank was organized and chartered in 1912 constructing a modern brick building on East Grayson Street next to the Bolen's Drug Store. The People's State Bank was successor to the Blair Banking Company established at Blair in 1904. H. M. Todd was President; Charlie P. Waugh, Vice-President. Cashiers were R. J. Cornett and B. D. Beamer. Directors were: Charlie P. Waugh, W. H. Bolling, H. M. Todd, W. K. Early. The People's State Bank of Galax defaulted during the depression of 1929. The bank was reorganized in 1934, renaming it the Merchants & Farmers Bank of Galax. Fred Adams was President; Collin Webb, Active Vice-President; I. L. Gray, Cashier. Directors were Fred Adams, I. Lee Gray, B. D. Beamer, Paul V. Dalton, T. N. Woodruff.

Thomas L. Felts, and E. L. Whitley in partnership organized and established the Twin County Motor Company on the corner of West Webster and North Main Street in 1915; Thomas L. Felts, President, Gordon C. Felts, Vice-President and General Manager: G. A. Holder, Secretary-Treasurer. Twin County Motor Company had the dealership agencies for the following automobiles such as Overland, Hupmobile, Chandler's, Model Ts touring passenger cars, Ford trucks, Federal trucks, Fordson tractors, farm machinery, car parts, tires. Thomas L. Felts donated to the Galax Volunteer Fire Department of the Town of Galax their first fire truck complete with fire ladders, fire hoses, equipment such as a foamite tank trailer.

The members of the Galax Volunteer Fire Department during the prior years of 1920's were: Walt Anderson, Ralph Todd, Walter Matthews, Clarence Todd, Tom Trimble, Willie Boaz, Garland Anderson, Emmon B. Todd, Ben G. Witherow, Dan Anderson, Lester Diamond, Walter Elliott, Herman Webb, Jim

Anderson, Sid Dotson, George Calloway, Paul Phipps, W. F. Worrell, Bob Morris, Lance Todd, Roy C. Manning, Gabe Lundy, J.W. Hortenstine, W. C. Roberson,

In 1916, D. A. Robertson was re-elected mayor of Galax. Councilmen were: C. A. Collier, M. E. McMillan, W. K. Early, W. C. Roberson, Charlie P. Waugh, J. F. Vass, Cliffside Farms under the management of John A. Faddis at Ethelfelts, Virginia, had for sale two mares, well broken, weighing 1200 lbs. Each. The Gillespie's Brothers, T. Gillespie, W. Gillespie purchased J. 0. Spea's saw mill and planning mill in 1911 producing mill [umber products. In 1919 the Gillespie Brothers opened their Gillespie Garage on the corner of Carroll Street (West side) and East Oldtown Street which became a local landmark by which the local motorist as well as visiting motorist were guided for their expert automobile services. The Gillespie Brothers garage were dealers for Hood tires, batteries and miscellaneous for automobiles, trucks. The business was repairing automobiles, trucks of every make. Their garage employed mechanics giving their customers complete services at a reasonable price owning their building that made their enterprise a substantial factor on the town of Galax.

A state doctor from the Virginia Health Board was in the Town of Galax looking into the causes for the outbreak of typhoid fever. Everyone is looking forward to attending the play drama Saturday night March 20th at the Galax Academy School auditorium, being played by the members of the Senior Class of 1914. Miss Elizabeth Scott has been directing and working diligently with the Senior students in promoting the school play.

For the best buy of nursery stock, visit the New River Nursery Company located off of Piper's Gap Road on Chestnut Creek.

The Prohibition Issue

A group of Galax citizens met at the Galax Methodist Church on Sunday, August 2, 1914, to listen to the Women's Christian Temperance Union. The group listened to the Commonwealth of Virginia Prohibition issue had become an alarming issue. The audience listened to local speakers discuss the state wide prohibition cause discussed by S. Floyd Landreth, Commonwealth Attorney for Carroll County. D. A. Robertson, Mayor of the Town of Galax and br. B. S. Dobyns, a local doctor of Galax, S. Floyd Landreth, talked about prohibition being a fight between true manhood, womanhood and righteousness on one side and the cause of wrong on the other side. Mayor D. A. Robertson made a point that everyone should take a stand for the rights in the matter of the state wide prohibition issue, which is in the findings of the right side.

Mayor D. A. Robertson stated at the present rate of destruction of the liquor business was demanding one son from every fifth family in the United States. Dr. B. S. Dobyns treated the subject from his viewpoint of being a physician: first refuting flatly and bluntly that alcohol was necessary to the physician's profession or to the human body at anytime. He stated to the group that in every instance it was a nerve destroyer and harmful to the human body.

D. A. Robertson, Mayor of the Town of Galax, and Manager of the Galax Buggy Company was elected to the House of Delegates of the Commonwealth of Virginia as a legislator representing the people of the fifth district in 1916.

Dan B. Waugh and Scoutmaster Lance Todd took a group of 14 Galax on a camping trip to Roaring Gap, N.C. for a camp outing. The Galax scouts started the trip in two model "T" Fords touring sedans and a covered camp wagon pulled by a team of horses hauling their camping equipment. The Boy Scout camp wagon made it to the selected camp

231

site at one of the springs located along the golf course range at Roaring Gap. The two Model "T" sedans finally arrived being pulled by hired wagon teams. Mr. Dan, being questioned by the camp wagon team said: "An amazing incident occurred at the forks of the road near Hooker, NC. Meeting a couple of wagons loaded with crossties on their way to Galax." Mr. Dan asked the head wagoneer "which was the best way of the three routes to Roaring Gap? I am lost and need some directions." The wagoneer answer was "it don't make no difference which way you go. You will always swear that the two other roads were bound to have been better." After a few days f camping and gassing up the Model "T" sedans, the Boy Scout group returned to Galax without any problems.

The winters in the Blue Ridge Mountains were rougher than some winters of prior years. When the New river froze solid with ice, when the warming trend began, the ice would began thawing creating ice chunks flowing on New River causing a constant worry to travelers, Wagoner's hauling loads of lumber, crossties, freight loads being pulled by oxen, major draft horses, creating a danger to their animals, which was the only source of transportation.

Mr. Harve Bayer ran a ferry crossing on New River called Boyer's Ferry, located on the main road from Galax to Independence, Virginia. The river was shallow in places above the ferry crossing. People familiar with crossing could ford New River with their teams without any problems. With the coming of the automobile, people began driving their Model "T"s, Whippets, Overland, or Hupmobile arriving at the Boyer's Ferry crossing on New River. Mr. Nerve Boyer would charge 25 cents to ferry their cars across New River. Some drivers would begrudge paying Mr. Bayer 25 cents, inclining to try and ford the river in their automobiles. When the magnetos and distributor became wet the car stalled out in the middle of New River. Mr. Boyer would sit on his ferry, thoroughly enjoying himself, watching the motorist wading out, going to hunt a team of horses or yoke of oxen to pull their automobiles out of New River to dry land.

Mr. John Honnecker of Bluefield, West Virginia, an earlier acquaintance of Mr. Thomas L. Felts during the years he lived in Bluefield, associated with the Baldwin-Felts Detective Agency, became interested in locating a furniture manufacturing operation in the town of Galax. Mr. Honnecker met with the business and citizen's groups in Galax taking option on land tract located on the corner of Railroad Avenue and East Oldtown Street close to Chestnut Creek. The business and citizen's group of Galax formed a joint stock company to raise funds, issuing stock certification shares to develop the Honnecker Furniture Manufacturing Plant opposite of the Galax Canning plant. Construction began on the Honnecker Furniture plant in 1916.

The Ward Brothers Brick Manufacturing Company furnished several thousand bricks for the construction of the Honnecker Furniture Company. The officers of the Honnecker Furniture Company were: John W. Honnecker, President and E.W. Dodd, Secretary-Treasurer. The furniture plant began manufacturing bedroom suites and dining room suites in 1916. Several experienced men who had worked at the Galax Furniture & Lumber Company in their earlier years became employees of the new furniture plant that became an asset to the town of Galax and the community area.

J. F. Vass succeeded D. A. Robertson as the Mayor of Galax in 1918. Councilmen were: B. D. Beamer, H. M. Todd, George Early, P. C. Martin, J. W. Hortenstine, and Charlie P. Waugh. Following the end of World War I, the Veterans were returning to Galax and the communities of Carroll and Grayson counties seeking employment in the furniture industry, General Chemical Company's Gossan Mines. Washington Mills, Bertha Mineral Company, timber operations, and farming. The Galax citizens and business people were looking ahead, planning more industrial developments in the area. The business people of Galax organized a joint stock company in late 1918 issuing stock certificates shares to raise $28,000 to build a new manufacturing plant called the Yancey's Brothers Extract Company located on Railroad Avenue (present location of the Webb Furniture Company] began constructing their plant. The Norfolk & Western Railway Company built track siding to the plant. The Yancey's Brothers began their manufacturing operations of extracting wood acids and color extract from the timber of chestnut, oak, and cherry used in the process of tanning leather, producing color base for the manufacturing of different colors of stain varnishes.

John W. Honnecker closed the Honnecker Furniture plant in Galax in Spring of 1919 due to financial difficulties. Mr. J. D. Bassett and Mr. B. C. Vaughan came to Galax in July of 1919 to look over the Honnecker Furniture Company's plant, talking to the local business people, and the Galax business group. Mr. J. D. Bassett and B. C. Vaughan called a meeting to be held at the Masonic Hall (located upstairs over J. C. Matthews & Company at the corner of West Grayson and North Main Streets) to discuss and express to the people holding stock share certificates, assuring them they would reclaim their stock share certificates and reissued new stock share certificates. Mr. J. D. Bassett and B. C. Vaughan purchased the personal, real estate properties of the Honnecker Furniture Company and began formatting plans to get the furniture plant in operation by September 1919. They renamed the furniture plant the Vaughan-Bassett Furniture Company.

Officers of the Vaughan-Bassett Furniture Company were B. C. Vaughan, President; T. G. Vaughan, Secretary-Treasurer; E. B. Lennox, Vice-President and production Manager. The Vaughan-Bassett Furniture Company was a success from the beginning of their venture from its inception with additions and equipment added from time to time during their expanding growth. Mr. E. B. Lennox came to Galax in 1919 when the industrial payroll in Galax was approximately forty employees in industrial manufacturing. Lennox took an active part in every phase of the Galax growing community by playing a large part in the developing furniture industry to the enviable position the furniture industries hold today. Mr. E. B. Lennox had one of those personalities that draw all his men to him, as well as being hard as a flint rock when the occasion demanded, but he had a heart big enough to cover the whole community. His fairness towards his men won him their admiration, which kept them going. In keeping their jobs secured when other manufacturing plants in the South were closing due to depressed times, Mr. E. B Lennox rose from a position working as a tail-boy on a cutoff saw in Martinsville, Virginia, to Vice-President of Vaughan-Bassett, Vaughan Furniture Company and President of Webb Furniture Company.

Warren B. Giersch opened a discount store on West Grayson Street. Floyd W. Williams opened the Palace Cream Parlor in 1919 on the West side of South Main Street across the alley next to the Galax Post Office (present Henderson Building). The Palace Cream Parlor became a prominent social center for the people of Galax and the surrounding community, because it had an inviting atmosphere giving the people the needed services at a reasonable piece. The Palace Cream Parlor merchandise was confectionary, carrying a variety of candies, leather goods, work baskets, fruit baskets, shaving sets, manicure sets, stationary, fiction novels, picture books, cigars, cigarettes, Christmas gifts, Kodak cameras, film, cards, fountain pens, magazines, gifts for all occasions, serving Clover Ice Cream and milk shakes.

Floyd Williams was very active in the Blue Ridge Post of the American Legion organization in Galax, having a very large number of Veterans from the counties of Carroll and Grayson. The post Commander was Roscoe Burnett, assisted by Garfield Childress service ad Adjutant.

The directors and stock holders of the First National Bank of Galax located at the corner of East Center, North Main Streets, made a decision they needed a larger banking facility. They purchased the corner lot on West Grayson and North Main Streets from Dr. J. H. Witherow who operated his Galax Drug Store for the past sixteen years.

The First National Bank began construction in 1921, building a two story brick building with all the modern facilities in banking to serve their customers in Galax and the Carroll and Grayson areas to the fullest extent. The new First National Bank opened for banking services in 1922, Thomas L. Felts, President; J. P. Carico, First Vice-President: S. Floyd Landreth, Second Vice-President; C. A. Collier, Cashier; W. R. Ballard, Assistant Cashier; Julia

Blair, Assistant Cashier. Directors were: J. H. Witherow, S. Floyd Landreth, A. C. Painter, J. P. Carico, W. D. Tompkins, and T. L. Felts. The directors and stock holders sold the old banking building to the Town of Galax, who changed the banking building into Town Hall, courtroom, Council Chamber, offices for the Police Department, Water Services, and Galax Fire Department.

The Galax Theater located on South Main Street next to the Galax Dry Goods Store was showing movies "Go Get 'em Hutch" and a western titled "Sand" starring William Hart, Dr. J. H. Witherow and H. C. Cox established the Cox-Witherow's Men's Clothing Store on South Main Street next to the F. C. Dalton building.

Thomas L. Felts was serving as a State Senator on the General Assembly of the Commonwealth of Virginia in 1922 representing the people of the 14^{Wt} District in Southwest Virginia. Tom Felts had been instrumental in converting a good road movement into reality forcing through the Robertson Act Loan that became responsible for the future road construction of the first hard service roads which evidence of several miles to be built in Grayson, Carroll, Wythe Counties being such routes #12 #18 changed to routes #58, #221, #52, and #89 becoming part of the state of Virginia Highway system. It was always stated by the people that no one worked harder or did a greater service for the people of Southwest Virginia that Thomas L. Felts while serving his years in the Commonwealth of Virginia Legislature from the fifth district.

D. A. Robertson succeeded J. F. Vass as the Mayor of Galax in 1920. Councilmen were: Charlie P. Waugh. H. M. Todd, B. D. Beamer, G. A. Holder, George B. Early, and Gordon Felts. Mr. Herman Boaz established his first studio on the West side of North Main Street. He purchased the stock and equipment of the Art Color Studio from Bedsaul, Rt. 8, Galax, and L. J. Stockner Studio, North side of North Main Street.

R. A. Anderson established the Blue Ridge Bus Line located on West Oldtown Street in the early 1920's, operating bus services to Mt. Airy, NC, Pulaski and Radford. The bus would leave Galax at 9:00 am, arriving in Mt. Airy at 10:45 am. Leave Galax at 2:30pm arriving at Pulaski at 3:45 pm; arriving in Radford at 5:30 pm. Besides hauling passengers, the Blue Ridge Bus Line hauled small parcel shipments and U.S. Mail. The regular bus drivers were Garland Anderson, Marcus Dalton, and Lawrence Bedsaul who attempted to maintain their schedule in getting from their destinations with their passengers, unless rough winter weather objected. The roads were a constant drag on their equipment. R. A. Anderson sold the bus line to W. F. Worrell in 1932, operating the Blue Ridge Bus Lines to 1937 when a devastating fire destroyed his bus garage and shop.

R. A. Anderson sold the bus lines to W. F. Worrell in 1932, operating the Blue Ridge Bus Lines to 1937, when a devastating fire destroyed his bus garage and shop. In 1922 Bill Mayhew organized and established the Mayhew Motor Company located on the North side of West Grayson Street having the automobile agency for Chevrolet cars and trucks.

Re-organizing the Town of Galax, Virginia

In 1922, the Town of Galax, Virginia, charter was amended and adopted to have a town manager form of government approved by the Commonwealth of Virginia, The Charter Amendment changed the term of Councilmen, so that only three Council members would be elected every two years, so the turn-over would not be that great. Mr. I. G. Vass, who was serving as Clerk of the Town of Galax, was appointed the first Town Manager to oversee the management of the Town of Galax, Virginia Police Department, Water and Sewer Department, and Street Maintenance Department. The Town of Galax began rebuilding the old bank building on the corner of East Center and North Main Streets, building a garage for the Fire Department to house fire trucks and equipment. They also laid out a court hearing room, used for Council Chambers, offices for Water, Sewer, street maintenance Departments; offices and jail for the Galax Police Department; for Town manager, and Tax Collection and Bookkeeping Department.

They moved their Town Offices from the second Town Office located on the corner of Carroll and East Grayson Streets. C. L. Dotson was Chief of Police of the Town of Galax. The Municipal Court Room was established in the municipal Town Hall building in 1922 ,located on the second floor, entering from East Center Street. The Domestic Court hearings were held by the Carroll, Grayson Justices to hear domestic cases. A remark was made when the first court convened in Galax by the trial Justices, they would have to move their Court hearings to their county side of Carroll or Grayson corners of the Court Room due to the Carroll and Grayson county boundary line that divided the domestic court hearing room.

The citizens of the Town of Galax living on the Carroll, Grayson County line created a two party political system in the town area, casting their vote either on the Carroll or Grayson side, which was evenly divided between the two major political parties in their political affiliations of their elected officials, having practically no bearing on their appointive candidates.

--- Judges and Attorneys serving Carroll and Grayson Court Systems 1900-1930's

Judges were: D.W. Bolen; S. W. Williams: R. C. Jackson; T. L. Massie: A. C. Campbell, William Kyle; J. C. Padgett; R. L. Kirby; and Horace Sutherland.

Attorneys were: J. S. Smith: John Alderman; J. L. Tompkins; W. D. Tompkins; B. F. Goad; Floyd Landreth; Ben Calloway; L. E. Lindsey; Heath Melton: Glenn Edwards; A. E. Cooley; S. F. Funk; William M. Foster; G. W. Cornett, William V. Wilson; H. Prince Burnett: S. M. Bourne; A. M. Cox; T. E. Brannock; J. H. Rhudy; John W. Parsons; H. A. Cox: J. D . Perkins; Joe W. Parsons; Gary Anderson; Jack M. Matthews; Pauline Bourne; Euna Gentry Campbell; P. L. Harrington.

The Town of Galax issued a sum of $75,000 for capital improvements due to the expansion of industrial, residential growth; having a total real estate value assessment for taxes in the year 1922, which amounted to $330,590. The rate of taxation was base at $1.70 per hundred value. The Town of Galax population had increased to 1700 by the census taken in 1920. I. G. Vass's first project to expand in 1923 was the improvement of the town's water system, sewers and streets. They began grading streets, laying storm drains, water and sewer lines, and contracting sidewalks. The first streets they paved with hard surface warrenite bitulithic pavement were the following: North Main Street from East Stuart Drive to the fairgrounds entrance on North Main Street; East Center Street from Main Street to West Stuart Drive; Lafayette Street from East Stuart Drive to West Murphy Street; East Grayson Street from Depot Avenue to West Stuart Drive: East Oldtown Street from Railroad Avenue to West Stuart Drive: East Murphy Street to West Stuart Drive.

Mr. I. G. Vass's second project was laying out plans for a modern water filtration plan due to the expanding growth of the industrial and residential area, which was outgrowing its current water works plant located off Gilmer Street, built in 1914. We need twenty to thirty men and ten teams of horses on the new modern Galax filtration water works. Construction of the plant approved by the Commonwealth of Virginia Water Board, located on the corner of Stockyard Road and Railroad Avenue. The new water plant was constructed having four concrete water holding basins for filtering the water pumped from Chestnut Creek for purifying, installing a chlorine injection pump to meter the amount of chlorine parts-per-million injected into the filter water, before it was pumped into large storage tanks at the water works plant, before being pumped to the holding reservoir located on Waugh Hill (just off of current Waugh

Drive). The water pressure from the reservoir to Main Street was at 150 lbs. of pressure per inch. The reservoir had a capacity of 500,000 gallons of treated water per day or more than 600 gallons per minute, The water when tested showed no presence of any vegetable, deleterious or foreign matter.

The Town of Galax had four and one-half miles of water and sewer main connections. The new water works plant began operating in late 1924 under the supervision of L. J. Stockner. Mike Crabill suggested to the public why not subscribe for the Galax Past Herald and the Southern Agriculturist Magazine at the going rate of $1.50 per year. They will be a weekly reminder of arriving 51 times during the year, giving you news of Galax and the community area. The Southern Agriculturist will offer instructions for the care of your radio, automobile, farm machinery, giving good continued stories on farm crops, orchards, nursery, livestock, sheep, hogs, and grains. The Post Herald will give you news on the local area of industries, farming, American Legion, social clubs, and gatherings; church and Sunday School Lessons; and the local schools that is very important for friends and neighbors.

J. H. Witherow and C. H. Smith established the Smith & Witherow Produce Company on the East Side of S. South Main Street next to Cox-Witherow Men's Store in 1923 dealing in produce, poultry, eggs, hams, meats of all types and a general line of groceries and staples. Mrs. P. R. Bedsaul had the honor of selling to Smith & Witherow Produce Company on April 13 the first crop of 25 spring chickens, weighing 42 pounds, paying her $21.84. They were hatched February 3rd. In later years E. E. Chappell purchased the store's stock, leased the building from J. H. Witherow, opening Chappell Grocery Store. E. E. Chappell opened a clothing store next to the Galax Electric Shop on North Main Street.

--- Dr. John Kingsbury Caldwell ---

Dr. John K. Caldwell grew up in early life on the family farm owned by his father, J. Barger Caldwell, located on the East side of Galax. He attended Stuart Normal Academy school at Woodlawn, Virginia. He taught classes after graduating to the young people at Stuart Normal Academy for five years. John K entered the Medical College of Virginia, Richmond, in 1896 receiving his medical degree in 1899. br. J. K. Caldwell joined Dr. S. M. Robinson in partnership established their medical practice and Crystal Drug Company at Blair, Virginia, in Carroll County serving a large area. John K. became active in the future developments of Galas, helping in organizing the Grayson Land Company and getting the Norfolk & Western Railway Company to complete their rail line to Galax. When the Grayson Land Company began selling lots December 17, 1903, Dr. John K. Caldwell purchased lots on the Southwest corner on West Center and North Main Streets. Bob Caldwell purchased lots on the North side corner of West Center Street and North Main Street opposite of the Waugh Hotel corner lots to the corner of West Center and North Jefferson Streets. Dr. John K. Caldwell opened his first medical practice in Galax in 1905 in the Dr. J. W. Bolen's boarding house building on the street level floor located beside the Harris Hotel of the East side of South Main Street. During the construction of the wood frame building at the corner of West Center and North Main Streets for their Crystal Drug Store and Medical offices owned in partnership by Dr. J. K. Caldwell, Dr. S. M. Robinson, Robert P. Caldwell, Ellis C. Caldwell owned the lots on the West side corner of West Center, North Main Street opposite Waugh Hotel, constructed a wood frame building housing medical offices and general store. They rented medical office to Dr. J. S. Hopkins who had a medical practice at Independence, Virginia, before moving to Galax.

Robert P. Caldwell was a shoe salesman for the International Shoe Company and Peters Shoe Company. He opened a men's clothing and shoe store in the corner building. In 1913, Robert P. Caldwell and Ellis C. Caldwell leased the Caldwell building to attorney H. Price Burnett moving his Blue Ridge Printing Company, Galax Post Herald, to the corner of West Center & North Main Streets. Dr. J. K. Caldwell and Charlie Muse operated a large apple orchard on the East side of Galax (current Twin County Hospital Tract) producing apples, selling local and shipping to distant markets via the Norfolk & Western Railway Company. Dr. John K. Caldwell always has a joke or story to tell. One story was about Bill Holderfield. Bill was a "herb" doctor, a neighborly fellow, but he had no use for a regular doctor. He cussed something awful. Bill had 27 "herbs" he used as a mixture to cure dropsy. One time he found his 28th "yarb" root, a nice yellar bush with a yellar root, trying it out. It liked to killed him and it did come nigh to scaring him to death. He cramped up till he was a sight to see. You can bet the old son-of-a-gun hollered for a doctor that time.

Another tale of Dr. John was Mike Crabill, publisher of the Galax Past Herald In 1919, we had the muddiest town in Virginia, we have one side walk, not a very long one, we talk a lot about the mud, but we put up with it because we don't have any money for paving. One day some of the town's rougher elements went seining in New River and I went along as pivot man on the net. We hauled in some water dogs, water lizards, bringing them back to town with us. Mike and the fellows dumped the water dogs and lizards into a large mud hole on South Main Street in front of the post office, putting a large sign up reading "No Fishing in the street mud holes without the permission of the Town Council".

Dr. J. S. Hopkins established the first hospital in Galax in 1920 on the corner of Monroe and Calhoun Streets (currently Bum Lindsay's home). His skill as a surgeon was such that he performed operations in Galax that would odd laurels to the reputations of the world's most eminent surgeons. As Galax grew, so did the hospital until the death of Dr. J. S. Hopkins; however under the management of Allie Hopkins, who had charge during the life of his brother, continuing the hospital operations and alleviating the sufferings. Dr. J. C. Sproule succeeded Dr. Hopkins as surgeon.

Dr. John K. Caldwell made several attempts with other physicians to organize a new hospital on a permanent basis. In 1924 Dr. W. P. Davis, Dr. John Phipps, Dr. Z. G. Phipps, Dr. Robert Kyle, and Dr. J. K. Caldwell formed a joint stock company issuing stock certificates. Construction began on the new hospital in the fall of 1924. The new Galax Hospital & Clinic was completed July 1, 1925. Dr. R. H. Edwards was head of the surgical department. Surgeons working under Dr. R. H. Edwards were: Dr. B. F. Eckles, Dr. Alex Caffen; other members of the hospital staff were: Dr. J. K. Caldwell, specializing in internal medicine; Dr. Glenn Phipps, a specialist in obstetrics and care of children; Dr. John Phipps, specialist in nose & throat; Dr. W. P. David in charge of the x-ray department; Dr. R. M. Cardwell. Mrs. Louise Bolen was in charge of the X-Ray Department. The hospital had 30 beds, complete X-ray equipment, chemical lab, and diet kitchen. Miss Mary Brintle was first head nurse, Miss Bertha Muse, first nurse, and 10 nurses in training. These doctors and nurses were engaged in one of the highest of all callings, ministering to the sufferings of those who could not minister to themselves. The Galax Hospital & Clinic was a big asset to Galax and the communities of Carroll and Grayson Counties.

Dr. J. K. Caldwell had dreams and visions in his early life in helping develop the Town of Galax into an industrial manufacturing center, creating employment for the women and men of the Carroll and Grayson areas who were the descendents of the early Scotch-Irish, English, and Quaker s that settled on the Chestnut Creek and New River areas before and after the Revolutionary War. They inherited a strong spirit of personal independence which made them fierce and frequently touchy at times, but they enjoyed a good laugh, parlaying a "ha-ha-ha" and a ho-ho-ho" as they work hard for the betterment of their community in developing businesses, churches, homes and industries. Dr. J. K. Caldwell's vision was developing the picturesque Blue Ridge Mountains areas into a resort mecca for the people and tourist that wanted an area to build summer homes and camping areas.

Dr. J. K. owned 1700 acres of land at Fisher's Peak where the head waters of Chestnut Creek tributary begin. What the Dr. saw pleased him, but it did not satisfy him, as he expressed himself, not enough people know what we have up here, from Fisher's Peak, you look down at the Piedmont on North Carolina, you see Pilot Mountain hump and the checkerboard pattern of plowed fields; you see the great white scar of the Mt. Airy granite quarry. The National Park Services would like to build a 50-acre wilderness lake of the middle prong of Chestnut Creek, but Dr. J. K. controls the property, having no use for the Park Service. "The sons of guns spoil every place they get their hands on. They make it so folks can't use it with their rules against walking on the grass and picking flowers", such nonsense made him snort.

Dr. J. K. has other visions and they were big ones. He wanted to develop a 1600 acre play ground at Fisher's Peak at the junction of the Carroll, Grayson Counties boundary line, roads come here from all parts of the country. Here on the Peak there is everything a man could want; scenery, climate, and wilderness of the old times. What I want is for people of all sorts to come here in the summer and enjoy the beautiful picturesque Blue Ridge Mountains country area. This area is magnificent, equal to anything you will find at Roaring Gap or Blowing Rock. One day it will be developed, whether I or the park service will call the shots. The impressive thing is that Dr. J. K. Caldwell was sincerely stirred by his visions of a major tourist development in the Galax area. Dr. J. K. Caldwell and Bob Caldwell opened the Galax Laundry and Dry Cleaning Business on the corner of North Main and Center Streets in 1928.

In 1922, Mr. B. C. Vaughan of the Vaughan-Bassett Furniture Company suggested to Robert P. Caldwell that Galax needed a modern up-to-date hotel for the many travelers, salesmen, tourist visiting the Galax area. Robert P., Ellis P., and the Caldwell family began making plans to build a new hotel, forming a joint stock company issuing stock certification raising funds to construct the Bluemont Hotel. The construction began on the new modern hotel with materials arriving by the N & W Railway. Completed in 1923, the Bluemont Hotel was a brick structure three stories high, modernly equipped, being steam heated, having all the conveniences that the most discriminating public could demand, including hot and cold running water in all the rooms, shower baths and private telephones. The Bluemont Hotel was one of the pleasantest hotels in the Town of Galax, serving the many travelers who had the pleasure of staying overnight. The traveling people would arrive by their own private automobile, the Norfolk & Western passenger train or by the Blue Ridge Bus Line, checking in at the Bluemont Hotel for good rooms and meals. The traveling people were tourist, salesmen, industrialist, entrepreneur, who were always welcome in the Town of Galax by the business and industries. Some of the visitors remarks were: "If you weren't so far from the center of the Commonwealth of Virginia, we would make our home here in the Town of Galax".

The local civic, social clubs, churches and other organizations would meet and dine weekly at the Bluemont. The lobby was always a gathering place to see friends. Charlie Muse managed the Bluemont Hotel. The Waugh Hotel was a landmark in the Town of Galax, for years it was headquarters for the traveling men and tourist. The Waugh Hotel was owned and operated by Lee and Della Baker. The Galax Inn Hotel (current Central Hotel) was leased and operated by Oscar C. Higgins. Robert P. Caldwell sold real estate establishing his Bluemont Company, Inc. office in the Bluemont Hotel.

Nancy Melinda Caldwell (nick-named "Vinnie"), sister of Dr. John K. Caldwell, Robert P. Caldwell, Ellis C. Caldwell, and sister to Bertha Muse, returned to Galax in 1912, which was then in its infancy. She became active in the advancement of Galax and Carroll and Grayson Counties. She had always been active in church and club work for the development of the Town of Galax and Carroll and Grayson Counties, She was a member of the Methodist faith and a strong Democrat. She entertained herself by studying the various religions that came under her observations, which converted her to an adherent of spiritual growth and reincarnation as a field of experience. She saw the need of all denominations, as necessary for the different stages in the development of mankind and was firm in her convictions that wash person should worship God as he or she saw fit from their stage of development. But the important thing of each life is that they worship God. She was a devout Bible student teaching Sunday School the greater part of her life.

Miss Vinnie was an active member of the Virginia Federation of Music Clubs, member of the Federation of Women's Business and Professional Club, and the Democratic Club of Galax. Her belief in equality made her an active politician since women were given the right to vote in 1920. In 1927 Miss Vinnie was elected a Delegate to the General Assembly from the Fifth District by the Democratic Party of Carroll County. In the 192B session under the leadership of Governor Harry Byrd, she became a very active worker in passing such bills for building the Blue Ridge Parkway, the Farm Market roads, the Jackson Ferry bridge, and a bill for educating and giving employment to the handicapped. Miss Vinnie was active in welfare during the depression of the thirties placing young children from broken homes into loving homes. She will always be remembered as "Miss Vinnie" to the people who knew her.

The development of the automobile business was one of the marvels of the modern industrial revolution that carried with it the development of the oil business, which has proceeded along just as efficient lines as has the development of manufacturing and distribution of automobiles. Mr. T. L. Felts after establishing the Twin County Motor Company in 1915, he and his son Gordon C. Felts organized the Felts Oil Company, an authorized petroleum dealer of Mobil gas, Esso gas and oil products of the Standard Oil Company of America, establishing a bulk distributing plant on the corner of East Washington Street and Depot Avenue.

The Felts Oil Company was distributors of Standard Oil Company products delivered to service stations in Galax and Carroll and Grayson area. Mr. McCamant Higgins established the Higgins Oil Company in December 1923 on the corner of West Oldtown and Monroe Streets distributing Sinclair gas and oil products from his bulk storage plant on Railroad Avenue, handling a line of automobile tires and accessories, delivering the products to his service stations in the Galax, Carroll, and Grayson area. In 1923 McCamant Higgins rebuilt and enlarged his service station on the corner of West Oldtown and Monroe Streets, changing his gas and products to Shell Brand becoming an authorized dealer for the Shell Petroleum Company building a larger bulk plant on the corner of Bartlett and Fairgrounds entrance, selling his Sinclair plant in later years to C. J. Sheffield who was authorized dealer for Sinclair Petroleum products. The Higgins Oil Company, distributors of the Shell Petroleum products delivered to their service stations in Galax, Carroll, and Grayson and parts of Alleghany County of North Carolina, was one of the larger distributors of petroleum products in Southwest Virginia. The business of the Higgins Oil Company showed a steady growth since being established in 1923.

The Blue Grass Hardware Company's stove drawing Saturday afternoon, November 9th a large group of people were present in front of the store. Garnett Largen's wagon drew up promptly as 2:30 pm, C. D. Martin, Mr. Fletcher and R. E. Jones climbed into the wagon with duplicate ticket stubs. Mr. R. E. Jones made a short talk on the business of the Blue Grass Hardware Company then proceeded with the drawing. The first prize was a range stove; second prize was a copper tea kettle; third prize was an aluminum stew kettle and aluminum percolator. The first lucky number drawn was 18571, but the holder was not present; another number was drawn; the number 3706 was held by Claude Hackler, winning the tea kettle. Another number 35870 was held by Ernie Funk, winning the aluminum stew kettle, another number drawn 15791 was held by W. W. Davis, winning the percolator. The last number drawn was 1444 by Kemper Wilson winning the stove range.

The new price of a Ford sedan was $595.00 F.O.B. Detroit, equipped with electric starter, lighting system, demountable rims, extra rim and non-skid tires all-around, the new Ford sedan is the greatest motor car value ever produced - an enclosed car of comfort. Buy now - terms can be arranged by the Twin County Motor Company, Inc.

A resolution of respect for the family of Dr. A. R. Grubb who departed life December 19, 1922, resolved that the Galax Chapter No. 47, O.E.S. has lost a good faithful member and a community citizen. Love and sympathy from the Chapter is tendered to the entire family in this scd hour from the ladies of the Eastern Star, Mrs. J. May Kapp, S. F. Welsh, Mrs. E. F. Cox.

The Galax Buggy Company has winter bargains, having received a new shipment of guaranteed horse harness. We have used and new buggies; we sell only first class goods, selling for less at the Galax Buggy Company.

For Sale: the Creed Felts home place on Virginia Street, the father of T. L. Felts; six room house with modern conveniences, good out buildings, corner lot, 150' x 150' in the best residential section of Galax. Seller: Joe W. Parson or I. W. Busic.

Notice: beginning January 1, 1923, no accounts charged to the Town of Galax will be paid unless goods were delivered on written order, property filled out and signed, or unless invoice was mailed to my office on day of purchase. I. G. Vass, Town of Galax Manager.

The Yancy Brothers Extract plant was destroyed by fire in the fall of 1922. Mr. J. V. Webb of Henry County came to the Town of Galax to establish a furniture manufacturing plant meeting with local business people and the Chamber of Commerce extending to them his plans to form a joint stock venture, issuing stock shares to raise monies from the local citizens of Galax, Carroll, Grayson area communities to finance the land tract of the Yancy Brothers, and construct the Webb Furniture Company plant on Railroad Avenue for the production of medium priced furniture in 1923. J. V. Webb, President, A. B. Gardner served as Secretary and Treasurer. The counties of Grayson and Carroll were similar to many other areas in timber resources in the United States with respect to quality of good timber, for there were few localities existing where the woodman's axe had not penetrated the virgin forest resources.

But notwithstanding the fact that timber resources in the Carroll, Grayson area had been systematically cut over in the prior years, there still remained thousand acres on which good timber existed, the predominating variety of timber such as oak, chestnut, pine maple, birch, ash, and poplar. A conservative estimate of good standing timber in Grayson and Carroll Counties was an average of 15,000 to 20,000 acres within the radius of twenty miles from the Town of Galax.

The Chamber of Commerce and the Galax Industrial Planning Committee were setting plans to establish the first textile manufacturing plant in Galax, negotiating with Mr. Robbins of High Point, N.C. to locate in a hosiery mill in the Town of Galax. J. T. Pollard came to Galax to organize the Galax Knitting Company forming a joint venture issuing stock certificate shares, selling to the citizens of Galax, Carroll, and Grayson areas in 1923 to finance the textile establishment. They began construction of the new textile plant on the current land tract of the prior Galax Furniture & Lumber Company on the corner of East Virginia Street and Railroad Avenue. J. T. Pollard rented a frame building opposite the First Christian Church behind the Polly Kinzer home on the corner of West Washington, North Main Streets next to the Bluemont Hotel, setting up knitting machines, training employees the principals of knitting socks and hosiery as construction was progressing on the new Galax Knitting Company plant. They began production in 1924 manufacturing a varied line of men's socks, ladies seamless hosiery and children's socks. The Galax Knitting Company was a modern up-to-date plant with the latest machinery, finishing, and drying departments. Their products were sold to the jobbing trades throughout the United States being one of the prosperous textile industries in Southwest Virginia. J. T. Pollard was over management Henry L. Harris joined the Galax Knitting Company in later years.

T. G. Vaughan of Galax was serving as Secretary-Treasurer of the Vaughan-Bassett Furniture Company in partnership with his brother B.C. Vaughan when he became interested in establishing the Vaughan Furniture Company forming a joint stock venture issuing stock share certificates, selling to the local citizens of Galax, Carroll and Grayson area establishing his furniture manufacturing plant in 1923, located at the corner of East Stuart Drive and Railroad Avenue, opposite of the Galax Knitting Company. The Vaughan Furniture Company completed their plant construction, installing modern wood working equipment and machinery far producing quality furniture, manufacturing a line of medium priced bedroom, dining room, dinette suites in 1924; shipping to distance markets via the Norfolk & Western Railway Company. T.G. Vaughan, the founder, President of the Vaughan Furniture Company, was a man of long experience in the furniture manufacturing industry. Officers of the Vaughan Furniture Company were: E. B. Lennox, R. S. Brown, R. V. Morris, serving as vice-presidents; J. G. Kirby, Secretary; W. M. Mayhew, Treasurer, F. S. Nuckolls, assistant Treasurer; and Gladys Landry, Assistant Secretary.

The Great Galax Agriculture Fair - September 9,10,11,12, 1924

The Great Galax Agriculture Fair held September 9, 10, 11,12, 1924 at the Galax Fairgrounds on South Main Street was planned as the biggest and greatest Agriculture Fair ever held in the town of Galax of the prior years since its beginning under the management of B. S. Roberts. G. F. Carr of the Galax Fair Association, who have spared neither time or money to make the 1924 fair celebration the most magnificent ever, offer to its patrons of Galax and the twin counties of Grayson and Carroll, from all of their indications of entries in livestock, poultry, agriculture exhibits will be the largest ever seen at the great agriculture fair. The Virginia Department of Game and Inland Fisheries will have exhibits of game, wildlife displays in itself will be worth the price of admissions. In front of the grandstand will be new free acts such as the "Grandsmiths" comedy acts from the Hippodrome of New York, the "Paris Alhambra" from England, and aerial stunt acts high on a swinging tower above the Grandstand.

In the afternoon during the week there will be hack racing, car racing, Model-T-polo ball playing. During the day there will be an airplane appearing at the Galax fairgrounds for the first time making flights over Galax giving the area people their first plane ride. The airplane will land at the North end in the center area of the racetrack. They will have a large variety of rides, games, and shows on the midway. The Norfolk & Western Railway Company will have an excursion passenger train from Pulaski picking up Fair passengers at Draper, Hiawassie, Allisonia, Barren Springs, Bertha, Foster Falls, Jackson Ferry, Austinville, Ivanhoe, Bylesby, Fries Junction, Chestnut Yard, Cliffview, to attend the Great Galax Agriculture Fair.

Special premiums were donated by the business people in Galax for the best agriculture displays:

Charlie

P. Waugh & Company - $10.00 ....best gallon of Bird Eye Beans

Blue Grass Hardware - $10.00.,.......best peck of Irish Potatoes

People's State Bank- $10.00............best six stalks white or yellow corn

W. K. Early & Son- $10.00 ....best ten ears of white corn

Mayhew Motor Company - $5.00... best sheaf of wheat

Joe W. Parsons - $5.00 ... .largest pumpkin

Mountain Loan Corporation - $5.00 ...largest number of entries in fair

Blair Grocery Company - $5.00 ....best factory made cheese

Twin County Motor Company - $10.00 ... best display of apples

W. C. Roberson - $5.00 ....best basket of grapes

J. R. Boaz& Son - $5.00 ....largest number of horticulture entries

Gillespie Garage - $5.00 .,............best pen of Rhode Island Reds or White Leghorns

Beasley & Boone - $5.00 ....best pen of Barred Rock chickens

Cornett-Parsons Auction Company - $5.00 ...best pen of Buff Orpingtons

Vass-Hawks General Store - $5.00 ... best chicken of any breed

T. C. Cornett - 1 bag Globe Scratch feed ... best dozen eggs

T. C. Cornett - 1. bag Globe Scratch feed ... best pound of butter

Farmers Supply Company - 1 bag Globe hog feed ... best Duroc Jersey or
                    Poland China Bull

Galax Bottling Company - $2.50 ... best Berkshire Boar

First National Bank - $5.00 ....best collection of canned vegetables
Blue Ridge Printing Company - $5.00 ...best display of preserves, pickles,
Jellies
T. F. Felts - $5.00 ... .best collection of homemade candies
Bolen Drug Company - Cara Nome Toilet articles ... best crochet luncheon set
Galax Knitting Company - $5.00 ....best pair knitted socks
Dan B. Waugh & Company - $5.00 ....best Royal Society luncheon set
Grayson-Carroll Real Estate - $5.00 _best collection potted plants & dahlias
C. L. Smith Furniture Store - $5.00 ,................best landscape water colors
Boaz Studio - $5.00 ....best pencil drawing
S. F. Landreth - $5.00 ....best collection of child's cookies
Tom Pearce 'Sanitary Plumber" - $5.00 ....best collection of child's handiwork
Galax Dry Goods - 1 pr. Mores-Rogers shoes ... ...largest number of entries
E. E. Chappell - 1 pr walk-over shoes ... .largest number of entries
Galax Electric Company - $5.00 ....best display of vegetables

The Vaughan Brothers Furniture Companies placed an ad in the Galax Post Herald wanting three hundred thousand feet of framing and rough lumber to be delivered between September r to December 1ST, 1924. David C. Newt purchased a building on Depot Avenue, next door to the Blair Grocery Company to open an up-to-date restaurant business named the American Cafe. The City Market opened in the Ward building on the east side of North Main Street carrying a full line of groceries, fresh meat, and vegetables. In 1924 at notice was issued: Lumbermen, owing to the heavy stock of lumber in our storage yard, we expect to buy only limited quantities; call for contracts before cutting for Vaughan-Bassett Furniture Company. date November 8, 1924, Dr. David Bolen, Dr. Paul Kapp, Dentists, opened their Bolen & Kapp Dentist Office on the second floor of the Bolen Drug Store.

Mrs. W. P. David entertained the members of the bridge club at her home Tuesday, November 15th. Mrs. Davis was assisted by Mrs. James, and C. Morris; her guest were: Mrs. E. B. Lennox, Mrs. S. F. Landreth, Mrs. C. L. Leonard. Circle No. 2 of the Presbyterian Auxiliary will have an apron and candy sale at the Galax Electric Company Store on North Main Street beginning Friday afternoon November 15th thru Saturday. They were meeting at Mrs. J. H. Witherow's preparing their merchandise for the sale.

Thanksgiving Union services will be held at the Baptist Church located on the corner of S. Jefferson and West Oldtown Streets at 10:30am the Rev. Sidney McCarthy of the First Presbyterian Church, will preach the sermon and there will be special music: everyone if cordially invited to attend.

To whom it may concern: On Saturday, the 22n^{d} of November 1924, my wife left me without any cause or excuse. I will not pay any of her bills made by her after. W. P. South.

The 1924 taxes for the Town of Galax are now due and must be paid prior to December 1"^{T}• to avoid 5 percent penalty. I will be in my office all day November 28" and 29t^{h} until 9:00pm, I. G Vass, Town Manager. A. M. Kirk was the Treasurer of Grayson County. George T. Blankenship was Treasurer of Carroll County.

The Galax Rotary Club was organized and admitted into the membership of Rotary International on May 24, 1924. President was C. L. Baumgardner, Vice-President was J. P. Carico, Secretary was Mike Crabill: Treasurer was W. C. Robinson; Sergeant -of-Arms was W. B. Giersch.

Mr. E. P. T Smith and Attorney Horace Sutherland in partnership established the Smith Drug Company, February 1924 in the Henry Brown building located on the corner of West Oldtown and South Streets. The Smith Drug Company was a neat attractive store stocked with a standard line of drugs, sundries, handling such name products of

Park-Davis, Lilly and Mulford Drugs, Kodaks, supplies having a modern soda fountain where the Galax people gather.

Galax High School – 1924

S. Floyd Landreth, Chairman of the Galax School Board Committee of the Galax High School Corporation of Galax, called for a meeting to be held at the Town Hall September 21, 1924, to discuss the needs of building a new Galax High School building, inviting the local citizens to attend this special meeting. Those present representing the local citizens governing body were: Mayor J. F. Vass; Manger & Treasurer, I. G. Vass; Councilmen Charlie P. Waugh, H. M. Todd, B. D. Beamer, G. A. Holder, George Early, Gordon Felts, E. D. Perkins, Secretary-Treasurer of the Galax High School Corporation and the School Board Committee; and school principal Stanley T. Godbey. The meeting began discussing the needs of the Galax School system, changing the present high school building to the elementary grade school building and constructing a new high school building, demolishing the old wood frame academy grade school building whish was in a bad state for repairs far the present school system for future educational use.

The members of the town Council, Mayor, Manager, School Board Committee proposed to build a modern up-to-date high school building replacing the old academy, having eleven teaching rooms, a large auditorium with stage, seating area, library room, science lab, school offices, equipped with a modern heating system, the high school will be a brick constructed building with all improvements to meet the requirements of the Commonwealth of Virginia Board of Education. The construction cost shall not be less than $10,000 or more than 40,000. The building fund will be raised locally and matched by the State of Virginia Literary Fund. The New Galax High School and the Elementary Grade School will have an enrollment estimated to be 560 attending students. The building contract was awarded to N. M. Ward, Arthur Lineberry, Contractors and Builders, to complete the Galax High School building for the opening of the 1925 fall term beginning September 5th

The school teacher's were: Mrs. Wythe Wampler, Ruth Tidwell, Mae Roberts, Lelia Cox, Eva Sue Sutherland, Grace Bishop, Susan Waugh, Mrs. W. F. Worrell, Mrs. J. A. C. Hurt, Luther Payne, Miss Elizabeth Boggs, Miss Willie O. Poole, Miss Thelma Lindsey, Miss Kathleen Leftwich, Mrs. Marcus Dalton, Mrs. Arthur Gardner, Mrs. Heath Melton, Mary Robinson, Mrs. J. H. Paisley, Nannie Parrish, Mrs. Charles Kanode, Bessie LaRue Jones, Mrs. Floyd Cox, Eula Cox.

Music teachers were Mrs. G. F. Carr, Mrs. Etta Brown, Rose Smith, Art Teacher; school Principal Stanley T. Godbey.

School principals serving from 1906 to 1932 were: G. F. Carr, S. W, Brown, Ned Hunger, S. G. Wright, J. A. Livesay, B. M. Cox, Mrs. Lee Beamer, W. J. B. Truitt, Heath A. Melton, Stanley T. Godbey, and Wythe Wampler, Principal G. F. Carr served the Galax school system seven years becoming the Superintendent of the Grayson County School system at Independence, Va. Mr. J. Lee Cox, Superintendent of the Carroll County School System at Hillsville, Va.

The Town of Pulaski was making an attempt to get rid of the roving cow "Bossie" who had a taste for the town's vegetable gardens and flower beds. Galax abolished the "Bossie" cow and "Porky" pig pens in earlier years becoming a fly-less town.

The first football game of the season for the football players of the Galax High School was played at the football field at the Galax Fair Grounds, Saturday, October 1, 1925, between Galax High and Jefferson High of Roanoke. The score was 26 to 0 in favor of the visitors, but the defeat in no way weakened the home team boys or dampened their ardor for the sport. They had been working faithfully under the direction and leadership of Coach

Bob Hoge.

Recent visitors to the new Galax High School and the Elementary School were: Prof. A. M. Gentry, D. S. Vass, J. F. Landreth, Rev. French Wampler, Mrs. R. B. Couch, Walter Anderson, Mrs. Walker Busic, Edwin M. Adkins, Mrs. J. A. Taylor.

D. S. Vass and C. W. Hawks purchased the R. A. Holbrook Grocery Store on the corner of East Oldtown and South Main Streets establishing the Vass-Hawks General Store in 1908 beside the prior Red Star Hotel and Boarding House of W. I. Harp, which was damaged by fire in 1907. The Vass & Hawks Store was a neat, attractive place with a large stock of standard line food brands, food stuffs, staples, fancy groceries including Maxwell House coffee, Blue Label products, Heinz pickles, Metropolitan Flour and many commodities recognized nationally. They had a strong faith in the future growth of the Town of Galax as an important trading center, fire destroyed their store building and stock September 28, 1925, damaging stock of the Galax Dry Goods Company owned by E. C. Blevins. Store building owned by J. H. Brown, Mr. S. Booker, State Agent and Adjuster for the Westchester Fire Insurance Company of New York were here days from the date of the fire, paid D. S. Vass and C. W. Hawks for loss of their store building and stock. On October 1, 1925, the Westchester Fire Insurance Company made a settlement to E. C. Blevins for his damaged merchandise stock, paying J. H. Brown for damages to his building.

W. A. Alderman, M. W. Zack purchased the building from J. H. Brown, establishing the A & Z Store, having a red front entrance in 1925. A public auction sale (Executor's sale) of the W. M. Gordon's real and personal properties-place will be on the premises Friday October 23rd, 1925, beginning at 10:00am. 28 acres of land, 8-room dwelling house, store building, woolen manufacturing plant, machinery, waterpower far operating mill and other buildings, good orchard and timber. Also: personal property such as stock of groceries, one lot of woolen goods including blankets, yarn, cloth, and misc, two cows, farming tools and misc. tools. C. F. Carico of Galax, the Executor of the Gordon's Estate. Lumber wanted, we are in the market for unlimited quantities of chestnut and poplar lumber to be delivered by November 1,1925 to the Vaughan-Bassett Furniture Company and the Vaughan Furniture Company.

The Woman's Missionary Society of the Methodist Church met Wednesday, October 28th at the home of Mrs. Walter Jones.

W. Dalton Store on East Grayson Street is having their final sales on all merchandise at cut prices to clear their stock due to closing their store.

Charles L. Smith and wife, Rose, came to Galax from Floyd County establishing the Galax Furniture Store and Smith's Funeral Home on the South Side of West Grayson Street. Rose Smith became an Art Teacher at Galax School. C. L. Smith organized and established the Galax Furniture Company Manufacturing Plant located on Railroad Avenue next to the Webb Furniture Company producing medium price d living room suits shipping to distance markets. Dean Gordon was Plant Manager.

The gross amount of freight tonnage handled by the Norfolk & Western's freight office under the management of Charles L. Baumgardner amounted to 57, 19 tons of incoming freight received in Galax. Outgoing freight tonnage amounted to 75,581 tons shipped from Galax.

The two banks, First National Bank and People's State Bank, had a combined capital of $95,500 resources of $1,281,367. The two banks were highly regarded for their able and conservative management. The growth of Galax in the past had been symmetrical, involving numerous lines of business endeavors, was shown by the records of the local banks, in investments in manufacturing, wholesale, retail business enterprises, showing a constant growth.

The Ladies' Social Club of Galax organized in 1910 was the oldest organization in Southwest Virginia being affiliated with the state and national Federation of Clubs, having a membership of 31 ladies, meeting twice a month at the homes of members. Aside from social gatherings that characterize their activities, they were active in literary work. The club established a circulation library for the people of Galax, placing bookcases in the Bluemont Hotel, which were filled with books of good reading matter for the traveling public. Officers of the Ladies' Social Club were: Mrs. W. K. Early, President; Mrs. J. H. Kapp, Secretary; and Mrs. S. E. Welch, Treasurer. Mrs. Rose Landreth, Mrs. Curtis Lindsey, Mrs. Hattie Whitley, Elizabeth Scott, Mrs. Katherine Reavis, Mrs. Mattie Hortenstine, Mrs. Sumners (Hillsville), Mrs. Jamie Robertson, Mrs. Viola Dodd, Mrs. Mamie Poole, Mrs. Tipton (Hillsville), Mrs. Jamie Waugh, Mrs. Blanche Early, Mrs. William Nuckolls, Mrs. J.H. Witherow, Miss Vinnie Caldwell. Mrs. J.P. Carico is the hostess for the next meeting of the Ladies' Social Club.

Mrs. Warren B. Giersh was appointed deputy Treasurer of the Town of Galax

The Galax High School football team will play their last game of the season at the fairgrounds Saturday, November 22n^d against William King High School of Abingdon, Virginia.

Special services were held this week at the Methodist Church celebrating the week of prayer beginning Sunday, November 23rd thru Sunday, November 30th. The Woman's Missionary Society is conducting these services under the leadership of Mrs. P. L. Vass. Sunday Services will be led by Dr. C. K. Wingo. The Rev. McGee, Pastor of the Baptist Church, is a patient in Roanoke Hospital.

An auction sale in Hillsville last Saturday was conducted by the Grayson and Carroll Real Estate Company of Galax selling more than $15,000 worth of real estate in the town of Hillsville.

Among visitors in Independence last week were: Mr. and, Mrs. Fred Wagoner, Mr. & Mrs. E. F. Cox, Mr. & Mrs. I. W. Busic, H. A. Melton, Mrs. J. H. Rhudy, Mrs. Horace Sutherland, Mr. & Mrs. R. L. Wright, Mr. & Mrs. T. W. Gillespie.

Millner's Variety Store was opened in the Dalton Drug Building on Grayson Street managed by Rixie Lineberry.

The Beasley-Boone Company Produce House on East side corner of Carroll and Bartlett Street was broken into Sunday morning April 17th, 1926, taking five cases of eggs, fourteen hams, coop of hens valued at $150.00. The firm was offering $25.00 for information leading to apprehension of the thief.

The Brownie Theatre located on East side of North Main Street, was showing the movie of the century called "Yolanda" staring Marion Davies, Leon Errol, and Holbrook Blinn. The movie was produced by the Cosmopolitan Picture Productions; admission 25c and 50c.

The Galax, Fries Council of the Junior O.U.A.M. held a flag raising at the Woodlawn High School building on Sunday, April 25th at 2:00om. R. E. Jones outlined the principles of the Junior Order. Rev. J. E. Larue presented a Bible accepted by Rev. F. L. Cox of Woodlawn School. Rev. French Wampler presented an American flag to the school accepted by Prof. R. S. Gardner for the Woodlawn School. Superintendent J. Lee Cox and others gave general talks. The public was a large group in attendance.

The black families of the Oldtown, Cranberry, and Galax areas became interested in establishing a school for the young black children. Contacting G. F. Carr, Superintendent of the Grayson School System, J. Lee Cox, Superintendent of the Carroll County School system, and the Town of Galax manager I. G. Vass, Mayor D.A. Robertson; Councilmen: Charlie P. Waugh, E. C. Cox, Shelby Vass, Gordon Felts, G. A. Holder, George Early, asking for the needs of a higher education teaching for the black children of Galax communities. Thomas L. Felts attending the meeting made a suggestion to the Black citizens, they should contact William Gershwin, a representative of the Rosenwald Foundation of New York and the Virginia State Supervisor for Black School Education. Tom L. Felts made a motion, he would donate a land tract and $500.00 towards the building of the school. Later William Gershwin of the Rosenwald Foundation, informed the concerned people the Rosenwald Foundation would donate monies for the construction of a black school in the Town of Galax, to be named the Rosenwald-Felts Elementary School.

The Rosenwald -Felts school trustees were: Rev. Calup Carson, William Martin, and Rich Garrett. The school opened for teaching March 1926, having two classrooms, James Isom served as principal, teacher. Mrs. Alberta Clark served as the second teacher. The enrollment was approximately 60 students from Oldtown, Cranberry, and Galax.

Fred Carter established the first modern steam dry cleaning shop in Galax on the East side of South Main Street beside the Waugh Building; later years selling the dry cleaning business to Roy R. Threatt changing the name to Galax Dry Cleaning Shop. Later years he sold the cleaning shop to Floyd Williams.

W. E. Lindsey and L. E. Lindsey established the Lindsey's General Store at Blair, Virginia, in 1897, selling all types of general merchandise such as hardware, dry goods, food staples, notions. They were dealers in lumber, cross-ties, tanning bark, wool, produce, shipping to distance markets via the Norfolk and Western Railway Company. In 1905 W. E. Lindsey sold his interest in Lindsey's General Store to L. W. Lindsey at Blair, coming to Galax establishing the Lindsey-Muse General Store in partnership with P. D. Muse located on the East side of North Main Street constructing a double width wood frame building, selling general merchandise including every product used in the home and on the farm such as the simplest utensil to dry goods, shoes, notions, groceries, feeds, farming implements, fertilizer.

W. E Lindsey and P. D. Muse were progressive public spirited merchants making their store an important factor in the growth of the Town of Galax. P.D. Muse sold his interest in the Lindsey-Muse store to W. E. Lindsey. After a period of years of operating the Lindsey Store on North Main Street, W. E. Lindsey established new General Grocery Store on Glendale Drive (Hillsville Highway).

C. L. Lindsey became interested in the produce business, buying the Galax Produce Company's business owned by E. L. Whitley located on the South side of East Oldtown Street. E. L. Whitley Produce Company had established the prior produce market dealing in hams, turkeys, poultry, eggs shipping to distance markets via the Norfolk & Western Railway Company. C. L. Lindsey operated the Galax Produce Company establishing a wholesale meat and staple grocery business, building an Ice Manufacturing Cold Storage plant named the Galax Ice Company, purchasing live turkeys, poultry, hogs, running a slaughter house; preparing turkeys and poultry packed in ice in wood barrels; processing bacon and hams; shipping to distance markets via the Norfolk & Western Railway Company, He established a delivery ice service to local merchants and residents.

T. N. Woodruff, a resident of Low Gap Community in North Carolina, began in prior years establishing his greenery business in Low Gay, N.C. Paul Dalton, T.N. Woodruff, W. A. Alderman, purchased from C. L. Lindsay in 1924, the personal and real estate properties such as the cold storage building, ice making plant and lot.

Paul Dalton owned the Dalton Wholesale Grocery Business on the corner of East Oldtown Street and Depot Avenue next to Bryant's Mill.

T. N. Woodruff established the Blue Ridge Ice Co, manufactures of clear crystal ice and commercial cold storage. Mr. T. N. Woodruff seeing the possibilities if the greenery business for the floral industry, began creating and expanding his line of decorative greens varieties, not only Galax leaves, but fancy dagger ferns, Leucothot, Laurel, oak sprays, boxwood, Magnolia, Smilax, Connie ferns, lycopadium, and other numerous forest products.

T. N. Woodruff and W. A. Alderman organized and chartered the W.M. Woodruff's Son and Company; T. N. Woodruff, President; W. A. Alderman, Vice-President; M. C. Goodson, Secretary and Treasurer. While most of these products were shipped in their natural state, the trade demanded a less perishable product, which cause Mr. Woodruff to build a dye processing plant at Low Gap using the perpetuating process to preserve the greens to be practically indestructible and fireproof. This plant was the only plant ever operated successfully in perpetuating the Galax leaves. As their business grew, new facilities were established, such as pack houses, cold storage plants at Galax, Old Fort, N.C.; Johnson City Tenn., and in Florida and Georgia. In connection with the plants at Low Gap, N.C. where the cooking and dying was done, they installed machines to make greenery raping such as pine, laurel, ivy, and other types of greens decorations demanded by the floral industry. The W. M. Woodruff & Son Company shipped their products via the Norfolk & Western Railway Company from Galax, from Mount Airy, N.C.; shipped via southern Railway Company; from Old Fort, N.C. the shipped via the Carolina Clinchfield & Ohio Railway Company.

The Post Office Department leased the brick building located at the corner of East Grayson and Carroll Streets owned by the Galax hardware Company for 10 years; from November 1, 1927, as headquarters for the Galax Post Office. The lease covers equipment, safe, parcel post, postal saving furniture, heat, light, and water. S. C. Cox was postmaster. Rural carriers were C. D. Higgins, Garfield Childress, and Emmett Ward. The Post Office building was beside the old town hall.

John A. Messer came to Galax in 1927 from Martinsville, Va. To establish his first mirror plant, beginning in a small way establishing his mirror operation in a metal storage building located behind Webb Furniture Company's plant on Railroad Avenue, producing mirrors for bedroom vanities and other misc. mirrors for home and business decorations. John A. Messer purchased the brick building of the Galax Buggy Company located on the corner of East Oldtown and Carroll Streets from the D. A. Robertson Company to establish and organize the Galax Mirror Company forming a stock company issuing stock certificates to raise funds for the mirror operations. The Galax Mirror Company made a popular line of mirrors for the furniture industry, shipping to distance markets via the Norfolk & Western Railway Company throughout the United States

John A. Messer established a mirror plant in Mt. Airy, NC managed by his sin-in-law J. M. Creek Jr. supplying mirrors to the furniture industry in the North Carolinas. John A Messer was president of the Galax, Mt, Airy Mirror operations. R. P. Nunn, son-in-law, managed the Galax Mirror Company. John A. Messer became Chairman of the Board of Directors of the Webb Furniture Company which was established in 1923, re-opening the operations in 1932, manufacturing a line of medium priced dining room and bedroom furniture, shipping to distance markets via the Norfolk & Western Railway Company contributing to the economic growth of Galax and t he counties of Carroll and Grayson. E. B. Lennox served as president, Dan B. Busic, Vice-President: A. B. Gardner Secretary and Treasurer.

G. W. Anderson, Town of Galax Police Sergeant, explained to the citizens that summer is almost here and the automobile traffic of our town is growing day by day. The Town has gone to the trouble and expense to provide parking zones marked off for the safety of your car keeping the traffic zones open. It is your duty as citizens of the Town of Galax to obey our traffic regulations and save the town sergeant the unpleasant duty of having to tag your cars, also the trouble of appearing before the town Mayor paying your fine. A visitor from out of town will see the orderly manner of our streets, proceeding to park within the zones. If they see our automobiles parked outside in a careless manner, they will park the same. We mean to be courteous to our visitors and instruct them to our traffic regulations. With all makes of automobiles, the Model T's, Whippet's, Hupmobile's, Overland's, Chandler's, Chevrolet's, Essex's, Star's, Dodge's, Willy's, we want the one-eyed automobiles to leave the streets of the Town of Galax, it is most dangerous to night traffic. Violators will be summoned to Town's Police Court.

While out on the road, if lights go bad, the law provides for you to go to the nearest garage for repairs. All one-eyed automobiles parking outside the parking zones, running cutouts opened, or speeding are all violators and must cease at once.

J. L. Thompson was caught by Sergeant G. W. Anderson stealing gas from a road tractor on South Main Street, bringing him before Squire Jennings, fining him $10.00 and cost.

C. H. Williams established the Galax Farmer's Supply Company, later sold to Omar Cox, who opened the business on the East side of South Main Street. T. R. Boaz & Son established a feed store on Carroll Street. Jones-Burge Motor Company was established on the South side of West Grayson Street by Newt Burge and Elmer Jones selling Dodge and Chrysler Automobiles.

Toni Apperson opened the Apperson Dry Goods Store in the F. C. Dalton building next to the Cox-Witherow's Men's Store of South Main Street. J. K. McKnight opened the General Store on West Grayson Street.

Charlie P. Waugh, son of J. B. Waugh, began at an early age in Oldtown working with his father at their John B. Waugh's General Store selling general merchandise such as utensils, dry goods, shoes, notions, clothing, groceries, hardware, produce and staples. The Waugh's traded for wool, animal hides, hams, bacon, bees wax, feathers, dry fruits, tallow, Seneca root, mountain herbs, ginseng, chestnuts, chinquapins, laurel, and ivy roots developing distance markets for these products. Charlie P. Waugh at the age of sixteen years, began managing the J. B. Waugh's General Store at Blair, Virginia, built by his father in 1896, expanding their business by purchasing lumber, crossties, tanning bark, shipping via the Norfolk & Western Railway Company to their distance markets. Charles P. Waugh came to the town of Galax from Blair in 1906 establishing the Waugh's General Store and Warehouse on Railroad Avenue, junction of East Grayson Street, opposite Galax Depot continuing the same type store operation of earlier years, buying and dealing in wool, animal hides, etc. Charles P. handled all types of fertilizer, farm seeds such as clover, timothy, red clover, orchid grass, oak wheat, rye, vegetable seeds, and farm implements. Through good and bad times Charles P. Waugh would initiate markets for anything that would bring in monies for the farmers and the citizens of the Carroll and Grayson area. One of the big money making crops in Carroll and Grayson counties for the farmers was the production of the Bird eye bean crop, which Charlie P. Waugh was due the credit for the immense production through his business enterprises, establishing cleaning plants in Galax and at his business establishment at Speedwell, Virginia, where bird eye beans were properly prepared for the buyer's market. Prior to this time the beans were shipped as they had been gathered and shelled, leaving many imperfect beans and trash in the lots of beans, detracting their appearance, lowering the commercial market price. With the cleaning machines, all imperfect beans and trash was discarded, creating a ready market for the bird eye bean industry. The bird eye bean was grown prior to 1915, farmers were growing bean crops of the bird eye bean family as early as the 1890's in Carroll and Grayson counties before being commercialized. Charlie P. Waugh established distance markets for the bird eye bean, shipping several thousand bushels via the Norfolk & Western Railway Company.

He served on the Town of Galax Council several years, always looking to the future development of the town of Galax, improving schools, municipal utilities such as streets, water-sewer, police department and volunteer fire department.

Charles P. Waugh gave generously of his time for the public good and his sound economic advice had much to do with the development of the municipal policies responsible for Galax's industrial growth. He was active in banking, commercial business, manufacturing, and the Chamber of Commerce.

Agriculture was the principal pursuit of the farmers of Carroll and Grayson Counties, having rich productive lands that were embraced in raising horses, mules, cattle, sheep, and swine that were in demand for the highest market price. These rich lands produced grass and feeds suitable for feeding livestock. While Carroll and Grayson counties compared favorably with other counties in the state of Virginia, in livestock raising for meat production: dairy stock for milk, butter and cheese production: chicken and turkeys for poultry production. Grayson was recognized as a large industry in producing eggs, meats, butter, and cheese. The Grayson County farmers established cheese production plants at Elk Creek and Spring Valley. In Carroll County a cheese plant was established at Hillsville in the mid-1920's producing high-grade cheese product in competition with the cheese made in Wisconsin and New York.

The Carroll-Grayson cheese products were given second prize at the National Dairy Show in Columbus, Ohio. The dairy farmers of the Carroll and Grayson area had a good outlet for their milk production selling their output to the cheese plants. The Carroll-Grayson cheese producers shipped their cheese products from Fries and Galax to their distance markets via the Norfolk & Western Railway Company. There was no section of the state of Virginia more adapted to fruit culture than the counties of Carroll and Grayson. The mountain soil of the Blue Ridge terrain was well suited to establish a fruit growing industry producing apples, peaches, pears, grapes, and cherries. Men of progressive ideas, with a desire to accomplish things, realized the opportunities, began planting orchards of apples, pears, peaches, cherries, plums and laying out grape arbor plantings. Fruit growing was established in the areas of Galax, Ararat, Lambsburg, Elk Creek, and Corners Rock. Apples and peaches were the best fruits adapted to the Carroll and Grayson growing areas. The varieties of apples grown were: winesap, stamen, delicious, Rome, Bonum, Sparger, and Mother. The varieties of peaches were: Carmen, Hiley, Georgia Belle, and Elberta.

Fruit growing developed into a large industry. The fruit growers shipped their fruits to distance markets via the Norfolk & Western Railway Company from Fries, Galax, and via the Southern Railway Company, from Mt. Airy, N.C. In the mid-1920's Guy Barger of Mt. Airy, Lafayette L. Gardner of Carroll County leased property on the South end of the Fairgrounds on the corner of Railroad Avenue, Pipers Gay Road opposite of H. P. Swartz Manufacturing Company (later years operated by Ben Lyons manufacturing poultry cops] from the Town of Galax, to establish the Carroll-Grayson Livestock Market constructing an auction building and holding stock pens. The Carroll-Grayson Livestock Market held livestock auction on Monday every week, selling sheep, beef cattle, milk cows, calves, hogs to livestock dealers and meat packers, shipping via the Norfolk & Western Railway Co. to distance markets.

Thomas L. Felts, Cliffside Farms, besides raising purebred Aberdeen Angus cattle and purebred horses, adopted part of his farming operations, establishing a modern, sanitary dairy plant pasteurizing milk from his dairy herd of cows, preparing bottle milk for delivery to the residential customers in the Town of Galax. In addition to supplying great quantities of milk, the Felts Dairy produced cream, cottage cheese, butter, milk chocolate and orange beverages. Selling to retail trade delivered daily by their trucks, the Cliffside Farms was famous for their Old Virginia sugar-cured hams and sausage made from their own raised swing herd.

Thomas L. Felts established the Produce Exchange in 1915 an the West side of Carroll Street opposite of the Galax Buggy Company (later Galax Mirror Company) operating a wholesale, retail, commission merchant dealing in farm products of all types. The Produce Exchange was an agent for Cliffside Farm's Old Virginia Sugar-Cured hams, sausage, and agent for the Garst Bros. Dairy Inc. buying cream and agent for Purina Checkerboard Feeds for poultry, livestock feeds. Hams were mailed by parcel post to customers in other areas; Gordon C. Felts, President: A. C. Dobyns, General Manager, E. G. Cummings, Secretary and Treasurer.

The Carroll, Grayson Counties farmers began to change their methods toward improving their dairy, beef herds, purchasing a better purebred stock of Domino Aberdeen Angus, Jersey and Holstein Herefords for beef and milk production, and changing their methods of farming by improving the pasture, grain lands by liming and creating a fertilization program for their producing land, which...hand in hand producing good livestock.

B. C. Vaughan owned and operated Hidden Valley Farms at Woodlawn raising whiteface Domino beef cattle. McCamet Higgins operated a livestock farm at Oldtown raising white face Domino stock beef cattle. Dan B. Roberts operated a dairy farm and a pasteurizing bottling plant at Oldtown, bottling milk, chocolate milk, and beverages for residential and retail delivery. Charlie Palmer operated the Richview Dairy Farms at McCamet Hill in Hillcrest area operating a pasteurizing milk bottling plant, bottling milk, chocolate milk, buttermilk, beverages for residential and retail delivery. Dr. John Phipps owned a dairy farm on Ballard Branch, Fries Road. John Moore Phipps established the Maplemoor Dairy pasteurizing bottling milk, chocolate milk, buttermilk beverages for residential and retail delivery.

In 1926 the Chamber of Commerce had been actively at work on the prospective cheese plant for Galax for more than a year. Mr. Noyes, Mr. Daugherty of the Kraft Cheese Company were in Galax January 31' to meet with Dan B. Waugh, President of the Chamber of Commerce and directors B. O. Beamer, J. P. Carico, Gordon C. Felts, J. F. Landreth, Mike Crabill, working out plans with Mr. Doughetry, at the request of Mr. Noyes, Mr. Sands representative of the State Dairy Development Board who was present with the assistance of D. T. Painter, Grayson County agent, Fred Kirby, Agricultural teacher and manager of the Cheese Manufacturing Plant at Hillsville.

A thorough check of pledged dairy herds in Carroll and Grayson counties, it was necessary for the business people of Carroll and Grayson to assist the Galax Chamber of Commerce in financing the project, which plans will be before them in the future. In the mean time, the Committee of the Chamber of Commerce recommends an immediately a written reply from the Cheese Plant owners at Hillsville. It was understood through Mr. Dougherty, if acceptable by the Kraft people to locate in Galax, the financing would be worked through the Chamber of Commerce. Omer Cox established the Farmer's Supply Store located on the East side of South Main Street selling all types of agriculture products and equipment o the area farmers of Carroll and Grayson counties.

The Georgia-Carolina School of Commerce established a business school in Galax to teach stenographic courses, commercial courses, commercial and type-writing courses, and secretarial courses. All those interested should see Verna Cox this week at the Mayor's office. Enrollment has started for the day and night classes. Next term will begin February 15,1926.

The members of the Missionary Baptist Faith have completed their new First Baptist Church on North Main Street in 1926. Rev. J.. R. Johnson was their new pastor, a noticeable awakening of interest in church work was manifested with a whole hearted co-operation in the church programs for the coming year. The Quaker Faith established the Friends Church on the corner of Jefferson and West Oldtown Streets in the first Baptist Church building built in Galax in 1905. Elizabeth Moon was the Friend's Church pastor. The members of the Methodist Church were rebuilding and enlarging their church on account of construction delay, the Epworth League Institute for Carroll and Grayson Counties was scheduled to begin December 5t[h], was to be postponed to the middle of April. The Methodist Sunday school classes were held at the Galax High School Auditorium. Circle #5 of the Galax Methodist Church, Mrs. E. E. Chappell, Mrs. C. E. Anderson will host a dinner at the Bluemont Hotel for the Public and Church members, proceeds to be used for the church building fund. An annual meeting of the W.M.C. (missionary) auxiliary of the New River Association, was held at the First Baptist Church in Galax, June 24[th,] 25th.

All Baptist Church representatives were invited. Mrs. E. B. Lennox, Chairman of the hospitality committee, request each delegate to be present. Please notify her that homes may be provided Sarah J. LaRue, Associational Supt ; Mrs. Reeves Gardner, Secretary. Mrs. T. . Vaughan was a hostess to the Ladies Social Club at the Bluemont Hotel June 26th. Dr. & Mrs. R. L. Jones, Dr. & Mrs. Paul Kapp, Dr. David Bolen were attending a meeting of the Dental Association in Roanoke.

Troy Goodson established the Goodson's Cafe on East side South Main Street next to Apperson's Store opening a modern restaurant serving three meals daily, later years opening his restaurant on the North side of West Grayson Street.

W. Letcher Porter established a furniture and appliance business on South Main Street next to the Levi Todd Store, naming the business W. L. Porter & Company. The Galax Merchants Produce market report for May 31, 1927: hens (not leghorns) 184; eggs 474 to 504 per dozen: butter 204 lb- No 1. by weight: 444 per lb.; cream No 2 by weight 394 per lb.

Real estate business DaCosta Woltz & Company offices over Galax Post Harold building, National Real Estate Exchange, managed by Gollie Stant Liff, offices were located over Smith's Drug Store. Todd Motor Company, agents for Pontiac, Oakland Automobiles, established a garage on West Oldtown Street (present Floyd Motor Company) owned and managed by G. W. Todd and L. M. Todd. R. A. Anderson of the Blue Ridge Buss Line added two twelve passenger Studebaker special busses to his first fleet of bus transportation. When R. A. Anderson began the Blue Ridge Bus Line services between Galax and Pulaski, it appeared as a small business, but the expanded growth of the bus line was a tribute to the traveling public riding the buses from Mt. Airy to Radford saving a day of traveling time between North Carolina and New York leaving Galax making connections at Pulaski on passenger trains going North and South. Traveling by Norfolk & Western Railroad passenger train was a rough ride and very slow from Galax to Pulaski. You could not ask for a better traveling service than the Blue Ridge Bus Lines.

The Bower's Ferry was purchased by Jackson Jennings having men on duty at all hours to transfer automobiles and wagons across New River.

The ladies of the Christian Church served dinner and supper Saturday, April 24th of baked chicken dressing, gravy, lettuce, creamed potatoes, apple sauce, and coffee at 504 per plate. Apple pie was 104 extra. At the Galax Knitting Company Café and in connection there will be a sale of children's dresses, aprons, and mist items to raise funds for the Christian Church. Rev. A .C. Meadows was helping with the dinner.

The Galax Progressive Baseball Club under the management of B.C. Lineberry opened the season on Saturday, May 27th with the Fries Mill Baseball League at the Galax Fairgrounds. The score was 16 to 1 in favor of the Galax Progress baseball Team. The Progressive ball team players were: Claude Henderson, Pierce David, Jim Anderson, Rex Williams, Baron Todd, Bert Wright, Joe Todd, Glenn Pless, Walt Anderson, Carl Kirby, Fred Roberts, Charlie Strader, Windy Morton, Baker. Couches were Dr. Dalton, and Bruce Todd; umpires Nelson and Lennox. On Friday June 3r[d] the Galax Progressives played the Pulaski Baseball Team at Pulaski, managed by a grand ole fellow, Doc Ayers, beating them to a tune of 6 to 5 in nine endings. Roy Williams pitched the first seven endings of the Pulaski game, relieved by Windy Morton, Williams, Morton, and Pless. Score in the ninth ending 6 to 5.

Judge Horace Sutherland, J. P. Carico, Joe Parsons, and other citizens were in Independence on Monday on business concerning the relief on the matter of the intolerable road condition now existing on the important link of the state highway route #12 between Galax and John Dickenson's place since a large amount of monies was spent on road grading and the erection of the new iron span metal bridge across the New River in 1927, lying idle more than one-third of the year due to the road conditions beyond the bridge span. The Galax Chamber of Commerce at their directors meeting May 23, 1928, appointed a committee who would personally visit state highway Commissioner Shirley at Richmond, Va. Monday, June 4, 1928. The citizens of Galax were J. P. Carico, Town Manager; I. G. Vass representing the Galax Chamber of Commerce, They were accompanied by representatives from the Business Men's Clubs of Fries and Independence to strengthen the presentation of their road meeting.

They were backed by letters and resolutions of several officials of Grayson County and many organizations of nearby communities.

Attorney H. P. Burnette remarked that Galax was a trading and shipping center for the people of Grayson County who have lost thousands of dollars due to the road conditions. As Letcher Wingate stated, Grayson County is entitled to a hard surface road. At the meeting of the Board of Supervisors of Grayson County May 24, 1928, present were W. R. Ward, Chairman; J. L. Bourne, E. J. Reeves, and W. S. Cornett when they discussed the road conditions and the need of highway #12 being hard surfaced, Joe W. Parsons, Clerk of the Grayson County Court, remarked that he was delayed 3 hours with at least twelve other cars stuck in mud costing him $7.50 to get pulled out. It was felt that this personal visit to Richmond to meet with the Committee of the Galax Chamber of Commerce expressing their strong sentiment for all the citizens of the Grayson and Galax area may result in favorable action of the Virginia Highway Commission.

Another Matter of the Galax Chamber of Commerce Committee would present to the Virginia Highway Commission would be the North Carolina State Line. The Virginia Department of Motor Vehicles of Richmond has received five rail cars of automobile tags to supply the automobile owners of Virginia for the year of 1928.

At the recent called meeting of the Galax, P,T.A., seven delegates were elected to represent the Galax Schools at the State Parent Teacher's Association meeting to be held in Charlottesville the first week of August. They were Mrs. J. L. Morris, Mrs. S. C. Cox, Mrs. B. C. Vaughan, Mrs. W. A. Davis, Mrs. J. S. James, Mrs. W. C. Roberson and Mrs. Gordon Felts. Money to loan, if its bond you want, or notes to sell, or loan or insurance of any kind, visit the Mountain Loan Company of West Grayson Street, managed by S. C. Cox, serving directors were Dr. D. W. Bolen, Horace Sutherland and others.

Jasper J. Allen established the Allen Motor Company on the south side of West Grayson Street in 1928 having the automobile agency for the Willys-Knight, Whippet, and Overland automobiles which contributed to the remarkable growth of Galax.

The Edwards Chair Company was taking bids for seven quarter oak and maple lumber.

DaCosta Woltz succeeded D. A. Robertson as Mayor of Galax in 1928. Councilmen were E. B. Lennox, Charlie P. Waugh, R. E. Jones, J. H. Brown, J. J. Allen, and R. F. Edwards. I. G. Vass ended his sixth year as Manager of the Town of Galax turning his office over to H. M. Todd. H. G. Vass had laid out the Town of Galax development in Modernization towards a bright future for growth expansion, accepting the Managership of the Town of Waynesboro, Virginia.

Judge Horace Sutherland was holding May term of Court at the Carroll Courthouse at Hillsville trying thirteen cases of violations of prohibition law. The 1928 graduating class of nineteen seniors of the Galax High School received their diplomas. Miss Helen Jones, daughter of Mr. & Mrs. Walter Jones of Galax delivered the welcoming address. Miss Marguerite Phipps, daughter of Mr. & Mrs. Con Phipps spoke of the 1928 Senior class motto The boor to Success is Labeled Push" all through life.

J. P. Carico, Chairman of the Democratic Party of Grayson County, called for a mass meeting at the Grayson Courthouse at Independence Saturday, June 9th at 1:00pm to elect delegates to the Virginia State Convention to be held in Roanoke on June 21'.

The Piedmont Salvage Company was selling the stock and fixtures of the Hines-McMillan Department Store on West Grayson Street.

G. W. Todd and L. M. Todd of the Todd Motor Company, south side of Oldtown Street, dealers of the Pontiac-Oakland automobiles were attending the Pontiac-Oakland Automobile Show in Roanoke, Virginia.

Edd Cox purchased the Mayhew Motor Company from W. M. Mayhew, located on West Grayson Street, renaming the business the Galax Chevrolet Sales Company being distributor and agent for Chevrolet cars and trucks.

Brady L. Jenkins opened his independent service garage in the Joe Reavis Garage building in 1928 located behind Henderson's Jewelry Store, servicing automobiles, trucks, and the bus fleet of the Blue Ridge Bus Line.

Peter Xenos established the Royal Cafe on the East side of North Main Street having a popular restaurant for the Galax area. Pete Xenos was active in political affairs. M. B. Jennings established Star Market, a modern grocery shop on the North East side of west Grayson Street. I. S. Atkinson Appliance Store was located on South Main Street. J. A. Langley operated the Electric Main Bake Shop.

The Rev. French Wampler, Pastor of the Galax Methodist Church, held the usual Sunday morning services well attended. A beautiful memorial service was held by Swift Waugh, Supt. Of the Sunday School Class in honor of Mrs. Sallie Sutherland, a life member of the Galax Methodist Church.

The Virginia State Highway engineers were surveying for the future Jackson Ferry bridge in 1928, changing the location of the road from the present ferry crossing. The tentative location is about 300 feet east of the Ferry Crossing on the south side of New River that will lead into the present highway under the Norfolk & Western Railway Company's trestle of the Cripple Creek Extension at mile post #24 Jackson Ferry. This would eliminate the present dangerous curve. The length of the Jackson Ferry Bridge will be 600 feet spanning over New River to the road approaches to both ends of the bridge which they will start on construction soon. The district highway department engineer was checking the flow of traffic passing through Hillsville on Wythe Turnpike (#52) getting a 24 hour tabulation, counting 426 passenger cars, 16 trucks, and 17 horse-drawn vehicles. At the station one mile west of Pulaski, the total record showed 664 vehicles.

The Town of Galax hosted their first convention of a large number of people when the District 1 of the Virginia Education Association composed of teacher's from the counties of Southwest Virginia between Roanoke and Bristol, about 600 teachers are expected in attendance. The Galax School facility held a meeting last Wednesday, January 23, 1929, appointing a committee. Those who were chosen to look after the arrangements and entertainment of guests were: Prof. S. T. Gobsey, Chairman: Mrs. S. C. Cox, Mrs. S. F. Landreth, Mrs. B. C. Vaughan, Mrs. Heath Melton, Miss Willie Poole, and Miss Gracie Bishop. The publicity committee is: Mrs. J. H. Rudy, Chairman; R. A. Anderson, President Parent-Teachers'' Association. Swift Waugh was appointed as chairman of the program committee. It was recalled at the 1928 convention, a meeting place for the 1929 convention was being discussed: the accessibility of Galax was mentioned by the educational group. Carroll and Grayson teachers were able to secure the next convention for Galax,

The Coca-Cola Battling Company was established in 1929 on East Oldtown Street opposite Galax Mirror Company. The Coca-Cola Bottling plant in Galax bottled Coke known as "the pause that refreshes" delivered to retail customers in Carroll, Grayson and part of Floyd Counties. Mr. R. J. Knisley managed the Galax Coca-Cola bottling operations.

Mr. Edwards sold the Edwards Chair Company on East Oldtown Street to W. A. Alderman, 0.S. Dalton, J. A. Lineberry and C. J. Dickens as the highest bidders for the chair manufacturing plant sold at auction Saturday, January 26". The price was $12,200, the purchasers intend to operate the plant formulating their plans for the operation. J. A. Lineberry will be in charge having an experienced background in hauling wood working machinery. C. J. Dickson, a past salesman for the R. J. Reynolds Tobacco Company will direct marketing. 0. S. Dalton, station manager of the Galax Depot of the N & W Railway, will render his valuable service as assistant in rail shipments. W. A. Alderman, a successful business man in partnership with M. W. Zack of the A & Z Store, a director of the Dalton Grocery Company, Blue Ridge Ice Company, Vice-president of the T. N. Woodruff & Son Company. The new owners have ample finances which will provide employment and best working conditions being a real asset to the industrial life of the Galax area community.

The Edwards Chair Company was the second wood working industrial plant to open after the establishment of the Galax Furniture and Lumber Company by J. B. Waugh and his associates. The Edwards Chair Company was established in the town of Galax in 1913 by the late J. N. Edwards and his brother A. M. Edwards who had been active in the chair manufacturing operation. After a few years of operation by L. A. Lineberry, 0. S. Dalton, W. A. Alderman, C. J. Dickens, they sold the chair operations to C. L. Smith.

The American Society of the Gideons were represented in the town of Galax by C. L. Lunford, Brooks Mormon of Roanoke placing their Gideon Bibles in hotels and hospitals encouraging Christian fellowship among traveling people and the hospital patients. They placed the Bibles in the Bluemont Hotel, Waugh Hotel, Galax Inn, Galax Hospital and the Rudolph Hotel in Independence.

Dr. W. M. Bunts of the Galax Methodist Church and Rev. H. G. Holdway of Fries attended the Holston Conference Board of Missions being held in Pulaski.

The Home Market Store operated by D. S. Vass and Norm Stocker, meat cutter; were having a special sale Saturday: 10Ib. Of sugar 53cents ; 6 cakes Octagon soap 25 cents, 2 cans of Dix sauerkraut 25cents 1 lb., Pure sausage 25cents, , 1-lb. Pork chops 25cents , 24-lbs. Honest Pride flour 90 cents.

Monarch Chain Stores managed by A. G. Bartlett, Grayson Street, is having reduced sales on ladies and men's fashion in clothing, shoes, curtain goods and misc. goods.

The Norfolk & Western Railway Company was blamed for the Fries wreck. The Safety Bureau of the Interstate Commerce Commission in Washington censured the Norfolk & Western Railway Company for the train wreck at Fries Junction on November 16, 1928, causing three deaths and eight injuries between the collision of the N & Ws freight #78 and passenger #57 trains on the Fries Branch Line of the North Carolina Branch Line of the Cripple Creek Extension (Radford Division) of the Norfolk & Western Railway Company of the New River Plateau. The Safety Bureau insisted that the operating methods of the Norfolk & Western Railway Company, which one train books down from Fries to the main line of the North Carolina Branch line was responsible, and explained that the conductors and engineers of the freight and passenger trains were primarily responsible. The reasons claimed to be contradictory in first placing full responsibility on the Norfolk & Western Railway Company and then part responsibility on the train's crew. The Safety Bureau of the Interstate Commerce Commission statement reads: "This accident was caused by No, 78 freight train standing on the North Carolina Branch Line without protection and by No. 57 passenger train leaving Fries Station ahead of time causing a collision under such circumstances was inevitable.

Claybrook Lester of Bluefield, W. Virginia, established the Texaco Oil Company petroleum bulk plant office on the corner of fairgrounds entrance and Bartlett Street. He was the authorized dealer selling Texaco products such as gas, oil, and handling other brands of tires, batteries, and misc. automobile products.

Abe Globman of Martinsville established the Globman's Store on the corner of East Oldtown and South Main Street in late 1929 managed by Rose & Nathan Potolsky . Clair and Joe Goldstein established the Claries' Fashion Shop on the East Side of North Main Street.

The Brownie Theatre name was changed to the Colonial Theatre and operated by Mr. Bawd.

Ellis Osborne was agent selling Essex Automobiles under the title of Osborne Motor Company selling cars from his home. 0. B. Hackler was agent for the Star automobile selling cars from his home.

The depression of October 29,1929, and the early 1930's slowed the development and progress of agriculture, industrial, and business growth in the Town of Galax and the community areas of Grayson and Carroll Counties. The area people having a strong determination joined together in reorganizing and establishing their priorities for the slow period ahead for a small town and the Carroll and Grayson communities of citizens who were characterizes by their energies being public spirited, patriotic Americans of religious faith, looking forward to better years in the future, which was certain to change as Galax had established and been recognized as one of the most important industrial centers in Southwest Virginia, having endowed its self to rapid progress, growth, in prior years nestled on the counties boundary line of Carroll and Grayson, which hold the Community of the Town of Galax between them in rich agriculture lands, abundant rich forest timber areas where businesses can prosper. The Town of Galax was progressing towards modernization with future developments of industrial growth in manufacturing products such as furniture, textiles, building materials, agriculture products of poultry, beef, cheese, milk, and other dairy products.

No town in Southwest Virginia near the size of the Town of Galax could boast of more modern public utilities that Galax was offering its businesses, residential households, and industry as purified water resources, sanitary sewerage, paved streets. Electrical power of the Appalachian Power Company was regarded as the largest single factor in the development of Galax, having a moderate low rate of cost favorable to their customers. The citizen's of the town of Galax accepted the expense willingly in prior years of developing their community into a town, seeing their neighbors succeed in manufacturing, farming, mercantile, and kindred trades in developing their business establishments, having churches of several religious faiths, educational schools and amusements. Transportation facilities of the Norfolk & Western Railway Company, freight trucking companies, Blue Ridge Lines and construction of hard surface highway roads, and bridge facilities were developed year by year aiding the industrialist, businesses, the Chamber of Commerce working out plans for a greater industrial center and community in their vision of the future torn of Galax, Virginia, continuing to attract and hold the citizens to be among the foremost town in the New River Plateau area as having the ability in their industrial manufacturing to distribute their products to the distance markets of their trade.

The high hills of the Blue Ridge Mountain section were drawing people from other areas to see the scenic beauty not to be found elsewhere in the Commonwealth of Virginia or even in the Southern States. Galax was strategically located to furnish the up-mast in enjoyment to all who visit the area. The Town of Galax elevation level is 2,500 feet above sea level, while its climate in winter is crisp and sometimes fairly cold, in the summer having mild days, cool nights, many visitors who visit Galax always return. The travelers of the present age of automobile, found highways to their enjoyment winding through the Blue Ridge Mountains to their delight. The visitors would find recreation and entertainment. The Galax Country Club has been established for entertainment and recreation purposes offering real advantages.

Hunting, fishing along the Blue Ridge Mountain and the tributaries empting into the New River was a great sport for hunters and fishermen. There was always an essence of hospitality among the citizens of Galax, Carroll and

Grayson in their attitude of always welcoming the visitors to their area observing their charming homes and community life style. The people of the Town of Galax were always anxious to greet the visitors.

Mrs. J. W. Bolen was hostess to the Women's Literary Club at her home on North Main Street

The formal dedication of the Southern Virginia section of the Appalachian Trail took place Sunday, June 1, 1931, at Norvale Crags located eight miles from Galax on the Low Gap Road at the top of the mountain, less than three quarters mile off the hard surface highway on a fairly good road readily accessible from Galax over the Low Gap Road, a short distance from the Galax Airport. The elevation of Norvale Crags is 3,400 feet above sea level, a greater elevation than any peak along the Blue Ridge Mountains, with the exception of Fisher's Peak which is 200 feet higher.

The Norvale Crags name was derived from its location, 'nor" from North Carolina, "Va" from Virginia and "le from the NC-Va state boundary line that runs through the resort properties. Crags name from the jaded granite rock. Norvale Crag was developed by DaCosta Woltz, Mayor of Galax, and through the co-operation of S. L. Cole, the resort is attractive in surroundings. The rustic club house, now almost completely will be the end point of the Appalachian Trail, the hiking and bridle route that follows the mountain tops from Main to Georgia, among the prominent persons expected to be in attendance were: Col. Avery, head of the U. S. Shipping Board and President of the Appalachian Trail Association; Ex-Governor E. Lee Trinkle of Roanoke; Lieut. Governor Sheppard of South Carolina; Governor Max Gardner of North Carolina; Cal, Jordon of Veteran's Bureau, Richmond, VA; Honorable Thomas L. Felts of Bluefield, E. Va.: Congressman Tom G. Burch: Rev. J. H. Fulghum, President of Mountain Parks Institute; S. L. Cole, President of Southern Virginia Appalachian Trail Association. "Bob" Angel of Roanoke will preside as Master of Ceremonies.

News comes from the Pipers Gap and Low Gap areas of Carroll County of unusually heavy rains and hail falling Sunday afternoon, in many instances large as a partridge egg, damaging roofs and windows and garden crops.

The Virginia Highway Department began mid-June 1931 hard surfacing the highway#12 from Independence to Galax. The hard paving in the town of Independence has been finished. When the hard surfacing was completes to Galax, it gave the people of Grayson a continuous hard surface road to Roanoke. Mr. E. L. McCove and Mr. McSpaddin of the State Highway Commission were at Independence checking on the roads progress. Carlen E. Cox purchased the Texaco Filling Station on W. Grayson Street and will continue to give first class services on automobiles, batteries and electrical repairs.

Members of the Epworth League of the Methodist Church enjoyed a picnic at Pot Rock Friday evening taking lunch which was spread beneath the trees, the Boy Scout Troop Training Class composed of interested citizens of Hillsville, Fries, and Galax met here Monday evening. This class was under the supervision of District Executive A. N. Asbury of Pulaski

The First Christian Church of Galax sponsors Boy Scout Troop #86; Galax Methodist Church sponsor Boy Scout Troop #59.

Active churches in the Town of Galax in 1931 were the First Baptist Church, Rev. J. R. Johnson, Pastor; Quaker Church (Friends), Rev. Elizabeth Moon, Pastor; First Presbyterian Church, Rev. D. S. McCarty, Pastor; First Methodist Church, Rev. W. M. Bunts, Pastor; First Christian Church, Rev, A.C. Meadows, Pastor; and Galax Primitive Baptist, Elder J. D. Vass.

A Decoration Service was held at the Old Quaker grave yard Sunday June 7th. Basket dinners were served on the grounds as usual, preaching at 11:00 by Rev. James E. Bartlett. The workers and singers from the Galax Quaker Church were present at the afternoon services at 2:30 p.m. Also a male quartette from Guilford College presented their song selections. The Rev. Lewis McFarland from High Point, N.C. preached at the 2:30 p.m. services.

Businesses Established in Galax, Virginia 1903

Art's Novelty & 5 $ 10 Store - located on south side of West Grayson Street

Ashburn Show Shop - Barber Shop;

Lou Ashburn - East side of Main Street

Blair's Pressing & Cleaning Shop; Fred Blair - East side of Main Street

Bryant's Barber Shop; Abe Bryant - East side of south Main Street [moved to the basement of the First National Bank Building - North side of West Grayson Street]

Smith-Beamer Produce Company; C. H. Smith & B. D. Beamer - South side on East Grayson Street (Blessings Building)

R. A. Holdbrook General Store: R. A. Holdbrook - corner East Oldtown & 5. Main

R. E. Jones General Store; R. E. Jones Funeral Home- R. E. Jones & Sons Furniture Company - West side North Main

Ward Brothers Gentlemen's Clothing Store; Marvin and Monroe Ward - East side North Main Street

McMillian Produce Market; E. R. and Lon McMillan -(Blessings Building, South side East Grayson Street

Blessings General Store & Produce; M. T. Blessing - South side East Grayson Street Smith-

Witherow Produce Company; J. N. Witherow & C. H. Smith - East side South Main Street

Bolen's Drug Company; Dr. J. W. Bolen - North side corner of East Grayson and North Main Streets

R. B. Couch Meat Market; R. B. Couch - West side North Main Street

Galax Produce Company; E. L. Whitley - North side West Grayson [2- East side of North Main; 3-East Oldtown & Depot Avenue]

Crystal Drug Store; Dr. J. K. Caldwell - West side corner of West Center & N. Main

Dalton Drug Company; Heath Dalton - South side West Grayson Street

W. Billy Dalton General Store; F. H. & W.0. Dalton - North side East Grayson Street

Ward's Brothers Plumbing & Heating Co.: Marvin & Monroe Ward - East side North Main Street

O. Donohue Brothers Plumbing Company ..?

A. E. Disher Grocery Store; A. E. Disher - (Roope Building) West Side S Main

Galax Drug Store; Dr. J. H. Witherow & Dr. W. B. Murphy - corner of W. Grayson & N. Main Streets

Galax Hardware Company; Sam Jackson, J. H. Kapp, Sam Kinzer - #1 store: W. Side N. Main; #2 store: S-side E. Grayson

Galax Department Store; E. M. Coffman & S. Schien - N-side N. Main Street

M. L. Henderson Jewelry Store; M. L. & Claude Henderson - W. side South Main

Hightower Studio; W. H. Hightower- S. side West Grayson Street

Stockner's Studio; Lester S. Stockner - W. side North Main Street

C. W. Hawks & Company (wool dealers); C. W. Hawks - E. side South Main Street

Liddle's Blacksmith Shop; Van Liddle - N. side East Grayson Street

L. L. Joines General Store; L.L. Joines - S. side West Grayson Street

W. G. Lowe & Company; W. G. Lowe - E. side North Main (leased to J. W. Stamey, [later sold to the C.H. South Brothers Store; C.H. & J.E. South who operated #2 store E. side of South Main St. leased to E. C. Nevins for the Galax Dry Goods Store

Vass-Hawks General Store (formerly R.A. Holdbrook Store); C. W. Hawks & J. H. Vass - corner E. Oldtown & S. Main Streets

S.. Atkinson Store; I. S. Atkinson - (F. H. Dalton Building) E. side S. Main Street

Apperson's Dry Goods Store; Tom B. Apperson - E. side (next to Cox-Witherow) S. Main Street

Star Market; M. B. Jennings - E. side South Main Street

H. Glasco Clothing Store; Jim Glasco E. side South Main Street

J. B. Waugh & Son Store; J. B. & Richard Waugh - S. side corner E. Grayson & N. Main

Dan B, Waugh's fashion Shop; Dan B. Waugh - W. side North Main Street

Charlie P Waugh's Store; Charlie P. Waugh E. side South Main Street

Charlie P. Waugh's Warehouse Supply - E. side Railroad Ave. & Grayson Street

A & Z Store; W. A. Alderman & M. W. Zack - E. side South Main (J.H. Brown Bld..)

Lindsey & Muse General Store; P.D. Muse & W. E. Lindsey -E. side North Main

J. C. Matthews & Company: J.C. Matthews & J. F. Vass - #1 Store: E. side East Grayson & Depot Ave; #2: E side corner West Grayson & North Main

F. H. Martin General Store & Harness Shop; J. H. Martin - E. side Webster Street

J. W. Poole & Company: J. W. Poole - Corner of S. Jefferson & W. Grayson

Perelman's Fashion Shop; Louie Perelman - W. side South Main Street

Produce Company & General Store; C. L. Lindsey - aside E. Grayson & Depot

Galax Ice Company; C. L. Lindsey - W. side Depot Avenue

Blue Grass Hardware Company; S. A. Kinzer, W. K. Early, G. D. Brown, M. L. Harrison – W. side N. Main Street

Vass-Kapp Hardware Company; J. F. Vass. J. H, Kapp, D. S. Vass, Charlie Dobyns – corner S. side West Grayson & North Main Streets

A & P Food Store - E. side North main Street

J. C. Matthews Hardware Company; J. C. & Edd Matthews - E. side South Main

J. C. Matthews Hardware Company; J. C. & Jeff Matthews - S. side East Grayson

Galax Meat Market; E. I, Robbins, C.I. Sutherland - E. side S. Main Street (next to
        Witherows)

Chappell Grocery Store; E. E. Chappell - E. side South Main Street

E. E. Chappell Clothing Store; E. E. Chappell - W. side North Main Street

Levi Todd's Store; Levi Todd - E. side South Main Street

Amburn Grocery Store; C.F. Amburn E. side South Main Street

Pennington Grocery Store; Bessie Pennington - E. side South Main Street

Witherow's-Cox Men's Store; Dr. J.H. Witherow, H.C. Cox - E. side South Main

J.K. McKnight Store; T. C. McKnight- S .side West Grayson Street

Farmers Supply Store; Omar Cox - E. side South Main Street

Y. B. Hall Farm Supply & General Store; Y. B. Hall - E. side South Main Street

Dobyn's Produce & Clover Creamer Company W. side Carroll Street

J. R. Boaz & Son; J. R. & Walker Boaz - N. side East Oldtown & Carroll Streets

Boaz Photo Studio; Herman Boaz - N. side East Oldtown Street

Smith's Drug Company; E. P. T. Smith, Horace Sutherland - W. side corner West Oldtown & South Main Streets

Carlan Drug Company; C. I. Carlan - W. side corner West Oldtown & S. Main

Palace Cream Polar; Floyd W. Williams – W. side South Main Street

Fred Carter Dry Cleaning Shop: Fred Carter - E. side South Main (Waugh Bid)

Threatt's Dry Cleaners; Floyd Williams - E, side on 5.Main (Waugh Bld)

Todd's Dry Cleaners; Blackie Todd - N. side West Oldtown

Cornett-Parsons Auction Company; Joe W. Parsons, T.C. Cornett - N. side E. Grayson

Morris Edwards General Store; Morris Edwards- aside corner a Jefferson & W. Grayson Streets

C. L. Smith Furniture Store; C. L. & Rose Smith - S. side West Grayson Street

Monarth Chain Store; Manger A.G. Bartlett –S. side West Grayson Street

Electrik Main Bake Shop; J. P. Langley - E. side North Main Street

Vaughan-Gwynn Funeral Home - corner of N. Jefferson & W. Grayson

DeHaven's Show Store; B. Dehaven: Walter Andrews - E. side North Main Street

Arlie's Shoe Store; Hurd/ Alderman - E. side North Main Street

Mick or Mack Store; G. A. Holder -N. side South Main Street

Berliner & Kyle Insurance Agency; B. O. Reamer, Cliff Kyle - W. Oldtown St.

Bower's Department Store; E. Bowers E. side South Main Street

E. C. Williams Jewelry Store; E. C. Williams - ??

Moore Brothers Store; Joe T. & Grover Moore - S. side cornet S. Jefferson & West Grayson Streets

Porter Furniture Company; Fletcher L. Porter - E. side South Main Street

Barr-Topin 5 & 10 Store; Manager Roxie Lineberry - E. Side 5. Main (Apperson Bld)

Globman's Department Store; Abe Goldman, Nathan Potasky - E. side corner East Oldtown & South Main Streets

Claire's Fashion Shop; Claire & Joe Goldstein - E. Side N. Main Street

Galax Electric Shop; Landreth & Rector - E. side North Main Street

Central Electric & Battery Shop; Claron E. Cox - W. side S. Jefferson & W. Grayson

Galax Electric Shop; Leftwich - E. side North Main Street

Millner's Variety Store; Mgr. Rixie Lineberry – S..side W. Grayson Street

Beasley-Boone Produce Company - E. side on South Carroll Street

Pless Furniture Store; Glenn Pless -W. side N. Main; 2"l- S. side E. Grayson

Home Market Store; D. S..- E. side South Main Street next to Apperson Bld.

Belk's Department Store - S. Side W. Grayson Street

Roses 5 & 10 Store - corner E .side E. Grayson Street- North Main Streets

Galax Florist; Alfred & Daisy Daub -S. side W. Grayson Street

Blue Ridge Office Supply; F. E. & Mary Lynn Nuckolls - S. Side East Grayson Street

Clover Creamery: Loy Phipps - N. side Carroll Street

Kyle & Williams Inc; Cliff Kyle and D. A. Williams S. side West Oldtown Street

Lesse's Superette & Laundrymat; Mildred Lesse - N. Side East Stuart Drive

Martin's Flowers & Greenhouses - S. Side west Calhoun Street

Martin's One Hour Cleaners; Rayburn Martin - North Main Street

Lineberry's Jewelry Store; E. E. Lineberry - N. side South Main Street

Peoples Drug Store; C. L. Schooley Family - corner E. Oldtown & S. Main

Truitts Fashion Shop; Helen Truitt - W. side S. Main Street

Rhodes Dry Cleaners; Amy Gladys Rhodes - West Grayson Street

Rex Supply; Rex Sage - S. side East Grayson & Carroll Streets

Vaughan Distributing Company; Harvey Vaughan - East Stuart Drive

Vaughan Shoe Store; Opal & Gene Vaughan - E. side North Main Street

Western Auto Store; Jack & Verdie Holt - N. side West Grayson Street

Newton's Dress Shop ? - E. side North Main Street

Ammar's Department Stare; ? S. side West Grayson Street

Winesetts Furniture Company; Davis Winesetts; South Main Street

Manufacturing Establishments 1906-1960s

Galax Canning Company,	Galax Furniture and Lumber Company,	Galax Knitting Company,
Galax Buggy Company,	Edwards Chair Company,	Galax Mirror Company,
Edwards & Scott Stove Company,	Ward's Brick Mfg. Company,	Carnation Milk Company,
H.M. Swartz Mfg. Company,	Honnecker Furniture Company,	American Concrete Company,
W.I. Harp Mfg. Company,	Vaughan-Bassett Furniture Company,	Bluemont Knitting Mills,
Yancy Brothers Extract Company,	Webb Furniture Company,	Galax Chair Company,
Vaughan Furniture Company,		Harris-Marshall Hosiery Mill,

Lindeman Wood Finish Company,
R. & H. Hosiery Mills,
Sawyer's Furniture Company,
Galax Furniture Company,
Galax Weaving Company,

American Mirror Company,
Dixon Lumber Company,
Hanes Knitting Company,
Joines Body Manufacturing
Company,

Perry Mfg. Company,
Ready Mix Concrete Company,

Lumber, Building Supply

Housmann & Kyle Building Supply,
J. D. Spec's Planning Mill
W. H, Taylor Building Supply

W..K.. Early & Son Building Supply
Gillespie Brothers Planning Mill
Reavis Brothers Lumber & Supply

Wholesale Grocery Suppliers
Blair Grocery Company Galax Mercantile Company Dalton Grocery Company
Galax Mercantile Company   Guynn Wholesale Grocery Company

Flour, Grain Mills
Spea's Roller Mill Adam's Flour Mill   C.M. Bryant Flour Mill
Adam's Flour Mill

Bottling Companies
S. F. Welch Bottling Company   Nuckoll's Bottling Company
Coomes Bottling Company   Galax Bottling Works

Restaurants and Cafes
American Grill   Royal Café
Goodson's Café   Bluemont Café
Midtowner Restaurant   Hub Restaurant
Red Barn Restaurant

_____ Movie Theaters
1st - Ward's Theater (E. Side N. Main St) operated by Ward Brothers
2nd Harp Theater (E. side S. Main) operated by W. I. Harp
3rd - Grand Theater (E. side South Main) operated by Claude Heckler
4th - Market Theater (E. side 5. Main St)   "
5th Galax Theater (E. side N. Main St. Operated by Mr. Dowd of Martinsville
6th - Brownie Theater (E. side N. Main St. "   "   "
7th - Colonial Theater (E. side N. Main St   "
8th - Rex Theater - S. side East Grayson Street

Real Estate Companies
        The Grayson Land Company - W. side North Main Street
        Twin County Real Estate Agency - N. Side E. Grayson (Bolen Building)
        Blue Ridge Land Company - (N. side E. Grayson St. (Bolen Building)

Galax Real Estate Agency & insurance Company – S side W. Grayson (Matthews BId)
DaCosta Woltz Real Estate Company -offices over Galax Post Harold Bldg. W. Main
National Real Estate Exchange; Gollie Stantliff; office over Smith Drug Company

<u>Live Stock Market</u>

Carroll-Grayson Livestock Market - 5.side Felts park on Railroad Ave., Piper Gap Oldtown Pike

N & Ws Livestock Holding Pens - Depot Avenue

Passenger & Freight Transportation

The Norfolk & Western Railway Company
Felts Delivery Stables
M. I. Bishop Delivery Stables
Blue Ridge Bus Lines
Stanley Transfer Company
Boone Transfer Company

Hotels

Central Hotel - name changed to Galax Inn
Harris Hotel
Red Star Hotel
J. W. Bolen Boarding House
Waugh Hotel
Bluemont Hotel
Midtowner Motel
Rose Lane Motel

<u>Newsprint</u>

Blair Enterprise   Galax Post Harold
Grayson-Carroll News   Galax Gazette

<u>Banks & Loan Companies</u>

Blair Bank   First National Bank
Peoples State Bank   Merchants & Farmers Bank
Penny Savings Company   Galax Savings & Loan Company
Home Credit Company

Telephone

Galax Telephone Exchange   Intermountain-Telephone-Company

Plumbing Electric Contractors

Utt & Wagner   Galax Plumbing & Heating Company
Diamond's Sheet Metal Electric & Heating Company
Fielder Electric & Motor Repair

Petroleum Distributors

Felts Oil Company (Gordon Felts)
McKnight Oil Company (Jene McKnight) Higgins Oil
Company (McCammett Higgins) Cockerham's Oil Company
(Mike Cockerham) Texaco Oil Company (Claybrook Lester)
Gulf Oil Company (N. G. Dixon)

Automobile Dealers & Garages

Twin County Motor Company; Gordon Felts - W. side of W. Webster & N. Main

Gillespie Brothers Garage - W. side corner E. Oldtown & Carroll Streets
Todd Motor Company Pontiac-Oakland Agency; G.W.; E. B; and L.M. Todd; S. side W. Oldtown &
        Lafayette Streets
Mayhew Motor Company Chevrolet Agency; Bill Mayhew - N. side W. Grayson Street
Jones-Burge Motor Company Dodge-Chrysler Agency; Elmer Jones, Newt Burge S. side W. Grayson
        Street
J. J. Allen Motor Company Willy's-Whippett, Overland Agency; Jasper J. Allen - S.side West Grayson
        Street
Galax Chevrolet Sales - Chevrolet Agency; Edd Cox - N. side W, Grayson Street
White Chevrolet Sales; Hubert White -N. side W. Grayson Street
Hackler Motor Company; O.B. Hackler, Star Agency- Home Dealer
Osborne Motor Company - Essex Agency-Home Dealer; Ellis Osborne
Dixie Morris Service Garage; Dixie Morris - Hillsville Highway
Brady L. Jenkins opened independent Service garage in Joe Reavis building behind Henderson's
Motor Company - Dodge-Chrysler Agency; F.L. Cochran - N. side W. Grayson St.
Mink Motor Sales; Jake Mink - West Oldtown Street

Hospitals

Hopkin's Hospital - corner W. Calhoun and Monroe Streets
Galax Hospital - S. side W. Center & N. Main Streets
Waddell Hospital; Dr. Robert Waddell - Painter Street

Mrs. W. T. Berry, Jr. was hostess to the Young Matrons' Bridge Club at her home on South Main Street Friday afternoon, having four tables arranged for play. Prizes were given to Mrs. J. V. Webb and Mrs. McCammant Higgins for the high and second high scores, respectively. Dainty and appetizing refreshments were served.

The American Legion Auxiliary met in the Legion Hall with Mrs. B. F. Eckles, President, presiding. The Secretary, Mrs. Jeff Matthews read the minutes of their last meeting. Mrs. Floyd Williams, Treasurer, made a report stating that the sum of $61.98 was received from their poppy sale. Those in attendance were; Mrs. Dan Roberts, Mrs. E. G. Cummings, Mrs. Garland Anderson, Mrs. R. A. Anderson, Mrs. Gordon Felts, Mrs. May Kopp, Mrs. T. G. Vaughan, and Mrs. E. R. Crabill. The officers made a motion that the Auxiliary contribute $8.00 to the Boy Scout Fund. They discussed the Girl Scout work and appointed a committee to help formulate plans for the organization of a Girl Scout Troop; Mrs. May Kapp, chairman, Mrs. R. A. Anderson, Mrs. E. B. Crabill, committee members. After the business meeting, a social hour was enjoyed with Mrs. B. F. Eckles, and Mrs. Garland Anderson serving refreshments.

C. I. Carlan purchased the Smith's Drug Store on the corner of West Oldtown and South Main Streets. L. Perelman Store was damaged by fire, having a big sale on all clothing.

The annual flower show under the auspices of the Galax Garden Club was holding their flower show at the Twin County Motor Company on North Main Street.

Hubert S. White of Cedar Bluff, Virginia, purchased the Chevrolet Sales Company from Ed Cox, establishing the White Chevrolet Sales of Galax on West Grayson Street in 1931 becoming one of the outstanding automobile agencies in Southwest Virginia. The repair and service department employed skilled factory trained mechanics, in addition to selling the popular Chevrolet cars and trucks. White had the exclusive agency for Frigidaire in Carroll and Grayson counties. Another service he established was a complete electric repair department, specializing in electrical motor rewinding, house wiring and general electrical construction.

Lawrence Bedsaul of Roanoke, formerly of Galax, driver for the Blue Ridge Bus Lines, was seriously injured in an automobile wreck at Marion.

The Bower's Department Store on Main Street was having a Ladies and Gents Clothing Sale.

The law offices of H. P. Burnett, J. M. Parsons, and Joe W. Parsons were located upstairs over the People's State Bank on West Grayson Street.

Fred and Omar Cox organized the Virginia Seed Services Store located across Depot Avenue opposite of the Blur Ridge Ice Company dealing in seeds, fertilizers, stock feeds, and all types of agriculture supplies for the area farmers.

Joining the Southern States Co-operative of Richmond, Virginia, in 1932, building the Southern States Store in Galax, was located on the corner of East Oldtown and Depot Avenue. Managers of the Southern States Galax Store were: Omar Cox, Fred Cox, and Elmer Davis, followed in later years by Ernest Cox.

The Business Men's Club held their monthly auctions and trading days, which was high spirited and all sorts of articles were sold to the large crowd present.

In 1932 J. P. Carle succeeded DaCosta Woltz for Mayor of Galax. Council members were: Herman W. Boaz, Dan

B. Waugh, E. A. Davis, E. B. Lennox, R. F. Edwards, Joe T. Moore.

Jack Stanley organized the Blue Ridge Transfer Company in Galax in 1932 for the primary purpose of serving the Galax furniture industries, having a fleet of trucks offering efficient delivery service to the furniture trade in fourteen states, operating under interstate permit. On their return trip, the Blue Ridge Transfer fleet would handle general freight and merchandise for the industries and businesses in Galax. Jack Stanley was President and Manager.

The Booze Trucking Company of Roanoke hauled furniture from Galax to distance markets returning to Galax with general freight and merchandise for the industries and businesses of Galax.

N. G. Dixon established the Gulf Oil Company on Railroad Avenue being the authorized dealer of Gulf Oil Company's petroleum products.

Dixie Morris moved into the old service garage, residence connected on the Hillsville Highway opposite of the W. E. Lindsey Store, operating his service garage repairing and servicing automobiles and trucks.

Grey Anderson, Chairman of the Red Cross, expressed the appreciation of the organization and the entire community for the generous contribution to Garnett Largen for hauling all the Red Cross supplies absolutely free on charge, at regular prices. This would have cost the organization $20.00.

Mrs. Joe Goldstein of Claire's Fashion Shop returned from New York where she scouted the market to find the newest and best fashions.

The Town of Galax was reorganizing their rock quarry operation at Rock Hollow, located on the Low gap Road, as a means of relief of unemployment in the Galax area. The Town Manager, H. M. Todd, had not forgotten the remarks made a few years prior by a State Highway construction person that "the Town has a gold mine in that rock". He added that it was exceptionally good quality for road building. Todd honestly believes that a good salesman could get sufficient orders to keep the quarry in continuous operation, and the proceeds would go a long ways toward paying off the Town's indebtedness. What a finer way to lower taxes since the State Highway Department has taken over the county road work there should be a big demand for rock in our own counties of Carroll and Grayson. Manager Todd received an encouraging reply to his letter to the Virginia Highway Commissioner Shirley, concerning the purchase of stone by the State. 2000 men applied for work as a result of this government loan for road work on seven work projects. Three were in the Fancy gap District of Carroll, and four districts in Grayson and Galax area. OF the 2,000 men applying for the jobs, only 600 were accepted. They were the ones who were in greatest need of work and physically fit for the laboring job. The work will be done on a stagger system, a different crew on the road work, working six days per week, being paid 12.5 cents per hour of work. Practically no machinery was used in order to give the applicants employment for a longer period of time during the depressed times.

The Galax Furniture, Textile plants and the General Chemical Company plant at Iron Ridge were working their work schedule to give their employees work due to the slow depressed economy,

Mayor J. P. Carico, members of the Town of Galax Council and some leading citizens were co-operating heartily and loyally with the Galax Community Welfare Relief organizations in their efforts to provide for the unemployment during the coming winter. The Welfare Relief Committee were: Miss Vinnie Caldwell as Chairman, Dr. W. P. David, Vice-Chairman, Mike Crabill, Secretary, H. M. Todd, Treasurer, and Swift Waugh, active Director of the relief work.

Many people responded to the campaign for funds, food, clothing and work or odd jobs in order to help care for the needs of the increasing number of unfortunate families in distress. Other committees were soliciting. It was becoming of Galax people to do all in their power to prevent or alleviate suffering of the unemployed. Swift Waugh made up a list of families who appealed for help. The Committee carefully investigated the family's situation where possible, to provide work in order that all able bodied men have an opportunity to earn their necessities. The Town of Galax and the local Red Cross Chapter under the direction of Grey Anderson combined in limited ways of helping forty-five families in Galax finding the unemployment more acute and the situation more serious than was realized by the average local citizens with the appeals for work and not for charity hand outs. More than ninety-five percent of the calls for help were people without jobs who were willing and anxious to accept any jobs or work through the depressed times was why the local business people and the local Red Cross Chapter of the Town of Galax were doing everything possible to list as much work, odd jobs, to help different families of the Town.

They placed a large stock of wood on the vacant Caldwell lot at the corner of North Jefferson Street and West Center Street, opposite of the First Presbyterian Church, past the Bluemont Hotel, which the unemployed men appealing for help could have a days work in the exchange for fuel and food supplies. Following the depressed years of the early 1930's in the Town of Galax and the Carroll and Grayson community areas, the members of the Galax Chamber of Commerce Industrial Planning Commission began looking into the future of more expanded industrial developments in the Town of Galax and the surrounding areas after their loss for the bid for the Kraft Cheese Plant, to attract more business such as retailing, industrial manufacturing, such as furniture, wood working industries, textile, and agriculture processing plants.

The members of the Chamber of Commerce and the Industrial Planning Commission of the Town of Galax approached the officials of the Carnation Milk Company of California in 1935, processors and manufacturers of evaporated condensed milk products, to locate one of their processing plants in the Galax area to serve the dairy milk producers in Carroll and Grayson Counties. The Carnation Milk Company purchased a land tract from M. L. Bishop located on the Chestnut Creek tributary facing Railroad Avenue to construct their milk processing plant. On May 10, 1937, began can milk production of evaporated condensed milk, The dairy farmers of Carroll and Grayson realized they had a dependable market for their dairy milk operations, which contributed to their agricultural farms economic conditions, selling all the milk they could produce, making progress in establishing new technology in their dairy operation and farming.

The formal opening ceremonies of the Carnation Milk Company was held July 23, 1937, at Felt's Park called the "Cow Day" ceremonies, opening the program by local members of the Chamber of Commerce, the Industrial Planning Commission and officials of the Carnation Milk Company and Governor George C. Perry of the Commonwealth of Virginia delivering the principal address.

The Norfolk & Western Railway Company purchased a large tract of land in prior years from M. L. Bishop and M. T. Blessing joining the Carnation Milk Company's land to build double track and turning wye used to turn their trains around to head back to Pulaski. The Galax Chamber of Commerce and the Galax Industrial Planning Commission began negotiating with the officials of the Burlington Mills Corporation of Greensboro, NC in 1936 to locate a weaving textile plant in the Town of Galax. The Galax Industrial Planning Commission and the Town of Galax purchased a large tract from L. L. Joine's fronting on the corner of East Oldtown (Poplar Knob Road) Street and Brickyard Road along the Chestnut Creek tributary for the construction of Burlington Galax Weaving Textile Plant. The Galax Weaving Plant, division of the Burlington Mill Corporation of Greensboro, N.C. began operation in 1937 producing drapery, upholstery cloth materials. The modern textile plant offers employment opportunities for area people of Galax, Carroll and Grayson providing fair wages and excellent working conditions.

The Norfolk & Western Railway Company's passenger and freight service has a vital interest in the establishment of industrial development of the Town of Galax and the Twin County area during the growth years from 1904 to the 1940's. There would not have been a town of Galax if the railroad and mineral investors from the states of New York, Pennsylvania, Delaware, and Rhode Island had not invested their interest in mineral resources such as coal, iron, zinc, lead, oxides, Pyrrhotite, sulphite ores, timber resources and railroad construction in the New River Plateau of Southwest Virginia in the prior years of the 1880's. Establishing mineral mining and railroad transportation following World War I, the mineral mining of iron ore and manufacturing of foundry pig iron ceased operations along the New River Plateau with the exception of the Four Mineral Mining Companies, who continued their mining and manufacturing operations such as the American Pigment Company of Hawassi, Virginia; the Bertha Mineral Company of Austinville, Virginia; the National Carbide Company, Ivanhoe, Virginia; and the General Chemical Company, Iron Ridge, Virginia.

The Norfolk & Western railway Company were hauling freight shipments of livestock, grains, crossties, timber, lumber, furniture, Pyhrrotite ores, textile cloth, carbide, limestone gravel, zinc, lead, lime, and oxide pigment over the Radford Division Rail Lines, North Carolina Branch Line, Fries Branch line, Cripple Creek Extension Line. The Norfolk & Western Railway Company began to see changes on the horizon in planning their future rail network system discontinuing their expansion of short rail branch lines into the small communities, as developments of better highway road systems linking towns and communities across the Country for travel by automobiles, passenger busses, freight trucking services, air travel, and air freight services. The Norfolk and Western Company began changing their rail line network rebuilding and upgrading their through rail lines to serve the public with more modern through passenger service, express services and upgrading their heavy freight hauling services over their large expanded rail network system.

On December 7, 1941, the United States was attacked by Japan. The United States declared war on Japan and Germany December 8, 1941. The developing growth of the Town of Galax was put on hold during the duration of World War II from December 8, 1941 until August 1945

These pages are dedicated to the honor and memory of my father, 0. C. Martin, founder of Martin's Flowers & Greenhouses operated in the Town of Galax from 1943 to 1979. O. C. was born in Carroll County between Woodlawn and Fancy Gap communities, August 28, 1904, son of Charles Lewis and Marietta Webb Martin growing into manhood in the Hillsville area with the exception of when he married Norma A. McGrady, making their home their first years in West Virginia and Ohio. He learned retail clerking being employed by George L. Carter and I. D. Webb in his earlier years. He moved his family to Galax in 1935, becoming employed as a shipping clerk by C. L. Smith of the Galax Furniture Company. O.C. first venture into the commercial flower business began when he established the Gladioli Dahlias Flower Farm leasing an acreage of land from the Norfolk & Western Railway Company in 1936 used as a turning wye turning their trains around to head back to Pulaski, located on Railroad Avenue above the Carnation Mild Company growing commercial crops of gladioli and dahlias cut flowers shipping by Railway Express to the New York flower markets and the Atlanta flower markets during the summer months from July to October 1[51].

He always extended a cordial invitation to the area people to visit his flower farm during the flower blooming time. In January of each year, O.C. would process and package dry flower bulbs to be distributed to retail stores in Virginia and North Carolina for their Spring sales. He could not resist the love of flowers had been part of his nature from early childhood, by plucking a thistle or planting a flower where ever he thought a flower should grow. D.C. gave up his position of employment with C.L. Smith making his second commercial venture with his wife Norma opening their first greenhouse, growing plants for the retail trade. In 1943 O.C. and Norma Martin opened their retail Florist

Shop at 209 Calhoun Street along with growing of flowers and the retail florist business there was within him a growing spirit far a greater achievement of business which had been founded on no other assets than sound character and grim determination slowly began to find its place in the business life of Galax, Carroll, and Grayson communities: surmounting obstacle after obstacle, often by trial and error methods, but always making progress.

O. C. saw his long dream of the flower business mature as a leading retail florist and a commercial greenhouse growing operation shipping roses, carnations, chrysanthemums to distance flower markets serving the retail florist trade. Not only did he achieve a little success and a lot of satisfaction from his chosen vocation, but his exemplary life and devotion to duty was such that his two sons, C. L. and Roger were influenced to follow his example by remaining in the retail commercial flower growing business. In 1946 C. L. joined the flower business operations bringing his wife, Lucy H. Martin, into the business in 1848 working the retail department. C. L. took over the management of the flower growing and marketing.

By 1957 the Martin's had expanded their greenhouse growing area to 29,500 square feet producing cut flower crops, pot plants, and bedding plants. In 1961 Roger joined in the flower business operations managing the retail business. Roger•'s wife, Pat, worked part-time. O.C. continued operating the flower farm growing gladioli for the flower markets cutting his acreage from forth acres to ten acres of gladioli per year. The Martin's began construction of the second greenhouse range on Kenbrook Drive building 42,000 square feet of growing area producing carnations for the retail flower markets in Virginia and North Carolina.

This photo was taken arouund 1910

4. Friends Church 5. Hotel Central 6. Bishop Livery 7. Blair Grocery 8. Blair Bank 9. J.B.Waugh & Son 10. Galax Drug Co. 11. R.E.Jones 12. Galax Hardware 13. First National Bank 14. Waugh Hotel 15. Crystal Drug Store 16.Presbyterian Church 17. Tom Roberts Home 19. N&W Depot 20. W.K.Early Home